Enemies of the Roman Order

Treason, Unrest, and Alienation in the Empire

Ramsay MacMullen

London and New York

First published 1966 by Harvard University Press

First published in paperback 1992
by Routledge
11 New Fetter Lane, London EC4P 4EE

Simultaneously published in the USA and Canada
by Routledge
29 West 35th Street, New York, NY 10001

Printed in Great Britain by Redwood Press,

British Library Cataloguing in Publication Data
A catalogue record for this book is available from the British Library.

Library of Congress Cataloging in Publication Data
MacMullen, Ramsay
Enemies of the Roman order : treason, unrest, and alienation in the empire / Ramsay MacMullen.
p. cm.
Originally published: Cambridge : Harvard University Press, 1966.
Includes bibliographical references and index.
1. Rome—History—Empire, 30 B.C. to 476 A.D. 2. Government, Resistance to—Rome. 3. Dissenters—Rome. I. Title.
DG270.M34 1992
937'.06—dc20 92–18399

Preface to the paperback edition

From *Enemies of the Roman Order*, after various reprintings in the original hardback edition, the life-giving infusions of ink were eventually denied by its first publishers; so it died. But demand for it, expressed to the author and others, remained unsatisfied. Accordingly, there seemed reason to make the book available again in this present paperbacked form.

The second publisher invites a word of introduction from me. That is not easy to provide without saying again what the book itself was written to say, or without saying what is extraneous or self-serving in some way. But a few details I can provide in the likelihood they will not be known: for example, that the title of the work, had the publishers agreed, was to have been *The Un-Romans*. In defense of the choice, from among the earliest as among the latest voices of the Romans themselves, one could demonstrate an explicit sense of Roman-ness, meaning a collection of qualities defining the dominant norms among that people; and the very term "unRoman" can be found today in the writings of so established a scholar as Arthur Darby Nock.* What I had in mind in *Enemies*, however, was something rather different from these usages: not deviation in individual character, but rather in group character, which would therefore represent something of historical significance. Significance might then be acknowledged by contemporaries through state action

*Scipio Aemilianus quoted by Polybius (31.23.11); Livy 1.53.4; *Epitome de Caesaribus* 38; or Nock in the *Harvard Theological Review* for 1952.

against what they saw as a threat; or it might be discerned only by ourselves, in hindsight, as having some genuine importance. In either case, it was worth writing about.

The selection of my subject was suggested by the period in which the book took shape. For years, back then, I lectured on modern European history, and came to feel that its evidence was not enough on the mind of classicists in arriving at their views about the past. Possibly the deficiency still exists, but it is less striking. I could assume as a matter of course that among all the people of the Roman empire, as in any population ever, there were bound to be manifestations of choice, meaning deviance, meaning freedom, which the ancient establishment took little notice of, and so partly hid from our modern view, or which the establishment tried to suppress, with the same result. A little digging should exhume the remains of *libertas*. At the same time, I was alerted to the possibilities of suppression, through having watched the House Un-American Activities Committee at work. From its actions, some of my older friends had suffered in their professional lives (I recall with special affection Val R. Lorwin); and I myself had first gotten my name into print in the early 1950s through a letter to the newspaper of the city I lived in at the time (Boston), excoriating that same committee. I was then (as still) well over to the Left in my politics. So I came to shape my curiosity and its findings in my own American, or un-American, way.

I was of course obliged, as every historian is obliged at every moment, to think like the subjects of my study, so far as I was able, and to try to do so from the very inside of their minds. Accordingly, I compelled myself at moments to think like—Nero, or like Domitian. Not a congenial task! It is an old question, whether one should condemn what is morally intolerable as one writes about it. But to do so can only unbalance and distract the attention of one's readers.

In due course, a student wrote a dissertation under my direction on a part of my subject, and while doing so illustrated extraordinarily that detachment from his subject, in conjunction with the closest involvement, which is of the essence in good historiography. The work was achieved by someone who had served his country, Russia, as a dissident in the 1970s, and who eventually found a second home in America. He therefore knew from personal experience what it was to speak "by code" (below, p. 41).*

There have also been works written more recently on other matters touched on in this book, too many to detail, for example, two long recent essays on bandits, a full study of one of the third-century Sibylline oracles, an international colloquium on cultural deviation within the empire, and a major study of that phenomenon as it can be seen in the north African provinces. To refer to these is not to claim them as descendants of *Enemies*. I recall Gaston Boissier's work in French on *Opposition Under the Caesars*, of 1875, of which I certainly do not see myself the great-grandson (nor ever read it, for my own benefit). All that can be said is that interest in the past redefines itself continually in the light of changing experience, and elevates to positions of prominence materials which are not new, necessarily, but appear so because no one had really looked for them before. Such recent developments now provide a far broader context, as well as correction and amplification for this present book re-issued.

R. MacM.

July 1992

*The dissertation developed as a book by Vasily Rudich, *Political Dissidence Under Nero* (Routledge, 1992).

Preface

In most minds, "Roman" indicates the institutions and way of life valued by the dominant classes in the late Republic and early Empire. It means the nobility, the senate, Mars and Jupiter; gladiators, too, giving the image its darker colors; and to contemporaries, whether admiring or detesting, it meant also conquest, and such characteristic public buildings as baths, bridges, and forums.

Romans, of course, not only built bridges but beat their wives. No doubt they did about as much of the one as of the other; and they stole, cheated, murdered, or turned their backs on the enemy in battle. Like any other people, too, they included the incurably idle, the illiterate, the impious, and, by the millions, rural and urban poor contributing nothing whatsoever to the façade nobly entitled "Rome." If anyone asked an ancient or modern historian whether all these types were really and truly Roman, in the charged sense that George Washington, but not Benedict Arnold, is "American," the answer would surely be no. They were in society but not peculiarly typical of it.

At a still further remove lay such phenomena as active treason, latent disaffection, brigandage, organized protest, and cultural deviation. Though these too were easily found in the empire, they must yet be called un-Roman—not Greek, or Syrian, or alien in that sense; rather, fully and by origin native, in spite of which they were marked off from what was "Roman" by a boundary of law, or at the least, by the prejudice, scorn, and defensive fear of those who made the law.

An Un-Roman Activities Committee, had the emperors established one on modern lines, would have pursued the investigation of the phenomena just listed; and if a history were to be written exclusively from the files of that committee, it would exactly resemble the present study, dealing with predictable unrest—mere ordinary violent wretchedness born of an imperfect world—and with more puzzling problems as well. The very strengths of the empire supplied characteristic weaknesses: among a proud nobility, tyrannicides; within the competitive patriotism of the cities, intercity angers; and because of Rome's toleration of local differences, local separation from the prevailing culture. These, and their like, constituted so many threats to the established order.

That the Roman order was established so firmly and grandly is what really counts, of course. Historians who write about it may be excused if they show little concern for the dissent it generated and overcame. Until the later Empire, what I describe were indeed failures: happenings that never quite happened, feelings or thoughts or actions that somehow could not inspire a universal imitation. Yet they do help to explain why the dominant civilization was changed in certain directions at certain times, they do show how strong it was and out of what jostle of competition it arose. Moreover, if these failures were to be altogether excluded, it could only be at the dictation of the ruling classes and under the spell of the outcome of events, whereas in real truth, at the moment of conflict, nothing is prejudged, anything may result, all competing forces in history are briefly equal and pregnant with the future. In this sense, without aiming at mere paradox, it was Roman to be very nearly, and very often, un-Roman, just as one can say of any ruling culture that it arouses an internal nonconformity perhaps essential to it and, in any event, characteristic.

Preface

Though there is little connection to be found between one aspect of opposition and another, they all belong under the covers of a single book. Their history, once it is viewed as a whole, suggests three interlocked conclusions. They receive a fuller treatment in the last chapter, and they are repeatedly noticed elsewhere, but they are outlined here to concentrate attention on them from the start.

First, opposition and deviation made themselves known by possessing a share in the power that also controlled the Roman Establishment. The fact may appear to be no more than a truism, or not even that, for, on the one hand, how else was prominence to be won except through the ability to make or modify events; and, on the other hand, unusual desperation occasionally summoned up great energy where little was suspected, as among the Jews in Hadrian's reign, effective beyond their seeming strength, or among the withered aristocracy of Rome in Symmachus' day. There are exceptions to the rule, then, but a pattern is discernible. The slave classes were never powerful, nor did they generate any movement that deserves inclusion in these pages. Consider in contrast the Roman nobility of the first century, clearly in control of the empire and supplying also the chief chapters in the opposition history of that period. The second century saw the passage of directing power to an elite drawn largely from the upper classes of provincial cities, especially eastern cities, and its rising importance to our purpose, as appears in the development, to its highest point, of Alexandrian protest literature and of intercity rivalry. The government was unable to control either of these sources of unrest. We need not test our first conclusion against the evidence of every other place and period in the empire, but it will be generally seen to hold good. Moreover, it accounts for the fact that opposition figures—first century senators, third century pretenders—fit so naturally into the context of their times. Brutus and Lucan are typical. The foes of the monarch rise from the midst of his friends. And when the value and honor of the eastern archer contingents stood highest in the army, and when their tutelary god Aziz appeared for the first time on the coins of the empire they so strenuously defended, in the third century, their close kinsmen, the bowmen of Palmyra, were challenging the empire by elevating their prince to the level of the throne. The loyal and the disloyal were brothers.

Second, if the history of the un-Romans could be put in the form of a table or graph, it would trace a steady downward course on the social scale. It ended in the third and fourth centuries with the Bagaudae speaking Celtic and Saints Anthony and Pachomius speaking Coptic, all drawn from groups that never before had had a chance to make events. The history of the Romans, too, traced the same course—that is, power passed into the hands of a widening circle in which the original holders were gradually overwhelmed and lost from sight.

Third, the empire was "democratized," to use a greatly exaggerated term. The civilization called Roman, in the sense defined above, yields to another, compounded of heterogeneous elements formerly suppressed and latterly vital. Styles of art latent in the masses in Augustus' day, but excluded from official monuments, emerged to full acceptance in the Arch of Constantine; beliefs about the supernatural, once illegal or contemptuously relegated to plowboys and servant girls, after the first century began to infect even the educated, and were ultimately embodied as a principal element in late antique philosophy. As a final illustration chosen from social and political history, the urban and rural poor began to be heard from, though not to control their own fates fully, through such forbidden activities as rioting and brigandage. In the end, the dichotomy on which this book rests breaks down.

Preface

There was little "Roman" left in the Roman empire. Rather, the "un-Roman" elements had come to the fore, and now controlled the world in which they lived. At this point our study properly ends.

The materials present special problems. Contemporary accounts are short or vague, the comments of modern scholars very scattered. There is no possibility of following a straight narrative line, since whatever has no success has no long succession. I have therefore begun my account with a single man, Brutus, and followed treason, unrest, and un-Romanism in widening circles to the senate; then to the students of philosophy among senators and to less than senatorial philosophers; next, to a more diffuse class of men who dabbled in forbidden magic; in Chapter IV, to diviners, and to popular rumors of the downfall of the emperor or empire; then into the turbulence of cities and urban poor, and at last into the peasantry and tribes in rural parts. This arrangement of my subject, aside from its convenience, is meant to bring out the three conclusions outlined above.

The notes refer not to everything I have read but to everything from which I have drawn profit. I generally avoid citing a work only to disagree with it.

I am much in the debt of those who criticized my manuscript. Professor Sir Ronald Syme read the first two chapters, Professor T. R. S. Broughton the next four. My profound thanks for their kindness, and the reader's thanks (if I may speak for him), for their valuable corrections and suggestions.

My work in its later stages was supported by a fellowship at the Institute for Advanced Study at Princeton and by a grant for study in Rome from the John Simon Guggenheim Memorial Foundation. To both sources of such generosity I am deeply grateful. At Princeton I enjoyed the chance to consult several Members of the Institute. I must particularly thank Professor A. Alföldi, whose door was always open and whose mind was always full. At the American Academy in Rome, it is a pleasure to recall with gratitude the help and hospitality of the director, of the Principessa Margherita Rospigliosi, and of Signora Nina Longobardi and her indefatigable aides in the library.

R. MacM.

February 1966

Contents

I. Cato, Brutus, and Their Succession 1

II. Philosophers 46

III. Magicians 95

IV. Astrologers, Diviners, and Prophets 128

V. Urban Unrest 163

VI. The Outsiders 192

VII. Conclusion 242

Appendix A. Famines 249

Appendix B. Brigandage 255

Bibliography 269

Abbreviations 293

Notes 295

Index 367

✧ I ✧

Cato, Brutus, and Their Succession

THE Ides of March, 44 B.C., set a great precedent. For the first time in Roman politics, virtue and philosophy joined hands with assassination. Their union was commemorated in the coinage of those strict constitutionalists, Brutus and Cassius: two daggers, and between them the cap of liberty that slaves wore on the day they won their *libertas*. It was a mighty word. It stirred men up, made them heroes; better still, it could be stretched to advertise almost any cause, if one were metaphysician enough. And Brutus, whatever might be conjectured of the other conspirators, was a deep thinker. He came to the murder of his friend Caesar fortified by long study and a life prolific in treatises on duty and virtue. No mere man of action; hence his fame: he stood for principles, and principles live on.

In the centuries that followed, until the fall of Rome, only a minority of emperors died a natural death. Of the majority, a dozen fell before assassins, not in battle. Those in the early reigns could not of course foresee the full peril of their position, yet it was clear even under Augustus that the principate roused the keenest and most stubborn animosities. Even Augustus had a liking for a breastplate when he entered the senate, little as he trusted that it might save him, and he unmasked or perhaps only wrongly suspected half a dozen plots against his reign. Rumor had it that his end was hastened by his kin. As much was said of the deaths of Tiberius and Claudius, among his descendants. Caligula was killed, Nero driven to take his own life. After Nero, the palace was fitted with heavy iron gates. Danger could still reach in. For Hadrian, it was a madman's rush from the garden shrubbery; for Commodus, the big hands of his wrestling companion. Knowledge that sooner or later one of their subjects was almost sure to try some desperate trick exercised an understandable influence on the policy and behavior of the emperors. They had all heard of Damocles. Some slid down the spiral of fear, persecution, plots, persecution, and more plots, to their death. Others like Vespasian trusted in their own popularity, or horoscopes. But for every one of them the throne was a dangerous eminence.

Most conspirators against the emperor hoped for some personal gain—to succeed him themselves, or get their candidate in, or prevent a threat of punishment. A few simply hated him. Our business here is with none of these, but with a different type that may in some sense be called the successors of Brutus—cultivated, literary, philosopher types.

The story of this succession can best begin with Marcus Junius Brutus and his background. His family enjoyed exceptional influence, and from his mother, Servilia, if from no one else, he might have learned to wield it. She was a woman of formidable character, powerful in politics, a friend of Caesar's long after she ceased to be his mistress. Rumor even said, wrongly, that her son was Caesar's, too. Her husband was treacherously put to death in the civil wars in 77 B.C.; the seven-year-old boy went to live with his uncle Cato, and in that house began the formation of his character. It was a house filled to bursting with character, both in the sense of eccentricity and of moral fiber. For Cato like many another Roman noble had at various times several resident philosophers as chaplains; unlike many another Roman noble, however, he did not need them, but could very well be his own spiritual adviser, and was willing to serve in that capacity to the entire aristocracy. Over the last fifteen years of his life—always brave, sometimes cunning, seldom wise—he struggled to correct and uphold the Republic, being its most steadfast pillar —a Doric column, Cicero more Corinthian, but both dedicated to the preservation of oligarchy.

The first full-length portrait of Cato is Cicero's. Cato appears in court against Cicero's client, and Cicero, to weaken the force of his antagonist's testimony, is desperately funny. Cato is the perfect puritan, advocating impossible standards with a sour face. If he left philosophy and mingled more in the world, his head might clear. Exactly the right line to take, this. Many in the audience would share the opinion that Cicero only pretended. Too much philosophy was a bad thing, too much thinking got in the way of doing. And with this thoroughly Roman view, Cato himself agreed, in part. Cicero, who knew him well, presents him as a model Stoic. He writes letters to him with a good deal of circumspection. But these are tributes, not to Cato's deep learning or force of mind, but rather to his moral nature. This is what speaks in a passage that Cicero puts into his mouth: "Most Stoics do not believe that pleasure belongs among the chief natural motives, and I strongly concur, lest a great many disgraceful consequences follow from supposing that nature placed pleasure among the things which are first aimed at." *Ne turpia sequantur*—so philosophy must be made to fit predetermined ethical ends. It is only valuable if it can be put to work.[1]

Between Pompey and Caesar, in the civil wars, Cato chose Pompey. Later admirers thought the choice needed explaining. "One might dispute whether in that period a wise man should have taken any part in public affairs. 'What do you mean, Marcus Cato? It is not liberty that is at stake now; that has long since perished. The question is whether the state shall belong to Caesar or Pompey. What have you to do with this dispute? It is no business of yours. A tyrant (*dominus*) is being selected. What is it to you which one wins?' " Cato's answer was imagined long afterward. War is bad, but virtue must follow destiny. "It will be a reproach to the gods," he said with monumental assurance, "that they have made even me guilty." He took up arms, then, on the side that was least un-Republican; fought at Pharsalus; survived that field and went on to fight at Thapsus; fell back on Utica; and there played out his last hours in a scene of artificiality and heroism. Plutarch describes it at greatest length: how friends gathered for the evening in a large group, going on from dinner to "cultivated and pleasant conversation," especially on the several schools of philosophy, and so to the Stoic "paradoxes" such as the contention that only the good man is free, which Cato defended "with extraordinary earnestness, so everyone perceived that he had made up his mind to put an end to his life"; how he tried to divert their suspicions with lighter talk; retired to his room, read the *Phaedo*, fussed about his sword (providently removed); discussed with Demetrius the Peripatetic and Apollonius the Stoic the necessity of seeking salvation in one's own way by one's own resolve; went to his bed, slept, and woke to thrust a sword into his side. Friends and doctors intervened in vain. He immediately tore open the wound again and died.[2]

His suicide aroused a mixed reaction. To a Greek mind, killing oneself was an act of cowardice, of desertion, as Socrates had said. Stoicism introduced a different view to be developed further in the century after Cato's death, but it was at this time not very prevalent. It emphasized motive: censure of suicide as retreat could not apply to an act that enabled one to retain one's position in the face of an insuperable threat to dignity or honor or country. To a Roman mind, this was an acceptable distinction. National heroes like Decius Mus or Regulus had often sacrificed themselves. Over the next two or three generations, for reasons that will emerge later, admiration was extended still more broadly. Cato was made the equal of Socrates. Together they had sanctified suicide, and schoolboys could recite set pieces on "Cato and the Contempt of Death." All this lay in the future. Meanwhile Caesar, at his triumph in 46 B.C., displayed cartoons of Lucius Scipio and Petreius committing suicide, and of Cato "torn open by himself like a wild beast." Caesar thus counted on popular prejudice against suicide, but he was wrong.[3]

The response was instant. At Brutus' urging, Cicero wrote a *Cato,* a eulogy of some sort, probably in 46, with a second edition the next spring; joined then by Brutus' own *Cato,* versus Caesar's *Anti-Cato,* in the summer of 45, and Hirtius' violent assault, of about September, these in turn meeting Fadius Gallus' and Munatius Rufus' rejoinders. What Cato's friends said on his behalf is not known, though no doubt we could make a good guess at the substance. His enemies ridiculed him as a fraud, all virtue on the outside, avaricious, eccentric, and sottish on the inside. To these opening rounds fired in the battle over his reputation, at least one more *Anti-Cato* was added by none other than Augustus, in extreme old age—what ripples of Republicanism in the salons elicited this last pamphlet, we do not know—and later historians and poets passed their judgments on the figure of dispute, almost all favorable. Though his standards had been too harsh, he himself remained the very type of virtue and the last defender of the Republic.[4]

It may well be that Brutus turned against Caesar in the course of this pamphleteering and in part because of it. Toward its end, after mid-45, he took a step that showed at the very least a lessening loyalty for his old chief: he married Cato's daughter. Porcia cannot have been his choice without sharing some of his attachment to the Republic and his affection for Cato—not that all children love their parents—and she is said to have supported him in the plot with the utmost courage. She may have influenced him; Caesar's adultery with his mother may have influenced him; vengeance for his uncle may have been in his mind; and so obvious and strong a motive as the desire for fame should not be forgotten. That, too, was attributed to him, by Cicero and others. All these are hidden reasons, however, beyond substantiation. Nor is it easy to guess at his general character and its inborn tendencies. Nothing appears in his features: a knobbly face, bearded in token of mourning for the decline of the Republic, on his coins, with heavy lines around his mouth. Written sources are hardly more satisfying. Brutus' own letters in Greek, where he speaks in haste to his inferiors, are extremely terse and businesslike, with an occasional grim smile. In Latin he spread himself more genially. Men of his own rank found him charming, able to use flattery (though himself immune to it), highly moral, rational, cautious, and even hesitant in making up his mind. Among the Roman nobility, especially among those whose sympathies lay with the Republic, it was wise to be conventional. Influence was in the hands of careful old men, who enjoyed deference, understood caution, and expected of the younger generation only that it might in the course of fifty years or so produce its own crop of careful old men. By these standards, Brutus' early character seemed to show great promise and no mark of a murderer.[5]

Nevertheless, he did lead the conspiracy. If his inner motives are really unknown, and if his outward character suggests no explanation of the role he played in 44 B.C., we can still look for light in the external forces that operated on him. We can certainly assume, to begin with, that he made many decisions by reference to family descent. Its weight lay heavy on the minds of every well-born Roman, heavier, perhaps, than any other sense or idea. A child was born into a *praenomen*, *nomen*, and *cognomen*, all parts of which committed him to the character of earlier namesakes—to whom, as he grew up, he offered sacrifices in his home, and for whose deeds he was ridiculed or respected by his friends as son (or grandson, or great-grandson) of the man who did thus-and-so. Career and marriage were in the gift of the family, and at his death his merits were recalled and his very few faults sunk to the bottom of a sea of rhetoric by cousins and adherents whose powers qualified them to deliver a eulogy. The embrace of the clan thus received him from the womb, shaped him, delivered him to his grave, and hallowed his memory thereafter. By a custom most extraordinary, it even brought him to life again at his funeral; for at this moment an actor who looked and talked most like him, or perhaps some relative who resembled him, put on his death mask of wax, exactly painted, and walked ahead of his bier accompanied by dozens or (for a great man of a great family) by hundreds of his ancestors represented in turn by their masks, and by the robes and rites of the highest office they had attained, so that the whole procession brought together praetors and consuls, generals and party leaders reaching back through generations. Since it was their position in public life that was emphasized, funeral oratory played on the same theme. Past achievements were praised, future loyalties hinted. At his aunt's funeral,

Caesar's mention of her democratic connections served notice of his own sympathies. When Cicero spoke in praise of Brutus' aunt Porcia, and distributed copies of the *laudatio* afterwards, it was "essentially a work of propaganda." And when the masks of these inspiring ancestors, their *imagines*, were taken home again, it was to a position of honor, hanging in the atrium, reshaped as busts, set in shrines, explained by epitaphs and biographies inscribed on the walls nearby, there to assert to every visitor the place of that particular family in Roman political history.[6]

Growing up in a house filled with one's own forebears, reading their stories and seeing them come to life and walk beside some relative's bier—all this must surely have had an effect on the stupidest boy. He would know what was expected of him with a vividness at times overwhelming. At the least he could continue the line with a carven correctness. He could be "a walking bust." But it was hard to stop there. The faces on the walls exercised a more powerful spell over the imagination. They made pride and obligation visible. Brutus would have understood as we cannot the phrase later used to describe his uncle, "the living image of virtues," *virtutium viva imago*, and Cato was only one among many. Servilii, Junii, Brutus' kin filled the annals of the state. He cultivated them carefully, with the help of that learned antiquarian Atticus, who constructed for him a family tree or something more. It traced the line back to the first consul, despite mean suspicions that there was a break somewhere. Cicero had no doubts. He refers to Brutus' long lineage again and again, basking in the glory of the acquaintance.[7]

"What do pedigrees accomplish?" asked a poet who had none (Juv. 8.1). For one thing, a pedigree could help to make a tyrannicide. There was a story that Brutus' uncle had offered his services as a boy, to rid the world of Sulla. Junii reached back with more certainty to L. Junius Brutus, assassin of the tyrant Tarquin and first consul, and Servilii (his mother's line) to Servilius Ahala, assassin of that would-be tyrant Spurius Maelius in 439 B.C. Everyone knew of Brutus' inheritance, and Cicero at least asked, with wisdom after the event, what need was there for anyone to urge tyrannicide on the Junii Bruti, "of whom one [Decimus] saw every day the bust of Lucius Brutus, the other [our Marcus] the *imago* of Ahala as well. Should these men with this lineage seek counsel from someone else?"[8]

It was not only in his home that Brutus saw his mission. Up on the Capitol was a row of bronze statues: the seven kings, and L. Junius Brutus, and Caesar as a recent ninth; "and it was this chiefly that led Marcus Brutus to conspire against [Caesar]." Such is Dio's opinion, for what it is worth. Perhaps others saw and exploited the connection. At any rate, in the spring of 44 that eighth statue was regularly decorated with signs and scrawls, "Would that you were living now"; on the ninth statue, "Brutus was made first consul for driving out the kings./ This man [Caesar], for driving out the consuls, was at last made king." On Brutus' own praetorian tribunal were the further daily taunts, "Brutus, you sleep," and "You are no true Brutus." Finally, there were letters from Cicero to Brutus, gently hinting, "We wish for you the kind of state in which you may be able to freshen and augment the memory of those two great lines"—of the tyrannicides! Their *imagines* had appeared on Brutus' coins of about 59 B.C., the year when he was officer of the mint, and the year too in which he was accused of plotting against the consul Caesar. The incident is obscure, the charge doubtful. L. Junius Brutus is pictured alone on the coins of 43, but very prominently, coupled with LIBERTAS.

The message that had penetrated to his descendant Marcus was thought to be an effective one for the widest possible audience.[9]

One force that turned Brutus against Caesar was his sense of family, operating through visible symbols. That is the argument so far. But immediately after the assassination he raised his bloody dagger on high like Lucius of the statue, and shouted to Cicero, "Freedom is found again," or some such words. His posturing had an explanation to be found in the conventional pose of one of the famous tyrant slayers of Athens; and when he and Cassius reached that city many months later, they were voted "bronze statues by the side of those of Harmodius and Aristogeiton, as for followers of those two." The Greek world thus acknowledged a true descendant of their own heroes in Caesar's chief assassin. His student life at Athens and a long-founded love of all things Greek had certainly given form and probably inspiration also to his act of tyrannicide.[10]

The Romans had no word of their own for tyrant; they had to make do with "king" or "master," or borrow from Greek. That they could do, because at least those of Brutus' class were generally bilingual, spoke to each other or wrote in either language, and so, for example, called tyrannicides *tyrannoctoni* or (in proper letters) τυραννοκτόνοι. The Greeks, on the other hand, knew all about tyrants. They might boast of having invented them, and their literature was filled with the figures of the monster on the throne, his victims, his guards, and at last his bold, radiant slayer. A Roman youth who came to Athens might learn too much of this mythology; he could not be safe even if, like Brutus, he went there to study under a Platonist; for in the national galleries of fame, among the heroes who stood up to tyranny, there was a special shrine reserved for philosophers. Their line could be traced, with some exercise of imagination, back to Solon confronting Pisistratus, then to Socrates, and so to Anaxarchus and Zeno.[11]

A story long famous in Brutus' own day told of the assassination of Clearchus of Heraclea in 353–52 B.C. by a pupil of Plato, one Chion. It was retold in the later first century A.D. in the form of seventeen letters, and with many changes and qualifications suggests what may have happened in Brutus' mind. The young Chion, of eminent family, came to Athens for study. He heard of what was going on in his homeland, and news of his opposition reached the tyrant, "who really does fear Silenus less, who captured his citadel, than myself, who pursue philosophy." The tyrant was a good judge. Chion did return, and did kill him, and without stepping out of character. That last is, in fact, the point of the whole correspondence: that philosophers are men of deeds. He used to think, writes Chion, that philosophy "dissolved the active, vigorous powers of the soul and made for weakness and softness," for, as his friend had always told him, "to be inactive and to stand apart were most marvelously praised by philosophers . . . It seemed to me very bad, then, if the pursuit of philosophy should make me better in other respects, but if I could not, upon need, be a brave man nor a soldier nor a hero . . . For I did not realize that those who pursue philosophy are better off even in regard to bravery, and only recently learnt this from Xenophon, not only when he spoke to me about it, but because he showed in action what sort of a man he is. For, though he was very much a participant in Socrates' discussions, he is still the man to save an army or a city, nor has philosophy made him one whit less useful to himself or his friends." His strength, and Chion's, comes from study that gives power to resist external force. "I consider that slavery subdues both body and soul, whereas what does not hold the soul but only the body does not seem to me to be slavery . . . Fear of suffering and of the pains arising from suffering are the worst evils to those who are not free. So then, can any one be a slave who does not fear future, and does not chafe under present, ills? . . . Clearchus will never make me a slave." A tyrant can inflict every kind of evil on the body but he can never subdue the soul. The only limit to Chion's utter freedom is the tie of affection that binds him to his country. That tie draws him to his native Heraclea and to fame.[12]

It is Platonism mixed with Stoicism that meets us in these letters. A mixture rather than the pure form of any one school was what prevailed among those who interested themselves in philosophy in the first century B.C. as later. Brutus himself is an example. On the one hand, Cicero calls him "an Antiochan," a follower of the Academic Antiochus; he praises his learning and dedicates *De finibus* to him. Brutus reciprocates with his *De virtute*. But then Cicero addresses the *Paradoxa Stoicorum* to Brutus, who writes a *De officiis* that has a Stoic sound, and a *De patientia* still more so. In all of his three treatises "the doctrines of the Academy were no doubt conciliated with Stoicism." There is no reason, however, to take the next step—to dismiss the author as a casual dabbler. What is mixed need not be diluted. Brutus' reputation for morals, by the standards of his own society, stood very high. Whenever he wrote on philosophy, "you know that he believes in what he is saying." So far as concerns the application of philosophy to political behavior, his last years certainly fit a Stoic-Platonic model. The decision to dedicate himself to action comes straight out of the thought-world of Chion's correspondence (or, for that matter, out of the lives of a number of fourth and third century philosophers). The mood of Chion's last letter matches that of Brutus' death scene, and if that is a conscious tableau, untrustworthy in detail, we can turn to a fact that is unquestioned. It was by Brutus' insistence that the plot was aimed only against Caesar. Some of his fellow conspirators thought Antony ought to be removed, "but Brutus said they would win glory by the death of Caesar alone because that would be the killing of a king." "Citizens should seek the blood of none but a tyrant (for to call Caesar by this title suited his ends)." He bore Caesar no ill-will except as one who aspired to rule by himself and above the law. Cassius hated Caesar; Brutus, tyranny.[13]

Among the external influences to which Brutus responded, philosophy was the second, then, along with a sense of family. A third is that influence most obvious in all the accounts, love of freedom. Nowadays people are suspicious of the word, an umbrella under which everyone shelters when the political weather looks uncertain. Most of the conspirators, if their innermost ideas had been examined, would no doubt have meant by it only "free" opportunity to exert the weight of their family in the old ways; "free" movement of power among all members of the traditional oligarchy, without constraint by faction or tyranny; in short, free access to the political trough for all the usual company of nobles and retainers. Had their leader permitted such ideas to dominate behind proclamations of *Libertas*, they would not have stopped short at the death of the dictator in the evident belief that the only difference between monarchy and a *libera res publica* was a single man. However, stop there they did, some very unwillingly, and anxious against their own protestations to force their faction on the state by a general purge of their enemies. About Brutus' purity of motive there was no question. A slogan that for others concealed selfishness and deceit was for him its own explanation. If his views on government were narrow and unimaginative, they were at least honest. He loved the Republic.[14]

One aspect of what freedom involved for Brutus requires a more particular explanation, and the best angle of approach lies through his own writings. Like others of his rank and education, he placed the most inflated value on literature not removed to a library or studio but injected into public life and history. History itself he pursued enthusiastically, and wrote about it: an epitome of Fannius' work, and of Polybius, and perhaps other studies at least begun. His letters were careful, so too his speeches, which Cicero praised extravagantly, adding as a further compliment the title for his own *Brutus*. It is an accidental but a true comment that, while Cato was dying in Africa, Cicero was polishing this latter treatise on the theory of talking. A literary family, Cicero's, to be sure: there was brother Quintus, dashing off four tragedies in the space of sixteen days while with the army on the Rhine. But his commander wrote history, and was an unmatched orator, and the author of an essay on Latin grammar dedicated to Cicero—the commander Caesar.[15]

It is hard to see how any of this devotion to *eloquentia* fitted philosophy. In fact, most schools refused to acknowledge it as one of the quintessential virtues—but not Stoicism,[16] and Stoicism predominated. It is hard to see, too, how *eloquentia*, or at least the finer points of its study, fitted with a public career. Nobody felt any doubts on this matter. Power over the written and especially the spoken word was believed to give power over the whole citizen body, and the needs and ramifications of this belief had been worked out very fully from Pericles' day forward. Absorption in the subject deepened in centuries to follow. Its whole history is crucial. From modern accounts of the Greeks and Romans, one would sometimes suppose that these gifted peoples, especially the Greeks, excelled in all the arts that we ourselves value—painting, drawing, sculpture, architecture; drama, poetry and the several forms of prose literature; even dance and music, so far as we can recover their remains; whereas in fact the one art in which cultivated people commonly expressed their cultivation, from the fifth century B.C. to the fifth century A.D., we no longer practice nor value, and tend to ignore. That was *eloquentia*. For a thousand years it remained at the heart of classical civilization, placing its heroes upon embassies, rostrums, richly endowed chairs, and the platforms of special theaters; at last, as statues, upon pedestals in the Roman forum itself. All other arts save poetry were left to slaves or to the lower classes.

The free exercise of this art went far beyond the merely political boundaries of what we call free speech. It engaged the idle hours of an aristocracy forever dabbling or pretending to dabble or seriously learned in literature as the support of their eminence in the state. They read or declaimed or memorized because they could expect such vital struggles in courts, senate, or assembly. They could see a relation almost hidden from us between their politics and what we would call their culture, and defended it as an extension of their freedom. When political freedom was curtailed, *eloquentia* declined. Tacitus and others traced the connection, and it has often been discussed in recent times. It will recur below, in Chapter II. Here it is enough to have mentioned the subject of free expression as manifestly important to Brutus and manifestly threatened by Caesar.

So much for *eloquentia* and the ideas that surround it. There is just a note to add on its Greek variations. Dio records the complaints of several of the tribunes, to the dictator, that they "could not enjoy παρρησία," free speech. The Greek word brings to mind the context in which it is so often found: the philosopher face to face with the tyrant, παρρησία against ἀνάγκη, force. To this picture, too, we will return; this too was present in Brutus' mind, once he had cast himself as a tyrant hater; and it serves to draw together two of the influences upon him, philosophy and the love of freedom.

The same influences operated on other conspirators and so help a little to confirm our analysis of Brutus. Decimus' family went back to the slayer of Tarquin; Cassius pursued philosophy—he was an Epicurean, however—and hated tyrants. No doubt he encouraged the story that he had tried to assassinate Caesar back in 47. But Brutus had to be swayed more powerfully, from one allegiance to its opposite. He may have studied the saying of a Greek sage: "So love as if you were perhaps destined to hate; and in the same way, hate as if you might perhaps afterwards love." At any rate, he led the plot, and there would have been none without him.[17]

The questions that confronted him and his fellows were how, when, and where. One idea they considered was to attack Caesar at the public games. They ultimately decided on a meeting of the senate where they could all be present naturally and get at him. They waited till the session convened in the stoa that ran along one side of Pompey's theater—his statue stood among the columns—since a spectacle was shortly to be given in the theater in celebration of a festival and on that account Decimus Brutus as urban praetor could command a large number of gladiators in the vicinity. He had them secretly in his pay, to guard the conspirators or do whatever else was needed. Despite portents, Caesar attended, and before the meeting was convened was attacked by the conspirators. Their heavy togas, lapping the left arm, made them clumsy, and some of their blows fell on each other, though without giving any serious hurt. Only two men started forward to Caesar's defense, too late, and none came to fetch his body for many hours. "Stone dead hath no fellow," as the old saying runs. The conspirators might rejoice that the liberation of the state was irrevocable, and carried the message and their bloody daggers to the heights of the Capitol. It was Rome's nearest equivalent to an acropolis, decorated with the bronze statue of L. Junius Brutus. Throughout the day's action, something Greek and stagy occasionally appeared.

At the dictator's funeral "somebody raised above the bier an image of Caesar himself made of wax (for the body, prone on the bier, could not be seen). The image was turned about by a mechanical device, and on the whole body and on the face could be seen the twenty-three wounds that had been dealt him so brutally. The people could not bear this pitiful sight longer, as it was shown to them, but groaned." Public anger, instead of the joy that the tyrannicides seem to have expected, produced acts of violence—to begin with, the burning of the senate house. An impostor turned up from southern Italy, proclaiming himself a relative of Caesar's and winning support on that account, until the consuls seized and executed him in April. Brutus still hoped to check the tide of public opinion, counting on an occasion in the summer when he would preside over the Apollinarian games. He scheduled a revival of *Brutus*, a drama on the subject of L. Junius Brutus, by a playwright once attached to the family. All his friends were to attend, money was spent lavishly on preparations, but at the last moment his enemies stepped in with their substitutions: for *Brutus*, *Tereus;* for the man Brutus, a brother of Antony to preside; for some other date, the nones of the month that bore Caesar's name. That hurt. *Quam ille doluit de nonis Iuliis! mirifice est conturbatus*, wrote Cicero of Brutus.[18]

With Rome too hot to hold him, he left for the East. Nothing further in his story is important to the purposes of the present study until we come to his death, of which later ages had much to say. The scene is given most fully by Plutarch, who describes his last acts, the meaning remarks that he uttered "smiling very characteristically," and the lines of

Euripedes that he quoted. After his suicide, his enemies found his body; his head, cut off, was taken back to Rome to be tossed at the foot of the statue of Pompey where Caesar had died. The symbolism of this and all the drama in the tale were worked up promptly in a hagiology of which Plutarch was only the last inheritor. Publius Volumnius, "a philosopher and fellow soldier of Brutus from the start," evidently published some account of the death scene which he had witnessed. A housemate and friend of Brutus, the rhetorician Empylus, described the plot, Asinius Pollio (d. A.D.5) "handed down the splendid record of [Brutus' and Cassius'] deeds." Lucius Sestius is known as another "enthusiastic follower of Brutus from the beginning, and a comrade in arms in all his battles, and even [in A.D. 23] keeping his memory alive, having busts of him, and delivering eulogies on him."[19] So began a cult with a long history, and a political use that was to be turned against the Roman emperors again and again in the course of the first century.

For generations that followed, the period of Rome's civil wars held a special fascination, full of the drama of the state at its most powerful rending itself in a kind of suicide. From the debates of epic poets and historians, the fame of Cicero emerged a little ambiguously; Cassius was remembered chiefly in connection with Brutus; and the other conspirators were names, or not even that. Two figures of particular refulgence stood out, Cato and his nephew. But praise of Cato struck at the memory of Caesar, founder of the Julio-Claudian fortunes; praise of Brutus did that and more, since he had not only killed Augustus' adoptive father but led the forces against Augustus and Antony as well, in 42. Anyone thereafter who wanted to show his hostility to the principate without endangering his life too much, or who wished somewhat covertly to reach out towards other men's minds and infect them with his opinions, turned thus to the cult of the two Republican diehards, and wrote about them or talked about them or in some other way advertised his allegiance to them. Discussion of this cult may focus first on Cato, though men who praised him were likely to praise Brutus also.

It should be said at the start, however, that the figure of Cato was so soon sanctified that his name might be harmlessly invoked as no more than a stereotype of virtue facing insuperable odds—so he appears in some passages gathered above and so he must be taken in the writings of Vergil, Horace, Seneca, and the poetaster Sentius Augurinus—while at the same time the official attitude toward his name, or other Republican recollections, was not always hostile, avoiding collision on such matters. Augustus, for instance, tolerated a predominantly Republican tone in current literature; the early years of Tiberius, Caligula, and Nero allowed considerable freedom of speech; and throughout the first century, inoffensive schoolmasters taught unpolitical schoolboys to recite the harangue that Cato might have made on his deathbed. Except for their parents, nobody listened.[20]

Brutus' cult attracted early attention, more difficult to ignore. An elderly senator, Aulus Cremutius Cordus, was brought to trial in A.D. 25 for a work of historiography in which he had sung Brutus' praises and called Cassius "the last of the Romans." That at any rate was the heavier part of the charges, but others were tossed in: abusive talk of the senate and the Roman people, insufficient respect for Caesar and Augustus. He committed suicide, and by decree of the senate his book was burnt. His defense before the senate, however, was remembered. He pointed out that his *Annals* had been written long ago, that they had been read without reproach by Augustus in the days when Brutus and Cassius were not yet reviled by such titles as "brigand" and "parricide," and that other authors too had once been free to write the truth about the past: Livy, or Asinius Pollio. What he did not mention were his sharp remarks against Sejanus, now at the height of his influence with the emperor, whose agents engineered the accusation. Cremutius' daughter Marcia hid away some copies of the dangerous *Annals*. Along with the works of other authors formerly banned, they were resurrected in a purified form by order of Caligula. Seneca praised them for their part in perpetuating the noble deeds of earlier generations and the knowledge of what it was to be a Roman, and praised their author for those two noblest things, *eloquentia* and *libertas*. These qualities, and impartiality in writing history, should not have cost a man his life, unless we want to attribute to Tiberius an insane despotism. Better to fall back on another answer, weak as it may seem at first sight: the association of ideas. For, to Cremutius' rhetorical question (Tac., *Ann.* 4.35), "Am I in arms with Cassius and Brutus on the plains of Philippi, or inflaming the people to civil war with my harangues?" the answer given by his enemies was an inward "yes"—"yes" in the legally inexcusable but politically colorable sense that people likely to make trouble for the regime were to be sought among Cremutius' friends. *Eloquentia* and *libertas* brought tyrannicide to mind. That was not the right kind of thing for senators to discuss. It connected the dinner parties and street corners, where Tiberius saw the origins of opposition, with more businesslike meetings, and ultimately with rebellion itself. Dangerous sentiments survived widespread among the vestiges of the Republican nobility, and the government took them seriously.[21] So, when Brutus' sister—the widow of Cassius, niece of Cato—died in A.D. 22, her family did not dare to advertise her historic lineage. At the funeral, *imagines* of Manlii or Quinctii were prominent, but "Cassius and Brutus shone forth the more because their images were not to be seen" (Tac., *Ann.* 3.76). As late as Nero's reign a descendant, Longinus, was indicted before the senate for venerating among his family *imagines* one of Cassius inscribed "Leader of the Cause."[22] It did not matter that such charges sometimes covered much more realistic considerations—that the accused was rich and worth plundering, or that he was one of the few surviving descendants of Augustus' line and so might serve as rallying point for revolt. What did matter was the popular belief, or mythology, that saw in Republicanism an enemy of the principate.

Connected with this Cassius Longinus by indictment and sympathies was Thrasea Paetus. He had been consul ten years earlier, in A.D. 56, and so late as the 60's the emperor could still be reconciled to him. At the beginning of his career his virtues and lineage made him eminent. His nature was gentle, social, and not unforgiving, and to the young Nero he showed a certain restrained loyalty—attended Nero's idiot performances, spoke conciliatorily in public, and yet defended the independence of the senate against the emperor's powers and agents. That in itself of course gave him a perilous prominence, and as the reign degenerated he became better known not for what he did but for what he did not do. He simply dropped the duties of a senator. This involved him in derelictions that could be twisted into treason, and at his trial, though no one brought in evidence of a plot, at least one accuser, the very formidable Eprius Marcellus, alleged that he meditated revolt. His friends later established the myth that he died for being what he was, for his censorious bearing and his schoolmaster's face. But there was really a great deal more to be said against him, given the atmosphere of his times. He wrote a life of Cato, for one thing. It probably suggested Plato's *Phaedo* and *Apology* and (in turn) the confrontation between force and virtue. His admiration for the tyrannicides was well enough known to be played on: "Let us revert to those ways of his, if they are better, or remove this leader and favorer of revolution. His sect produced men like the Tuberones and Favonii [Stoics of Cicero's time]. To overthrow the empire, they wave *libertas* aloft; if they succeed in subversion, they will attack liberty itself. You have in vain cleared Cassius away, if you allow followers of the Bruti to spread and flourish" (Tac., *Ann.* 16.22).[23]

"And he has disciples or rather partisans," the same speaker continues. Yes, indeed. Consider the congenial circle around him: a father-, mother-, and son-in-law, all treasonous; the latter and Thrasea and Seneca friends since they had enjoyed office together in A.D. 56 (as suffect consuls and tribune); his house the resort of disaffected men, conspicuous, critical, or entangled in the loyalties of previous conspiracies: Arulenus Rusticus, Domitius Caecilianus, Avidius Quietus, Persius, Paconius Agrippinus. No doubt a dozen other names of a similar reputation could have been found at the kind of dinner parties on which the emperor Tiberius had frowned.

Moreover, Thrasea was a philosopher. That explains the reference to the sect of the Favonii and Tuberones; it explains Thrasea's supposed censure of Rome's law and empire and Nero's eagerness to be quit of him. For if Nero was to murder his mother or amuse himself on the stage *à la grecque*, he wanted no Stoic scowling in the wings. He allowed Thrasea only to choose how he would die, and his victim chose suicide. The scene was his own garden. "He had brought together a large party of distinguished men and women, himself especially attending to Demetrius the teacher of Cynic doctrine, with whom, to judge from the concentration on his face and what could be overheard when their voices rose, he was discussing the nature of the spirit and the separation of body and soul." When the moment came, he cut his arteries and sprinkled his blood on the ground with the words, "We are making a libation to Jove the Liberator." The thought followed Stoic belief, and a later version of the events expanded on them. He was reported to have said, "We can pay our debt to nature in freedom. Nero can kill me, but he can do me no hurt."[24]

The poet Lucan belonged to the coterie that included Thrasea Paetus and Lucan's uncle Seneca. His immediate family hailed from Spain, two generations back, and had reached a higher position through the study of *eloquentia*. His grandfather was a famous rhetor who combined an admiration for speakers like Cicero with a love of old-fashioned ways in general, and described them in a book of Roman history from the civil wars to the reign of Tiberius. His views will be discussed a little later. He had three sons, one an outstanding rhetor who rose to the consulship; a second, the dramatist, philosopher, and prime minister Seneca; a third, Lucan's father Annaeus Mela, whose thoroughly unheroic complaisance toward things as they were, even under Nero, and whose lifelong enthusiasm for money, kept him a procurator of the imperial private finances. Lucan was thus brought up in the lap of loyalty; education was added to prepare him for the same line in life that had rewarded his forebears; and he responded with a success that dazzled his teachers. By the time he was twenty he had entered the choicest literary society. Persius was his friend along with another man of letters a year or two older, Nero. Their studies had brought them together. Lucan and Persius shared the same instructor in Stoicism, Annaeus Cornutus, who was perhaps Seneca's freedman; and Lucan and Nero shared, though no doubt not literally in any single classroom, Seneca himself as guide to philosophy and eloquence. Mutual regard among the three young men fed upon their interest in their studies and was certainly not darkened by any vision of Nero's later behavior. The emperor that Lucan first saw was in fact no figure of fear: a rosebud mouth, a fat face, a fat body, and a nature blown hither and thither by gusts of enthusiasm. He liked Lucan and at the first chance (in 60) made him quaestor and augur. Lucan answered with a eulogy delivered at the Neronian games, won a prize for his *Orpheus*, and began to map out an epic in which the emperor and his ancestors received the most flattering tributes. It contained other passages less flattering, but Nero was tolerant. "A remarkable and especially notable fact . . . was that he bore nothing so patiently as the curses and jeers of men, nor showed himself more merciful to anyone more than to those who attacked him in their remarks or verses." The first three books of the *Pharsalia* appeared without censure, presumably with applause.[25]

Then came a breach. Apparently before a special meeting of the senate in 62 or 63, Nero was exhibiting his talents, and Lucan walked out. As a result, he and his work were banished from favor. He was soon heard "making great talk about the glory of tyrannicides," and this, or the emperor's resentment and jealousy, linked him further to the Pisonian conspiracy of 65. In April he was seized, questioned, tortured; forced to inform against his mother among other confederates, and then to cut his veins, with some lines from the *Pharsalia* on his lips.[26]

His poem presents a puzzle which scholars have been debating since the twelfth century.[27] The heart of it is, how to fit together the passages that are anti-imperial, with those that flatter Nero. He chooses a perilous subject, in the first place —the civil wars beginning in 49 B.C. His work, unfinished, might ultimately have stopped at the winter of 48/47, where it now does stop, or was perhaps intended to go further—to 46, even to 44. The exact shape of the whole is unknown. But its *dramatis personae* are clear: on the abstract level, *libertas* doomed by tyranny; on a lower level, Cato and his cause against Caesar. For illustration: "Thy name, Liberty, and thy empty shadow will I follow," Cato declares (*Phars.* 2.302f); and to his troops, "Do you refuse to offer your throats and swords to your country, now that liberty is near?" (9.264f). Yet there is something fatal in wars fought only to choose a master. Pompey and what he stands for are consistently favored over Caesar the *tyrannus* (8.835; 9.279) or *dominus* (6.262); yet Pompey too is *dominus* (9.257). Rome endures tyranny, liberty has fled beyond her borders (7.433) whence it has never returned. Which side was right? "It would be impious to ask, *scire nefas*" (1.126). Both are tyrannies. And to know the nature of tyranny, read a courtier's speech: "The whole strength of scepters vanishes if it begins to weigh considerations of justice, and regard for virtue overturns citadels. Free rein in crime and boundless slaughter guard hated rulers. No one can do all things cruelly and unpunished, save by that very cruelty itself. Let him who would be righteous leave royal courts. Virtue and autocracy cannot be mixed" (8.489f). No more can peace and liberty; "peace will come with a tyrant" (1.670), though as second best, and "you may retain the illusion of liberty by desiring whatever is enjoined on you" (1.146f).

All this is bad enough, one might think, yet it represents only the clichés of the rhetors' schools, worth quoting to show the kind of thing that schoolboys learnt but hardly treasonous. To balance the blame between Caesar and his enemies was acceptable, too, and certainly no one could defend tyranny. Was it, however, wise to insist quite so much on Caesar's bloodthirsty ambition? On Cato's virtue, in Books 2 and 9? On Brutus, so noble, "the ornament of the empire, last hope of the senate" (*Phars.* 7.588)? Perhaps the Stoicism evident throughout the epic, and its colors used to identify its heroes, might have been toned down, and, given Nero's extravagant Hellenism, the *Pharsalia* surely contained too much of the old Roman, especially the Octavianist, suspicion of the East. Worse, there were derogatory remarks that an ingenious reader, ancient or modern, could turn against Nero himself, and some unmistakable assertions that in Lucan's own day freedom was dead.[28] The wars turned into the struggle "which we have still, between *libertas* and Caesar" (7.695f).

But if fate could find no other means save through the civil wars to arrange the advent of Nero—so says Lucan—then all the crimes and horror were worth it. Upon this incredible adulation he piles still more, taking refuge at last in visions of his emperor as a god tipping the world off its axis by some careless shifting of his great bulk (*onus*—true enough, *that*). The eulogy is utterly at odds with much else in the poem, just discussed. It cannot be dismissed as ironic; no one doubts its genuineness, and, what is more, it cannot be set aside as part of a pro-Neronian first three books, published before the break in relations. In fact, there is no corresponding break in the poem. Ideas expressed later are, where appropriate, expressed in the first three books as well. The whole epic builds to a climax of opposition—through the concepts of tyranny, liberty, the Stoic hero, and so forth—in an organic fashion.[29]

Lucan's views on the principate developed rather like his poem from an attitude vaguely loyal and no more than conventionally obsequious toward the emperor into an attitude of violent disapproval which he vented in revolution. His political career, like his literary one, had been ruined by Nero; Nero's passion for the theater by itself made Roman senators shudder; and past events proved that Nero was perfectly capable of turning some flash of fatal petulance against anyone at all—mother, wife, mistress, friend, or tutor. Lucan thus had good cause to act. The point is, however, that, when he was drawn into opposition, it was by means of the ideas that he had written about for a long time without ever understanding or believing. The external situation accounts for the fact of conspiracy while the form of it—his loud talk of tyrannicide, and the manner of his death—was strongly traditional. The same may be said of Seneca, if he was a member of the plot, and no doubt of other men too, while on the other hand Nero's willingness to suspect Seneca, and even Seneca's brother the rhetor, sprang from a recognition that an empty political cliché, the mere husk of an idea, might become filled with passion and energy, shaping and directing them. In Cato, husk and substance were one. He did what he did because of what he believed, and allowed his actions in turn to shape his beliefs. By Lucan's day, a man could begin a poem glorifying the Republic without being for a moment disloyal to the emperor, though how he and his poem ended was a question for the emperor to decide.

Curiatius Maternus is the last of those who got into trouble for their love of a Republican hero. He wrote a *Cato* in about A.D. 74. Rumor said that "he offended certain powerful individuals, by so forgetting himself in the theme of his tragedy as to think like Cato." Just so: write what you wished provided the clichés remained that and nothing more. What was required, and more often found, was a man like Titinius Capito, loyal servant of the regime and exemplary citizen. He cultivated the busts of Brutus, Cassius, and Cato "with wonderful veneration and zeal." "No suspicion of Republican sentiments incriminates the life and career of Titinius Capito, nor does any link of propinquity explain or extenuate his behavior. Not a noble, not even a senator, but merely a Roman knight, Titinius is a document of social mimicry."[30]

A sense of family that inspired Brutus needed continuity. His own kin, however, withered by closeness to the imperial house. Cato's luster was transmitted to no descendants, and that of Cassius was diffracted among collateral branches. After A.D. 22, we hear of no great funeral in which their *imagines* figured. Their principles lived on for a long time. They retained their outer form while gradually losing their substance, becoming in the end not much more than a part of a conventional aristocratic education. But into their form, a century after the great battles of the civil wars, some ephemeral power could still be poured, some genuine anger. Emperors were to this extent right in suspecting their subjects who showed too noisy an affection for the last Republican heroes.

Cremutius Cordus, Thrasea Paetus, Lucan, and Curiatius Maternus have come forward in order of their age, covering the period from about A.D. 25 to 75, and with them have appeared in their acts and writings the heritage and cult of the Republic. It is now time to turn to their background and political opinions. If the subject were treated properly, it would take in the whole history of the early principate and of its reception recorded in detail by Tacitus and others. Here only two questions may be raised. What did the opposition not like in the constitution of the state? What did they want instead? Obviously they were no democrats. Their enemies once or twice accused them of rabble rousing, but the charges are vague and unsubstantiated. In trouble, they might look to popular sympathy for a great name. Generally they despised the lower classes and provincials. They themselves were of the new nobility, or as near to it as they could possibly get: senators like Cremutius Cordus, or, at the least, members of the imperial bureaucracy. For illustration, take Seneca and his brothers, two of them consuls, one a procurator; a nephew (Lucan), fairly started on his career by way of the quaestorship; a relative or descendant of a freedman, prefect of the City Watch; or again, Thrasea Paetus, consul, marrying the daughter and sister of consuls, leaving his daughter the wife of a praetor and the mother of a consul. Against one of this coterie it was even charged that he had not chosen to go beyond the quaestorship. He had disloyally abdicated a birthright.[31]

So, in a way, had Seneca's brother the procurator—to get rich.[32] In this aim he succeeded not half as well as Seneca himself, who combined the posture of a philosopher with perfectly gigantic wealth. His enemies thought this was most amusing. In a later generation, Pliny belonged to the fringes of the opposition, and he too was rich. The Stoic Junius Mauricus asked him to look out some young man as a possible nephew-in-law. Pliny begins his reply with an encomium on Junius' martyred brother, and then turns to his subject. There is a certain Minicius, modest, frugal, of an antique rusticity. Odd for Pliny to recommend such qualities, himself a millionaire and having boasted in the previous letter that he had almost never missed a literary recitation (*Ep.* 1.13). But he goes on: Minicius is a handsome lad "who will cost you nothing, having already passed through his quaestorship, tribunate, and praetorship. I hardly know whether or not to add that his father possesses ample resources" (1.14). Such delicacy—but no more than due to his virtuous correspondent.

Riches, then, and public office marked the followers of Brutus and Cato (who had themselves, for all their devotion to philosophy, loved riches and public office). Naturally the great majority of this opposition were to be found in the senate. The fact explains why emperors—Augustus, Tiberius, Claudius—sometimes feared to attend its sessions.[33] The last of these three gave as his reason the forces unleashed in the overthrow of his predecessor, and a description of these will help to explain the character of the opposition that we are studying. The source is Josephus, at least the immediate source, in his *Jewish Antiquities* 19.1–273, which is here severely condensed.

Gaius, that is, Caligula, attended the horse races, where the Romans love to gather, and where their petitions are usually granted. This time, however, when they asked for lower taxes, the emperor sent his soldiers among them to arrest and execute the insolent. His tribune Chaereas was assigned to investigate further, and to collect the taxes in question, but his manner of proceeding only earned Gaius' ridicule for a lack of manly severity. Angry, and afraid of worse punishment, and eager, too, to win fame for a deed befitting a free man,[34] Chaereas began to form a conspiracy. He enlisted other soldiers, senators, and knights. Some felt shame as he did for bearing arms "not for the freedom and empire of the Romans but for the safeguard of the man who enslaved them"; others chafed under the injustice of the reign. One shouts, "Give me liberty as the password . . . I have no leisure to consider the dangers to myself while I am so grieved by the slavery of my country, once the freest of all, and by the complete subversion of the laws." Delay can only deprive their fellow citizens of liberation from tyranny. Accordingly, the next time the games are held in the palace they set upon Gaius and kill him. The good news is announced to the senate by Gnaeus Sentius Saturninus: "We are now in possession of liberty" in a state rendered "independent and governed by such laws as it once flourished under. As for myself, I cannot remember our former times of liberty," but I now see and rejoice in our present freedom. "Virtue alone can preserve liberty"; tyranny, on the other hand, "discourages all virtue and deprives the noble-spirited of freedom." Julius Caesar decided to destroy the democracy, and overstepped "the order (κόσμος) of the laws, making himself greater than the laws but less than [that is, slave to] his pleasures." All his successors have vied with each other to overthrow the ancestral laws of our country, and to strip it of all citizens of noble principles. But liberty, hateful to all tyrants, now allows us free disagreement with all proposals, since we no longer have a master. Yet beware! "Nothing of late has so much engendered tyranny as sloth and the failure to contest what tyranny desires." All credit to Chaereas, vindicator of liberty! "Brutus and Cassius laid the foundations only of civil war, Chaereas has ransomed our city from all evils." Whereupon the hero steps forward to receive the password "Liberty" from the consuls. After a hundred years, the right of giving it has returned to them.

No one, of course, imagines that a Hellenized Jew transplanted to Rome was the first to gather the materials for this tale, though he could doubtless recognize how glorious was the subject. Instead, Josephus can be shown to have drawn on an account in Latin by someone almost surely a senator, probably of the generation of Vespasian. After reading the long speech toward the end, we can see why Claudius trembled to enter the curia, for the tone is wildly pro-senate, and the climax of the entire story and its most essential element is the explanation of motive and achievement offered by Sentius Saturninus to his fellows. Granted, his thoughts are not very original. That is precisely the value of the whole account. It is linked to similar ones of Brutus and Cassius, summarizes half a dozen passages from Lucan, recalls sayings of Seneca and Thrasea. Some elements come from Greek romance: in general, the prominence of Chaereas, perhaps also the fact of the senate's ascending to the Capitol directly after the assassination, like good Greek heroes to the Acropolis. Much of the picture of the tyrant's vices and cruel behavior, his isolation, his placing himself above the laws, is no more than naturalized Roman, which we have met before, and the relation between him and the servitude of his citizens introduces a topic of Greek philosophy that we will meet again. Despotism makes men slaves not only to political *force majeure* but to the worst in themselves. The very ones who should exemplify nobility (τὸ γενναῖον) cannot rise above self-indulgence (τοῦ τερπνοῦ ἡσσώμενοι; below, p. 64). They are "trained to live the life of slaves," preferring "rather to await their end in the uttermost degradation than to die with virtue" (Jos., *Ant. Jud.* 2.181). Sentius is indignant to discover how easily men can get used to tyranny and in this way lose the power to throw it off—exactly what Chion points out in the letters attributed to him, and what Tacitus and Pliny so lament. With enough arrests and spies and butcheries and shouts of rage, any tyrant can work his will. The end is horrible. Men do what they are revolted to find themselves doing. They should then in justice hate themselves. But the human reflex spares them that, with any luck, and they turn their redoubled hatred against the outer cause of inner rottenness.[35]

This is what joins politics and morals, liberty and virtue. Another connection exists between the love of liberty and free speech (above, at notes 15f; below, p. 65f). Sentius rejoices in the return of debate to the senate, where all had been acquiescence. But while his periods lengthen and his audience takes heart, outside the curia events are decided by men in arms, without hearing what the noble senator says, and another emperor is discovered hiding behind a curtain. History prefers the most scorned of the Julio-Claudian line to the best candidate the senate can produce; and the irony in the situation is not lost on the reporter whom Josephus follows. Similar misgivings about a Republican restoration and the real fitness of the senate to take over the reins of government can be detected perhaps in Lucan, certainly in Seneca, Tacitus, and Pliny; after all, the principate has its redeeming features.[36]

What then did the opposition want? In essence, security to speak their minds. That meant the rule of law; hence the emphatic hostility to a ruler above law, as the Josephus source describes him. Next, more power and dignity for the senate, where that free speech might find its focus. The senate was the center of protest. And third, that the ancient magistracies should be more than merely decorative. The password *Libertas* must return to them. As for the principate, modified thus to the form it actually had at scattered times throughout its first hundred years, there was an early and almost unanimous agreement that Rome needed it. Possibly in Augustus' reign someone like Cremutius Cordus would still have preferred the Republic in its pure form, whatever *that* was, but later figures that have been discussed were willing to support, even to enjoy and flourish under, any rule that was supportable.

They still proclaimed the old slogans of their heroes, but the words had changed meaning. The key was freedom, but not the freedom of a nobility operating through senate and magistracies without check, as the tyrannicides had demanded; rather, freedom, especially of speech, guaranteed under monarchy. It was possible for the same motto hallowed by Brutus' coinage to be stolen and repeated by aspirants to the throne: Libertas personified, with the cap of liberty, in Galba's program, recalling legends of 43 B.C.; or LIBERTAS (PUBLICA) alone, or with SALUS or PAX. Vespasian boasted LIBERTAS RESTITUTA SC, even that antinomy, LIBERTAS AUGUSTI SC—"the freedom of the emperor by vote of the senate." By Trajan's time, we know that the ancient reality had become only a phrase, for his coins go right back to LIBERTAS, BRUTUS of 59 B.C.[37]

In their criticism, the opposition chose their standards from the past. They wanted to turn the clock backward. Their words of praise were "ancient" or "ancestral," in Sentius' mouth. They longed for a world that, as Sentius admitted, they had never seen, known to them only through books and busts. They cultivated the memory of men who had fought against the future—Brutus, Cassius, Cato. But, as toward the principate, so toward the Republic their attitude wavered. Its last age, that of the civil wars, drew conflicting views from men like Sentius, Seneca, and Lucan, to say nothing of Tacitus' circle later; and opinions prevailing among Cicero's contemporaries, that the great days were past, were revived and elaborated by other Romans of the Empire. "It is astonishing how quickly, after the flowering of belief in Augustus' mission, a change to a total historical pessimism succeeded, and how axiomatic, even for Julio-Claudian historians, was the idea that Rome had fallen on irreversible decay." A single example may suffice. Seneca the elder, in his *History* written under Caligula, distinguished several epochs in Rome's past: under Romulus, infancy; childhood under the remaining kings; youth, down to the end of the Punic wars; maturity from 146 B.C. on, until it turned its powers against itself; and "this was the beginning of age . . . for, having lost the liberty that it had defended under the leadership and inspiration of Brutus, it began to grow old, as if too weak to sustain itself had it not been supported by the application of monarchy." An interesting view for the elder Seneca: the principate had come in the nick of time. Interesting, too, that he should see the civil wars not so much as a struggle for liberty, but as the fatal misapplication of enormous forces. "Rome was destroyed by her own strength," said Horace (*Epod.* 16.2). That was a common interpretation in his generation. Seneca the elder's grandson Lucan repeated it in a more developed form. For him, the decline of the Republic was a moral one, working through general causes—luxury, arrogance, self-indulgence, greed—upon the specific instruments of national suicide. Bad men were typical in the society of that time; bad men actually hacked the state in pieces, fulfilling their wicked destinies. But Lucan believed that all great things must decline, anyway.[38]

Roman emperors cannot have liked being told that what they ruled was a civilization in its second childhood, to which they served, by one view, only as a kind of dry nurse, or by another view, as the continuing cause of its decline. Historiography under the principate was indeed almost unremittingly gloomy. Its gloom deepened as time multiplied examples of rulers whom it was safe, after their death, to paint in the blackest colors. Here too was reason for imperial displeasure. By way of contrast, a new regime might allow the damning of its predecessors, but, after all, until 69 the emperors were all members of the same family, and lurid accounts of Caligula or Claudius reflected on the Julio-Claudii in general as on the very institution of monarchy. In this sense, historiography offered to the opposition a common disguise for attack, at least for criticism. Criticism was also possible if historians reached back farther to the very origins of Julio-Claudian power, in events surrounding Caesar and Augustus. Under the wrong emperor, any kind of approach could be dangerous. Domitian killed Hermogenes of Tarsus "because of certain parallels he had drawn in his *History*, and crucified the amanuensis who had written it out."[39]

But we have now described what ideas, catch phrases, and partisan retrospection inspired the enemies of the throne, from Augustus to Nero, or a little beyond, and what weapons of propaganda they could draw from the past. It is time to survey quickly the vehicles of literary attack.

To histories, declamations may be added. Dio records under Domitian an incident to serve as transition: capital punishment for "excerpting and reading aloud the speeches of kings and other leaders recorded in Livy." A certain sophist Maternus died about the same time for delivering a school exercise on tyrants, and a similar case occurred under Caligula. Everybody knew what to say on the subject because everybody had learnt the same themes in school. Remarkably silly, they were: "He killed the tyrant" (give him his reward); "He killed the tyrant, his father" (tyrannicide or parricide?). What if two physicians both claim the reward for tyrannicide? Or if you kill him when he takes you in adultery with his wife? Distinguish between different degrees of difficulty in the enterprise, the types of law applicable, and so on. Fine phrases ring out: *publica vindicta cruentum gladium.* It is amusing to think of an emperor, Vespasian, subsidizing a chair of rhetoric from which these exercises were taught, and still taught later under his son Domitian, the very one who punished antityrant declamations with death. Men of sense protested: "What incredible compositions! And what follows next is the application of bombast to topics that have nothing to do with real life . . . 'The Rewards for Tyrannicides,' 'The Choice of Evils,' " and so forth.[40]

The needs of schooling excused almost anything said on the subject of foul despots. Occasionally we hear of particular speeches before a real audience that brought understandable penalties, and occasionally veiled or quite innocent remarks were taken amiss.[41] On the whole, however, people were very careful. If they really intended to oppose the emperor's power, then they said so, or did so, and perhaps suffered; but to rebuke or ridicule him *viva voce* would have been insane: either he did not deserve it (like Titus) or would punish it (like Domitian).

Criticism (in contrast to opposition) therefore preferred the written word, and spoke in code. Given the audience to which it was primarily addressed, an upper class of men all sharers in the same traditions, culture, and education, there was a good deal one could say without seeming to say anything at all. There had been other tyrants long ago. Whoever chose could aim at the emperor through Agamemnon, with unexceptionable and unmistakable detestation. Accius' old tragedy on the Thyestes theme, filled with the most useful targets—Thyestes himself and Atreus for tyrants, a family entangled in murder, adultery, and horrible hatreds—had been a favorite for many generations, and was rewritten so often that it became a kind of joke—a risky one. Seneca's version survives, some parts of which indicate what might be done with the material. We hear of enmities between brothers, or between fathers and sons, or wives and husbands; of exiles and mistresses—for which substitute Titus and Domitian, Claudius and Nero, Agrippina and Claudius, Tiberius and Messalina. Another passage tells us that tyrants do as they will while the people must applaud. That thought could be used ad lib. To Domitian's divorce, a comedy on Paris and Oenone could apply. But some emperors had no sense of humor. Playwrights were punished. It was safer to hide in a crowd. Pointed lines in the theater might be received with roars of applause, and repeated to more roars, right in the emperor's face. This happened not only in Rome but in Greek cities as well.[42]

Some explicit works of the opposition have survived, brave after danger had passed. One is a short dialogue once attributed to Lucian, the *Nero;* another is the drama *Octavia*, sometimes attributed (I think wrongly) to Seneca.[43] Its publication satisfied hatreds that could be vented at leisure after Nero's death, but it was nonetheless pretty uninspired. Platitudes fill up the better (or worse) part of it; Nero shows the stock character of the tyrant; his tutor Seneca gives him the most obvious moral advice in the flattest tone; for example, "It is most improper to make up one's mind in haste against one's friends" (line 440; Rubellius Plautus is meant). Still, there is plenty of material: all of Nero's crimes from matricide to the execution of his wife Octavia, despite his improving conversation with Seneca on the topic of "The Good Ruler" (lines 440–491). At the end comes the comfort of the chorus: "Humankind are ruled by fate, nor can anyone make any promise to himself firmly and surely. . . . Let many examples that your [Octavia's] progenitors suffered fortify your spirit. In what way is fate crueler to you?" (lines 924f). Other lines seem a little more venturesome. "We too are unmindful of our leader [Augustus] since his end, whose descendants we betray under the influence of a violent fear. The virtue of our forebears once was truly Roman, and truly the race and blood of Mars in those men. They drove proud kings from this city and fully avenged your [Virginia's] spirit, slain by a parent's hand" (lines 288f).

Seneca's authorship of one work of criticism, the *Apocolocyntosis*, seems certain.[44] Its exact purpose, however, is obscure. Since it piles up the names of some thirty victims of imperial persecution, it falls a little below the level of pure comedy. It belongs rather in the long line of broad, harsh Roman satire, here directed at Claudius. A similar piece is Juvenal's picture of the council of state meeting to decide what to do with a gigantic fish presented to Domitian (4.37 f). It was of course written after that emperor's death, nor was Juvenal troubled with such a despot in his own life. If he eventually suffered exile, as some late biographical notices say, it was for attacks on private enemies.

Earlier poets had other troubles. Under Augustus, anonymous or pseudonymous literary attacks were declared actionable, and the emperors sometimes protected themselves behind this law. Late in his reign a new policy extended the definition of treason to words as well as deeds. The door opened to charges against writers whose books were occasionally burnt by the authorities and whose lives were forfeited to the emperor. Several minor poets published abusive verses against Tiberius, Caligula, and Nero, one of them choosing a banquet as an audience. All were prosecuted for treason, two escaped. More notable victims include Phaedrus. In the first two books of Phaedrus' *Fables*, Sejanus felt secret slander, and brought the poet to court. His punishment is unknown, his humiliation evident in the repentant preface to the third book. After him came Lucan, whose fate has been described; but his friend Persius may also have been one of Nero's victims. He died in 62, *vitio stomachi*, leaving some encomiastic verses on the elder Arria which his literary executor advised his mother to destroy. That executor was L. Annaeus Cornutus, whom we have met before as instructor in Stoicism to Persius and to Lucan, while the Arria in question was wife and fellow sufferer to Thrasea Paetus, and relative (*cognata*) to Persius. Persius, according to the biography of him attributed to Suetonius, "was for some ten years one of the closest friends of Thrasea Paetus, even accompanying him sometimes in his travels." Persius thus moved familiarly in the most Stoic circles, and his poetry reflects the philosophic views that we would expect, especially the fifth book of his satires (lines 83–99, 153). This alone would render him distasteful to Nero, and his friends and family were suspected of subversion. Moreover, parts of his writings could be interpreted as hostile to specific features of the reign. It is not inconceivable that he was poisoned by Nero's doing.[45]

Suppression of sections of Persius' poetry by his friends helps to explain why so little opposition appears in our sources till long after the events they describe, though it is obvious from materials preserved in Suetonius, for instance, that there were at least plenty of short pieces—the martyrologies and "last words," to be discussed later, and satirical bits and sketches, and miscellaneous "hate" literature—ready to emerge from hiding when it was safe. Safety was not really certain, despite false promises, except in Vespasian's decade, and then again after Domitian. Meanwhile there circulated in the utmost secrecy the works of Cremutius Cordus, Titus Labienus, and Cassius Severus, and of others whose names are lost. Seneca before his death erased from what he had written anything that might result in censorship or suppression. Authors like Curiatius Maternus were advised by their friends to steer clear of dangerous subjects. Tacitus considers what choice of topic is safer, and in fact did keep silent for many years. Even men generally associated with subversive circles could be discreet: Seneca, for one, fawning on Claudius' minister, in his early *Consolation to Polybius*—he later wished it to be forgotten—and Lucan, for another, in the opening sections of his *Pharsalia*. It would be pointless to condemn them for a certain acquiescence. They demonstrated a truth well known to other centuries: terror works. And besides, theirs was a group not blindly hostile to the principate. They were willing to play a part in it, they had their careers to think about. So too for Martial, a typical figure: proud of special favors and rank bestowed by the genial Titus, ready to flatter Titus' successor with the whole *Liber spectaculorum*, in the first year or so of the reign, and later, too. "If truth may be trusted, greatest Caesar [Domitian], no age can be set above your times. When could we view more noble triumphs? When have the Palatine gods more deserved our thanks?" (*Epigrams* 5.19.1–4). If a certain nobleman ended a burdensome disease with his sword, that reflected honor on the emperor. Brave Festus "with dry eyes cheered up his weeping friends, though determined to approach the Stygian lake." Nothing so unheroic as starvation or poison for him, but "a Roman death" which "fame might prize over Cato's end, for Caesar [Domitian] was this man's friend." So says Martial (1.78). Yet his own circle included Lucan and Pliny, and he hated Nero with the best of them. He hated Domitian, in due course.[46]

Finally, opposition of a lower order—smart sayings and jokes for the crowd, anonymous squibs, or some pretty unpleasant remarks on Nero's sex life written on walls. One graffito in Pompeii says, "Mr. Poison takes care of Nero's finances," in reference to the six or eight profitable deaths by that means that Nero had allegedly engineered. "In many places," says Dio (62.15.2), speaking of Rome, "people wrote on walls, 'Nero, Orestes, Alcmaeon, matricides,' " presumably pointed at Nero by someone well educated.[47] References to

Greek mythology take us back to what we mentioned earlier, communication by code among the upper classes.

Code depends on decoders. Over the first hundred years of the principate, people lumped together as the "opposition" shared the same kind of background in any one generation, though it was a slightly different one at different times. They were alert to the same ideas, under the same dark skies, a close group. On the periphery stood men of views and courage similar but not so extreme: Curiatius Maternus or Pliny; at the heart, someone like Thrasea Paetus. It was their receptions and banquets that emperors feared, where, after the slaves had left the room, voices got lower and zeal hotter for revolution, for "new things," in the usual phrase, *novae res*. Here too was where men praised old things: the Republic, Brutus, and the ancestral way of life, *mos maiorum*. Sympathies were woven tighter by kinship. The charts on pages 42–43 show this best, but a few details are worth adding: how often people were friends, how common it was to exchange the dedications of works of literature, celebrate each other's martyred fathers and brothers and husbands in eulogy and verse, and strengthen cordiality with ties of marriage or guardianship. When Helvidius' daughter was left fatherless, she was brought up by Cornutus Tertullus, defender of the opposition in the senate. From him she would learn the proper view of things; so Lucan and Persius from Annaeus Cornutus, Helvidius from his father-in-law Thrasea, or Seneca's friend Marcia from her father, Cremutius Cordus. No doubt we could trace much more extensive loyalties if we had for Nero's and earlier reigns the kind of intimate accounts preserved in Pliny. From his letters (*Ep.* 3.11) it is enough to draw the mention of "seven of my friends killed or exiled: Senecio, Rusticus, and Helvidius killed, Mauricus, Gratilla, Arria and Fannia exiled, and I myself half scorched by so many strokes of lightning

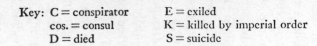

RELATIONSHIPS AMONG THE DISLOYAL OPPOSITION

Key: C = conspirator E = exiled
cos. = consul K = killed by imperial order
D = died S = suicide

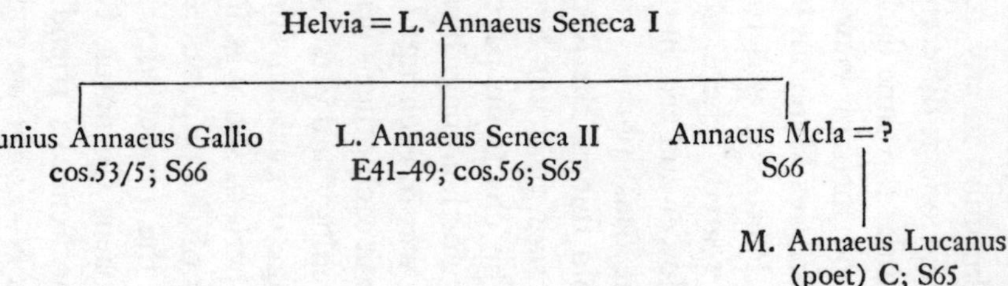

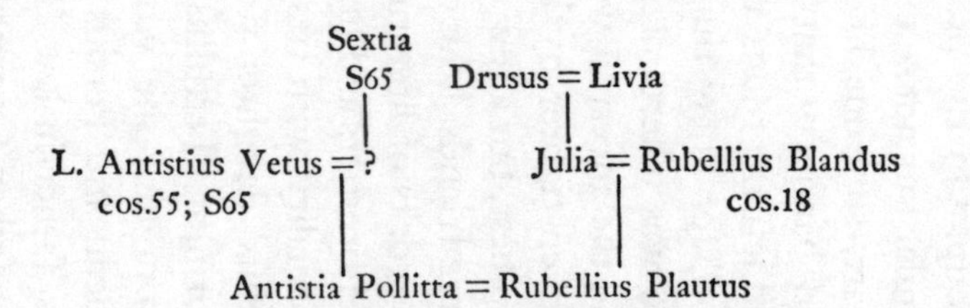

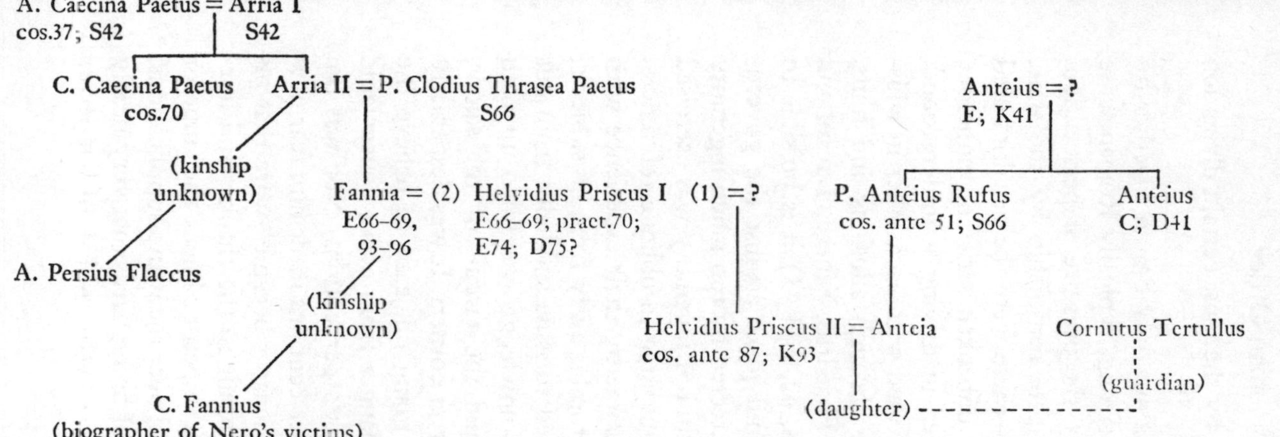

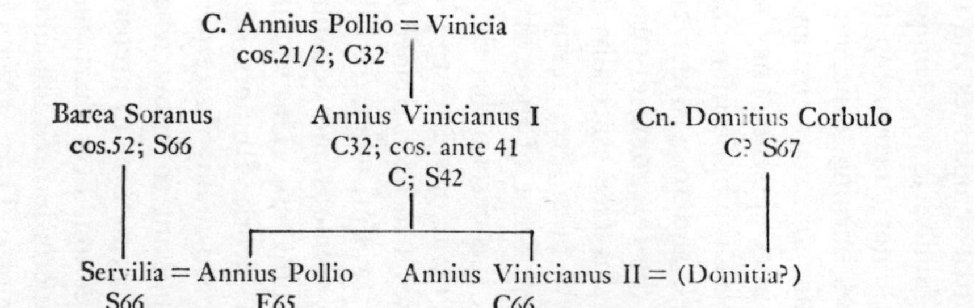

Note that the groups above are partially connected through their teachers and spiritual advisers: Verginius Flavus (C; S65), to Persius; L. Annaeus Cornutus (E62–65), to Lucan and Persius; and Musonius (E62–65), to Thrasca Paetus and Rubellius Plautus.

hurled about me that I foresaw by the most certain divination that the same fate threatened me."[48]

The group he deals with was not only drawn together by mutual sympathies and by the strong, typically Roman sense of family; it was compacted by the pressure of persecution. Voluntary censorship to anticipate censorship by the state, book burning, exile, and death—these were the penalties used in fits and starts by an almost unbroken series of emperors, to bury dissent. They succeeded in driving it underground. There the opposition communicated with each other in whispers, and to a wider audience through allusions and hints. In the foregoing discussion of Phaedrus, Seneca, Lucan, and Persius (see especially notes 28, 42, and 45) it is possible to show or suspect furtive jabs and jokes against the government. Some of these may be detected by too much ingenuity but it is certain that the same kind of ingenuity was exercised by contemporaries to pick up meaning in oblique references. They had been trained to the game by their experience with terror. For, when the ruler got too far away from his subjects, his opinions and decisons seemed to issue suddenly from out of nowhere. The vacuum of knowledge was filled up with guesswork. Rumors raced round the circuit of the salons, buzzed among the crowds at street corners. It was desperately important to know what was going on, easy to believe the worst, natural to prepare for danger from every conceivable direction. Fear sharpened people's perceptions. Nor was the emperor himself immune. His persecutions made him fear new enemies. Thus, when a certain senator became aware that his remarks had been taken as an insult to the throne, and hurried to fling his arms around the emperor's knees, the emperor started as from an attack, tripped over the man's supplications, fell, and was rescued by a rush of bodyguards that very nearly killed the senator. Instances could be added of emperors angered by wholly imaginary slights, fearful of assassination from wholly innocent quarters, convinced of disloyalty where no evidence existed. Hence the extremely loose nature of many charges against men accused of treason and the tendency to throw together, in allegations of guilt by association, all sorts of talk of Stoicism (or at least of strict morality), hatred of the throne (or at least a father once suspected of that), and similar stuff the truth or falsehood of which it is now idle to investigate. At the worst, emperors took into account the fact that the execution of one man for a plot turned his brothers and cousins into plotters who might as well be removed in advance by still further executions. Entire families in this way fell under a general suspicion, not quite unjustified, since as we have shown, suspicion itself increased their solidarity. And they for their part were as quick as the emperor to see a threat. There are instances of unnecessary suicide in anticipation of indictments that never would have been lodged. This was a consequence of trying to outguess a tyrant, of giving room to one of the anxieties that beset men in bad times: "What will the emperor think?" "If he summons you, what does it mean?"[49]

Tacitus' *Agricola* and *Annals* contain descriptions too good to condense, of the atmosphere under Tiberius or Domitian. One passage (*Agr.* 2) is specially interesting because it reveals a sense of guilt to be shared among all the nobility: "Truly, we afforded great proof of our submissiveness." It was a guilt felt most by those like Tacitus who could neither resist tyranny nor surrender completely to it. In periods of terrible fear, the moral problems for an aristocracy priding itself on its leadership became truly excruciating. To these and to their relations with politics we turn next.

✧ II ✧

Philosophers

OPPOSITION among Roman nobles had a literary tinge under the Julio-Claudii, a philosophic tinge under the Flavians. Why this was so no one knows. The fact is probably connected with the gradual dilution of the nobility, earlier upholders of a more Republican balance retaining a genuine family claim to the idea of a strong senate, while a later, rootless aristocracy relied on theoretical claims. Talk of the change requires a great deal of qualification, and recognition of the overlap between the two periods and the two approaches to protest. It is a change only real enough to justify the division of our material into the preceding and the present chapters, though a figure like Seneca reminds us of the strong ties that bound the satire of the *Apocolocyntosis* to the deeper sense of the *Moral Epistles*. The same ties appear in Cicero, if we compare the *Philippics* with the treatise *De officiis*. It was not much in the Roman character to speculate on higher things without taking account also of current realities.

With Socrates the focus of philosophy turned from the universe to man. Those Romans who were of the class to be patrons, students, or dilettanti brought it down further, from ethics to conduct, and further again, to its relations with the ordinary objectives and obstacles of their own life. This last is our interest, as it was also the interest of Cicero and Seneca. So they asked, What limits should one set to the acquisition or use of wealth? Of power? Of luxury and ease? These were not questions that much perplexed the peasantry (see above, Chapter I at notes 31 and 48, on the exclusiveness of opposition views). Or again, What should be the form of the constitution? The spirit of law and justice? The role of the citizen and the degree of his participation in politics? More sharply, for our purposes: What was virtue, for a descendant of oligarchs, under an autocrat? The answer was sought wherever rather casual study might direct a man, toward any of the great schools, most often to Stoicism, but generally in an eclectic and unsystematic fashion. If Cassius was an Epicurean and Brutus an Academic, both were subsequently revered by Stoics, especially Brutus, and what can be known of his views suggests that he himself was no narrow adherent of Plato. Specialization in one school, even what we would call real competence in any, belonged to pedants, not to gentlemen. Consider the close escape of young Agricola, who "would have plumbed philosophy more deeply than is permitted to a Roman and a senator." His mother, and reason and age, checked him. "He retained from wisdom—and this is the most difficult thing—moderation." Or consider the opinions of Quintilian, foremost teacher of his day: a man who is a citizen and truly "wise," will give himself up, not to idle disputations, but to the running of the state; if he is Quintilian's product, he must be wise in the Roman way, showing the qualities of a citizen not in the logic chopping of a studio but by applying himself to the experiences of real life.[1]

As a result of these attitudes, distinctions between different schools became very blurred, not only in common parlance but in the minds of serious students as well. Stoicism was favored first, without a close second, but it had learnt much from its competitors and had almost forgotten parts of itself. Its development is typical of what happened also to the teachings of Epicurus or Diogenes. Ethics lost their necessary firm anchor in physics; organized systems and derivations of thought were dissolved; all was open to choice, and hodgepodge handbooks encouraged everyone to be his own metaphysician.[2] That was just what everyone wanted; for the prevalence of lax logic meant no decline in philosophy, rather a great popular interest in it. To have no opinion on the subject at all was unheard of; to be hostile put one in a decided minority; and most richer men, from Petronius' egregious Trimalchio to senators of older wealth and cultivation, seem to have picked up at least a smattering of the chief terms of dispute. Many continued the studies of their youth into later life through attendance at lectures. Others enjoyed the distinction of having a resident philosopher or merely some tame thinker. Foremost was Musonius, who died toward the end of the first century, sought out by such important men as Rubellius Plautus, Thrasea Paetus, and Seneca; a teacher to Euphrates, Epictetus, and Dio Chrysostom, and founder of a line, for his son-in-law Artemidorus was a well-known philosopher and an acquaintance of Pliny; Pliny also knew a pupil of Musonius just mentioned, the famous Euphrates, in turn known to Apollonius of Tyana; while Epictetus established his own school including Arrian (consul, 129?), as did Dio Chrysostom with Favorinus. Further ramifications will concern us later, but the immediate point is clear. These were figures of the *haut monde*.

Augustus himself had a special favorite and preceptor, the Stoic Athenodorus of Tarsus. A few turncoats supported Domitian.[3] But, leaving them aside, there seems to be no prominent philosopher from the death of Athenodorus to the reign of Trajan who sided with the emperors against the large number of "opposition" philosophers. The *haut monde* to which these latter belonged was, we might deduce, the enemy of emperors; but that, of course, is obvious anyway.

Patrons or students of these men were in a position to pick the philosophy that suited them. They often mixed elements of several brands—Stoic the favorite, but also Epicurean, Peripatetic, Pythagorean, Academic, or Cynic—in a manner that showed their ignorance of the strict connections that ought to exist among all parts of a chosen system. It is, however, not too relativistic to doubt whether people generally choose any view because of its logic. It must instead form a harmony with economic interest, political bias, and social custom. We would not, for instance, expect from an aristocracy a delicate regard for the lower classes. Despite the most explicit teaching of Stoicism, later to be admitted to a changed situation, the Roman nobles of the first century did not look on all the world's population as their brothers—far from it. Nor was it they that would succor the slave. "Slavish" was the most common term of contempt among them; in contrast, "liberal" studies were "those that were fit for a free man," and the best of them was the study that "makes men free"—wisdom, in the Stoic sense. It was not for every man, only for the educated. Opinions of the masses should be ignored. As to a second point of Stoic orthodoxy, that men are ruled by destiny, it was distasteful to Roman nobles who had been at pains over some centuries to subdue the entire civilized world to their empire, to be told then that neither this nor any future act was really within their power at all, that they were, in the words of Zeno or Chrysippus, bound to their fate as a dog to a wagon. In their struggles with this doctrine, Roman Stoics achieved a most typical adaptation. Fate, they said, could be controlled by actively engaging one's will in its commands; its hold could be loosened by abandoning to it the possessions and desires by which one's will is deflected; or it could be (as some thought) confronted head on, and compelled to give way by strenuous courage. *Pugnare, luctari*, and such violent words are used to describe the belief.[4]

As Stoicism predominated in the upper classes, it must predominate in our discussion. It was aristocratic and aggressive, that much is clear. But did these two qualities combine to produce a philosophy of leadership? That should have been their tendency, but in fact men argued for an apparently individualistic or passive life. It was a moral problem. "Is a public life recommended? Even under a tyrant?" asked Quintilian (*Inst. orat.* 3.5.8). The questions were debated in the schools. Seneca answered (*De otio* 1.4), "Your Stoics certainly say that we shall be active to the very last moment of our lives, we shall never cease to work for the common good." But this we can do without making a great show of it.[5] We have, after all, two areas of common good, two homelands—our own country and the whole universe. Though we are under orders here in this life to be of service to others actively, we may choose our field of action. Our country may be corrupt beyond cure, so given over to evil that our efforts would be wasted on it. "The wise man will not struggle uselessly." He will struggle only "if nothing else prevents," such as ill-health, or lack of talents, influence, or leisure. He will struggle if his actions seem genuinely important and honorable. But none of these conditions may be met, and he must then turn quietly and softly to retirement. Why so discreet? Wisdom does not make a parade of itself. Besides, if the wise man encounters unconquerable violence, even withdrawal has its dangers. "A part of safety lies in not seeking it openly; for what one avoids, one condemns"—a very revealing remark. "Let him who would be righteous leave court life; virtue and power supreme go ill together." That second country, the cosmos, deserves our efforts, and to it we may devote ourselves. "Nature has begotten us for two purposes, contemplation and action." The founders of Stoicism, Zeno, Cleanthes, and Chrysippus, themselves kept aloof from the state, and sent no one into public life. Properly ordered, there is no higher life than can be lived in private. There, by thought and study, we can frame better laws of conduct for all mankind, by putting the life of the state, and our state of mind, in correct perspective. "The work of a good citizen is never vain. By being heard and seen, by his expression, gesture, silent stubbornness, and by his very walk, he helps." This is the conduct of Herennius Senecio or Thrasea Paetus, a protest through inactivity perfectly intelligible to their fellow senators. It was part of the formal charges against them that they had withdrawn from politics.[6]

Moreover, some parts of virtue can be attained, or pursued, only by oneself. To distinguish real from apparent good is the prime business of philosophy, the first step along the road, and we are surrounded by choices that demand the most exact and thoughtful analysis to separate reality from appearance. Meditation provides the key. And it is by oneself, too, that one can best practice virtue. Retirement may be only preparatory to action, for action is the end, not study by itself. Between the two, no contradiction in motives or thoughts. The ultimate powers are the inner ones. They require constant training, implied in favorite metaphors drawn from the field of battle or the arena. "To live is to serve in arms"; we are "athletes" fitting our minds "for the contest of public life" by "exercise."[7]

At this point we pick up lines of thought leading, not to the conclusions generally favored by Seneca, but to other conclusions that suited more venturesome natures. The life of mental struggle is defended as the best because it can direct itself toward either contemplation or activity. "The wise man will not live in solitude," but will readily answer the call to honorable deeds. He will recognize the demands of civic duty—so say Panaetius and Athenodorus, Dio Chrysostom, Euphrates, and many others of the time. The letters of Chion quoted earlier are written chiefly to prove the adaptability of philosophic training to the needs of patriotism, offering Xenophone as an example of a man who could be both thinker and leader. The same name, with those of Socrates, Plato, and Dion, recurs in a later list drawn up to show the double roles of statesman and sage.[8] It is important to collect and emphasize this testimony, since it is sometimes said that Stoicism and philosophy in general drew men away from the political sphere. No contradiction, however, necessarily existed between the studies and the deeds of Cato, for example, but rather a positive connection. They fortified each other. A person might keep to his library, if that was his natural love, and find encouragement to that choice in various writers; he might equally avail himself of the range of philosophic loyalties, in late Republican and early imperial times, to pursue a more vigorous life, relying on models and precepts scattered through the same popularly accepted corpus of instruction. To read and reread, to "train," "exercise," "arm," and "drill" under one's teachers added great strength to inborn tendencies. It is here that one can begin to sense the overt, historic power of philosophy.

Mention of Cato introduces another matter. Romans habitually taught duty through examples. Roman philosophers did the same, using figures like Xenophon. But among the fraternity of Stoics a special halo surrounded their own champions, from Cato on, and his spiritual descendants believed that they and all good men were obliged to add the witness of their own lives as a chief means of service to humanity. They could aspire to join a sort of Faculty of Moral Philosophy whose full professors taught through their immortal writings and whose more humble instructors taught only through their conduct. "Let the soul have someone whom it can venerate, whose authority may sanctify even its inner parts . . . Choose therefore Cato"—that was Seneca's advice (*Ep.* 11.9 f); and he was loyal to the same method of instruction at the end of his life, the image of which he left to his friends "as the only thing, and the fairest, that he possessed. If they bore it in mind, they would retain the glory of his noble pursuits as the reward of such a steadfast friendship."[9] No extravagant hope. He was indeed added to a distinguished company as a model of behavior, like Cato, or Thrasea Paetus, Helvidius Priscus or Musonius, and long remembered with them. His ambition verges on conceit, but it was a world of different values from our own, with different, prouder, hopes. As Musonius said, "If you do anything both noble and difficult, the noble part remains after the toil is gone"; or, in the metaphor of Epictetus, "The purple thread adorns and stands out from the white cloth." The prominent act wins renown, perhaps death, "yet I want to be purple." "What good is the purple in the mantle?" he asks, in another passage. "What, but to stand out in it *as* purple, and be a goodly example to the rest?"[10]

To the chief question of this chapter, Why philosophy and subversion went together (as they undeniably did), the answer so far seems to be that Stoicism in particular sharpened the impulse and the courage to say what one felt, without supplying any specific political program. It made missionaries, but missionaries with very little more than the vague idea that men—*other* men—could be roused to revolution, or the emperor recalled to an antique virtue, by a great deal of defiance. Tacitus has a sour smile for all this. It shows mere greed for glory, "a passion that even the wise shed last."[11] His views cannot be dismissed as envy. What was needed for a successful attack on the throne was arms, such as Corbulo could command; for assassination, the physical courage of a soldier, not the moral courage of a philosopher. Hence the division of labor in the year 41: Chaereas did the dirty work, Sentius made the speech; or again, the double plot (as it seems to have been) called "Pisonian" after the candidate it put forward, in which the really dangerous elements held aloof from the assistance offered by Lucan's circle—and quite rightly. People who seriously intended to conspire against the ruler would never, like the latter group, have drawn attention to themselves in public, and in private communicated their antimonarchic sentiments to so vocal and prominent a coterie of sympathizers. This is not to detract from their courage. They took their chances, and knew it, and paid for it. In their number (to include some already discussed in another connection) were Lucan; Persius and his teachers Verginius Flavus and Annaeus Cornutus; Seneca; Thrasea Paetus, his daughter, her husband, and another of her kin, Anteius Rufus; Demetrius the Cynic; Barea Soranus, his son-in-law Annius Pollio, and the latter's brother; Rubellius Plautus, the pupil of Musonius, and three of Rubellius' relatives. All but one adhered to Stoic principles, all but two (Rubellius Plautus and Persius, both dead in 62) died or were exiled in the wake of the Pisonian conspiracy, along with Seneca's two (presumably innocent) brothers. They had accomplished absolutely nothing.

These heavy blows decimated the opposition without putting an end to it. After 66 a second generation had a measure of revenge and its own trials. No need to unravel all threads in the complicated story, but some links must be shown between the events of Nero's reign and later. Thrasea Paetus had chosen for his daughter a suitable revolutionary, Helvidius Priscus, exiled in 66 as his alleged accomplice. Helvidius, with a number like him, returned after Nero's death thirsting for revenge. In the senate he spoke against his father-in-law's once formidable foes; Musonius spoke against a traitorous Stoic teacher of Barea Soranus. The brother of Arulenus Rusticus, Junius Mauricus, demanded the opening of the imperial archives where more evidence of informers lay hid. What began well soon ended. The new regime forbade any thorough rooting out of former delators, and frustration made an enemy of Helvidius Priscus. He turned to violent Republicanism vented in extravagant rudeness to Vespasian—refusing him his titles, and the like—and in repeatedly pressing the senate to take business into its own hands. When Vespasian sent him word not to attend a meeting of the senate, he answered (as Epictetus imagined the exchange), "It is in your power not to allow me to be a member, but till then I must attend its sessions.' 'Yes, but keep quiet, then.' 'Do not ask my opinion and I will keep quiet.' 'But I must ask.' 'And *I* must answer what seems right.' 'But if you answer, I will put you to death.' 'When did I ever tell you that I was immortal? You will do your part, I mine—yours to kill, mine to die without fear; yours to banish, mine to go without complaint.' What did Priscus accomplish by himself? What good is the purple in the mantle?" He at least earned exile, and some time thereafter, death, in about the year 75. Vespasian regretted his fate, being a merciful man, perhaps also forseeing the embarrassing consequences to the Flavian house. Under the far harsher rule of Domitian, Helvidius received the tribute of a well-publicized eulogy, for which its author, Herennius Senecio, was executed. His father-in-law was praised by Arulenus Rusticus, and *that* author killed, his brother exiled, and the younger Helvidius Priscus put to death for writing too pointed a farce.

At the same time, philosophers, including Epictetus, were driven from the city. Thus within a year (93–94) a second circle of opponents to the throne, narrower than the circle of 65–66 but linked to it, was destroyed.[12]

Their fate turns us back to the question asked a little earlier, What was it in the study of ethics that drove men into opposition? Their philosophy gave them strength for open defiance. Beyond that, it made them see and hate the inner, moral consequences of subjection to any ruler or higher rank. There lies the answer. Thrasea Paetus, though from northern Italy and the first of his family to attain prominence, still defended the oldest Republican bastions, the senate above all; Helvidius Priscus was descended from a mere centurion, yet he too in his time championed the same causes.[13] Both men had become entangled in the kinships of the aristocracy, and evidently in its slogans and toasts as well—*quale coronati Thrasea Helvidiusque bibebant/Brutorum et Cassi natalibus* (Juv. 5.36f). They belonged to the succession of the tyrannicides. The succession, however, with a good deal of reason on its side, had grown more radical as the principate grew more settled and authoritarian. If Vespasian, personification of common sense, had the epithet "tyrant" hurled at him, part of the explanation might be sought in the still extant bronze tablet defining the scope of his authority. This conferred on him in a block all the grants, privileges, rights, and power built up through precedent, usurpation, or senatorial decree by all five Julio-Claudii. Contemporary historians barely mention this law. So much had subordination become a habit of the Roman people. Worse yet, as some quotations that follow will show, the upper class from which the opposition once drew its best recruits had, for the most part, made their peace with the principate, had become sharers in its benefits, feared commotion, and waved aside any questioning of the new order with an indignant hand. Philosophers might fear subordination as leading to the loss of inner independence. They might point to the corrupting effects of a monarchy with powers too much taken for granted. All this sounded rather theoretical. So Helvidius was obliged to shout louder and louder to an increasingly indifferent audience. Others in the fight may have looked for reinforcements in a lower class. At any rate, they were charged with appealing to the people against monarchy —true, perhaps, though it would certainly be wrong to call them "democrats."[14]

Further charges directed at them were interesting, too: puritanism and philosophy, defenses needed against "the inner moral consequences of subjection." No doubt about the virtue of these men, nor (in the minds of their supporters) that precisely this contributed to their fate. It was actually made a sort of crime to "philosophize" or to "Stoicize," partly because a censorious bearing seemed to rebuke the government. We may guess, too, that Romans with hides no thicker than Athenians welcomed the chance to condemn gadflies that behaved too importunately. The banishing of philosophers in 71 was attributed to the urging of an adviser of Vespasian who spoke hotly of their "virtue," their boasting, and their easy indignation: "They despise everyone, calling the wellborn man a mollycoddle, the lowborn, a halfwit, the handsome, immoral, the ugly, a mere innocent, the rich man, grasping, and the poor man, servile." Epictetus confirms the charge. He is discussing how one makes converts in the streets. "But," he says, "nowadays this activity is not a very safe one, especially in Rome. For the man who engages in it obviously cannot do it off in a corner, but he must go up to some rich ex-consul, perhaps, and ask him, 'You there, can you tell me who takes care of your horses?' 'Certainly I can.' 'Some chance fellow who knows nothing of the care of horses?' 'By no means.' " So the conversation goes on through gold, silver, wardrobe, and body, to the soul. " 'It is not likely, especially with so wise a man as yourself and held in such respect in the city, that you would stand by and watch your most precious possession go to rack and ruin?' 'Certainly not.' 'But have you provided for that possession yourself?' At this point the danger arises that he may ask first, 'What business is it of yours, good sir? Are you my master?' And if you pursue the matter, he may raise his fist and give you a punch. I myself used to be very zealous in such inquiries, once upon a time, before I fell to my present estate."[15]

Philosophy, in defense of integrity, might thus turn out to be a kind of leveler. That was all right when senators or equestrians were considering the moral price they paid for their subservience to the emperor. Their awareness lost its edge over the course of the first century, they paid the price with increasing indifference, and talk of inner value and "subjection" began to seem too challenging, possibly revolutionary. Among the upper classes admiration of philosophy grew somewhat rarer, or more guarded. Many people obviously disapproved of the whole thing.

The "present estate" that Epictetus spoke of—exile—was, in their view, just what such a pestilential fellow deserved. What men of dignity would withhold their vote against him, or regret his loss? His kind were known, everyone looked on them with contempt and anger. Let Seneca dispute popular opinion: "Stoics shut themselves off from the state only to devise laws for humanity without offense to anyone in power. The wise man will not disturb the ways of his country nor draw the attention of the populace to himself by any novel course of life." And elsewhere: "I think people are wrong who believe that the serious devotees of philosophy are mutinous and refractory, scornful of the magistrates, or of their kings, by whom the state is governed." Those were Seneca's views. Others disagreed. Philosophers in the late first and second centuries, Stoic or Cynic, "used a façade of philosophy to discuss in public many subjects not suitable to the times." "They howl against your customs, rites, cults, and ceremonies openly, publicly, and with every kind of bitter speech, some of them flaunting their freedom unpunished against the very emperors." They "engaged in relaxing everything and in slackening the serious pursuit of practical affairs." They quibbled about the fine points, without really believing anything; hence Nero's game of calling in the teachers of wisdom after dinner to amuse his guests with their disputations—and there was no lack of competitors, wearing their most deliberative frowns. Their patrons bought plaster busts of Stoic founders, indiscriminately jumbled with Aristotle or Pittacus; their students affected gloom and virtue, while still preferring gauzy clothes to the honest toga. Such were the sneers and charges against them. Teachers themselves, those of the rougher sort, appeared in every part of the empire from Italy eastward, in one of the commonest of literary clichés: identified by their long hair, beards, bare feet and grimy rags, their wallets, staffs, and knapsacks; by their supercilious bearing, paraded morals, scowling abuse and rodomontade against all men and classes; shameless they seemed, and half-educated, vulgar, jesting; beggars for money, beggars for attention, parasites on patrons, or petitioners at the door, clustered at temples or street corners, in cities and army camps; loudmouthed shouters of moral saws driven to a life of sham by poverty, Cynics, Stoics, "philosophers," all alike. Their special saints were men credited with a common touch, Socrates and Diogenes, the latter especially. Where mendicant philosophers were given a name, they were likely to be Cynics—but not always; and Cynicism has been well described as "a kind of radical Stoicism." From Nero's reign to the death of Antoninus Pius, the century of their chief prominence saw them scattered the length and breadth of the eastern Mediterranean, concentrated most in Athens, Rome, Alexandria, Corinth, and (every fourth year) Olympia. They were to the ancient world what palmers and friars were to the medieval, a familiar sight everywhere, both suspect and sacred, but more rightly suspect, since the whole movement, like any vogue, drew in recruits who had the least suitable talents and motives. The many imposters dirtied the good fame of such as Epictetus or Musonius precisely because these latter few enjoyed, and deserved, great honor. Even the worst frauds could make a living off some village, if they did not stay too long. Clever men could impose on a more important and discriminating audience, in Rome, for example. Their victims were willing because they could hardly tell the genuine from the false, and longed for what the genuine could bring them: fortitude, peace, understanding. But the gains of philosophy were made only at the price of recurrent disillusionment.[16]

The style of speaking of these philosophers was adapted to other ends than display. Orations dazzled, discourses or "diatribes" (in the Greek sense) gave instruction. Examples from Epictetus survive almost verbatim, dramatic, charming, penetrating. Passages have been quoted above. Musonius, on the other hand, cultivated a more even style, closer to rhetoric, though he forbade applause. He wanted to reach the soul, and by the purity of his character he did so. These were Stoics, and the problems they dealt with and the manner of their address were suited to rich, educated people. As one moved down the social scale from salon to street corner, philosophic discourse retained its fundamental aim, to instruct and comfort, and its fundamental moral positions; but its expounders were more often called Cynics, and their style lower and simpler. Galen (*On the Errors of the Soul* 3.71) says of the Cynics of his lifetime, and of "some other philosophers also, that they shun the exercise of logical reasoning." This was an extreme claim of the "proletarian" teacher: to avoid pedantry, to stick to essentials; and Galen's statement, at first sight extraordinary, might be duplicated ten times over from descriptions of other figures of the same type. Cynics spoke very directly to their audience, often using the second person singular, so that everyone who heard would think he alone was intended. They used dialogue, jokes, invective, a wealth of illustrative incident borrowed from personal experience or from mythology. Especially they relied on satire to make the targets of their attack seem suddenly shocking or disgusting. Many of their barbs were borrowed by Roman poets; many remained quivering in the fat flanks of the bourgeoisie, even of ex-consuls. Nothing, alas, was sacred.[17]

An early, famous Cynic was a certain Demetrius, whose intransigence Caligula tried to soothe with a gigantic bribe—so the story ran. He was the man with whom Thrasea Paetus spent his last hour discussing the soul's immortality. Seneca befriended and admired him for virtues almost divine. A scene in the anonymous *Nero* links him to Musonius, though afterward he opposed that philosopher before the senate. His activities and views are typical: scorn of luxury and convention, insulting challenges to everyone in power. He was expelled from Rome in 66, returned, and was expelled again in 71 for exasperating the patient Vespasian. His ranting did the most to rouse the emperor's anger, and resulted in the decree of exile for all men of the same profession in that year. Some of them "somehow slipped into the city" four years later, obviously not a bit chastened by exile, and resumed (one of them in the theater) the game of emperor baiting. Under Domitian, Dio Chrysostom was barred from the capital, and some ten years later, about 93, in direct connection with the "philosophizing" and writings of Arulenus Rusticus, all philosophers were once again swept out of the city.[18]

Philosophy at Rome, as the sources show it, thus meant a loose complex of ideas adaptable to the prejudices of various classes, fortifying them against risks and inclining them to criticism. Its practioners included many of distinguished rank who clung to the ideal of a monarchy limited by increased power for the senate and Republican magistracies. It was impatient of authority, at this highest level, and something more than impatient, certainly very turbulent, among the poor. Prejudices against philosophy of this latter, "proletarian," degree strengthened the hand of a government grown more oppressive as the century wore on. Documents of secret opposition like the letters of Chion and the pamphlet on Caligula's death, quoted in Josephus, seem to belong to Flavian times, and must have angered the emperors further. More serious charges, however, may have explained the periodic expulsion decrees. Philosophers claimed to have an opinion not on specifics but on the general ethical intent of government, which did not exactly meet Domitian's specifications.

Cynics of the old school would have defended anarchy, but their descendants were very far from being strict students of classic doctrine. Just what they said to some throng in the market place is nowhere recorded. Philosophers of a more Stoic color saw three choices: disregard of government of any kind as a mere distraction or encumbrance; the mixed constitution of the middle Stoa of Panaetius, Cicero, and others; or benevolent monarchy favored by the early Stoa. The first alternative only claimed that what one rendered unto Caesar was of no great importance. Such a doctrine, short of being used (as it was by Thrasea Paetus) for pointed retirement from public life, constituted not even an indirect attack on government. The second alternative presumably underlay some of the plots of Augustus' day, and the increasingly dreamy Republicanism of later reigns; but modern authorities agree that restoration of the Republic had lost significant support very early in the first century A.D. This left only the third alternative, monarchy, to which in principle Stoicism had no objection. Seneca and others are at pains to make that perfectly clear. Yet the king must be a just one, able to control himself and his ministers, moderate and prudent, ruling by example and persuasion rather than force, obedient to the laws, strenuous for the common good. This is the ideal of the Stoics.[19] They were asking a lot, to be sure—a lot more than Nero or Domitian could give. Yet for nearly a hundred years after Domitian the principate did achieve just this level, through adoptive succession. That solution, perfectly accidental, did not appeal to Vespasian. "My son succeeds me or no one," were his words (Dio 65.12.1), after an unusually bitter exchange with Helvidius Priscus. Possibly Helvidius had been suggesting the election of an emperor by merit (and by the senate), a device that was in people's minds in 41 and 69, to be revived in the third century; possibly the remark was tangential to some attack on Domitian, with whom Helvidius had collided in 70. At any rate, there is no other hint in the sources of any Stoic or Cynic program to revise the form of the constitution.

What we do see, instead, is the interpretation of the whole struggle in which the opposition engaged in terms increasingly inward and philosophic. The position of emperor is acknowledged by Seneca, Lucan, Curiatius Maternus, and Tacitus, all counted more or less among the opposition. They will grant the emperor an eminence above the law of the state so long as he remains accountable to the laws of nature and reason; citizens, for their part, must retain a freedom no longer political but moral. A good ruler and, by consequence, a legitimate ruler in the Stoic sense, is one who does not corrupt his subjects, does not insist on servile behavior or adulation or betrayal of friends. Restrictions on his power—that meant, in effect, the independence of the senate—could alone prevent him from turning into a destroyer of virtue. So Epictetus reasons with the tyrant, Take my body, or property, do not try to rule my moral purpose. Many like Epictetus, who consider the ethical problems of the time, analyze them in terms equally dramatic, often personifying their elements for heightened effect: "Tyranny hates wisdom."[20] The contest between them is a commonplace of ancient thought, given a real arena, and flesh and blood—plenty of blood—during the reigns of Caligula, Nero, and Domitian. Tyranny resorts to force, wisdom retreats into truth, or something of the sort. Only truth shall set you free from the thrall of the body, its desires, its pains and pleasures and possessions, its delusions of what is the good. Servitude—the word and its cognates occur again and again in the chief sources—is no more than ignorance of the truth. He who values what is really of no importance one way or the other, or downright evil, is to that extent a slave. The flatterer of a tyrant may be such a man, or the tyrant himself; vices and delusions are tyrants (another very common metaphor, seen in Sentius' speech, above, Chapter I). Freedom, on the other hand, knows and clings to essential things: moral purpose, courage, equanimity, justice; and the man possessed of these is beyond the reach of force. No threat or compulsion can have any effect on him. Nevertheless, he is not obliged merely to await and endure force, but should rather speak out. This is his duty, and his chief weapon against the tyrant, who hates it. "What is the best thing of all?" someone asked of Diogenes. "Free speech, παρρησία"— chief instrument of protest and enlightenment, so often joined to freedom, ἐλευθερία. Moreover, it was the principal characteristic of Cynics and of street philosophers in general, who meant by it, at its best, the kind of informal, unstudied style of speech exemplified in Epictetus, and, at its worst, the licentious ranting and verbal shock tactics of the mendicant frauds. In a political sense, it served as last defense to liberty. All else taken away, if men could still speak their minds they might count themselves free. "You command us to be free—we will be," cried Pliny to Trajan, in an extraordinary bit of self-contradiction. "You command us to publish what we think—we will do so . . . Relying on the support of your right hand and your promises, our lips, locked in a long servitude, we now open"—in a panegyric. Not quite the same παρρησία that Thrasea Paetus and Helvidius Priscus displayed, but a remote descendant.[21]

Oppressive rulers tried to shut men's mouths by punishment, most often by exile. It might bar the victim from Rome, or Italy, or from his home province. Artemidorus simply retired to the Roman suburbs, where Pliny saw him in 93 when he was praetor. Artemidorus' father-in-law, Musonius, suffered exile earlier, but at least one friend chose to go with him, as Musonius, a few years before, had accompanied Rubellius Plautus to Asia. On the tiny island of Gyaros, Musonius even assembled a kind of school, counting as a pupil Epictetus, who, in his own long relegation to Nicopolis from 94 on, attracted Arrian with many others. Demetrius the Cynic while in exile received a visit from Pliny, who noted the distinguished company around him. Moving into the generation that flourished under Trajan and Hadrian, we know of Dio Chrysostom's punishment that drove him from his native Bithynia while he was still a young man and sent him on wanderings physical and spiritual; for it was in this period of his life that he renounced rhetoric for philosophy, moving from place to place over Greece, speaking and teaching everywhere. After Domitian's death he settled in the capital, a friend of emperors. Favorinus studied with him, was banished by Hadrian to an island, probably Chios, and there continued the pursuit of philosophy. What emerges from these stories is the continuity of view among the intellectual leaders of the opposition while undergoing punishment for their leadership. The same point can be illustrated by the apparent license accorded to men under ban to talk to each other or to vilify their betters. They still clung to their παρρησία, quoting Euripedes, at the lines where Jocasta asks her son what is worst in exile: "One thing above all, not to enjoy free speech." She agrees: "This is slavery, not to say what you think." The passage appears in Musonius' treatise *On Exile*, where he asserts the possibility of retaining free speech even under such circumstances. Other writers, in a series that begins with Teles in the third century B.C. and includes (besides Musonius) Seneca, Plutarch, Dio Chrysostom, Dio Cassius, and Favorinus, discussed the same topic, offering comfort. Their discussions met an obvious need of earlier times, but degenerated to a genre later.[22]

The pains of exile were pains of the spirit often supported in no great degree of discomfort. Tyrants also attacked the body, with torture or death, and the regularity with which confessions were extracted from brave men, and occasional tales of sufferers like Epicharis who died on the rack, suggest that what went on in the cellars of the palace was fairly efficient and perfectly horrible. Philosophy was obliged to fortify its followers against this as against any other trial. Torture, or rather endurance under it, could be made to seem positively desirable, upon careful reflection. The wise man would accept it, even advance to challenge it, for it touched no vital inner part of his soul, only his flesh. Anyone not convinced might try another way of escape, by suicide, the ultimate guarantee of freedom. Of this no despot could deprive the weakest victim. The point is driven home repeatedly, and used, too, for solace in illness or sorrow. Not all Romans admired suicide. It was a last step, to be taken by deliberation with one's self and friends, not an act of hasty, animal courage, nor a short road to fame. Yet it brought fame, on the model of Cato. It was the way out chosen by a large number of Romans, sanctioned by philosophers before them: Cleanthes the Stoic, Menedemus the Academic, and, after a fashion, Socrates himself.[23] His death gives the clue to the literary treatment of martyrdom, to which we turn shortly.

But before going on, it might help the reader to reach back into the material presented so far, to pick up the main threads. Many names, for one thing, have been mentioned, not all of them familiar in other contexts. They have been introduced here to give substance and boundaries to a certain group that had its origins in 44 B.C. The plot of that year, like those of A.D. 41 and 65, presented two aspects, idealistic and practical, and when from the latter point of view there was no reason to plot any more, under Vespasian, idealistic men still indulged in insult and agitation to show that they were not to be bought off with realities. Their last outburst came in the 90's, after which, though emperors still suppressed conspiracies, like that of 117, and still banished philosophers, like Favorinus, the motives and circumstances involved were entirely different. Opposition ended in 96, partly because of Domitian's thorough persecutions, partly because of the satisfaction of the opposition's chief aims, partly because the more passive audience to which they played had been almost wholly replaced by men really loyal to the principate.

The opposition presented a spectrum of opinions ranging from dissatisfaction through disloyalty, and so to the darker colors of irreconcilable conspiracy. At the extreme, the most dangerous end, ties of sympathy were not enough. Close friendship, discipleship, marriage, and descent made a tighter knot. Consider, for illustration, the Annaei: two Senecas, and Gallio, Mela, Serenus, perhaps Cornutus, and Lucan. At the other end of the spectrum one could find men like Martial who hated tyranny after it was gone, or Pliny during the worst years of terror hastening upward through various magistracies like Domitian's most devoted subject, while still retaining his friendship with Helvidius Priscus the younger and his sort, as well as the proper enmities, of Regulus for one. Yet Pliny is not unique. Men with more violent views than his nevertheless entered on the career normally expected of senators or prominent equestrians. Some went on to a consulship. Magistracies could be looked on as Republican. One, the quaestorship, gave access to the senate, if other ways were lacking. And the senate provided the opposition with a home. If they could imagine that they received the emperor into it as a guest, that it retained its place independent among the arches and temples honoring the Caesars, then all was well. Here they gathered to assert their dignity and power, here at the northwest corner of the forum they could stand where Cato had stood, and see on the walls of the curia scenes painted to honor victories achieved under senatorial leadership, when Rome was great.

With purges and the natural senescence of aristocracy, men who had a family attachment to the Republic died off. A sentimental attachment took its place. Its password was *Libertas*, at the center of a complex of ideas. One line led from *libertas* in a political sense to the freedom of the clans, which under the principate lost most of their significance; another line led to the contrast between free people and master, demos and despot, and to the rich mythology of tyrannicide; another, to the Republic in its social aspect, where men neither succumbed to the luxury of established empire and wealth nor cowered under a tyrant, a Republic where all was pure, strenuous, and proud; still another line led, through the teachings of Greek philosophy, to the notion of freedom as moral certainty, servitude as ignorance, and tyranny as the force that binds us to our own vices. *Libertas* included, too, the right to discuss all these things aloud, in the tradition of the historic senate debates, or in the traditions of παρρησία that alone could teach true virtue.

These ideas, when actually applied to the world around them, revealed their hidden tendencies; but looked at in isolation, they appear harmless enough. Not revolutionary, not necessarily political at all, they were rather moral in some extremely wide sense, though entangled also in political protest, social ambition, pride of history, and philosophy. If a ruler outraged people's sense of decency by his relations with his wife, he would be pilloried in an *Octavia, Paris and Oenone*, or *Apocolocyntosis;* if he turned against his family, and put them to death, he would hear about it from a *Thyestes*, or from some scribbler on walls and statue bases. It is significant that Nero was hated for playing the lyre—harmless hobby in our eyes, but shocking to Romans—and that a member of the Pisonian conspiracy recommended attacking him while he was singing on the stage, "the very presence of a crowd to be the fairest witness to so great a deed" (Tac., *Ann.* 15.50).

Since the Pisonian conspiracy led to the death of everybody concerned except Nero; since the opposition that we are talking about were just on the fringes of it anyway; since, moreover, they included a young firebrand who informed on his mother, and a philosopher-chamberlain who had somehow managed to condone matricide by the emperor; since that same Seneca so obediently ended his life at the emperor's command, like dozens of others, without any final explosion of desperate, violent, *active* courage, we may wonder why Nero or Domitian, or other emperors earlier, took them seriously at all. The question immediately answers itself: the opposition were persecuted because they supplied dangerous ideas and stories to dangerous men, just as the intelligentsia of more recent times—the eighteenth century, let us say—were persecuted. No one imagined that Voltaire was likely to try his luck with a dagger, words failing him, yet it was quite right, from the government's point of view, to hound him out of France. Our own century is not without parallels. We too have our ideas and stories.

To men operating in the realm of ideas, as a suppressed minority, the stories of their own deeds offered a natural weapon. The philosophic opposition used not only a literature of attack, described in the preceding chapter, but one also of memorial. They publicized their heroes' overthrowing the hated master of the state or enduring his cruelty. Publicity was essential to their cause if they were to make converts. If possible—that is, if it was not too dangerous—they sought notoriety through strident accounts, at times even through the most exaggerated and loudly trumpeted actions. That is the motive evident behind the quotation above: Nero should be killed before a crowd. For the same reason, the conspirators of 44 B.C. and A.D. 41 considered the theater a proper setting for their plot. They were not thinking only of better access to their victim. They wanted spectators and glory. Their weapons must be waved on high, as Brutus', for example, in the porch of Pompey's theater; and they must pick the right one, too. For Nero's death, one of the plotters got a dagger from out of the temple of Safety, or Fortune, as some accounts said, "and wore it regularly as consecrated to some great work" (Tac., *Ann.* 15.53). When he ordered a slave to give it an extra edge, one evening, and to get ready a supply of bandages, suspicions were not unnaturally aroused, the whole scheme exposed, its principal actor immediately arrested. He died the martyr of an exaggerated sense of theater, victim of too much reading. We can sympathize with him. Tyrannicide indeed offered a thrilling drama, and the full descriptions which appear in Nicolaus and the Josephus source, and which were evidently available to chroniclers of last hours of the Athenian Hipparchus, or Nero, or Commodus, belonged to a genre. Literature in this way exercised an inspiring and formative influence over men's imaginations, as it did over the Republicanism of Lucan. Its didactic purpose was as old as its very beginnings. Stories were meant to teach ideas, *exempla* were handed down for the improvement of the young, history itself was, or was supposed to be, no more than a collection of models studied for the purpose of "calling to our minds illustrious and courageous men and their deeds, not for any gain but for the honor that lies in praising their nobility by itself" (Cic., *De fin.* 1.10.36).

Plutarch's *Lives* contain many good tyrant-killing tales. The point of them comes out in the comparison between Dion and Brutus (pars. 3f): "For what stands most to the favor of both men is their hatred of tyrants and of base conduct alike." He goes on to weigh the merits of their strategy and courage, and the respective dangers they faced, in just such an analysis as we have seen Quintilian's students practicing. Declamatory patriotism, often somewhat abstract, was a Greek tradition, naturalized in Roman schools and fed to Roman boys who would grow up to be consuls. They kept their national preference for action but ornamented it with the trappings of Harmodius and Aristogeiton. Plutarch knew that tale as well, and in the 90's it was turned against Domitian.[24] The contemporary *Letters of Chion* bear on the same general themes of tyrannicide, so there was plenty for a Roman audience to enjoy.

Not every plot succeeded. Accomplices might prove traitors, suspects might be seized. Proceedings then varied, according to the importance of the accused and the fear or impatience of the government. Some men were brought before the senate, where the heavier charges leveled by the speakers for the prosecution were set down in the minutes (acta), as well as parts of the defense, thereafter available to any person who took the trouble to consult them—Tacitus, for one, who added his own colors: Thrasea Paetus' "venerable appearance" confronting an enemy "grim and threatening, fire kindling in voice, visage, eyes." The agon was of a familiar type, enacted less often before the senate than before the tyrant himself in scenes more intimate and chilling. For these, the models were well known, giving cast and *dramatis personae:* A cruel interrogator stands ready. "Yet amidst these tortures, some men have not groaned. 'Not enough—' but he does not entreat. 'Not enough—' but he does not give answer. 'Not enough—' but he laughs, genuinely." "Can anyone then prevent my smiling, my being cheerful and calm?" " 'Tell your secrets.' I keep silent, for that much is left to me. 'But I will fetter you.' What do you say, fellow?—*me?* My leg you may fetter, but Zeus himself cannot overcome my moral purpose." The victim somehow managed to have the last word, too, either by suicide, making his torturer rage that "he has given me the slip," or by repartee: "You have within your power a half pint of my blood; for as to burial, what a fool you are if you think it matters to me whether I rot above or below the ground." "You threaten me with death, but nature threatens you." Or again, by rousing the people to revolution with his last words—*that* the philosopher could do; he could turn the tyrant's suspicions against his most loyal henchmen; he could (favorite stories) bite off the tyrant's ear, bent to catch a whispered confession, or his own tongue, to prevent involuntary disclosures. Zeno did this, and Anaxarchus, Theodotus, and Leaena, long enough ago to excuse some vagueness about detail. This was the stuff that fattened a book *On the Courage of Philosophers.*[25]

It was not all romance. As there were minutes of the senate, so there were minutes of trials and hearings before the emperor, for in his capacity as a kind of supreme court with an appellate power constantly increasing and the bureaucracy to go with it, his decisions, his very exchanges with witnesses or accused persons, were noted down in shorthand, to be filed away, sometimes to be released on request to interested parties. Testimony before Constantine on the Donatist controversy provides the fullest illustration; testimony before Caracalla meets us in an inscription; and the *Digest* is full of imperial responses copied by secretaries assigned to the purpose—law clerks, we would call them. Minutes resembled the scenes of literature to the extent of preserving dialogue. Exchanges at these sessions were surprisingly informal, direct, even familiar. Emperor and subject spoke to each other quite on the same level. We turn, then, to a trial under Domitian, with no reason to call it mere fiction, however much it may reflect the influence of the genres just described.[26]

Apollonius of Tyana, says Philostratus at the beginning of the seventh book of the *Life of Apollonius*, may best be judged through a description of his attitude towards despotism. This is the touchstone for any philosopher, Zeno or Plato, Phyton, Heraclides, Python and Callisthenes, Diogenes and Crates and so on and so on—the full list. Apollonius, then, was a friend and edifying correspondent to Nerva and Orfitus; they were exiled on suspicion of conspiracy; and he was summoned to Rome in the hope that his testimony might justify further steps against them (Philostr., *Vit. Apoll.* 7.9). Outside of the capital he stays with Demetrius the Cynic—we have met him before—who warns him that "wisdom has become a crime" (7.11) and that the accusations trumped up against Apollonius are those of sorcery and divination by human sacrifice, by which he allegedly encouraged Nerva's ambitions. The praetorian prefect, secretly friendly, puts him on guard against the same charges, but dares not help him further. Apollonius must stay in prison until he is called to the palace for a first hearing. There Domitian and he talk together in a civil fashion for a while (7.32f), Apollonius defending himself and his friends in high places; but as he goes on without fear though without truculence, Domitian grows angrier and ends by consigning him, shorn of his philosopher's long hair, to closer confinement. Shortly afterward he is brought by a court clerk to "the agon of his soul," the contest for his life (8.2), in the presence of a crowd of notables, with Domitian as judge. Apollonius refuses obeisance to the emperor, but raises his eyes upward to Zeus. Questioning begins, concentrated on four points, the first three of which the prisoner answers so convincingly that Domitian comes to the fourth after considerable hesitation, incoherently, indirectly, and is answered by Apollonius "as if he were rebuking a child" (8.5), to loud applause. Domitian, "somewhat struck by the responses," acquits him till a further interview, though not in time; for Apollonius, first calling him to account for the corruption of his councilors, the ruin of his cities, the hordes of exiles and mourners in his empire, the alienation of the senate, and the cowardice of his armies, suddenly vanishes into thin air. Domitian proceeds to the next case in a distracted way.[27]

No one knows just how much the description deserves belief.[28] In outline it is probably true. To it is added, however, a very long speech which, like Cicero's *Verrines* and *Pro Milone*, the orator would have made if circumstances had allowed, and which is certainly pure invention. It harks back to a much earlier and much more famous tableau in Athens, the court crammed, the philosopher defending himself against charges of atheism launched by the enemies he had made through his continual behavior as the city's gadfly. Apollonius must have the record of a gadfly, too, he must have his Anytus, must confront the accusation of impiety, above all, must deliver an *Apology*. The parallels are pointed. Not unnaturally, other philosophers or their followers recalled the example of Socrates: Musonius, Epictetus, Seneca, and Thrasea Paetus.[29]

Their trials, like Socrates', led to their deaths. Seneca had "prepared long in advance the poison with which Athenians condemned to death were executed" (Tac., *Ann.* 15.64). Thrasea's libation imitated that other which Socrates would have poured from the cup of poison; and in writing a life of Cato, Thrasea had studied the example of a man who made ready for suicide by reading the *Phaedo*. These Roman martyrs were all philosophers, in a broad sense. Their philosophy lent resolution. Seneca "turned [his friends'] tears toward firmness, now through his conversation, again through a more insistent, almost coercive, tone, asking 'Where were the maxims of wisdom, the views reasoned out against impending evils over so many years?' " (Tac., *Ann.* 15.62). To his questions, his own writings gave answer: "It is no great thing to live." And philosophy lent comfort, too. Its votaries in their last hours discussed the afterlife, as Cato had done, and Julius Canus also, the Stoic philosopher under Caligula, as Thrasea was to do in his day with Demetrius the Cynic, and as Petronius did *not* do. But Petronius was eccentric; Epicurean, at that; and while protracting his life, talked "not on grave matters nor on topics by which he might establish a fame for steadfast courage. He listened to [his friends] as they discoursed not on the immortality of the soul and the pursuits of philosophy, but to their light songs and witty verses." A hint, here, of something else that philosophy contributed to these scenes: the dramatic script, and hope of renown. Tacitus doubted the motives, with reason. It was easy to detect a note of ambitious self-satisfaction in remarks of Seneca, for instance, or in the typical words of someone nameless (by a nice irony) in our fragmentary manuscript. " 'I go to meet my peril retaining my freedom and my self-respect. I call on you to remember me not with sorrow but rejoicing, adding my name as well to those who escaped calamities of state by a noble end.' He now spent part of the day in detaining or dismissing his visitors, as each was inclined to take his leave or speak with him, and while there was still a crowd around, all witnesses to his intrepid face," he killed himself.[30] The classic moment had its style: a kind of party or reception, self-restraint and usualness of manners (full of pride), death delayed whether by timing of the blow or interruption of the effects of bleeding or fasting, perfect courtesy to the agents of the tyrant who intruded, talk of philosophy, perhaps some tags of verse—Brutus quoted Euripedes; Lucan, himself —all this very Athenian yet also very Roman, and most extraordinary.

Seneca dictated a long discourse to his private secretaries at the very end. It was published and much read. Other Stoic martyrs relied on their friends and disciples to preserve their writings. A son-in-law of Barea Soranus is the most likely author of reminiscences and maxims of Musonius. L. Annaeus

Cornutus served as literary executor to Lucan; and after Helvidius Priscus the elder died, his widow Fannia persuaded Herennius Senecio to write up his life, she to supply the materials. A different kind of tribute was dictated by the Roman veneration of the dead: the martyr's birthday became the occasion for poems commissioned by his survivors—so Martial's and Statius' verses to Lucan. They were meant to be displayed near the *imagines* of their subjects. Funeral eulogies, as we saw in our first chapter, provided still another occasion for praise.[31]

Thus families, natural custodians of fame in the Roman mind, immortalized a good life and a splendid death. The means they employed were the special property of the Republican aristocracy. Times changed, old names disappeared, old customs of grandiloquent mourning gave way to less public demonstrations. Big funerals were reserved for the members and kin of the imperial house. Private clans, on the other hand, though retaining some of the close bonds that we have seen uniting the Annaei, for instance, lost the appearance of factions, lost the greater part of their political strength, loosened their hold on their remoter cousins and marriage connections—began to resemble, in short, about what we mean today by "private clans." As blood counted for less, political and philosophical persuasions counted for more: coteries formed on the basis not of descent but of like-mindedness. These were the changes one could see if one compared the Republicans of Lucan's epic with those of that author's own generation. One consequence was a more abstract quality of fame. Lucan was the hero not exclusively of Annaei but of all whose views of the principate resembled his own, as Cato, perhaps the first clear example of the process of abstraction, aroused the devotion of men not connected in the slightest degree with the Porcii Catones or with any other branch of the ancient aristocracy at all. They added Cato to that language used among the opposition in place of explicit and dangerous speech: Cato, Brutus, Cassius, all symbols, all in the public domain. Not that the habit of communication by political myth was anything new. Greeks and Romans alike cherished their heroes, both (we have said) taught succeeding generations by the use of *exempla*, to whose number men of Seneca's and Tacitus' day consciously added.[32] Protagonists specifically of the opposition, however, differed in owing their fame to their championing of intangibles. They stood for ideas, not actions. Their natural descendants were simply those who held the same opinions.

A second point: opposition heroes, unlike Decius Mus, Horatius Cocles, even Harmodius and Aristogeiton, won glory passively. Fighting over matters of belief, their "actions" on that field could only be symbolic—true especially of the later, more purely philosophic figures of Domitian's reign. They wanted to demonstrate the loss of free speech. How else than by getting their mouths stopped? How better demonstrate the tyrant's depravity than by provoking torture and death?

And for a third point: opposition heroes deserved their fame, against a background of widespread hypocrisy and fear. Political protest attracts more adherents because it can be abandoned at will. It has relatively clear-cut boundaries. Moral and philosophic protest, over intangibles, moves in half darkness, where one may encounter dangers without realizing it and cannot relinquish the fight without actually joining the enemy, like those senators who danced for Nero, those others who showered Caligula or Domitian with wild adulation. In contrast, under the worst emperors, merely to stay away was treason, for "he who flees, condemns"; one must applaud actively, and control every facial expression. A frown was actionable as being too Stoic, and woe to those who wore the costume of philosophers. Their very presence in the city from 66 on was repeatedly forbidden, and, cowering in the provinces, they still felt the chill of Domitian's displeasure. These were the men pledged to make others brave. Some held to the pledge. "A primary motive in the teaching of Epictetus was to free men from the *fear of force*."[33]

Death, then, and specifically dying as opposed to boldly acting, qualified men for a wide admiration, from the 60's to the 90's, because death was no longer the affair only of one's kin, nor scorned as passive, nor matched by the competition of general courage such as one would find in some battle line. With those three points by way of explanation, we may turn back to the more notable features of commemoration among the opposition.

It is striking, though not surprising, that the opposition made such frequent use of literature to honor those who fell for their cause. Stories were handed down by word of mouth (see note 31), praises were sung in anniversary poems, writings were preserved. That was not enough. Special short prose eulogies were commissioned, distant from the earlier Cato pamphlets by a century but connected in form and intent, and by one further fact: Thrasea Paetus, whose *Cato* was counted against him, became himself the hero of just such a work written by Arulenus Rusticus in 93 or 94. A friend of the latter, Herennius Senecio, wrote on the elder Helvidius Priscus at the same time, and Pliny on the younger Helvidius Priscus a decade or so later. Under Nero, a relative by marriage of Helvidius the elder attracted suspicion for undertaking a biography of a friend accused of treason. He was put to death, and Arulenus Rusticus, and Herennius Senecio after him, evidence enough that eulogy of traitors could be called treason itself. After Domitian, we come to Pliny's work, just mentioned, and to Gaius Fannius, relative of Helvidius Priscus' wife, who died of natural causes in the early 100's while in the midst of his *Deaths of Those Executed or Exiled by Nero*, of a style "in between dialogue and history." An admirer of the same circle, Titinius Capito, completed his *Deaths of Illustrious* Men;[34] another wrote the *Agricola*—Tacitus.

The introduction of the *Agricola* here is of course too abrupt. While none of the works on which it might have been modeled survive, the few words describing them in ancient sources suggest that they were not long, nor biographies, nor balanced historical treatments at all, such as the life of Tacitus' father-in-law, but rather short pamphlets, episodic and eulogistic, embroidered rhetorically, strongly emphasizing the subject's last hours. They did, however, have this in common with the *Agricola:* their subjects held the center of the stage as victims of tyranny, and their tone was one of filial piety. No doubt, in a general way, they inspired the *Agricola;* possibly, too, certain facts and aspects of Agricola's life were bent to an imitative shape, especially in his relations with Domitian. By a typically tendentious ambiguity, Tacitus goes so far as to hint that Agricola was hurried out of life by poison. And Tacitus' liking for this style of commemorative literature appears in his use of it for source material in his proper historical works. The fact is not surprising. His chief heroes are losers in the unequal struggle against force, his affections (or nostalgia) Republican: natural, then, that he should return to a genre first imported to Rome in the days of Cicero and Cato. It drew partly on the age-old fondness for recording what a man said as he died, as if summing up his life, or already half filled with some divinity from beyond. Last words recur again and again in both Greek and Latin literature. But to last words, Romans added as a postscript something further, the funeral oration. That too seems to offer a model for the description of a life's end. *Ultima verba* and *laudationes funebres* thus combined to produce the genre of *exitus*, and that in turn had as a giant offspring the *Agricola*.[35]

If commemorative pamphlets had seemed to contemporaries as artificial a problem in source criticism and as indirect a form of revenge as they seem to us today, they would never have been published at such risk nor repressed with such severity. We should remember what passions, sensitive to the slightest appeal, charged the minds of the Roman aristocracy in this period. Little shows in the sources or in the conduct of men who prided themselves on their self-control; much may be imagined. We have one fragment of conversation filled with the icy hatred and grief that years of persecution leave behind, between a relative of someone attacked by a pamphlet and the ex-informer who wrote it. "What business have you with my dead? I did not get in your way with Crassus and Camerinus, did I?" (Pliny, *Ep.* 1.5). It was in this atmosphere that the warfare first waged over Cato's death through pro- or anti-martyr pamphlets seemed worth continuing as late as Domitian's reign.

Much in these pamphlets was imported from Greece. The fact is surprising but the explanation clear. Granted that Sentius or Thrasea, heroes of a deeply national antimonarchism, would have returned to a form of state more traditionally Roman and less ecumenical in its outward implications —a monarchy can absorb alien elements more easily than an oligarchy. Granted also that some of the conservatives who disliked the principate disliked the newcomers to Rome from not very distant Italian townships, to say nothing of immigrants from the provinces, and indulged in the same kind of anti-Hellenism—Lucan shows signs of it—that Octavian aroused for his war against Antony. All this has little significance. The opposition were indeed a rather ingrown coterie, sharing with other members of the Roman upper classes a suspicion of foreigners. They drew a line around themselves to keep out most of the world of their own day. The line emphatically did not exclude *classical* Hellenism. Several figures explain the paradox: Cato, so absurdly traditionalist in many ways, so ardently Roman, reading Plato on the eve of his death, Brutus reciting Euripedes, Seneca talking (in Greek, we may be sure) with Demetrius the Cynic. Greek elements run through the history of the opposition from start to finish. Motives for resistance, justification of tyrannicide, hatred of despotism, all the preliminaries show Greek colors; conduct in the killing of the tyrant, or in confronting his interrogation, or in the scene of suicide—the same; and the same again in the cult established for the martyr by his family and his friends, in the written memorials that brought together Cremutius Cordus and Epictetus, or Pliny and Plutarch; in busts that raised comparisons with Socrates. He and Cato were named in the same breath, he and Seneca carved back to back in double herms (Plate I).[36]

How strong a spell the Greek tradition cast over the most diverse audiences appears not only in Rome but elsewhere too. It drew on a regular library of works now known to us more through their later debtors than through themselves—works of a type hardly developed before Alexander's day, suddenly flourishing under his successors, who, by introducing to the world their ceremonious courts, their resplendent autocracy, and their oppressive strength, made protest almost impossible and almost inevitable. It was, to be sure, expressed only through words and ideas, in default of physical resources. It could be only a protest through the dramatic confrontations, diatribes, and "last words" which have been already discussed so far as they bore on the history of the Roman opposition. Yet the use of these same words and ideas spread beyond the boundaries of a single city to every circle where Greek was read and spoken, and to any group or class pressed down by too strong a government. For the present study, the whole subject of Greek opposition becomes important.

A sort of introduction to our wider search can be found among the Jewish Apocrypha, in the Fourth Book of Maccabees. Much about the work is strange or obscure: author unknown (some Hellenized Jew); place of composition unknown (very likely Antioch); date uncertain, though lying somewhere in the century after Augustus' death. In form it is a commemorative speech on the sufferings and deaths of nine Jews punished by King Antiochus for refusing to break the Law. Their conduct is used to exemplify the victory of right piety over natural weaknesses, in a curious interweaving of philosophy and religion to which we will return in the next chapter. Here it is rather the trial that concerns us, particularly the first scene involving a certain old man, Eleazar, "well known to many of the tyrant's courtiers for his philosophy," dragged before "the tyrant sitting with his councilors upon a high place, and surrounding by his soldiers stationed round about him in arms." Eleazar responds to pleas and threats alike with noble courage, at some length: his not to give in, the tyrant's to compel—if he can. Do your worst with wheel and fire, Eleazar challenges. "You guards of the tyrant, why do you hang back?" Torture by new and strange devices, nothing avails. He stands it all, "straining his gaze upward to heaven," endures even while unconscious; for, though fallen in a faint, "his reason remained erect." So, "like a noble athlete, though struck, he conquered his torturers;" and so, after him, in further scenes of defiance, seven brothers successively "antiphilosophize against the tyrant" (ἀντεφιλοσόφησαν τῷ τυράννῳ, 8.15). What is true of one is true of all: the guards "were keenly angered by his παρρησία" (10.5), "the tyrant himself and all his council were astonished by their endurance" (17.17). Readers, shuddering, share their astonishment. The martyrs indeed submit to a variety of tortures not matched for ingenuity or for detailed effect in any earlier piece of ancient literature nor in subsequent works until the second century *Passion of Polycarp*. The latter fact points to some influence, direct or indirect, or from a common source, on Christian martyrologies, and speculations along that line, though beyond firm substantiation, receive support from the popularity that 4 Maccabees later enjoyed not among Jews, who cease to mention the work, but among such writers as Jerome, Eusebius, Augustine, and John Chrysostom. We can follow its fame into the period in which Christian martyr acts were being composed. If we turn back in the other direction and seek its sources, we find, mixed together with other proofs of the author's Hellenic culture, continual little hints of Socrates in the person and words of Eleazar, and much of Stoic doctrine: brotherhood of all men, sovereignty of reason over passions. Despite the fervor of the author, it is clear that 4 Maccabees is a work of conscious art—he is, after all, describing events two centuries past, recollected in tranquillity—to which he can at leisure adapt the resources of his wide reading. What is particularly interesting is his dependence on the antityrant motifs that were developed for a similar service by the Greeks, and which a most aggressively patriotic and pious Jew felt no embarrassment in using against Greek enemies. For him as for Romans of the same period, the alien tradition nevertheless appeared an attractive weapon of opposition.[37]

This same tradition is found next in the Acts of the Pagan Martyrs, surviving in longer or shorter papyrus fragments from Egypt, and for the most part recounting the collisions between Alexandrian Greeks and their enemies over the first two centuries A.D. Some bits belong to a period only a little later than the events they describe; others reveal several re-editings. They were still being copied and polished, and their drama heightened, in the first third of the third century, but retain at least something, generally a great deal, of the form of original trial minutes (acta). Aside from scattered short narrative passages, they consist of dialogue only, with more or less rhetorical embroidery depending on the authors. Evidently a great many persons contributed to the corpus of the Acts at different times, and it would thus be vain to look for uniformity either in style or in content. Actually, the audience for which these pieces were produced, the well-to-do Greeks of Alexandria, looked on the local Egyptians with scorn, the Jews with dislike rising to hatred, and the Roman emperor and his representatives at times with approval, at times with anger. Anti-Romanism took the form of cultural snobbery, accusations of injustice, or charges of fiscal oppression or dishonesty. So various were the topics and points of view to be handled. In general, the themes that recur are three, and fit what else is known of the Greek population in the city: namely, their exclusive pride, anti-Semitism, and restiveness under Roman rule. Several speakers in the Acts emphasize their cultural heritage. Consider this exchange between a certain Appian and Commodus:

The emperor called him back. The emperor said, "Now do you not know whom you are speaking to?"

Appian: "I know. Appian speaks to a tyrant."

The emperor: "No, to the monarch."

Appian: "Don't say that! For your father, the divine [Marcus Aurelius] Antoninus, was fit to be an emperor; for—listen to me—first of all he was a philosopher; second, he was not avaricious; third, he was virtuous. You have the opposite qualities: you are tyrannical, unvirtuous, uncivilized." Caesar ordered him to be led away [to execution]. As he was being led away, Appian said, "Grant me this, my lord Caesar."

The emperor: "What?"

Appian: "Order that I may be led away in my noble insignia."

The emperor: "So be it."

Appian took his headband and put it on his head, and putting his white shoes on his feet, he cried out in the middle of Rome, "Hurry up, Romans, and see the sight of the ages, an Alexandrian gymnasiarch and ambassador being led off!"

The *evocatus* immediately ran up and stood before the emperor, saying, "Do you sit idle, my lord? The Romans are murmuring."

The emperor: "About what?"

The consul [beside him]: "About the execution of the Alexandrian."

The emperor: "Summon him again."

Appian, when he entered, said, "Who calls me back a second time as I was about to greet Hades again, and those who died before me, Theon and Isidorus and Lampon? Was it the senate or you, you brigand?"

The emperor: "Appian, we are accustomed to chasten raving and abandoned men. You speak only so long as I wish you to."

Appian: "By your *genius*, I am neither raving nor have I forgotten myself entirely, but I am rather appealing on behalf of my noble rank and rights."

The emperor: "How so?"

Appian: "As one of noble rank and a gymnasiarch."

Or consider Isidore's damning of Jews and Egyptians in one breath:

Against what you, Agrippa, declare concerning the Jews, I will make answer. I accuse them of wishing to stir up the whole world . . . We must consider the whole crowd of them. They don't think the same way as the Alexandrians, but more like Egyptians.

And a similarly rancorous passage pits two embassies from Alexandria against the emperor Trajan.

And the Jews, entering first, saluted the emperor Trajan, and his Majesty saluted them most warmly, since he had already been won over by Plotina. After them the Alexandrian envoys entered and saluted the emperor. He, however, did not come forward to meet them, but said, "You say, 'Hail!' to me as though you deserved to receive a greeting—you who dared to do such wicked things to the Jews! . . ."

[Trajan]: "You must anticipate dying, being so contemptuous of death that you answer even me so boldly."

Hermaiscus said, "Yes, but we are grieved to see your council filled with impious Jews."

Caesar said, "I tell you for the second time, Hermaiscus, you answer me boldly, relying on your high birth."

Hermaiscus said, "What do you mean, boldly, greatest emperor? Tell me."

Caesar said, "Pretending that mine is a council of Jews."

Hermaiscus: "Do you then object to the word 'Jew'? You should then rather help your own people and not defend the impious Jews."

As Hermaiscus was saying this, the bust of Serapis that they carried [on their embassy] suddenly broke into a sweat, and Trajan was astonished at the sight, and in a little while crowds gathered in Rome and very numerous shouts rang out, and all began to flee to the highest parts of the hills.

Here the text breaks off. The rest is lost, by mischances which have beset the whole corpus, and from which not a single example has escaped entire. Still, considering that any papyri from Alexandria are rare, almost unknown, and how discreetly these particular ones had to be circulated there and in the countryside, lest they incriminate their authors, we are lucky to have as much as we do. For the Acts of the Pagan Martyrs plainly exalt the enemies of the state, glorify men persecuted by the Romans, and preserve the memories of heroes "who died before—Theon and Isidorus and Lampon." Whoever copied or so much as read such literature would have something to explain to the governor. In this respect, the Acts invite comparison with that other type of commemorative literature created in Rome itself, involving several men in the death penalty. Alexandrians resented the emperor's rule just as the Roman nobility did, and championed a senate—a boule of Alexandria—not granted to the city until Septimius Severus' reign. Like Roman senators, the *gymnasia* class of Alexandrians looked on the very existence of the empire with mixed feelings, though what they would have preferred instead hardly appears: perhaps Athenian hegemony combined with local independence, or something equally farfetched. In this very vagueness of political intention, parallels with the opposition in Rome hold good, too. As to the Acts in their literary character, the influence of earlier works describing philosopher-heroes is limited but plain. The tyrant, called "brigand" (λῄσταρχος), presides in court with his nobles around him, his guards at his back; a preliminary hearing is followed by a second, at which the subtle culture of his victims, φιλόλογοι, challenges despotic force with παρρησία. They display their intrepidity in bold talk, θρασυτολμία; they lecture their oppressor on their beliefs, and when he orders them burnt at the stake, they go calmly, or at the last moment escape his cruelty by the intervention of some divine manifestation. Readers here will catch the echoes of sources quoted above, the "last words" and trial scenes of philosophers, especially Domitian's trial of Apollonius of Tyana; and if all the surviving Acts contained only these features, it would be fair to trace their formal inspiration to just these genres. Such connections in their various aspects have often been defended. The Acts, however, are a most miscellaneous collection. To the pride of office and obvious wealth displayed or implied in so many passages can be opposed the mention of a hero who "did not criticize the emperor, since he was a judge of kind temper, easily against the rich, easily angered at those in any way of noble rank." This has a thoroughly proletarian sound. And to the anti-Roman sentiments that predominate can be opposed those others that flatter the emperor as beneficent and upright. Beyond the political, many literary elements can be detected: minutes of real hearings, notes taken by sympathetic spectators, artistic embellishments drawn from various common forms of Greek fiction.[38]

Some coincidental likeness between the descriptions of Hermaiscus, or Isidore, or Appian, and of Socrates, Zeno, or

Apollonius, can be accounted for by external circumstances which imposed their own character on the forms of defiance. The fact must be kept in mind when we turn to a third genre, Christian martyr acts. These too were written and circulated covertly among persecuted groups to glorify their heroes and blacken the names and conduct of their oppressors; these too have as their setting a trial, and concentrate so decisively on dialogue that the actual death scene may be entirely omitted or hurried over in a sentence or two; and, by judicious culling, these too can be made to yield most of the features already noticed in their pagan parallels. A warning is needed here, however; for the number of really early accounts—that is, of the second and third centuries—is small, comprising perhaps a dozen that have come down to us without serious contamination, and of these in turn the oldest and truest seem to conform least to any single pattern. Moreover, if we look for outside influences, our findings may be deceptive. Strict bureaucratic form encloses the drama: for example, "In the fourth consulship of Valerian and the third of Gallienus, the third day before the calends of September, at Carthage, in his office, Paternus the proconsul said to Cyprian the bishop, 'The most divine emperors Valerian and Gallienus have deigned to send me a letter ordering . . .' Cyprian the bishop said . . ." and so on—thus begins the *Acta S. Cypriani*, very much on the scheme of the Alexandrian Acts with their repeated εἶπεν's. The similarity arises from no literary borrowings but from the dependence of both types of document on official acta emphasized for the sake of credibility; and everyone acknowledges that both pagan and Christian martyr tales really did draw, some more, some less, on court minutes. These would of course preserve little more than date, place, names of judge and witnesses, and interrogation. If spectators kept their own minutes, they would follow the same form. A later editor wishing to add art and drama from other genres thus had little to turn to except other question-and-answer literature, that is, Cynic diatribes, with as much of Stoicism as had been accommodated to that form. A few key words shared by Epictetus and Diogenes, and by Christian hagiographers, once led to theories of dependence later disproved, nor could any direct link be established joining early Christian acts to the *exitus* stories and the Alexandrian Acts, whatever might be said of the possibility of a common source. The exuberance of first discoveries and arguments had to be pruned down.[39]

Some arguments nevertheless resisted correction. In their exchanges with Christians, Roman judges always got beaten, going so far as to shape their questions to a devastating repartee. Aphorisms sparkled on the lips of innocent priests and still more innocent peasants as much as if they had been the sharpest sophists, and this and other tricks of presentation rapidly spread among martyr acts of the fourth and fifth centuries. It was indeed inevitable that the style of address skillfully adapted by popular philosophers for a vulgar audience, over previous centuries, should be later reused, and that Christians under persecution should take from literary models traditionally turned to violent social criticism. In the more authentic martyrologies, dependence on Stoic-Cynic writings was never decisive and at first hardly detectible. Its later development can nonetheless be traced through further details. In the very process of rebutting sophistic eloquence, martyrs echo their enemies. "A certain Rufinus, standing near—one of those reputed to excel in rhetorical studies—said, 'Cease, Pionius, to deceive yourself.' Pionius answered, 'Are these your speeches? Are these your books? Not even Socrates suffered such charges at the hands of the Athenians. Everyone now is an Anytus or Meletus. And I suppose Socrates and Aristides and Anaxarchus and the rest deceived themselves, among your citizens, in practising philosophy, justice, and bravery.' Rufinus, however, hearing this, was silent." By implication, the martyr resembles the philosopher-heroes whom he mentions; surely, then, the persecutor must be a "tyrant" —and so he is, τύραννος, in a number of even the early and relatively unadorned accounts.[40] By Eusebius' day, the development had advanced much farther: witness his tale of five Egyptian martyrs,

led before the tyrant [Firmilian the governor], where they gave rein to their παρρησία; they were then thrown into prison. On the next day —the 16th of the month Peritius, or, by Roman reckoning, the 14th before the calends of March—they were led before the judge . . . who first made test of their invincible perseverance with all types of torture, by instruments strange and differently devised. The spokesman for all of them he [Firmilianus] struggled with in these contests. He asked first, "Who was he?" And in place of his true name, he heard him give the name of a prophet. And so it happened with all of them: instead of the names which had been given by their fathers and which were in some cases the names of idols, they called themselves by other names: Elias, Jeremiah . . . [The spokesman] answered that Jerusalem was his country (no doubt thinking of that of which Paul had spoken, "There is a free Jerusalem on high, which is our mother," and, "You have come to Mt. Sion to the city of the living God, the heavenly Jerusalem"). And he had this in mind. But [Firmilian], casting his thoughts lower, upon this earth, and inquiring closely and curiously what this might be, and where it lay . . . he answered, "It was a city to be the homeland only of the righteous, for none but those should have a share in it; and it lay toward the east, toward the rising sun." And so again he philosophized about these matters . . . [Turning his anger next against another victim before him, Firmilian renewed his interrogation], for he was not a man but a wild beast, or whatever is more savage than a wild beast . . . But this [second martyr] Porphyrius was a fair sight to see, with the bearing of one who has conquered in all contests of the Sacred Games . . . truly filled with the divine spirit. And in the manner of a philosopher he wore a mantle like a tunic around him, looking upward . . . [At the moment of his death] with a calm untroubled determination, the hero made disposition of his possessions to his friends.[41]

Here in Eusebius can be seen, sometimes obvious, sometimes a little more deftly hidden, almost the full range of perfectly alien motifs imported into martyrologies from pagan writings. The events described really took place, in some sequence now obscured by dramatic ornament; the date survives as witness to the original protocol; but, to begin with, the general atmosphere of a battle of wits, of παρρησία, in which both judge and persecuted engage and from which the one emerges triumphant, the other baffled even in ways that he does not realize, is quite false and quite in the style of Cynic debates. It is typical, too, that the judge should not only be called τύραννος, but should display the cruelty, dullness, and lack of culture regularly attributed to the tyrant. In the end, his very barbarity avails nothing against his victims, whose smiles in the midst of their agony defeat him—smiles and victories common in the martyr literature and suggestive of a debt to reports on the trials or deaths of Zeno, of Seneca, or the like. What gives the Christians their triumphant power is their relation with God. They are "truly filled with the divine spirit." As descriptions of cruel questioning and tortures are elaborated in Eusebius' lifetime, they speak increasingly of the dramatic operation of mysterious forces. The martyr, by his nearness to death, his inner sanctity, his purpose in enduring, anticipates immortality by a few hours. Divine grace is granted him; a heavenly aroma and light spread around him; and with superhuman gifts he is able to tame the beasts of the arena, to encounter Satan and subdue him, to speak with Christ or be spoken to by him, to see visions and make prophecies—hence the names of prophets that Firmilianus' victims take to themselves. A well-established kind of story, the aretalogy, to be discussed in the next chapter, must at least be mentioned here, since it seems to tie to a common heritage the miraculous powers of Apollonius of Tyana, vanishing suddenly from Domitian's court; the Alexandrian envoys, whose cult image of Serapis bursts into sweat at a crucial moment in their trial; and, a century later, the persecuted wonder workers granted the strength of God to defy or baffle their enemies. In this latter role the Christian need not put aside his philosopher's "mantle like a tunic," for in the later Empire the philosopher had become, from logician and scientist, a communicant with the beyond. It was thus not surprising, though the stricter Fathers found it very reprehensible, that monks should go about dressed for all the world like the older wandering Cynics, with bare feet, mantle, staff, beard, and dirty matted long hair. Certain stereotypes of superhuman virtue were too deeply fixed in the ancient mind to be eradicated.[42]

It is the philosopher that most clearly connects all four kinds of protest pamphlets that we have surveyed, Roman, Jewish, Alexandrian, and Christian—that, and the fact that the groups giving rise to these pamphlets confronted an enemy infinitely beyond their strength to defeat or even to challenge openly. Had the odds been different, opposition would have shown itself in action. Facing the overwhelming power of the Roman state, its opponents had little choice of weapons. They were obliged to strike only through ideas and words, that is, through the philosopher, whose message and attributes changed over the centuries, but whose formidable figure embodied anger and reproach.

The phenomena reviewed in this and the preceding chapter suggest a conclusion to be developed later, namely, that the history of those who held up the Roman Establishment, and of those who sought to tear it down, traced parallel lines. Just as it was a truly Roman nobility who ran the empire and made the laws, in the first century, and who retained for some generations an inherited tendency to exercise their influence through family ties, so the anti-imperial were also nobles, with their roots in the capital and the Latin plain; and they too expressed their opposition through memorial cults, marriage alliances, and prejudices bequeathed to sons. In all respects but the political, these two groups were the same. After a time, less pedigreed but still decidedly upper-class figures were admitted to the imperial civil service and the senate. Julio-Claudii were succeeded by mere Flavii. But similarly, the line of Cato and Brutus devolved upon Annaei. When, in a sort of epilogue, the story of the unconquerable martyr is traced into other surroundings, it is seen passing from a Roman into a provincial aristocracy, more precisely into an Alexandrian circle, and finally into the community of second and third century Christians, who represented quite undistinguished classes. In the same period, as is well known, the same lower strata of society were obtaining their share of power and helping to form and control the empire's laws by such routes as the equestrian civil or military career. The conclusion that follows seems necessary, even if somewhat unexpected. Internal opposition in the empire was not a matter of enemies aiming at each other across a gulf of difference but rather of hostility between persons who were close neighbors in a cultural and social sense; and, though the types and appearances of opposition are for the most part unrelated to each other, they moved steadily down the social scale much as did the dominant classes in just these centuries.

✧ III ✧

Magicians

ONE might believe, if one read only superficially in ancient or modern sources, that the philosopher in classical times was very much like his counterpart today, that is, essentially a metaphysician, a thinker, a Plato or (if Plato's private demon and his ultimate mysticism should offend) perhaps an Aristotle. The type at any rate could be known by the achievements of the mind. Yet challengers to the same title "philosopher" existed, building their fame not on the creation of a rational system but on the exercise of the powers of their souls—powers derived, it might be, from a previous existence in some other form of being, or from an ascetic regimen that enabled them to learn and to do more than other mortals. They were the descendants of Pythagoras. In a long line, they perpetuated his inspiration, however misapplied or misunderstood. For Pythagoreanism, after a temporary eclipse in the fifth and fourth centuries, revived, and carried down into the Hellenistic age and to popularity in Rome from the first century B.C. an image quite different from that of Plato, more resembling the pursuit and the person respectively called "philosophy" and "philosopher" in the preceding few pages. On the changed meaning of the two words, as the chief matter of this chapter, we will focus later, but the background must first be sketched in, beginning with the early history of Pythagoreanism in the Empire.

Thus (not to mention two or three Pythagorean senators of Cicero's day) Seneca, a young man in Tiberius' reign, as a result of his studies under a Pythagorean teacher, entered timidly on the ascetic life and might have continued the experiment but for an unlucky conjuncture of the times: "Foreign rites were then afoot, and abstinence from certain animal foods was taken as a proof of superstition. So, at the request of my father," he gave up a choosy diet.[1] He had been at it a year, and thought he could already detect improvement in his intellectual processes. That had been promised by his teacher, and the promise helps to explain the attraction of Pythagoreanism for so very unvegetarian a nature as Seneca's. There were still richer rewards in the doctrine. The believer could conquer death. Under the emperor Caligula, Julius Canus, called a Stoic, was condemned to die, and in approved fashion, gathering his friends about him and discussing the immortality of the soul with them and with his special spiritual adviser, he awaited arrest. When the final moment arrived, Canus revealed an unexpected side of his philosophy quite alien to Stoicism. He promised his friends to return after death and report whatever he had learnt that was especially interesting. Thus far Seneca's account. Plutarch adds that Canus before execution foretold the same fate within three days for one of his friends (who died as predicted), and himself did reappear from the beyond to another of his circle to "discourse on the survival of the spirit."[2] The incident reveals the penetration of obvious Pythagoreanism into the more conservative circles and the higher social classes with which Seneca and his like were acquainted.

Just what was involved in this penetration must be learnt from the life of Pythagoras. Details reach us through the biography by Iamblichus (ca. 300), in which he draws on earlier biographies by his own master, Porphyry, and, most of all, by Apollonius of Tyana. These two in turn depend on traditions first fixed in writing, it seems, by Aristotle and by other reporters of the late fourth century B.C. Pythagoras, then, appeared as a wanderer on the scene where he was to win his fame, in south Italy—a god, so his followers believed, a benevolent demon, Apollo, or the moon, in the form of a man (Iamb., *Vit. Pythag.* 30). His five senses, however, and his intelligence were all of a keenness beyond that of any mortal (67), and, even more, he could work miracles of prediction (36). In one encounter with an angry peasant, he was able to speak to the man's ox and persuade it not to eat his crops again (61). Stories of this sort drew to him a certain Abaris, priest of Apollo from Thrace, who believed that he could recognize Apollo in Pythagoras—and rightly, for Pythagoras by way of proof gave him a glimpse of his thigh of gold (92, 135). Abaris had a wonderful arrow taken from Apollo's shrine by which, with muttered spells, he could ride where he would or deflect plagues and hurricanes from suppliant cities like Sparta (92). This he gave to Pythagoras—gave *back*, since Pythagoras was Apollo—and the new owner used it as Abaris had. He averted plagues and wind- or hailstorms, banished monstrous serpents from the countryside, smoothed raging seas, or merely foretold shipwrecks (135f, 142)—all "proofs of his piety," in Iamblichus' phrase (137). He made himself invisible to escape his enemies, or appeared in two places simultaneously to two groups of friends. As to the source of all his lore, some he gathered as a youth when he went to live in a temple, some in a descent to Hades, some from Egyptian priests, some from eastern Chaldeans or Magi, and Brahmans. Wherever he went, he was revered—save at the court of Phalaris. But every philosopher must meet a tyrant and, in his very teeth, pronounce a long and edifying speech.[3]

The incidents clustering round the life of Pythagoras, most of them receding into legends of the fourth century B.C. or earlier, some added as late as the third century A.D., served to raise him above the run of men. He was a figure much like Solomon or Merlin, each answering to the tastes of a certain audience by which, in the course of generations, the life of the hero was slowly, lovingly, naively, and at last almost unrecognizably transformed into a work of folk art. The story spoke to those who desired to be fooled, who wanted (as men have always wanted) to stare or shiver; and so, quite without embarrassment, it embroidered incidents if it did not steal them outright from the lives of other heroes. In Herodotus could be found, for instance, the nucleus of the Abaris story. Within a century it was attached to Pythagoras. But Herodotus made popular another rich source of romance: the encounter with peoples of the East. Pythagoras shared in this, too. It was a commonplace. Greeks, so arrogantly contrasting themselves to most "babblers," βάρβαροι, nevertheless acknowledged their youth before the much older wisdom of certain other lands. They never outgrew their awe. They could at the same time despise a western race like the Romans and yet say, "Bronze-bound is the road toward the gods, high and rough, whose many paths the barbarians have discovered where the Greeks became lost . . . The god revealed the way to the Egyptians and the Chaldeans (for these are Assyrians) and the Lydians and Hebrews." This was the canonized list. The curious therefore read of Egypt, or traveled there. Serious inquirers would try to reach Persia. Adventurous devotees occasionally got as far as Alexander the Great had gone, boasted of more distant journeys still, and returned to ungrudging admiration. They had seen the gymnosophists, the Brahmans, the very fonts of wisdom. Pythagoras drew on them; everyone respected their learning, sanctity, and miracles. To reach them, the last great pagan philosopher, Plotinus, joined the Roman invasion forces of 243–44 against Persia—in vain, the attack failing—while Christian contemporaries sent their saints, in imagination, to the same source, lest they should fall behind in reputation.[4]

A truly spectacular display of Brahman influence was offered in the great tourist town of Olympia at the conclusion of the games of 165, by Peregrinus Proteus. He went up in smoke. According to Lucian, who tells the tale to make us laugh (choosing, readers feel, a rather grisly subject for humor), Peregrinus had begun life in unnatural vice and patricide, advanced to the role of charlatan, passed briefly through Christianity and imprisonment as a much pampered martyr and "new Socrates" (*De morte Peregrini* 12), turned Cynic and declared his allegiance by the usual dirty mantle, long hair, and shocking manners; procured his banishment from Rome, next, and then, slowly losing the notoriety on which he had managed to support himself, decided to end it all in a blaze of glory. To this point, his career is, if strange, not uncharacteristic of the age he lived in. Dabbler in a forbidden religion, Christianity; in the least respectable of philosophies, Cynicism; in Pythagoreanism, as appears in some details of his final scene, and in his advertising of himself as the avatar of Proteus—everything prepares us (if anything can) for the manner of his death. He had himself burnt alive on a great pyre, by previous arrangement well advertised and well attended. Lucian's friend, being present there, was reminded of the Brahmans. It had been a century and more since one of their order, Zarmanochegas, had immolated himself before a Greek or Roman audience, and much longer ago than that since Alexander the Great had witnessed the ceremonious exit of Kalyâna from this world; but people still remembered. Peregrinus was the last in the line. He had no successors, despite the rewards: fame, and cult statues, and the testimony of at least one disciple who saw him after death "clad in white, radiant, garlanded in olive, walking about in the Stoa of the Seven Echoes."[5]

Peregrinus' posthumous reappearance was not unique. As much was attributed to Pythagoras in variant descriptions of his death.[6] No ordinary end could have terminated the story of a being somehow compounded of a mortal body and an Apollonian spark. It was this that set Pythagoras apart. Later followers indeed studied his philosophy, but turned more and more to that part of his heritage that could be called religion, or even magic. He was accordingly described as being wise through some supernatural receptivity; receptive by the exercise of ascetic piety; pious by the denial of the body toward the liberation of the spirit for travels into new and wider realms of truth. Neopythagorean beliefs in the soul as an entity capable of independent motion, of action upon the physical world, and of response to invocation in turn contributed to a literature increasingly popular in the second, third, and fourth centuries. With help from other sources and doctrines, it created a world in which anything might happen. Men might be given to see some great philosopher's soul passing into a snake, like Plotinus' at his deathbed; or, like Plotinus again, they might see their own soul summoned by the incantations of an Egyptian priest in the temple of Isis in Rome. The demon that then responded turned out to be not of the usual quality found in most men but the spirit of a god, thereby explaining the outcome of a curious struggle with another philosopher from Alexandria, one Olympius. This rival tried to "crush Plotinus with star spells" and astrological enchantments. "When he sensed that his attempt was recoiling on himself, he told his associates that Plotinus' soul had a great power, able to retaliate every attack upon those who attempted to hurt him. Plotinus, however, perceived the attempt, saying that Olympius' body was at that moment contracted like a purse pulled tight, with his limbs compressed against each other."[7]

The participation in the contest of an Alexandrian, and the use of the temple of Isis, "the only pure place in Rome," belong naturally in these episodes. Egyptian worships had taken hold on the world, the ancient Egyptian primacy in the whole field of the occult was accepted with more absolute conviction. To date this rising popularity would not be possible. A single mark of its progress may be mentioned. Hadrian was the first to honor Serapis on imperial coinage, picturing himself in the Serapeum of Alexandria face to face with the god; and to his reign belongs that influential priest of Isis, Pachrates, who spent twenty-three years in the crypt of the temple apparently learning everything the goddess could teach; for when he emerged, he had mastered the trick of riding on crocodiles and of transforming a door bolt into a robot helper, and, to the visiting Hadrian as further proof of his powers, he "brought a man to the spot in a single hour, made him take to his bed in two hours, killed him in seven hours, and caused a dream to come to the emperor himself, demonstrating the entire truth of the magic through him. Hadrian, marveling at the prophet, ordered double salary to be issued to him." Magical recipes of Pachrates' devising survive in papyri: "A spell with incense, to draw"—that worked in one hour. "If you wish to cross riding on a crocodile, sit down and repeat as follows." Pachrates turned up in Greece, and Lucian speaks of him. He had a pupil, the Pythagorean Arignotus, himself "a marvel for wisdom and admirable in everything."[8]

Pythagoras had listened and learned in Egypt; there, too, Peregrinus enrolled himself in "that remarkable course in asceticism" (Lucian, *De morte Peregrini* 17). Plotinus was an Egyptian himself, and student of another (the famous Ammonius Saccas), and in his own school in Rome in the third quarter of the third century he gathered around him Egyptian friends and students. At the other extreme from these notable men were "the pupils of the Egyptians, who for a few pennies make known their sacred lore in the middle of the market place and drive demons out of men and blow away diseases and invoke the souls of heroes." All of these figures together demonstrate the radiation of influence from the one province, not only to distant places—Rome, Athens—but to eminent circles. The emperor himself was their convert. These same figures, however, demonstrate also the prevalence of a most singular belief: that, through force of piety, like Plotinus', or of some unspecified virtuosity, like Pachrates', or of more vulgar tricks, like the market place Egyptians', one could wage war on weaker spirits. Within the second, third, and fourth century world of mixed eastern magic or religion, and Neopythagoreanism, collisions of fantastic powers could elevate or destroy a reputation. They took place not only in mere romances for the entertainment of readers, but, as people of the time were convinced, in actual fact. That much is known from nonliterary evidence. One category comprises the very large number of curse tablets, generally of lead, buried and left to do their work on their victims, in all parts of the empire. Their inscriptions curdle the blood: for example, "Let him be picked out, for you to take away his senses, memory, reason (?), marrow." Though the text is fragmentary, a picture of a devil armed with a hook shows who is invoked. A second category is made up of magical papyri. They survive from every century of the

Roman Empire, most of all from the fourth; they indicate different levels of literacy in their compilers; they have often been found in bunches, that is, in libraries, belonging to regular practitioners; and among recipes for every conceivable wish that might be answered by the black arts, they include prescriptions for the cleansing away of evil spirits and for the words and secret signs to be written on amulets: Kmephis, Chphuris, Iaeô, aeê, Iaô, oô, Aiôn, with the picture of a dragon devouring its tail. "Go away demons, ghosts, illness." The amulets themselves, thus to be engraved, also survive in hundreds, increasingly common from the first century on. Like magical papyri, amulets reflect the dreads and desires of all social ranks, raking around wildly in the rubble of eastern and classical superstition for any formula that would do the job. To the resulting muddle, the principal contributor was Egypt, from which, for example, come amulet spells to kill or mutilate the enemies of the owner of the stone. One shows a horse-headed demon torturing a man, and on another, in addition to the lapidary's work, beside a picture of Isis holding a whip and a torch, some rejected woman has scratched with an angry needle, "Either bring him back or lay him low." Papyri, amulets, and curse tablets remain; incantations, gestures, incense, and sacrifices cannot reach us, though they are often enough described in written sources; the total of the evidence affirms the belief of people of the time that the strength of their spirit could be increased by the right practices or that another spirit could be engaged to reach out against their enemies. The ancient world was as tangled in a crisscross of invisible contacts, so it might be thought, as our modern world is entangled in radio beams.[9]

Aggressive magic was only one of many kinds, and by no means the most common. Among amulets, it was pain and sickness that were most often aimed at; among curse tablets, the wrong horse or chariot in the hippodrome. Nothing so very horrible here. And the picture of star spells and of demons with whips or hooks in their hands, ready to strike where they were told, should be further corrected by mention of magical powers used for good purposes. Exorcism of unclean spirits occurs familiarly in the New Testament. They caused disease, especially madness, and experts could prescribe for their removal in various ways. More serious demonic forces caused plagues, earthquakes, floods, storms, or droughts. Occasion for such invasions might be offered by the presence of unholy people —Christians, said the pagans; Arians, said the Christians— or perhaps simply of "Jonahs," κακοποδινοί. One madwoman, toward the middle of the third century, even announced herself as an active agent of bad luck, able to cause, not prevent, earthquakes. This Christians interpreted as the boast of a demon within her. It was eventually driven out, and earthquakes ceased for a time. A better reputation could be built on the power to avert disaster. Julianus the Theurgist took credit for the rainstorm that routed the Quadi armies in 174. It was recalled to contemporaries by the sculptures of Marcus Aurelius' column and so was an unquestionable historical fact, whoever was really responsible. Julianus was also said to have tried to turn the plague from Rome—the incident recalls chapters in Pythagoras' life—and to have "repelled the Dacians from the borders; for he shaped a human figurine out of clay and set it up facing the barbarians, who, when they drew near it, were driven back by irresistible thunderbolts." Though the source for the story is late, it may be called the first of a line. In 394 the pretender Eugenius erected against the emperor's troops a statue of Jove brandishing golden thunderbolts, to block the passage of the Alps. A generation later, inhabitants of Thrace discovered in a "sacred area, sanctified there by ancient rites," three silver statues barbaric in dress and posture facing north; as soon as the emperor ordered their removal, the Goths, Huns, and Sarmatians swept in. "The three statues seem, from their number, to have been dedicated against all the barbarians." A last feat of apotropaic magic may be added: the dream of the Neoplatonist Nestorius, telling how to save Athens from earthquake by making a statuette of Achilles and sacrificing to it. The magistrates laughed at him, but not the people. He had his way, by hiding the statuette under the cult image of Athena, to which (and so unwittingly to Achilles) the town fathers regularly rendered homage. Such were the tricks to which pagans had to resort. The times were hard. Influence was passing into the hands of Christians inclined to ask their own God and their own heroes to defend the empire and its cities.[10]

In some of the episodes just reported, sources speak obscurely but emphatically of the rites needed to endow statues with power to act, move, respond, or befriend. As little a thing as a pinch of incense and a hymn might bring a smile to the stone lips of Hecate; it might be some far more complicated procedure making use of a hollow statue in which were placed plants, stones, animals, roots, gems, and symbols chosen as appropriate to the god involved. Sometimes written requests were inserted in the statue as into a mailbox, to be posted to the infernal regions. The same range, and many of exactly the same details, of invocation raised the dead or deities to be questioned without need of statues. When Plotinus saw his own soul, the priest had an assistant handy, who terminated the interview too soon by wringing the necks of birds used (it is not clear just how) in the ceremony. Other animals sometimes interfered—really demons in animal form, demanding to be bought off by certain special attentions. Sometimes gods had to be summoned with moos, clucks, hisses, and other animal noises, described most elaborately by Lucan, but by magical papyri as well, and finally by Proclus in the fifth century. Beyond such direct appearances, epiphanies, or autopsies, as they were called, and beyond the materialization of supernatural powers in statues, a third common way of consulting spirits lay through the use of mediums, most often boys.[11]

In these three or in any other methods (leaving aside further details), the great object was to attain truth guaranteed by its source, since the later Roman inquirer was more likely to value knowledge according to its giver than by his own critical judgment. Teachers for their part were obliged to present their philosophic or religious revelations wrapped up in the most absurb claims: an exclusive interview, μόνος πρὸς μόνον, with Hermes, perhaps, or with Isis, or some other deity. In the preface to a treatise on astral plants, an author describes how widely he had pursued his researches, always in vain, even at Alexandria; but how at length through the magical offices of a priest in Thebes he obtained an introduction to Asclepius, and learned all that he now discloses to the dedicatee—apparently the emperor Claudius.[12] This is an early example. Somewhat later, the elder Julianus, known in Rome as a "Chaldean philosopher" and author of a work on demons in four books, turned his lore to the benefit of his son of the same name. He "demanded for him an archangel's soul," and "conjoined him, when he was born [under Trajan], to all the gods and to the soul of Plato that abides with Apollo and Hermes." The boy grew to a man, incredibly wise, and together with his father published the *Chaldean Oracles*. The collection is a disjointed essay announcing a whole philosophic system in which Platonism predominates. It purports to have been dictated by Apollo, Hecate, and others; in fact, such is the bizarre, obscure, bombastic, and incoherent content that it may rather have been dictated by a medium in a trance. It stood in need of more than the exegesis that Julianus (the younger) supplied: Proclus added further commentary. Julianus enjoyed great fame. His accompanying Marcus Aurelius to the northern wars and his rainmaking there have been mentioned. In Rome he headed a sort of community for philosophic and magical initiation. It endured for a century at least. Porphyry then learnt of it, brought the *Oracles* out of obscurity, published his *Doctrine of Julianus* and *Philosophy from Oracles*, and passed on the enthusiasm to his pupil Iamblichus. Iamblichus wrote more on the subject, and his disciples in turn introduced the emperor Julian to it—which brings us to the heyday of oracular philosophy, or philosophical oracles. The mid-fourth century indeed abounds in figures taking the name first introduced by Julianus, "theurge"; abounds in doctrines emanating from mysterious sources, promoted by mysterious beings half divine, as they claimed, able to work wonders, to warrant salvation, to reveal all truth.[13]

Such revelations were in theory addressed only to initiates. Secrecy enhanced their attraction. From Pythagoras to Proclus, anyone who wanted to impress spoke in riddles and whispers, bound his hearers to silence, promised them elevation in knowledge far above the common herd: "Do not reveal this lore to all men," it is "a wisdom unknown to the crowd." In actual fact, much must have been widely circulated and often copied, because much survives to the present day. We have the *Chaldean Oracles* of the second century and the Hermetic Corpus, mostly of the third. We can trace, too, the progress of Neoplatonism toward theurgy, through the abundant writings of the school, beginning with the vast treatise of Plotinus, the founder of Neoplatonism; then through Porphyry, and so to Iamblichus. Both of the latter left works on a variety of subjects. The extent to which all three reached beyond Plato to alien sources is not easily determined. Neopythagoreanism contributed rules for abstinent diet and regimen and some tincture of its views on the soul. Porphyry and Iamblichus showed their special interest in Pythagoras by composing histories of his life. Neopythagoreanism, in truth, may be said to have died in the arms of Neoplatonism. There is evidence, too, for Oriental influence of growing importance over the course of the century after Plotinus' death. But on a level above particular details, it is clear that the whole intent of Plotinus' teachings, still more of Porphyry's and of Iamblichus' after him, differed from Plato's fundamentally. It was not a matter alone of demonology, astrology, and magic, though toward these the Neoplatonists offered at least a cautious homage, and, at the worst, total surrender. Neoplatonists rather differed from the school they claimed to continue in making a religion out of philosophy. They hoped for salvation, not wisdom, for mystic union, not moral learning. A vegetarian diet helped Plotinus four times to attain nirvana; Iamblichus (*De myst.* 3.14 and elsewhere) preferred divination. Neither believed it possible to establish philosophic truth by use of the mind unassisted. "It is not thought that links theurgists with the gods," Iamblichus said, "else what should hinder the theoretical philosophers from enjoying theurgic union with them? The case is not so. Theurgic union is attained only by the efficacy of the unspeakable *acts* performed in the appropriate manner, acts which are beyond all comprehension, and by the potency of the unutterable symbols which are comprehended only by the gods."[14]

It would be well to pause here and consider this last quotation. It returns us after a long detour to our starting point at the beginning of the chapter, and to the type of philosopher described at the end of Chapter II, that is, to the man in whom the seat of power is the soul, not the mind. The mind, in fact, from the second century on, comes under increasingly open, angry, and exasperated attack. Perhaps Quintilian's earlier impatience with scholarly disquisitions meant nothing; perhaps Seneca's dislike of theoretical arguments, and Dio Chrysostom's plea to strip education down to the bare bones of moral philosophy, were no more than commonplaces traceable to far earlier Greek sources. The Cynics of every age were ready to throw away logic, physics, geometry, music, letters, in sum, all liberal studies. But a figure like Sextus Empiricus is a new phenomenon. In the later second century he "sat down to administer the intellectual *coup de grace* to the world of reason which Greece had created from chaos." Methodically though without originality he turned the batteries of skeptic thought against grammar, philology, rhetoric, the sciences, everything, leaving a great vacuum; and in preparation to fill it again with the kind of revealed philosophy we have been talking about, a writer of the third century, in the Hermetic Corpus, puts these words into the mouth of Hermes Thrice-Greatest himself: "Philosophy is nothing else than striving through constant contemplation and saintly piety toward the knowledge of God. For many have rendered philosophy incomprehensible and have confused it, with manifold speculation . . . mixing it up in different unintelligible studies through their clever treatises on arithmetic, music, and geometry . . . [True philosophy] is unsullied by restless inquisitiveness of spirit."[15]

Prejudices discoverable in these passages infected the whole Roman world. Proof lies in word changes. Linguistic evidence of this sort is particularly weighty because it implies a corresponding change of ideas in the minds of all people who spoke either Latin or Greek. The conclusions that emerge are, moreover, particularly clear. To cover the spectrum of men ranging from the semieducated charlatan to the most profound scholar in philosophy, including between these extremes various degrees of sober integrity or gullibility, and of various shades of philosopher, diviner, or magician, the words that should have indicated one type or another came to be used almost interchangeably. Some terms—γόης, ἀγύρτης, *magicus*, *ariolus*—were always perjorative. They occur, however, joined casually with *philosophus*, *theurgus*, *mathematicus*, and *astrologus*, in the third and fourth centuries. In the second century some allied changes had already appeared: specific equivalences between *philosophus* and *magus*, "in common parlance" (Apul., *Apol.* 2.7); also between *astrologus* and *mathematicus*, and then between *mathematicus* and *philosophus*. Cicero (*Tusc.* 5.7.18) specifically distinguished between the latter two terms. His sense of their difference was evidently lost a few generations afterward. Philosophers became astrologers; and astrologers went by a host of names: "dream diviners," "Magi," "Chaldeans," etc. The treasury of words carrying honor was being depleted by unjustified borrowings, very much as today the title "scientist" is usurped by anyone who turns tabulator or puts on a white lab coat. For the same reason, too, people outside Greco-Roman paganism reached in and filched "philosophy" as being properly descriptive of their own religion. We have seen this happening in 4 Maccabees and in Philo too. To draw the comparison between *philosophia* and Judaism, the former term had to be applied to any life of piety, even to gnosis or revelation. Christians of the second century followed suit, naming their religion a "philosophy" because it called for a way of life that led to God. Not that the old meaning disappeared among church writers. They might draw a sharp line between their faith and philosophy in the classical sense; they might, like Justin, turn from vain studies with Platonic and Stoic teachers to the "sole sure and profitable philosophy" of the prophets and Christ, or dismiss all Greek wisdom as merely propaedeutic; but their tendency was to apply the prestige of the word to all good believers, eventually (in John Chrysostom) to people of the simplest, the most illiterate piety. By Chrysostom's time "philosophy" had come to designate a life of Christian asceticism as well. Monks "philosophized"; so did martyrs, by their victory over the weakness of the flesh.[16]

That noble image of Plato, cherished without major change for so many centuries, simply dissolved in later Roman times. Where there had been cultivation, derivative pedantry succeeded, or contemptible imitation; in place of calm, extravagant behavior to catch the crowd; in place of mind, force of personality and claims to revelation. It is instructive to compare the philosopher of an Augustan painting (Frontispiece), a face and pose to remember, surely, but no more than a man, or to compare the self-comfortable ordinariness of Seneca's appearance (Plate I), with the late fourth or fifth century bust of a philosopher (Plate II). He is shown at the moment of gnosis, head tilted back, long locks flying, mouth slack. His eyes above all focus attention. They are enormous and visionary. Like Maximus, instructor to the emperor Julian, "the very pupils of his eyes were, so to speak, winged; he had a long gray beard, and his eyes revealed the impulses of his soul."[17]

Men of this nature joined a parade of wonder workers filing through the pages of Lucian, Diogenes Laertius, Philostratus, Eunapius, Porphyry, Iamblichus, Athanasius, and Palladius—pagan or Christian, philosopher, sophist, or saint. They had, of course, miraculous powers—of levitation or of communication with animals in their own language, to name two. These were favorites. Such powers as well as the individual acts of exercising them were called ἀρεταί—hence the name "aretalogies" for the accounts in which they were incorporated.

Many circulated in Greece and Egypt in Hellenistic times—their earlier roots need not be traced here—and in imperial times still more were recounted or extemporized at the temples of Serapis by the priests, or at Roman dinner parties, or at Syrian martyrs' shrines. Some had a serious intent to edify or convert. Others, like Lucian's parody *A True Story*, were meant only to amuse. If there were perhaps these two general types, they drew on each other freely, and offered inspiration just as freely to Jerome's or Athanasius' or Rufinus' lives of various early monks. The distinguished trio of debtors should not give the wrong impression. Aretalogies of at least the secular, entertaining variety grew up and flourished best among the people. Jerome in one of his biographies "for less educated readers, strove for a much lower tone," as he tells us, and modern scholars strongly sense the "vulgar" or "folk" quality. What educated person, after all, could swallow the tales of umbrella-footed men, of giants, of the raising of the dead to life, exorcisms, ghosts, werewolves, transformations of men into animals or hay into gold? And where was the plot? It was a favorite device to string everything on some picaresque line without pretense of plan. The hero and some faithful companion were turned loose to roam over half the world, so as to touch all lands known for their marvels, or unknown entirely, and thus an unchallengeable setting for whatever marvel the storyteller chose to invent.[18]

The biographies of Pythagoras by Porphyry and Iamblichus must be classed as aretalogies. They fully belong in the genre and help to define it. Episodes were recalled at the beginning of the chapter. Still better, we have the very substantial biography of Apollonius of Tyana by Philostratus. Philostratus' long career really began in the early third century, when he won the patronage of the empress Julia Domna and entered her literary circle. It was she, according to his story, who drew his attention to material on Apollonius deserving fuller treatment. The result (though she did not live to see its completion, shortly after 217) was the biography that has come down to us. Like others of the kind, Philostratus' work makes a determined effort to convince readers of the hero's actual existence. Effect depends on reality; and nowadays no one doubts that a kind of wonder worker called Apollonius did in fact flourish in Domitian's reign. In some ways his fate suggests that his accomplishments and character were out of joint with the times and would have brought greater fame had he lived, say, in the third century. While his story had then to be exhumed from quite forgotten records, once it was recovered it convinced and interested. People accepted the miracles, held his memory in honor, went on to write more lives, or referred to him in related works as late as the fifth century. He owed his second lease on notoriety in part to his being chosen a champion in the intellectual struggle between pagans and Christians; in part, to a tendency of the times to accept and venerate the kind of person he was.[19]

Apollonius seems to have been two kinds of people; or rather, two aspects in his character can be easily seen and separated. The division began immediately after his death with his first biographers, one critical of him as a charlatan, the other admiring of him as a philosopher. In the latter role he stood up to Domitian and for the occasion wrote but never delivered a (wholly Philostratean) speech full of the rhetor's art. He also wrote a life of Pythagoras on which Iamblichus is thought to have drawn heavily, and a book on the forms and best hours for prayers and sacrifices, "in his own tongue" (Cappadocian), that Philostratus had seen in use in several temples and cities; moreover, says Philostratus, Apollonius enjoyed the close friendship of that real man of letters Dio Chrysostom. Apollonius amply qualified for the title philosopher, easily rose above the term of abuse, γόης. Notwithstanding, "charlatan" he was called. It was his own fault. The tales he told of Pythagoras were too good to be forgotten, and seem to have influenced the treatment of his own career when Philostratus approached it. No doubt the real Apollonius lay under Pythagoras' spell, though to what extent he may have been a conscious imitator no one knows Without some tendency to the occult, he would have afforded to his detractors, immediately after his death, no basis for abusing his memory.[20]

Philostratus' *Life of Apollonius* is far too long to rehearse here, and yet too important to pass over entirely. A selection of episodes will draw out a few of the Pythagorean and miraculous elements.

"Votaries of the Samian Pythagoras," the book begins (1.1), say that he was a reincarnation of Homer's Euphorbus; ritually abstinent in diet and clothing; and in direct communication with the gods. "Quite akin to all this was Apollonius' way of life" (1.2). Townsfolk of Tyana believed him the son of Zeus, Sparta honored him as "the Pythagorean" (*Ep. Apol.* 62), and (*Vit. Apol.* 4.16) he himself refers to Pythagoras as "the progenitor of my wisdom." From the labyrinthine caves beneath the oracle of Trophonius in Boeotia he emerges after seven days, holding a book of Pythagoras' doctrines (8.19), the god's answer to his question, Which is the best philosophy? Among the Brahmans he discovers a "semi-Pythagorean" monastery (3:13 and 19) and upholders of Pythagorean tenets amid the Ethiopian gymnosophists (6.20). Like Pythagoras, Apollonius is enabled to foretell the future by his ascetic practices (8.5; 8.7.9); like Pythagoras, he can recall a previous incarnation (6.21), predict a shipwreck (5.18), avert earthquakes and famines (6.41; 8.7.8), and appear to followers in two places at almost the same time (8.12). Dying in confused circumstances, he comes back to a doubter in a dream (8.30f).

Like Pythagoras, too, he travels very extensively in the East, sees ghosts and men twelve feet high (2.4) and exorcises demons (3.38; 6.27, in Ethiopia). Similar encounters take place within the Greek world. He restores life (4.45), combats wicked spirits (4.20 and 25;

6.43), and at Ephesus (4.10) detects the essence of the plague in an old beggar woman, whom he persuades the Ephesians to stone to death. Under the stone pile, her body is found turned into a great dog the size of a lion, "vomiting foam like a mad dog."

He enjoys popularity and authority among all the cities, settling their disputes, receiving honors, hobnobbing with the great (1.15; 4.1–8; 5.13, 24, and 26; 6.34). Titus, Nerva, consuls, prefects, proconsuls, and senators all listen to him (6.30; 7.11 and 16; 8.7.7; *Epp. Apol.* 30; 31; 54).

In all this, no one can distinguish for certain between stories current in the lifetime of their subject (not strictly historical, of course) and others added by his biographers, especially Philostratus. Everything hangs suspended, as it were, between the early second and the early third century. To this general period, as a reflection of beliefs and tastes, the Apollonius legend unquestionably belongs; unquestionably, too, it tells a great deal about the mentality of the times; but its testimony commands a greater respect because of the confirmation in the kind of material discussed earlier in this chapter, entitling us to consider the legend as typical of its period in a dozen ways. Moreover, from just this legend period—more precisely, from a little after 180—comes another source available to its own contemporaries, capable of being treated as a historical document: Lucian's *Life of Alexander of Abonoteichus*.

In the small, partially Hellenized town of Abonoteichus on the Black Sea, Alexander was born (about A.D. 105) and raised. He was a tall, handsome youth, quick-witted and evidently unscrupulous. He attached himself early (Lucian says as lover) to a public physician from Tyana who had once been a follower of Apollonius, and who (Lucian is again the poisoned source) sold philters, spells, and inheritances. After some time, the boy switched masters, to an itinerant entertainer, and the two went about "practicing quackery and sorcery" (*Alex.* 6), ending in Macedonia, where Alexander for the first time saw the local custom or superstition of keeping tutelary pet snakes in the house. This gave him the idea for a stupendous trick. He planted oracles at different cities, some giving Asclepius' promise to move to Abonoteichus, some announcing that Alexander the descendant of Perseus would appear. Claiming this parentage, our Alexander duly came to his home town—alone, his companion having died—extravagantly costumed, proclaiming himself the indicated prophet. The Abonoteichans meanwhile had begun a new temple to house the promised Asclepius, and in its foundations Alexander first hid and then dramatically discovered an egg with a baby snake inside. To the wild excitement of the whole populace he showed it, took it home, and a few days afterward revealed it again (or rather, one of those Macedonian pets) miraculously grown to full size. Its head he kept under his robes, showing instead as the snake's continuation a false marionette arrangement resembling a human head that he could manipulate to speak and move. "Now then," Lucian cautions his readers, "imagine a little room not very bright and not much open to daylight, and a crowd of heterogeneous humanity, excited, wonderstruck in advance and exalted by their expectations" (16). That was the beginning. Fame came immediately, and pilgrims and petitioners from Bithynia, Galatia, Thrace. Glycon, as the snake was named, would return versified answers to questions submitted in writing, even to sealed and never unsealed questions, at the inconsiderable price of 1 drachma 2 obols. The administrative staff naturally grew apace: information collectors, to supply Glycon's omniscience; hexametrists as his ghost writers; clerks to gather in the money, and apostles to spread his fame. A few skeptics scowled. Lucian and his fellow Epicureans tried to expose the fraud, and the campaign reached the point of physical violence. The chief priest of Pontus, one Lepidus, was no convert. Everyone else, however, thronged to the temple to which Glycon had been removed; whole cities begged for oracular guarantee of immunity from plague, fire, or earthquake; and he entered into diplomatic courtesies with the old oracles to buy their support. He obtained for the city, from Marcus Aurelius, a new name, Ionopolis, destined to a long life (modern Ineboli), and a three-day yearly festival marked by choral hymns, initiations, and Alexander's mystic union with the moon, represented on one occasion by the wife of a local Roman official. Abonoteichus began to issue coins "bearing on one side the likeness of Glycon and on the other that of Alexander wearing the fillets of his grandfather Asclepius and holding the curved knife of his maternal ancestor Perseus" (58). He was now rising in the world, borne on the back of Glycon. A Roman senator's brother came to the shrine, and a former consul whose importance could be judged from the length of his name: M. Sedatius Severianus Iulius Acer Nepos Rufinus Tiberius Rutilianus Censor, asking Glycon whether Rome should attack Armenia. An unlooked-for triumph was the acquiring of a son-in-law Publius Mummius Sisenna Rutilianus. He published his career in an inscription from Tibur: the son of a consul, himself consul in 146, proconsul of Asia about 170, and so forth; also augur in Rome, Salian priest in Tibur, and curator there of a temple to Hercules. Rutilianus it was whose influence availed with the governor of Bithynia and Pontus to check Lucian's campaign of ridicule and exposure, and on Alexander's death, it was Rutilianus who settled a quarrel about the succession to primacy at the shrine. He is described by Lucian (*Alex.* 30) as "quite diseased on the subject of religion," and died insane.[21]

Lucian does not explain and probably did not fully understand just what a tangle of ideas Alexander had woven together to clothe his deceit. Asclepius worship is explicit, and

Asclepius was a god of healing; hence (probably) Ionopolis, from ἰᾶσθαι, unless it be "the city of Ion," brother of Asclepius. Asclepius was also a benevolent god, γλυκύς. That may have been the inspiration for "Glycon." And he had a son, Podaleirios, to whom Alexander traced yet another branch of his exuberant family tree. Above all, Asclepius was associated always with a snake, and at his temples in Ephesus, for example, had a sacred snake; but there may have been a similar, older cult at Abonoteichus to explain the *two* snakes on the coins of the town; and the snake lying across the initiate's lap or bosom was a feature of the worship of Thracian Sabazius. A human-headed snake god, Serapis or Isis, is common on coins, gems, and other minor works of art, and one carved emerald shows a rearing serpent, head haloed, inscribed "Chnoumis, Glycon, Iaô," explained by an Egyptian snake god Chnumis (Chneph), by our Glycon, and by Iaô, one of the Seven Angels among the heretical Gnostic sect, the "Snakeites" (Ophites). Ophitism attracted a following in the second century throughout the eastern provinces. Epiphanius described the chief rite. A snake symbolic of the Benefactor or Savior was released from a box on the altar and allowed to entwine itself around the bread of the Eucharist. "They call the snake Christ," Praedestinatus tells us. "Against them rose up the priests of the province Bithynia . . . and killed their serpents" in a sudden raid. To the popularity of these several snake cults in northern Asia Minor Alexander's creation owed its easy success. Still further traces of Glycon can be picked up in the coins of other cities in the area in the mid-third century.[22]

Beyond his Asclepianism, Alexander also makes explicit his attachment to Pythagoras. He calls himself the master's reincarnation. In his itinerant career, long hair, and vegetarianism, he makes good the claim. He can even match Pythagoras' golden thigh. On the other hand, the mysteries that he established at Abonoteichus borrow from Eleusis and from astral and Apollo worship.[23] Had he intended from the start to sum up and embody the syncretism typical of the later Empire, he could hardly have exceeded his actual success. He reaped the harvest of that rich dark mixture from which a new enthusiasm could grow to maturity overnight. People could repair to his cult because it was so cleverly compounded of the old, though indeed the old could and did yield a dozen further inventions, distortions, contaminations, and unpredictable, passing alliances in the realm of religious ideas.

One further point: there was evidently nothing to prevent Alexander's rise into the favor of the imperial aristocracy. Consider the high position of his later clientele; consider the rank of his son-in-law; see how naturally Rutilianus fits into the circles which, in loyalty to older Roman traditions, should have rejected Oriental oracles and totemism but which nevertheless supplied Alexander with his most influential supporters. Alexander, however, made capital of a widespread development: the very marked rise of oracles to popularity and honor in the second century. Asclepieia profited most. Aelius Aristides describes the crowds of wealthy nobles hanging around these shrines in hopes of enjoying good health, or good company, reminding us of eighteenth century men and women at Bath. Other trends aiding the acceptance of Alexander's fake snake were the current enthusiasm for Oriental worships, whether Egyptian or Syrian or Iranian, and the greater willingness to believe in the physical manifestation of divinities, or at least of spirits and supernatural beings. Both of these well-known trends have already been illustrated in passing, but the second should be underlined. In literature it represents nothing new. Invocation of the spirits of the dead, for example, occurs in Homer, Theocritus, Lucan, Lucian, and

Heliodorus, to name no more. When we come to real personal beliefs about demons, the picture changes. In the first centuries B.C. and A.D., skepticism prevailed among the educated and to some degree among the uneducated; in the second century, Plutarch and Pliny believe, and the use of apotropaic or spirit-raising amulets spreads in all classes; in the third century Dio can soberly record an event of his own time: "A certain demon in the form of a man," sent to tell of Caracalla's approaching death, led a donkey to the Capitol and into the palace, and, being arrested, disappeared in Capua. This is not one of the ordinary portents. So far as they are concerned, Dio believed implicitly, but so also did Romans throughout the Republic and Empire. Phlegon's work *On Wonders* is no less credulous in recording monstrous births and the like, in his own day (the earlier second century), than the Augustan History (SHA) in the fourth. Portents, then, were always taken seriously, while demons were something else again, and had to wait till a later date for their acceptance. Their position in the writings of Porphyry and Iamblichus has been indicated. Neoplatonists, however, who taught the communication between the material and the immaterial world, could not logically deny what ignorant folk had long accepted, namely, the reality of a middle class of spirits between men and gods. Somewhat reluctantly, certainly without emphasis, Plotinus opened the door to a grosser gullibility. His followers succumbed abjectly to what we would call mere superstition. They represented the intellectual elite—scholars, philosophers, and a large number of high officials and senators.[24]

So much for the changing attitudes of the aristocracy over the first four centuries A.D. They were willing to grant the importance of portents in the first century, of oracles in the second, of apparitions in the third and later, though to put the matter so shortly and schematically is no doubt a little misleading. One further subject remains: magic. One would assume its practice among the great mass of the population everywhere, even if there were no evidence at all. Of course evidence does exist very abundantly. There is the large find of north African curse tablets ensuring the victory of the right horse in the hippodrome; but for the same purpose Egyptians consulted the books of professional spellsellers, and Jews in Palestine read the *Book of Secrets.* Let these racetrack incantations stand for magic as a whole, practiced by ordinary people on their day off. The well-to-do and educated were not all devotees of magic. There were some who smiled. Pliny the elder, ready enough to credit omens and prodigies, drew the line at spells against hailstorms or the occult gibberish of the *magi.* Yet Nero his contemporary "tried to summon [his mother's] shades, through rites performed by *magi*, in order to obtain forgiveness" (Suet., *Nero* 34.4); and still a third person of the times, our friend Lucan, showed in his *Pharsalia* a depth and detail of magical lore that could have come only from long study, perhaps from repeated practice. As time went on, all doubters disappeared. A universal darkness prevailed.[25]

It is through individuals that the general is best described. Julianus, Pachrates, Apollonius, Alexander—all the men whose acts and ideas have been touched on, however lightly—stand like so many boundary markers to show the range of the possible. One final figure now comes forward. He is Apuleius, author of the *Metamorphoses*, and of the less-known *Apology*. The latter undoubtedly presents a true story.

In the 150's, on his way to Alexandria, Apuleius came to the unimportant coast town of Oea. It was winter, his journey thus far from Carthage had tired him. He decided to stay for a while. His presence impinged on a local imbroglio, with results that brought him to court for the practice of black arts. There was a rich widow, Pudentilla, about forty, with two grown sons. Herennius, father-in-law of one of them, hoped to control Pudentilla's riches through his daughter; Aemilianus, brother to Pudentilla's deceased husband, hoped she would marry the third brother of the family, a man of good country stock, after all.[26] When the widow chose Apuleius, Aemilianus and Herennius, both balked, joined forces, determined to have their revenge in court. They accused Apuleius of having pressed his suit by magic, and by magic of plotting his stepson's death.

They could allege that Apuleius was too suspiciously handsome, a charge to which he pleaded *nolo contendere;* that he wore his hair too long, kept a mirror by him, knew the secrets of tooth powder and mouthwashes, and wrote love poems. If he was as he claimed a philosopher he hardly fitted the part. He was obliged to defend his right to the title because it alone could explain graver charges of questionable conduct. It was an understandable case: a dandy from the big city, widely traveled, highly and arrogantly educated. People brought their prejudices to the aid of their dislike, making him the target of the distrust "commonly felt by the ignorant toward philosophers" (*Apol.* 3.6), "of whom they think some are impious for investigating the elemental and unique causes of bodies, and declare that they deny the gods . . . while other philosophers they call, in vulgar parlance, *magi*, for searching too curiously into the plan of the world" (27.1). Why had he particularly asked local fishermen to procure him three rare kinds of fish? Surely for some philter to overcome the widow's virtue. But no, Apuleius explains, he had already published a work on animal reproduction and was presently pursuing researches on anatomy, in the course of which he had discovered a new species unknown to Aristotle. His interest in medicine had brought him, at different times, visits from two epileptics for a cure. Both had fits in his presence, and one of them, being a boy, malicious gossip turned into a medium in a trance "enchanted by some spell" (42.3). "They should have added that the same boy had predicted many things by prophecy; for this is the reward that we receive for our chants: presages and oracles. Not only vulgar opinion but the authority of the learned recognizes this phenomenon performed through children."

As a serious accusation, the story fails completely. The child involved was an epileptic, impure, whereas even the most ignorant know that such rites require a person whole in mind and body (43.4). It may seem a strange piece of knowledge for Apuleius to admit to; but his ambitions of "philosophy" committed him to the entire range of accomplishments implied (in the common mind) by that word. Soon after he had entered Oea, he displayed himself in a set speech as a master of the Latin tongue (*Apol.* 73.2), and in his *Apology* some fifteen times quotes Greek philosophers and poets in their own language to *épater les bourgeois* (as in 31.5; 38.3). He refers to all the stock figures of the past, from Cato to Zoroaster, as proof of his historical learning; he knows something of animal dissection, astronomy, geography. Medical science belongs in the list, as part of his stock in trade, as something expected of his profession.[27] So the jurist Ulpian (*Dig.* 50.13.1.2f) asks whether doctors are truly professors of liberal studies, and answers yes, excluding only practitioners of incantations, prayers, or exorcism—"although there are some people who affirm with commendation that these men have been of help to them." For Apuleius the rhetor to have acquainted himself with epilepsy and spells was after all not so odd.

Other tales were told about him—that he worshiped certain mysterious objects in his home; that he had commissioned the carving of a little skeleton figurine. In truth, everything had an innocent explanation, distorted by the "ignorant." Apuleius speaks very contemptuously of them. In contrast, he flaunts his own wide learning. When examined, it appears rather close to theurgy. Mediumistic trances he accepts as perfectly undeniable phenomena. Plato he cites for the belief in spirits intermediary between men and gods, through whom spells are worked (*Apol.* 43.1). He reconciles knowledge with superstition by ascribing to demonic power the sole means of attaining the higher verities, the essential foundations of philosophy. "What captures Apuleius' attention, in the life of a Pythagoras or Plato, are the great voyages by which they were able to knock at every door of wisdom and science, and from which they returned laden with pillage and riches of learning." In short, he blends very easily into the company of Julianus or Apollonius. The reason he finds himself in court is because of the gradual *rapprochement* already discussed between the various meanings of "philosopher." Popular and educated views, philosophy and magic, were drawing steadily closer.[28]

Were this not true, Apuleius of course would never have had to argue for his life. It was a capital crime to "commit" magic, if that is the right way to put it. His enemy is "bringing charges of magic . . . That magic of his, so I hear, has been forbidden in the laws long since, by the Twelve Tables" (*Apol.* 47). Nothing could be clearer. We can check his reference to the Twelve Tables. That ancient Republican code indeed threatened the man "who enchanted with an evil incantation" or magically destroyed a neighbor's crops. To the list of things earlier prohibited Sulla in 81 B.C. had added philters, assimilable under laws against poisoning. *Venenum*, however, meant "philter" before it came to mean "poison" (like φάρμακον, both "poison" and "medicine") showing the confusion between harmless and harmful potions, much as we have seen two sides to the word "philosopher" and as we will later see how astronomy and mathematics blended into astrology and numerology, the ancient sciences being in all these ways thoroughly contaminated with superstition. Legislators when they approached the subject of magic consequently experienced difficulty in making clear their intention; but it should be remembered that they were in the grip of just the same prejudices as anyone else, numbered a Pliny or a Rutilianus among their friends, and could only express in law the prevailing atmosphere of their age. Hence Gaius (*Dig.* 50.16.236) is aware of the distinction that must be made clear between good and bad *venenum*, between *medicamenta* and poison; Paul, in the early third century (*Sent.* 5.23.14), notes that draughts to induce either abortion or love are illegal, and goes on to list related crimes—human sacrifice, spellbinding (*qui . . . defigerent obligarent*), "nocturnal or impious rites," "magic arts," the very possession of "books of magic arts"—among which at least one further item (*mala sacrificia*) had been brought under Sulla's law by Modestinus' time (ca. 240) by decree of the senate (*Dig.* 48.8.13). Two points emerge: that the foundation of antimagic legislation was laid by Sulla, and that it could support a broad structure of prohibition and punishments because of the very looseness of thought on the whole subject. Once the use of *venenum* became illegal, the ban was bound to spread by confusion of thought to all kinds of occult practices.[29]

Constantine upheld the traditional ban on "magic arts" used either to hurt people or seduce to love (adding that there was nothing wrong about medicinal magic or spells to prevent bad weather). Constantius legislated specially against necromancy and "magic arts employed to disturb the elements [or] undermine the lives of the innocent." Still later, magic to influence the outcome of a horse race was specified, with the appropriate penalties, and nocturnal prayers or sacrifices.[30]

There was thus no period in the history of the empire in which the magician was not considered an enemy of society, subject at the least to exile, more often to death in its least pleasant forms. How then to explain his open circulation in all social circles, the wide and apparently public use of ring stones magically endowed, the boasts of occult revelations in published books, and the survival of many magical papyri? Set against the whole picture of magic in Roman society, the official attitude is a plain contradiction—resolved, however, by the very importance of magic. Not only could it not be eradicated from the common mind but the most enlightened people took it seriously, attributing to it (they would have said) many specially valuable aspects of that same enlightenment. A law against the like of Thessalus, Pachrates, Julianus, or Maximus—to recall a figure from each of the first four centuries A.D.—would have been plainly unenforceable. Compromise followed. Laws said again that what defines the crime is the intent to hurt. There was black magic and white, there was the γόης and the scholarly or benevolent practitioner. Insistence that one was not a γόης turned out to be, after all, more than a terminological quibble. It might prevent arrest. Hence the tenor of some passages in Philostratus' *Life of Apollonius* (5.12; 8.7.2) and much of Apuleius' *Apology*. At times the law was tightened up. Caracalla and Constantius punished wearers of antifever amulets with death; theurgists were intermittently in danger. There are instances of the actual application of the laws against winning a woman by magic or possessing magic books, and Tacitus records, among other famous cases, the death of Germanicus, in whose house were afterward found, it was said, "incantations and imprecations and the name 'Germanicus' scratched on lead tablets, half-burned cinders smeared with blood, and other maleficent objects by which it is thought that souls can be consigned to the powers below."[31]

Like philosophy, magic thus presented two aspects, one accepted and even characteristic among good Romans, the other feared and unlawful. Initiates were found in the senate house or in the palace, and yet also in darkened crypts and temples, or dragged forth to face arraignment before the civil authorities. There is a further point of comparison with philosophy. As figures from progressively lower classes appear in the history of the *philosophus*, so magical superstitions characteristic of a steadily lower class come to prevail throughout the empire. Vergil left it to a peasant to melt a waven image of his rival (*Ecl.* 8.80f.); Petronius laughed at an ex-slave, Trimalchio, for telling a story of werewolves (*Cena* 62). By Dio's time, such beliefs were no joking matter. To their level had fallen the very leaders of culture: senators, imperial councilors, consuls—in short, the governing classes. Hence the ever widening legislation to protect society from magic; and from the same cause, the decay of rationality among the best-educated men, followed a closely related effect. More and more stringent measures forbade the unriddling of the future through appeals to supernatural powers. This is the subject to be discussed next.

✧ IV ✧

Astrologers, Diviners, and Prophets

In the Roman empire, a universal confidence that the future could be known either through rites of official priests on public occasions, or privately, produced an infinitely combustible audience for predictions. Against these, as sometimes dangerous to public order, it was correspondingly important for the state to defend itself by legislation. The means of determining the future were, first of all, study of the stars acting especially on men in a position to shape events; then, study of the entrails of sacrificial animals or of birds' flights or the like; lastly, by direct revelation. The three methods were employed respectively by astrologers, diviners, and prophets or seers, whose titles supplied the vocabulary of legislation: *astrologi* (also called *mathematici* or *Chaldaei*); (*h*)*aruspices* and *augures;* and vaguer terms like *vates*, *vaticinatores*, *coniectores*, (*h*)*arioli*, προφῆται; later, *magi*, and, pejoratively, γόητες. Usage was inconsistent, ideas blurred. Tacitus (*Ann.* 2.27 and 32; 12.22) and Tertullian (*De idol.* 9; *Apol.* 35) show the tendency to jumble prediction and magic together apparently in official documents. We have seen the wizard Pachrates called a prophet, and a similar confusion is clear in laws of the fourth century (*Cod. Theod.* 9.16.4 and 6). By then, too, people had begun to confuse prediction on the one hand and geometry and philosophy on the other.[1] In actual fact, men who claimed occult powers in one field often claimed them in all: witness Julianus and Apollonius, or the practitioners who assembled recipes for inducing dreams or epiphanies, for compelling love in someone else, and for foretelling the future, all in the same magical papyrus book. Mixed roles and suspect associations thus provided a further reason for bringing seers, astrologers, diviners, or prophets within the reach of the authorities, beyond the plain need to enforce public tranquillity.

In A.D. 11, being then 74 years old, Augustus became the focus for upsetting speculation about the nearness of his death, and accordingly he forbade divinatory consultations without the presence of a third person, and any prediction on a person's death. His successor, Tiberius, repeated the universal prohibition against "consultations in secret and without witnesses." Antoninus Pius took up the subject again, and Ulpian in the early third century could look back and say, "Very often and by almost all the emperors it has been forbidden to anyone at all to involve himself in this sort of folly, and those who practice it have been punished in different degrees . . . For those who consult about the health of the emperor are punishable by death or some still heavier sentence; and about their own or their relatives' affairs, by a lighter sentence. Among the latter are counted *vaticinatores* . . . since they sometimes exercise their dishonest arts against the peace of the realm and Roman rule." Aurelian forbade soldiers to consult *haruspices*. Diocletian thundered against the whole *ars mathematica*, Constantine warned practitioners not so much as to set foot in a private house, Constantius commanded "the curiosity of divination" to be silent, "the wicked revelations" of "those whom the vulgar call 'maleficers' from the greatness of their crimes" to cease, in court circles as well as elsewhere. At the end, harshest fate of all, *mathematici* had to choose between empire-wide exile or conversion to Christianity.[2]

As Augustus pointed the way for the control of divination, so he did for prophecy, confiscating and burning in 12 B.C. more than two thousand books on the subject, Greek and Latin (Suet., *Aug.* 31.1). Henceforth their private ownership was forbidden (Tac., *Ann.* 6.12), and under Tiberius the Sibylline oracles were closely scrutinized and their circulation checked, so far as was possible. For some date unknown before the mid-second century, Justin mentions an actual law on the whole matter: "Through the agency of evil spirits it was proscribed by death to read the books of Hystaspes or the Sibyl or the [Jewish] prophets." By the early third century, the jurist Paul declared, "Those who introduce new sects or beliefs unacknowledged by reason, by which men's minds are disturbed," are punishable by relegation or death (*Sent.* 5.21.2), evidently referring to prophecies, since he is discussing *vaticinatores et mathematici;* and a generation later Modestinus knew of legislation according to which "if anyone should do anything to terrify the flighty minds of men with superstitious dread of the divine, the deified Marcus [Aurelius] decided that such men should be exiled to an island" (*Dig.* 48.19.30). It has been suggested that this was what Melito meant in 177, referring to "new decrees" against Christians, though it is more likely that the "new decrees" are lost to us, and what was really in Modestinus' mind was Marcus Aurelius' exiling of "the man who, at the time of Cassius' rebellion, prophesied and told much, allegedly under divine influence." The last clear reference to the subject of illicit prophecy comes from Diocletian's reign, directed at the Manichaeans, men of evil religion and wicked wills, who draw their views "from that nation, our enemy, Persia . . . to stir up quiet people," and who are to be burnt at the stake together with their writings.[3]

Astrologers, Diviners, and Prophets

With help from the applicable parts of the antimagic laws reviewed in the preceding chapter and with all the laws just now described, the Romans were thus well equipped to defend themselves against the closely allied crimes of divination and prophecy. Inquiries through occult arts into the destinies of the royal house or of the state were illegal; clandestine attempts to get around the law were barred by insistence that any probing into the future—permitted as late as 371 (*Cod. Theod.* 9.16.9)—must be carried out with witnesses present, in some public place; furthermore, oracular literature might be confiscated according to decrees laid down by Marcus Aurelius if not earlier. The emperors' motives can be guessed almost with certainty. Themselves believing in the efficacy of the arts they proscribed, they wanted no meddling with their own stars or lifelines. Cases cropped up, too, in which divination raised disloyal hopes and encouraged conspiracies. So far as concerned the legal basis of the government's policies, it had always possessed the right to prevent or repress civil disorders, a power often appealed to in the laws just cited. The public mind must not be "disturbed." General police power was fortified by a further development. Any act hostile to the imperial family came to be defined as treason, *maiestas* (*minuta*). Hostility displayed through occult practices, at first only added to other charges, soon provided a basis by itself for a charge of treason.[4] This remained the law throughout the period of the Empire.

Emperor and subject both took precautions when they investigated the future. In official consultations, the evidence was destroyed after it had been analyzed, and royal horoscopes were if possible kept secret. Augustus', cast by a senator who studied such things, offered so clear a promise of pre-eminence that its owner published it on his coins—perhaps before he attained sole power, as Suetonius says, perhaps only in his declining years, to put an end to people's wondering how long he could live, as Dio says. A large number of emperors were later credited with horoscopes that foretold the throne —several have come down to us. Either ancient astrology had an accuracy lost, alas, to the modern world, or half the Roman aristocracy were at one time or another promised great things; or, still a third possibility, the stories of imperial horoscopes were invented after the event. That last is surely the answer. In any case, though Romans sometimes did know their friends' horoscopes, it was a decidedly risky matter to advertise one too ambitious. Even after attaining power, Severus wisely kept his horoscope to himself, in its details, though he divulged its general intent. Astrologers, for their part, from Augustus' reign on, pretended that their vision could not pierce the majesty of the imperial fates—an unctuous disclaimer that fooled no one—and advised their students, "You will give your answers in public and will take care to warn those who come to consult you that you are going to respond in a loud voice to everything they ask you about, so they will not ask questions that they should not and which it is forbidden to answer. Be careful to say nothing about the condition of the state or the life of the emperor, if anyone should inquire; for that is forbidden; we must not, moved by criminal curiosity, speak of the condition of the country; and he who answers questions on the destiny of the emperor would be a wretch deserving of every punishment."[5]

But there was really no stopping astrologers save by driving them right out of the capital. Their expulsion from other cities is never mentioned; the *Roman* crowd, on the other hand, could on occasion make or break an emperor. Accordingly, first in 33 B.C. by action of the aedile Agrippa, later by senatorial decree, and after 52 by imperial edict, the city or all Italy was repeatedly cleared of *mathematici*, *Chaldaei*, *astrologi*, *magi*, γόητες, or however they were called, perhaps ten times over the period 33 B.C. to A.D. 93, and possibly once more under Marcus Aurelius. These were temporary measures called forth by particular circumstances. In 33 B.C., wars with Antony impended, in A.D. 68–70, four emperors came and went; in 16, 52, 89, and 175, plots or pretenders used astrology to unsettle the populace. A connection between these sudden expulsions and their causes was no doubt understood by contemporaries. Tacitus (*Ann.* 2.32; 12.52) makes the point clear; so does the specific provision that astrologers who kept away from forbidden subjects might register with the authorities for exemption from the decrees. Moreover, war with astrology being ultimately fought for the possession of the mass mind had to be correspondingly explicit and well publicized. The government punished with the ancient formula, "interdiction from fire and water," hurled its enemies from the Tarpeian rock, or put them to death "in the ancient manner" outside the Esquiline gate, to the sound of trumpets. Astrologers responded with spirited—because anonymous—replies. As the date in 69 approached on which they were obliged to leave Rome, according to Vitellius' command, they posted the pasquinade "The Chaldeans say, It is Our wish that Vitellius Germanicus should quit life before the last day of the calends." The stars, with aid from massed Danubian regiments, brought that emperor to an ignoble end—just on the day predicted, said the astrologers. They drifted back into the city. Vespasian drove them out; they returned; Domitian expelled them again. They suffered little by an occasional turn in the provinces, even gained some increase in fame, as by official endorsement. "Hence the practitioner's repute, if manacles clank on both wrists, if he has been in the prison of some distant camp. No *mathematicus* can boast true inspiration without having been condemned—only the man who has almost died, who barely won an exile to the Cyclades"

(Juv. 6.560f). So it went, quidnuncs and charlatans against prefects and judges, rumors against stability, neither side able to win a final victory. Ill health or weakness in the ruler encouraged the one, a popular reign upheld the other. After Domitian, astrological disloyalty ceased to be a serious problem.[6]

Broadside action against the whole class of astrologers was supplemented from Augustus on by the threat of laws applicable to individual offenses. Records of a dozen trials survive from the first century in which persons connected with the very highest nobility stood charges of inquiring into the destinies of the emperor or of his family. This was treason, whether done through diviners or (most often) through astrologers. The same period produces six trials of the astrologers themselves. Much of this evidence is well known, coming from the more lurid parts of Tacitus' *Histories* and *Annals;* a recent treatment has illuminated them systematically. From the later Empire two cases are given to us by contemporaries. The first belongs to about 205, that is, to the reign of a convinced believer in astrology who had himself once been indicted "for consulting seers and Chaldeans." It was a certain Apronianus, proconsul of Asia, who was accused. Septimius Severus personally forwarded the evidence to the senate. A nurse of the defendant had dreamed that he would some day be emperor; he was reported to have "employed some magic toward this end"; such were the contemptible charges. Dio was present at the senate meeting where they were presented. A witness under torture had stated that, from the room where the dream was first divulged, he had seen "a certain senator peeping in, a bald man . . . When we heard this," Dio goes on, "we were in a wretched state; for the witness had not spoken nor Severus written anyone's name, but fear paralyzed even those who had never visited Apronianus, not only those who were bald but those too with somewhat receding hair . . . I was so disconcerted that I felt with my hand for my own hair. Many others did exactly the same." Further testimony narrowed suspicions, and their victim, identified by the witness with help from the furtive nods of the senators, was executed almost on the spot.[7]

The second case, of 371–72, was known to Ammianus in great detail. It began with the interrogation of a hireling poisoner and a horoscopist who earned forgiveness of their own crimes by revealing a worse: the discovery of the ruling emperor's successor "through detestable presages." They pointed to three men. Of these, one betrayed "many others" not specified by Ammianus, and a second betrayed three more, of whom one thereafter betrayed Theodorus the Notary; and so on until the jails were jammed. Ammianus mentions fifteen suspects by name. The whole investigation was pursued with unspeakable savagery, under which one man, being taken to the witness stand, dropped dead from terror, while Ammianus himself, fumbling in his memory years later "as among shadowy things," yet recalled the racks and scourges and the brazen shouts of the torturers echoing in the prefect's palace, by which the tale was wrung out. Two among the accused had made a tripod of laurel wood, consecrated with incantations, placed in a room purified with incense. On the tripod was a metal plate inscribed with the letters of the alphabet around its rim. "A man clad in linen clothing, shod with linen shoes, garlanded and carrying twigs from a tree of good omen, after propitiating the Divine in prescribed verses," set swinging over the letters a ring on a linen thread. To the question "Who will succeed Valens?" it successively stopped at Θ, Ε, Ο, Δ; and there the inquirers stopped, too, certain that Theodorus was meant. He soon learned the outcome of the séance and the secret spread beyond him—presumably no further than Valens' thorough cruelty could later reach. All whom he discovered—a chancellor of the treasury, a vice prefect, proconsul, Palatine trooper, ex-governor, including also men of outstanding culture and the theurgist Maximus—were executed. Of two "philosophers," one was sentenced to the stake. Still "laughing at the sudden collapse of human destinies, he died unmoving in the flames, like Peregrinus Proteus the famous philosopher." Ammianus continues, "Next, innumerable books were piled together, many heaps of volumes drawn from various houses, to be burnt under the eyes of the judges as prohibited." In fear of the widening investigations, "throughout the oriental provinces owners burnt their entire libraries. So great was the terror that seized everyone. For, to put it shortly, in those days we all crept about as in Cimmerian darkness."[8]

Ammianus leaves out the connections of his thought as being too obvious to need telling: book burning belonged inevitably to the whole inquisition because divination was a very bookish skill—how much so can be seen in the description (only a small part of which has been quoted) of the tripod and the rites that made it work. "Philosophers" belonged to the scene as well because, in the fourth century especially, they were likely to have studied the magic arts. Maximus at least was a known wonder worker, teacher of the emperor Julian, and Iamblichus was said, in a subsequent variant of the whole story, to have engaged Libanius in an inquiry into Valens' succession, using a cock and a piece of corn before each of the letters of the alphabet. The order of the cock's pecks spelled Θ, E, O, Δ, and ruin for many persons implicated in the affair. A sophist, a Neoplatonist, and a theurgist—Libanius, Iamblichus, Maximus—could thus be suspected of exactly the views implicit in the meaning of their general title: *philosophi*—the word has been discussed above often enough. They may be taken as typical not only of their several branches of the learned professions but of the educated classes as a whole, from which they drew their students, disciples, or accomplices: Julian, Proclus, the enormous acquaintance of Libanius among the aristocracy of the eastern empire, and all those great officials named in the "Theodorus plot." No different picture meets us if we turn back to Dio's time. Senators among whom he sat listening to a capital charge of dream interpretation never questioned the reality of the crime, whatever they may have felt about the guilt of their fellow, Apronianus; nor, for that matter, did their predecessors under Nero, when Servilia was on trial. To determine if her family would survive investigations in the wake of the Pisonian conspiracy, she had sold her dowry in payment to the *magi* who would assist her. Her purposes were innocent. "I have called on no unholy divinities, no spells, no other thing in my unlucky supplications than that you, Caesar, and you, Senators, should preserve in safety this best of fathers. My jewels and gowns and signs of my rank I gave as I would have given my life and blood, had they been asked." Just these were in fact demanded. She was permitted only to accomplish her own death. But what chiefly distinguishes her case, beyond its pathos, is the insight it allows into a circle we have met before. Her husband was Annius Pollio, her father Barea Soranus. She belonged to the very heart of the Stoic opposition, and yet believed, to the last penny she could raise, that knowledge of the future, perhaps a faint control over it, could somehow be purchased. In every period of the Roman Empire, this confidence inspired even the most enlightened minds.[9]

Astrology and allied arts could only be mastered through long study. That claim underlay the price experts put on their skills to strip Servilia of her dowry. That underlay the book-burning that Ammianus mentions, and the general willingness to attribute occult learning to a person learned in anything at all. Without the semischolarly façade of the astrological profession, there could never have been a profession in the first place, nor could its members (in contrast to the entire mass of the people who dabbled, say, in healing magic) have been singled out for exile from Rome and Italy. Laws against individual crimes of illegal divination spoke equally of "consultations," pointing to the fact that the average man could not avail himself of what the legislators admitted was an art without expert assistance. Naturally, different degrees of proficiency were found. Juvenal (6.582, 588) tells his less wealthy readers to take their custom to the Circus Maximus. There they would find a *mathematicus* whom they could afford. A natural resort. In the preceding chapter we have seen the urban poor concentrating their gropings in magic upon horse races and gladiatorial combats. So with astrology. The hippodrome was thought of as a universe in miniature: its circuit, the year; its twelve starting gates, the months; its four usual teams, the seasons. "Saturn, Mercury, and Venus have affinity to the Blue party; Sun, Mars, and Moon, to the Green; Jupiter is common to both," says a handbook on the subject. Being organized in this way, the course of the horses came under the ordinary pretensions of astrology to predict and control. Even here, one can see the outlines of a true body of learning which could be lowered to the level of the racetrack crowds but which in its more technical forms came close to a science—perfectly unintelligible to a popular audience, indeed to the average classical historian today. Rules, tables, calculations, and commentaries now known from a vast corpus of astrological writings lay far above the reach of casual charlatanism. Its masters earned their fees. Through Vettius Valens, for example, of the mid-second century, we can still follow the history of more than a hundred of his clients from the precise hour of their birth through star-drawn vicissitudes calculated with rigorous discipline, to their deaths: "This person was drowned in bilge water," "was killed by wild beasts," or "was banished and committed suicide." A hint here of an interesting fact: since no tuppenny-ha'penny criminal suffered exile, the last-named client belonged to the upper classes. The deduction finds support in some though not all of the other case histories. They deal with men high in the government, with owners of slaves and large estates. Vettius Valens himself ran a school, perhaps not a successful one. At any rate, he complained that astrology "is nowadays dishonored and rejected." A few generations later things looked better. An emperor friendly to astrology sat on the throne, "and so certain *mathematici* by his order held forth publicly in Rome and professed their art."[10]

From hippodrome to lecture room, from poor to rich. An equally wide audience for astrology appears in Juvenal. He turns from the Circus Maximus to wealthy believers who, he says, must repair instead to some Phrygian or Indian soothsayer "skilled in the stars and the heavens"; "a greater trust will lie in the Chaldeans" (6.533f, 585). He pictured Tiberius at Capri "with his Chaldean herd" (10.94); but then, Nero delayed his coronation on the advice of his Chaldeans, Otho consulted *his*, indeed the great majority of emperors of every century were either credulous or studiously respectful to the claims of astrology. Their attitude of course reflected that of the upper classes generally: of Seneca, Tacitus, or Apuleius. From Hadrian on, for a half century, skepticism gained strength among the educated, yet for humble folk of just this period there always remained "those who give a prophecy to any comer for two obols," those others "who display their secret lore in the market places . . . to adolescent boys and a crowd of slaves and a company of fools." Later yet, in the third century, new enthusiasms and a prevalent antirationalism slowly won first place in men's minds, but there were still proconsuls and high functionaries to take an interest in astrology, and scholars to explore its depths.[11]

A single remarkable family indicates the rank that practitioners could reach. Tiberius Claudius Thrasyllus appears in Juvenal (6.576), full of fame. An Alexandrian grammarian, he carried his researches to Rhodes, where Tiberius met him. The future emperor possessed an unusually steady judgment and bestowed his friendship on no shallow deceivers. In Thrasyllus he had found an astrologer, to be sure, but one who added to his studies in that area the editing of Plato in the form traditional to this day and the composition of long-remembered essays on Platonism and Pythagoreanism. He acquired Roman citizenship with the help of his powerful patron, and the hand of a Commagenian princess in marriage; his granddaughter Ennia married Macro successor to Sejanus as praetorian prefect in 29, and aspired still higher, through an adulterous liaison with the heir apparent to the throne. That Caligula actually became emperor was due in part to her help, though, of the triangle Macro-Ennia-Caligula, it is unclear who was dupe to whom. Thrasyllus' son, Tiberius Claudius Balbillus, kept apart from these adventures, returning to Rome only upon the accession of Claudius, who proclaimed him "my friend" in an official document. He accompanied Claudius to Britain, being then a legionary tribune. He was decorated for his services, shortly advanced to high priest of the temple of Hermes in Alexandria, head of the university (the Serapeum), and overseer of the imperial properties in Egypt, and under Nero became prefect of the province (59?). This was the second highest office open to equestrians. His astrological treatise and services to Nero were remembered from the 60's, but he played no prominent role. His daughter's second marriage was to another prefect of Egypt; by her first, she had renewed ties with the royal house of Commagene, and had borne a son destined for a consulship in Trajan's reign and a daughter Julia encountered later in the entourage of Hadrian. On November 20, 130, Julia stood with the emperor before the Colossus of Memnon, hoping to hear it speak to the rays of the rising sun. Such were its powers, tradition said. She rebuked its silence in verses carved on its pedestal. On the next day, obediently it responded "out of the ringing stone." Her inscribed poems are the last-known record of Thrasyllus' line.[12]

No need to underline the obvious: a world in which men principally known for their astrological lore could rise to such influence and could found such a dynasty was a world quite dedicated to astral fatalism. Had it been otherwise, the rapid development of the treason laws to embrace divination could not have taken place, nor the trials that so often darken the pages of Tacitus. These and the relation between legislation and religion are what concern us, not religion or superstition or pseudo science for their own sake. Those subjects must be left to other books. Yet a curious connection should be drawn with our earlier chapters on the philosophic opposition. Stoicism of the stricter school went hand in hand with astrology. Astrology could best flourish as a serious science when men believed, as Stoics of the first century did believe, in the power of a fixed, universal destiny. Servilia's frantic consultations with diviners are, after all, not out of place in a daughter of Barea Soranus, nor is it strange to hear Seneca's emphatic praise of Balbillus. Seneca believed in astrology and no doubt taught Nero to do so. His fellow tutor, the Stoic Chaeremon from Alexandria, like Seneca, wrote a treatise on comets, and earned great renown for his learning in astrology.[13] With such a pair to shape his views, Nero turned naturally to an even higher authority, to Balbillus, to advise him about a comet seen repeatedly in 65. Balbillus told him that "rulers usually expiated such signs by the death of some distinguished man, and thus diverted them to the heads of the nobles." The result, continues Suetonius (*Nero* 36), was to strengthen Nero's implacability against the conspirators of that and the next year—Seneca, Barea Soranus, and the rest. The whole circle of relations and effects here is very strange.

With Nero's reign, we may turn from stars and horoscopes to the second broad area of prediction that the authorities tried to control: prophecy. In 64, fire destroyed a vast part of the capital. No suspicions could have been directed against the Christians of the city had the general public not reacted to the catastrophe with irrational conjectures. A second fire in 69 burnt down the Capitoline temple, Rome's most sacred. That was a portent. In the rebellious Gallic provinces, "more than anything else, it drove them to the conviction that the end of the empire was at hand. 'Once the city had been taken by the Gauls, but Roman rule endured so long as Jove's home remained intact; now a fatal flame had given sign of the divine wrath and of the transfer of the control over men to the tribes beyond the Alps.' Such were the vain and superstitious prophecies of the Druids." The Gauls were at the time in an unusually excitable condition. A little before, they had listened to a seer from the Boii who claimed divine favor, claimed even to be a god himself; and a little later, when revolution had spread openly, they invited the aid of another prophetess from the Bructeri whose "authority was growing, for she had predicted a German success and the annihilation of the legions." Such were the great dangers concealed in predictions. From experience of this sort, the Romans learned the necessity of the laws we have already reviewed.[14]

But the Year of the Four Emperors threw the whole Roman world into a sort of fever. The empire was proving mortal; all things were possible, or thinkable. A symptom of the times came in the form of a fantastic vision: Nero had not died but would return. By way of background to the story, it should be remembered that twice before members of the imperial house had emerged from darkness to a double or second life: Agrippa Postumus in A.D. 14 (or rather, his slave taking his name) supported by many relatives, by knights, and by senators, until his arrest in Rome on the very verge of inciting a civil war; then, twenty years after, a false Drusus who appeared in the Cyclades while the real Drusus lay in chains under Tiberius' palace. The impostor traveled to Greece, then to Ionia, and was thought to aim at the loyalty of the Syrian and Egyptian legions. Recruits flocked to him, cities welcomed him. The governor intervened in the nick of time. "Drusus" was captured unresisting, and went to some uncertain fate. What his adventure seemed to prove was the combustibility of the Greek provinces, at least of the youth of the cities there; perhaps also the popularity of the Julio-Claudian line. This, Nero may have enjoyed like his predecessors. He had wooed Greece with his extravagant visits, more flatteringly with his philhellenism. He had made the province of Achaea "free." Discounting honorific inscriptions, we should nevertheless trust the Greek writers who admit his crimes and yet speak of his death with regret. Many wished him back; and the obscurity of his dying, too oddly contrasted with the fanfare of his living, permitted them to hope that he lay concealed somewhere, awaiting the right moment. In 69 Greece and Ionia "were terrified by a false belief in Nero's advent" (Tac., *Hist.* 2.8), the object of the rumor being a slave from Pontus—others said a freedman from Italy

—who not only looked like Nero but was his equal in talents. He went about singing and playing and recruiting people who desired revolution (this was no doubt what "terrified"). Turning pirate in the islands, he was caught by a trick and killed. He had had all Greece in a ferment. Ten years passed, a second false Nero appeared—an Asiatic Greek "winning some followers in Asia and raising a much larger number on his way to the Euphrates. At last he found protection with Artabanus king of Parthia, who, because of his anger with Titus, both received him and made ready to restore him to Rome." In 88, yet a third Nero appeared, and taking refuge with the Parthians was handed over to the Romans very reluctantly. The line of pretenders ended with a false Alexander the Great of 221, a demon, Dio can only conclude, who came from the Danube provinces "into Moesia and Thrace in a Bacchanalian company of 400, with wands and fawnskins, doing no harm. Everyone then in Thrace agrees that accommodations and provisions were given him at public expense. No one—magistrate, soldier, procurator, governor of the communities—dared to say or do a thing against him, and he got as far as Byzantium in a sort of formal progress, traveling by daylight and serving notice of his coming. Then he crossed to Chalcedon, and there, after some nocturnal rites, burying a wooden horse, he vanished."[15]

No doubt these half-dozen impostors—Agrippa, Drusus, the Neros, Alexander—threatened the peace of the areas they visited. The two later Neros, however, presented a special danger arising from the character of their original. Beyond his resorts to astrology and magic, reported in the preceding chapter, he had a taste for prophecy as well. He had been told that "someday he would be repudiated . . . But some [diviners] promised him the rule of the East, when he was cast off, a few naming specifically the kingdom of Jerusalem, several others the recovery of all his former fortunes" (Suet., *Nero* 40.2). His eastern hopes, more likely his uncontrollable appetite for experiment, led him in 66 into conversations with Tiridates, present in Rome to be crowned king of Armenia. Tiridates was a good Mazdean, probably a priest, certainly surrounded with priests; and he won Nero over and initiated him into the sacred meals of Mithraism. When he kneeled to the emperor for his crown, in a scene immensely advertised, it was to Nero as avatar of the Iranian god of light endowed with a halo of Mithraic messianism.[16] That was why a Parthian embassy begged for honor to be paid to Nero's memory, in the 70's in Rome, and why pretenders to the name found instant welcome and support beyond the Euphrates in the 80's. One or the other of them, the sources are agreed, came very near to attaining a triumphant return, backed by Parthian arms.

Among the Jews and Christians, the myth of Nero's return received a different notoriety. He would come—that was already known in thc 80's and 90's—but as Beliar "in the likeness of a man, a lawless king, the slayer of his mother," or as the Beast with the number 666, "who was and is not and shall come," in Revelation 13 and 17. It was knowledge born of hate, vivid and plausible only to an audience which saw in Nero either the first of the persecutors or the emperor under whom the revolt in Judaea broke out, with frightful flames. He was well suited, according to one version of his role, to lay waste the world at the head of an army of revenge—Parthian, that would be; according to another, to be chosen as the form of an embodiment by the Antichrist himself. Details and repetitions of the legendary coming meet us in the 3,400 lines of the *Sibylline Oracles*. They circulated thoughout the diaspora, closely imitating their pagan namesakes' meter, form, atmosphere, and language, in order to borrow authority. The fourth book (lines 119f), though dating to the year 80, already mentions Nero's return. He is "a great king as a fugitive" fleeing beyond the Euphrates, a matricide and a sinner, sheltered in Parthia, from which (lines 137f) he will reappear at the head of a great army. Perhaps a decade later, the fifth book pictures Nero as a king equal to Zeus, a sweet singer, but the killer of his mother and hated by all. The agent of divine purpose, at the end of time, he will receive the satanic powers needed to destroy the whole earth with fire. About A.D. 180, the eighth book (lines 70f) for the last time speaks of the return of the exiled matricide to establish Asia's rule over the world. In the early fourth century, Lactantius quotes the Sibyllines—"The matricide in exile will return from the ends of the earth"—only to rebuke believers. What Christian, he asks, can conceive of Nero as the first and therefore the last scourge of the faithful, and precursor to the Antichrist, when such an idea attributes to this "evil beast" an eternity and prophetic rank equal to Christ's?[17]

Prophecy is one of the several literary shapes in which hopes can be cast and wishes fulfilled. Like the imaginary interviews between "tyrants" and martyrs, described in an earlier chapter, or like Lactantius' horrible work just cited, so the *Sibyllines* projected into an unreal world hatreds that could not find direct expression. As God tortured Lactantius' persecutors, as pagan or Christian heroes triumphed in spirit over their adversaries, so what actually had not happened could be made to happen by oracular verses. It would be wrong to see in any part of this dream literature only a purging of animosities. Especially for the Jews, during many centuries too weak to confront their enemies in arms, dreams could keep alive the image of ultimate victory. Roman authorities were therefore, according to their own lights, quite right to enforce peace with an iron hand.

Jesus was not the first nor was he destined to be the last sacrifice. In A.D. 45, "a certain seer" (γόης) called Theudas persuaded a great part of the people to follow him to the river Jordan. He said he was a prophet and could divide the river. The procurator prevented the attempt with a force of cavalry, cut up the crowd, and executed Theudas. The incident widens our focus on anti-Roman rumors, beyond those that center in the person of Nero, though it is still the eastern provinces that must monopolize our attention. For Theudas was only one of many from the same area. Less than a decade later, the whole of Judea was filled with "bandits and seers" (somehow accomplices to each other, in the view of a contemporary) "who delude the people," infiltrated the restless crowds of Jerusalem in order to intimidate or murder their opponents, and at last "persuaded the population to follow them into the wilderness." They promised to work miracles by God's power. This movement too was checked by troops. But next, "a man from Egypt arrived in Jerusalem at this time [A.D. 54], saying he was a prophet and advising the masses to go with him to the Mount of Olives." There they could witness in safety the overthrow of the city's walls at a word from him. Again: troops, butcheries, arrests; and after this, yet one more γόης "who promised salvation and an end of ills" if people would but go with him into the wilderness.[18] Offenses to religions by the Romans, schismatic zeal, class warfare, and the clash of cultures all added to the ferment in the province in this period, but over all hung the atmosphere of prophecy like premonitory smoke, until Judea took fire. An army of fifty thousand was needed to restore the *pax Romana*.

"But the thing that most aroused [the Jews] to war was an obscure oracle, likewise found in their sacred writings, foretelling that at this time [the 60's] someone would come from their own land to rule the world." Just what oracle this was that triggered rebellion cannot be known. The most likely candidate, or at least the closest parallel, is the one that circulated under the name of Hystaspes. It should be remembered that the Near East in Hellenistic times was already astir with promises of revenge against many other rulers and intruders besides the Romans. Sometimes the source of prediction was Iranian, sometimes Old Testament prophecies. In the first century B.C. or A.D., what scholars call a work of syncretism, that is to say, a muddle, drew together many rebellious eastern beliefs into a single picture of the Last Days. This picture was attributed to a figure of an age infinitely remote, Hystaspes.[19] He had foreseen six thousand years of bad times, one thousand of good, and then the destruction of Rome; rule of the world would pass to a savior from the East; thereafter (apparently) a breakdown of all power among many kings, and the annihilation of the world to the accompaniment of tremendous portents: the moon bloody, the sun checked in its course, mountains leveled, an all-wasting fire, and the Last Judgment at the end. From the welter of ideas, Jews picked out something to comfort them: the certain coming of a conqueror from their own land. For this, they rebelled. Rome's laws prohibited the reading of Hystaspes (see note 3). The prohibition may have been imposed as a result of the lessons of the first century. Those four figures, Theudas and the rest, who troubled Judea in the 40's and 50's, and Hystaspes in the 60's, arose naturally in the midst of a people whose religion so much emphasized their prophets. Roman governors would have had to be very blind indeed not to see the danger of the tradition.

At the time of the rebellion or within a few generations of it, a rabbi wrote, "This empire gnaws at our substance through four things: its tolls, its bath buildings, its theaters, and its taxes in kind."[20] That was part of the trouble made explicit—cultural smothering, economic exploitation. While the Greeks suffered alike, and said so in speeches, Jews inevitably turned to prophecy. They incorporated their charges in the *Sibyllines:* Rome imposed her laws on all (8.13), yet spread an insane avarice throughout the world that set children at odds with their parents (8.17f). Someday—so said a late first century book—Rome would give back her pillage to Asia (4.145f). "Effeminate, criminal, ill-starred among all, vile city, thou hast used adultery and foul intercourse with boys. Woe to thee! . . . who hast a blood-guilty heart and godless spirit. Knowest thou not what God can do?" (5.162f). His day approaches when there will be "no judge-rhetor nor archon giving decisions by bribes, nor sacrifices on altars," no drums, cymbals, flutes (8.110f), but "the race of the Hebrews will come forward . . . for Rome's empire will be destroyed then (8.141f) . . . when thrice three hundred and forty-eight years are fulfilled" (8.141, 144, 148f).

Prophecy, however, was used as an expressive weapon in other circumstances than those of rebellious Judea. A majority of the *Sibyllines* were composed in Alexandria by Jews exulting in the hope of Egypt's destruction by civil war, and in the hope of the neglect or expulsion of Isis, Serapis, and Apis. As the Jews for their purpose took over a pagan oracular genre and wrote in Greek, so also could the Egyptians, to strike back. Fragments of a third century papyrus describe a golden age to come, under soft skies and soft winds, when "the tyrant shall join with the Egyptians in their worships." There is mention of the coming of the Jews and of their annihilation of Alexandria, a recollection, apparently, of events of A.D. 115–116. Where the city once stood, only sand and hippopotami will be found. The true intention of the text emerges only obscurely—it is a prophecy, it remembers the evil done by the Jews, it champions Egyptian religion—but a longer *Oracle of the Potter* in the same period takes up the note of protest directed against Alexandria as an intrusive *Greek* stronghold. It is an "apocalyptic vision of the troubles of Egypt under foreign soldiers, of their expulsion by a 'King from the South,' of the subsequent restoration of an Egyptian golden age marked by the destruction of the 'city by the sea' and the return of the gods to their old abode of Memphis." Finally, we have a part of the Hermetic corpus in a later fourth century form foretelling, as some native Neoplatonist feared, the desertion of the old gods for new, that is, for Christianity. "Do you not see, Asclepius," Hermes is imagined to be saying, "that Egypt is the image of the heavens . . . and our land the temple of the whole world? Yet, since the wise should properly foresee everything, you should not be ignorant that a time will come when Egyptians will appear to have honored their gods in vain, though with dutiful hearts and careful piety . . . The gods quitting the earth will return to the heavens, leaving Egypt and the earth, the seat of piety that was . . . Worse yet, it will be decreed as by laws that piety, observances, and divine worship are prohibited under pain of punishment. Then this most holy land, the seat of sanctuaries and temples, will be filled with graves and the dead. O Egypt, Egypt! . . . to be left desolate of men and gods. And to you, holiest of rivers, I call, and foretell the future to you: filled with streams of blood, to your very banks, you will burst over them." The note is one of nostalgia and retreat; and it sounds in the prediction of another man of the same time, and country, and philosophy: that "when he died [ca. 390] there would be no temple, and the great holy temples of Serapis would depart into formless gloom, and be changed, and a fabulous and insubstantial darkness would hold sway over the fairest things of earth." Events confirmed him. Christianity conquered, as it was bound to. Constantine could prove its triumphant destiny from oracles. To the assembly of bishops in 325, and with extensive interjections and strident exegesis, he read aloud about a hundred verses of the *Sibyllines*. The history of prophetic literature in the Roman empire thus ends fittingly in the confrontation of pagan and Christian.[21]

Outer enemies have been seen surrounding Rome: a king from the South, in the *Oracle of the Potter;* Nero, or some other Antichrist figure or great destroyer, from the East. "The Assyrians will be masters of the Roman world"; a king will come at the head of a huge host, the sea white with his sails, Tyre and Sidon and Beirut in ashes at his feet. Danger loomed from a third direction: "A king of another race will arise in the West, master of a great force, godless, murdering, restless . . . hating the faithful, a persecutor. And he will be ruler of barbaric nations and shed much blood . . . In every city and in every place will be pillage and the raids of brigands and the shedding of blood." With such kings, or with those of Revelation, or of the *Sibyllines*, events would move on to the utter overthrow of the empire. The prediction shook men's minds and could be whispered about by Rome's inner enemies.[22]

The first were the Jews, after 66, made yet more bitter by Hadrian's destruction of the Temple. With them we move on from the specific figure of a conqueror and from his championing of specific national groups to a different topic: the general prediction of the overthrow of Rome. After Revelation under Domitian, equating Rome with Babylon, and Baruch and Ezra in the early second century, the angry vision was taken up in the eighth book of the *Sibyllines* (lines 141f), fixing the doom of Rome in A.D. 195. A few years later, Hippolytus, one of the chief Christian writers of the third century, reacted to an outbreak of persecution with a three-barrel blast at the world he lived in. He wrote treatises *De Antichristo* (ca. A.D. 200), *In Danielem* (ca. 202–204), and *On Revelation.* True, he foresaw no immediate Second Coming. The world had had six thousand years allotted to it, the last five hundred dating from the birth of Christ. Three centuries of safety stretched ahead. It would have been impious to await the end too impatiently or to try to reckon its advent in precise years, as his audience in Rome sought to do (*In Dan.* 4.21.4). Yet the end of the world was a thing desirable in itself and in God's time. How else could Christians feel, when they were struggling under persecutions (*De Antichristo* 49; 60)? Earlier terrestrial powers had been oppressive, but Rome was worst of all. It was the part of iron, in Daniel's statue; "It is the master now; it subdues and drains strength (λεπτύνει) from all, and reduces all men against their will. We see these things now ourselves." It is a serpent, perhaps the Beast of Revelation with the number 666, certainly intended as the fourth Beast of Daniel (*De Antichristo* 25). It unifies men only for war and pillage, achieving nothing but a hodgepodge nation of many tongues and races "called Romans" (*In Dan.* 4.8.7); and the figure at its center, demanding worship, is like a statue of the Antichrist himself (*De Antichristo* 49). In time, as Daniel envisioned, the empire will break up into ten warring nations, δημοκρατίαι, antecedent to Christ's coming.[23] Hippolytus will not be sorry.

Other men looked on the Roman empire differently. Not one of those after Hippolytus who offered their eschatological views, nor the much-quoted Irenaeus in the generation before him, shared his exultant expectations, even though these writers—Ephraim, Commodian, Lactantius, Cyril—drew equally on Daniel and Revelation and the rest of the traditional body of images. Take as an example the protest of Tertullian against accusations that Christians were disloyal. "There is another greater need why we should pray for the emperors and for the whole condition of the Roman empire and interests, for we know that by the respite that the Roman empire affords us, the great force hanging over the whole world, and the end of time itself with its menace of horrible sufferings, are kept from us." People could imagine what the sufferings might be (though each story differed from the next): flood, fire, pillage, wars foreign and civil, portents, darkness. "The heavens will no longer send dew, the earth no more bear fruits, the streams disappear, the rivers run dry, plants no longer grow"—and so on, a complete mirror image of the Golden Age. Most naturally, the very thought of an end to everything, accompanied by who could tell what horrors, brought pleasure only to the suicidal anger of the Jews and early Christians, terror to everyone else.[24]

And terror is a stimulating emotion. It draws wild fantasies and conjectures from the brain. Amidst extreme social and cultural tensions in first century Judea, all sorts of prophecies were heard. Rome in that time had its own troubles: two brief moments of excitement when seers managed to attract attention to themselves. Later, in Trajan's reign, and evidently in connection with his Parthian campaign, danger was foretold along the Syrian borderlands and "a war between the angels of unrighteousness in the North, through which all the kingdoms of unrighteousness shall be confounded." The source of the news was allegedly a certain Elchasai (the name is Aramaic, "Secret Power") from Parthia, who received it in a book from an angel 96 miles high and 16 miles wide. Though the story was doubtless a fabrication, it was listened to and spread about in Syria for some generations, ultimately reaching Rome. Its apostle, Alcibiades, was then able to arouse considerable excitement and to attract a considerable following, partly by his promise of a remission of sins. He vanishes from history obscurely. Marcus Aurelius' reign, at the time of the Marcomannic wars, provided a similar though less important episode: some silly rabble rouser delivering oracles from a tree in the Campus Martius warning of a universal conflagration and world's end. He was arrested but pardoned.[25]

With these incidents in Rome, having traversed two centuries of the Empire without encountering more than a handful of examples of specifically millennial hysteria, and arriving now at Alcibiades and Hippolytus, we have entered on a short era of sharper fears, for which the explanation must lie jointly in the acceleration of political history and in the changes in the spectrum of beliefs. Antonine tranquillity had declined through northern wars into a second Year of the Four Emperors; and much that was said in the chapter on magic should be applied here. A twilight of irrationality had begun to close in on the "enlightened" classes, while at a lower level slaves prophesied and God spoke through wandering beggars.[26] In Rome, eschatological speculation called forth Hippolytus' *In Danielem*, our oldest treatise on a book of the Bible; and the author illustrated the pastoral problems he was trying to meet by referring to two recent and extraordinary movements that he had heard of: one in Syria, where a bishop had led into the wilderness a good part of his flock, with their women and children, to meet Christ, and the whole lot of them had been very near to massacre as brigands at the hands of the governor's forces; the other in Pontus, where a bishop had likewise predicted Christ's coming within a year, according to his visions, and the faithful had thrown up their jobs, sold their belongings, and wandered about like lost sheep (*In Dan.* 4.18f). Toward Hippolytus' date, the year A.D. 194–95 had been picked for the appearance of the Antichrist, on the basis of Daniel's prophecies, by the *Sibyllines* (8.141f), and a certain Judas, a Christian chronographer, had chosen 202 (Euseb.,

Hist. eccl. 6.7). Montanist revelations were disturbing Rome, too, and a writer Gaius, in combating them, went to the lengths of declaring all eschatological ideas chimerical and Revelation itself a forgery. The birth of Montanism comes pat to the period, with the emergence of Montanus suddenly in Phrygia in 172 (the less likely date is 156); his oracles collected and published; and more added by his equally inspired disciples Prisca and Maximilla. He spoke half in a trance, in riddles; yet he was, he asserted, God's mouthpiece. God would send the heavenly Jerusalem to earth, to the tiny town of Pepuza nearby, whither all the faithful should repair—this was the message, and Pepuza was still a holy place in the fourth century. Maximilla for her part foretold horrible wars and revolutions, summoned all to repent their sins, and closed her life with the announcement that she was the last of the prophets. Quite wrong. The predictive habit had taken too strong a hold on her fellows, and in the course of time, as a frequent feature of holy services, seven virgins would enter among the worshipers "to prophesy to the people."[27]

No ruler could look kindly on these many visionaries who, from the later second century, increasingly spread unrest and perplexity in the towns, and whose staring followers might be found adrift on the countryside. Individuals could be seized or executed—that is attested. Books could be burnt or put on an Index to which no one paid much attention. "Hystaspes" was read by the authors of the *Sibyllines;* the latter were openly quoted by Lactantius and Constantine. Gallic Druids, once troublesome and long shorn of real power, went on prophesying, at least to individuals, more in the later Empire than in the earlier.[28] From the ruler's point of view, the difficulty lay in framing the right decrees, not too broad but broad enough; harder yet to put decisions into effect. The Romans, subordinating their love of order to their distrust of "big" government, had entered on the business of running an empire with habits of mind almost impossible to eradicate, and not at all suited to their responsibilities. They compromised with necessity. Their law, occasionally aroused by particular crimes or crises, declared in gathering detail what a person must not do. If he did it anyway, without causing disturbance, the law slept on. *Quieta non movere*. If he did it, and caused complaints registered in proper form with the proper authorities, the law awoke, laid about it with the weapons of arrest, fines, imprisonment, or execution, and, having made all peaceful, resumed its slumbers. This in general is the picture that meets us in Pliny's famous exchange of letters with Trajan, and earlier, too, in Tiberius' hostility to Judaism and Isiacism alike. The one had begun to infect the nobility, the other had excited a particular scandal. Christians suffered similarly as a cause of disturbance. Before Decius, the administrative formula seems to have been "no riots, no persecutions." It was not until events of the 170's and later had revealed the dangers of predictions and eschatological rumors that the state—unwillingly, no doubt—took cognizance of persons who threatened the stability of opinion. Legislation of the later second and earlier third centuries has been quoted above (p. 129f). Though not without precedent (in 186 and 139 B.C., to offer only those two Republican examples), it represents the entry of law into somewhat wider spheres. A statesman of the time —Dio, who had first commended himself to Septimius Severus by a treatise on dreams and portents, and who went on to become consul—suggested as part of a program for the empire that traditional worships be cherished and their rites enforced on every citizen, while "those who introduce some foreignness into religion you should abhor and restrain . . . because from this arise conspiracies, factions, and cabals . . . Do not therefore permit anyone to be an atheist or γόης." And he goes on to warn against the misuse of "prophetic arts" by private individuals. His point of view fits very well with the spirit of alarmed censorship apparent in earlier quotations from his contemporaries, Paul and Ulpian.[29] It fits equally well into the context of seers and prophets listed above: bishops of Syria and Pontus, Montanus, and the rest.

As the third century stumbled through its destined wars, its economic vicissitudes and dizzying dynastic changes, a merely repressive attitude toward millennial visions appeared more clearly inadequate. It was necessary to go a step further. Propaganda was accordingly unfolded more widely to reveal abundant promises in the very near future. The year 248, being the thousandth of Rome's history, was celebrated with games of extraordinary richness and advertised by a variety of coin types throughout the empire not only by the emperor on the throne, Philip, but by his successors Decius, Hostilianus, Trebonianus Gallus, and Volusianus, all of whom stressed the notions of victory, concord, and, above all, of renewal. Hence the phoenix shown sitting on the Temple of Eternal Rome, the temple itself owing its consecration to this glorious *birth*day. Rome was indeed eternal. Another thousand years had been guaranteed, a *saeculum novum*. The motif and meaning of the phoenix can be found again in 348, on the birthday of the birthday, so to speak, sitting on a globe (the *orbis* of world rule) held by the emperor, and proclaiming the "Renewal of Happy Times." Once more *Reparatio temporum* appears, on Gratian's coins, along with the phoenix on the globe indicating the empire's recovery from the Gothic catastrophe of 378. As for *Roma aeterna* and *Renovatio Romanorum*, in 290, with the wolf and twins, these hark back to Rome's birth and to the worship of the city, linked to the *Perpetuitas* of the ruler. Various other notes of renewal are sounded more in the late third century than ever before, with repetitions in the century to follow, and the myth of the Golden Age is held out for the first time in a century by Gallienus and his dynasty, and thereafter in fourth century court poets. Scattered signs in that period, Gallienus to Gratian, point to a widespread longing for some sudden amelioration of affairs, by however extravagant means: projects to be undertaken by the emperors for the reform of the entire government, for a philosophic utopia to be established in Campania, or simply for an end to all wars and taxes. Imperial propaganda, though its promises were vague, hyperbolic, and of course never made good, nevertheless spoke to a most desperately receptive audience.[30]

For different reasons, over the second, third, and fourth centuries, Christians like the emperors tried to meet and counter eschatological conjectures. Their attempts rested (notably in Melito) on the historical parallelism between the Church and the empire, Christ and Augustus, whose fortunes were thought to be divinely conjoined. To wish for, even to speculate on, the end of the one was to attack the other. The idea of parallel histories lasted long among those Christians—the great majority, at all times—who trembled less under their Roman persecutors than under the fear of the Antichrist, of universal fire, and the Last Judgment. They were taught by their intellectual leaders to look on the empire as something fixed and good, to take its stability for granted, and thus to relax from their visions. Moreover, a weakness in their method was pointed out to them. Predictions relied on such parts of scripture as Daniel and Revelation; but a spiritualized and allegorical interpretation developed by Origen and theologians after him removed the prophetic quality from these Old and New Testament passages. A kind of chiliastic number juggling did continue to be popular. Eusebius attacked this, too, with indignation. It was presumptuous to probe God's will, nor could the human intellect in any event avail to solve such questions. There was hardly a need for Eusebius to be so emphatic. In the century before he wrote, there had been a pause in millennial speculation, no one knows why, though Melito, Origen, and others of their views must have had some repressive effect. Jewish and Christian *Sibyllines* (Books 12 and 13) stuck tamely to *vaticinia post eventum*, no new Montanus arose in the eastern provinces. On only one occasion had the Church been required to exercise a restraining influence. Bishop Nepos in the Fayûm had used Revelation to refute the allegorists like Origen and to foretell "a certain span of a thousand years of delights of the body," ending with the Second Coming. The work was "most persuasive," so much so that "schisms and apostasies had occurred in entire churches." The allegorist bishop of Alexandria, Dionysius "the Great," saw his duty. Some time in the second quarter of the third century, he went into the area, summoned the elders and teachers of all the villages to a debate, and in three days argued them back into the orthodox fold.[31] It was not long afterward, however, that Manichaeism began to spread into Egypt. A new prophet stood forth to trouble the empire. His emergence brings us back to Eusebius' day and to Diocletian's threats of vengeance by fire against Manichaean books and worshipers (see p. 130).

The potency of prediction in the Roman empire has now been passed under review from Nero's reign to that of Diocletian, with chronological detours into the earlier first century, or backward or forward at various points; but it has been generally clear that *pagan* eschatology aroused relatively little interest until perhaps the 170's, and thereafter intermittently in degrees controlled by such factors as the stability of the throne, the pressure of national misfortunes, and the prevalence of irrational credulity. Another factor steadily increased its influence. Among first the Jews and then the Christians, an ancient tradition of apocalytic writings made natural the use of predictions as a weapon of the oppressed and a relief for hatred, felt most by the Jews before the mid-second century and by the Christians from the later second century onward in times of persecution. This tradition, through the spread of Christianity, widened its hold on the population of the empire. It should come as no surprise, then, to find more millennial conjecture and hysteria in the fourth century—a century both Christian and politically troubled—than in any previous age. Numerology played a good part. The Basilidian heresy invented a god the letters of whose name totaled the mystic 365, and on the model of the week of Creation, as we have seen, a world life of six or seven thousand years was built, and commonly credited. That would put the world's end (according to reckonings that we may pass over) in A.D. 500, or 1000, or 1029, or some other year. The wide currency given to millennial notions is both illustrated and resisted by fourth century pagan and Christian writers. One specific prediction dates to the mid-fourth century, referring with oracular vagueness to the death of one emperor under whom all was tyranny, oppression of the poor, and protection of the guilty, and the accession of another of heroic mien and pure heart who will reign for 112 or 120 years in an age of plenty. He will defeat Gog and Magog, and thereafter hand over his crown to God. Another prediction was known to Augustine's see, though it probably originated in Italy. In traditional Greek verse it foretold the collapse of the Church after a span of 365 years obtained by St. Peter's sacrifice of a child of one year, that is, 365 days old, each day by magical means extorting from God one year of life. Like other oracles, this must have been composed very shortly before the date to which it pointed, but whether that was in the 360's or 390's depends on whether the *terminus a quo* was Christ's birth or ascension. At any rate, the inspiration was obviously pagan. In the long struggle against Christianity, this was not the first or the last appeal to the supernatural for aid.[32]

A readiness to believe in the possibility of universal catastrophe underlay the imaginings of Augustine's generation. Their roots reached far back in time, drawing on ideas developed in Rome independent of eastern chiliasm. In Augustus' reign, Romans could think their civilization already declining. Vergil and Horace resisted despair, confidence slowly returned. To the very end of the empire, poets and panegyrists still promised it eternal life. But doubts crept back in the third century, in the form of a cycle theory that first century writers had discerned: a Roman childhood under the ancient kings; youth during the conquest of Italy; maturity during the expansion overseas; and a long, long old age verging to the grave. "The world now is shaken and driven, because your gods are not worshiped by us"—so a pagan said to Cyprian (*Ad Demetrianum* 3f). "But," he answered, "the world grows old, it rests not on the same strength as of yore nor has it the same robustness with which it once prevailed." All things grow old by a universal law proved in our own era of wars and dwindling resources. And in the same way others in Cyprian's day and in the century that followed felt themselves dwelling in a time of senility, *iamque vergens in senium*.[33] It was a feeling strong in 378 and needed (along with Judaeo-Christian apocalyptic) to account for a most remarkable event of 398 at Constantinople. Following on alarming floods and earthquakes, God revealed to an army official in the city that it would be destroyed, and that he should carry the report to his bishop. The latter preached to his flock, who wept and repented. At sunset, a red cloud spread over Constantinople, a great flame issued, and the smell of sulphur. Everyone rushed to the churches demanding baptism; there were terrified conversions in the streets and squares. On the ensuing Sunday, again it was revealed that the city would be destroyed. A mass exodus took place, with the emperor among the crowd, to a point a few miles away. A pall of smoke could indeed be seen hanging over the city, but as nothing else appeared, they returned to their homes.[34] Utter panic sweeping magistrates, bishops, the emperor himself clear out of the city, had something medieval about it; or at least we sense that the history of prediction, ending in this episode, has carried us a long way from the sane, steady world of Vespasian or Antoninus Pius. They had heard apocalyptic rumors, but they and their like responded only with irritation or ridicule.

✧ V ✧

Urban Unrest

DISLOYAL writings, abusive speeches, unsettling predictions, maleficent magic, contumacious heterodoxy—though the crimes described so far were forbidden by the law, yet they lay outside its usual realm. Their instruments were invisible: ideas, fears, beliefs, beyond the competence of the village constable to repress or even understand. They were not, like ordinary crimes, violent: they threatened neither life nor property; the weight of charges often teetered on some point of definition—what *is* a magican or a philosopher, what were the defendant's motives, reputation, associates?—or on factors perfectly irrelevant—the healthiness of public opinion or the stability of the throne. The Un-Roman Activities Committee that we imagined in our Preface would have turned with a sigh of relief from all these matters to the subject of the present chapter: acts visible or tangible, riots, shouts, blows and bloodshed.

These were checked or punished by authorities probably as effective in the second century as in any European country prior to 1830, when measures developed in London began to spread more generally; yet a detective force was at that time still in its infancy everywhere, and riots, for another generation or two, had to be put down by the army. We forget how recent are our own better defenses against crime. The Roman solution was extremely mixed and hard to describe. In the capital, praetorian guards, *vigiles* or night watchmen, and the urban cohorts made up a number very large compared to the size of the population and more than adequate until the third century. Thereafter, for another hundred years, though there were ungovernable outbreaks, they were few and uncharacteristic. In the fourth century, all three troops of guards were dissolved, step by step.[1] With them went the power to restrain mob disorder. Crowds, with a kind of wild logic, more than once laid siege to the residence of the chief of police (the urban prefect) and obliged him to spy out the return of peace from the safety of his suburban villa. "Do you not remember, Emperor, how many houses of the prefects of Rome have been burnt, and no one avenged them?" asks Ambrose (*Ep.* 40.13).

Individual as opposed to mass crime, however, presented no insuperable problem. For its control, in all periods, *agents provocateurs*, plainclothes men, and secret police circulated in Rome, as the latter agents did also in Italy and the provinces.[2] Detachments of praetorian guards (before 312) were scattered in stations throughout the city, and the *vigiles* went about at night—though a man in the streets alone after dark took his chances. Juvenal (3.278f) mentions the dangers. On the whole, we hear little of people attacked or of houses broken into in the accounts of the time. This is the more surprising because the swollen garrisons in Rome were rather meant to prevent any challenge with political overtones, such as had shaken the Republic, and were adapted only partly and gradually to the punishment (very rarely the detection or prevention) of ordinary crime. Therein lay the reason for disbanding them when the emperor chose a new capital. His subjects there, and in the old capital, he expected to defend themselves against theft or violence, or to bring before his courts the names of those who had done wrong. In this way, through complaints and informers, Seneca, Apuleius, and Theodorus, in our earlier chapters, came to trial.

In western provincial cities, evidence for police arrangements hardly exists. Inscriptions give us the names of army units assigned to urban garrisons, and stories of the persecutions mention Christians arrested by soldiers, with whom municipal magistrates cooperated. Troops in Carthage in the days of Tertullian (*De fuga* 13) kept lists of notorious undesirables: sneak thieves, barkeeps (*tabernarii*), and the like. Tertullian protested the inclusion of Christians. Other troops suppressed a riot in Carthage in 347.[3] Beyond these few facts, nothing tells us how citizens of Trèves, London, or Vienna protected their lives and property.

In the East, the picture is far better lit, though confused by changes and variations. Large-scale disturbances called for the army—witness the course of well-known events at Alexandria under Claudius, Trajan, and Caracalla, or at Thessalonica under Theodosius; or again (though less famous) at Antioch in 387; and soldiers singly or in small companies became increasingly common after the first century, doing duty as constables, sometimes acting with local municipal agents or proconsular aides. Among purely municipal police officials, bearing many different expressive titles—Warders, Pursuers, Night Commanders, Street Chiefs—the most usual were the so-called irenarchs, who are discovered acting like their military colleagues against the early Church, and sometimes at the head of small bodies of assistants: young men of the better classes in course of military training, mustered for emergencies; public slaves diverted from their ordinary business with drains and sewers; the Carpenters' Benevolent Association brandishing hatchets; or councilmen chosen as bulwarks to peace and property only because they were rich enough, or old enough, or in some cases even young enough, to have no other pressing occupation. If these arrangements seem makeshift and amateur, it is clear that the regular government forces also could be criticized. Soldiers for police duty were assigned in better times with extreme parsimony; in worse times, they so bullied and stole that the emperor might be urgently petitioned for their recall to the colors, or irenarchs be mobilized to make them behave.[4]

As to the civil authorities, most of our evidence bears on a single province. Egypt suffered under a bureaucracy especially clumsy, and the frustrations awaiting the unwary entrant into the labyrinth of official appeals and appearances, affidavits and triplicates, should not be taken as typical of the whole empire; yet lengthy litigation from other provinces appears in entire files of correspondence copied out on stone. It is worth noting as a testimonial to Roman justice that its pursuit through the proper channels went on despite the difficulties evident in those same inscriptions, went on even into the period of widespread administrative breakdown. Inadequacies clear to us, in the enforcing of law and order, were not so clear to the Romans, and the authorities set over them were still looked on as effective friends, through sheer habit of loyalty, when in fact they had turned into enemies.[5]

Any discussion of urban police must emphasize the shape of the ancient city, which tended to concentrate crime in certain areas: street corners, theaters, squares, market places, and forums. While the density of population might approximate what we are used to nowadays, the ratio between public and private space was strikingly different. Crowded parts were very crowded, open parts and public buildings very generous. The climate of most of the Mediterranean basin invited people to live out of doors. Their homes held out no conflicting attraction: cramped, dark; for furniture, straw beds and a chest containing clothes and valuables; on the floor a brazier to cook the soup, sending savor and smoke up to the ceiling, from which, in a hammock contraption, were suspended a baby or two. Turning from such depressing quarters, men satisfied their sociability at cookshops and taverns, gathered at street-corner fountains, or, where the blank walls of houses fell back to form a market place, idled their way through the day's buying and selling. Wealthy people provided all open points of the city with ambitious amenities, very pleasant to enjoy during most seasons of the year; but it was just at these points that brawls and riots might start. The days of serious slave or gladiator insurrections were over, and a source of tumult new to the fourth century, the students of rival schools of rhetoric, disturbed only Athens. Taverns and cookshops, however, like those along the streets of Pompeii—118 of them can still be counted—lay under a more enduring suspicion as dens of criminals and prostitutes, centers of extravagance and loose living. From the 30's to the 70's A.D., the governing classes, heavy eaters themselves and sometimes, like Nero, addicts of dives and bars, tried to improve the character of the lower classes by intermittent legislation to shut up taverns and to prohibit the sale of cooked meats and pasties. That left vegetables, their definition at one time being narrowed to peas and beans. After Vespasian, public morals were given up as a bad job for three centuries. In the 370's, urban prefects renewed the war. They limited wineshops in what they could sell and in the hours they could stay open. Tavernkeepers who had trafficked in citizens' tickets to free bread and to the amphitheater were listed publicly and somehow punished. They had been organized in a guild since Vespasian's time, and in 403–407 numbered at least 120.[6]

A reason for these various attempts at regulation is suggested by common sense, though it is not mentioned by our sources. Troubles begin when men congregate, especially drunken men. So in Pompeii political arguments were continued on tavern walls by those who were determined to have the last word, for example, the inscription "The dyers support X" (*CIL* 4.7812). The local association of tavern-keepers themselves electioneered for their candidate (*CIL* 4.336, 1838). One declaration on a tavern wall serves as transition to a different subject: "We urge you to make X aedile. (Signed) Porphyrius, with the Paridiani." The Paridiani were the local fan club of a *pantomimus* and dancer, one Paris, wildly admired by all circles in Rome, even by the empress. Accused of adultery with her, he was executed in 83. He must have put on a show in Pompeii shortly before the town was buried.[7] The ardor of his supporters introduces us to the theater, a center of unrest more serious than taverns in this Campanian town as elsewhere throughout the empire.

A traveler to Arles or El-Djem, or one who stands before the Colosseum in Rome, knows for the first time the importance of theaters in a Roman city. The truly spectacular bulk, capacity, and disregard of expense obvious even in their ruins give proof of that disproportion, mentioned earlier, between public and private amenities; proof, moreover, of just what amenities were prized beyond bath buildings, forums, or temples. Drama and triumph in the life of the masses reached them most directly in the theater. Here they experienced excitement, here they felt their power a little, and a kind of patriotism. A grand showplace made everyone bigger, more important, consequently boastful, consequently offensive to his neighbors. That, precisely, was a part of the reward of putting so much money into so uneconomic a structure: it aroused envy. People in Placentia suspected enemies in nearby cities of using an opportunity of war to burn down the Placentian amphitheater, "because there was not in Italy another building so capacious" (Tac., *Hist.* 2.21); and at a time when, in common sense, ancient angers should have been long suspended, under Hadrian the Athenians were still to be found debating the staging of a gladiatorial show "out of rivalry against Corinth." In Pompeii, amphitheatric competition produced a sudden tragedy known to us from a passage in Tacitus (*Ann.* 14.17) and from a well-known painting. It survives on the wall of a house that was decorated in other rooms with arena scenes—the owner may have been a gladiator retired to rich respectability—and it shows an aereal view of contests going on in the amphitheater, while in the seats and in the streets outside, other battles rage among spectators and citizens. The occasion was the gladiatorial exhibition put on by a controversial and ambitious magnate of the city recently expelled from the Roman senate. In the audience were men from the next town, Nuceria, earlier fallen from its primacy, taking the other side from Pompeii in the Social War, and rewarded by the winners with an increase of territory at Pompeii's expense. Nucerians had their own amphitheater, which Pompeians probably visited for the shows, like the Nucerians who came to Pompeii—not as friends. All the Campanian cities were embroiled in quarrels with each other, reflected in Pompeii by scribblings on walls: "Bad cess to Nucerians"; "Good luck to all Nucerians and the hook for Pompeians and Pithecusans." This was the background to the year 59. In the amphitheater, people who began with taunts now took to arms, and in the general massacre that followed the Nucerians had the worst of it. An inquiry by the senate resulted in exile for the magistrate who gave the games, the disbanding of illegal associations (see below, pages 176f), and a decade's prohibition of further shows in Pompeii. That last was the worst part of the penalty, invoked on other occasions when the emperor wanted to punish a whole city with special severity.[8]

Amphitheater crowds might take fire not only with city rivalries, but with their enthusiasms for some star or team of gladiatorial combat, chariot racing, or dramatic dances and plays. Ephesus in Severan times had a club organized like Pompeii's Paridiani: the "Vedius Fans of Gladiation." Vedius was owner of a local troupe, and the cognoscenti of the sport who borrowed his name erected statues in the market place to honor the givers of two gladiatorial exhibitions. Followers of horse racing were clearly grouped as early as Caligula's reign, and in Antioch as in Rome. Ordinarily, four teams competed, but partisans ranged themselves only behind the two principal ones, the Greens and Blues. To the first belonged (we happen to know) Caligula, Nero, Domitian, Martial, Lucius Verus, Commodus, Elagabalus; to the Blues, Trimalchio, Vitellius, Caracalla. In the Byzantine empire, perhaps people chose their colors to reflect political views, but in Roman times they cheered, uncomplicatedly, for the horses they had bet on. The final category of entertainment, drama and dancing, had its admirers, too, beginning with Augustus, who made a point of attending and openly enjoying the shows. So did Tiberius, in his younger days, and Drusus, and Nero most of all.[9]

Lesser folk made their weight felt in the theater by disciplining their cheers to a unison, sitting in compact armies of support under acknowledged leaders, or coming ready-organized as guilds.[10] There was a danger in this. Men by the five thousand in Pompeii, by the fifty thousand in Rome, tossed on waves of enthusiasm, on waves of rhythmic shouts, on storms of applause and excitement, did together what they would never have thought of doing each one by himself: howled, cursed, jeered, and fought in unpredictable outbreaks of passion. Emperors repeatedly tried to keep the crowds in order. At the start of his reign, Tiberius issued an edict to curb the actors, but by A.D. 15 it had already proven ineffective. A bloody riot swept the theater, "not only some of the plebs being killed, but soldiers and a centurion, and a tribune of a praetorian cohort being wounded." In A.D. 23, dancers had to be banished "because they kept debauching women and fomenting factions." Troops like those that suffered casualties in A.D. 15 continued to be stationed in the theaters, both before and after Nero's reign, but that emperor, either as a test of the situation or because he so keenly enjoyed watching brawls in the audience, suspended the guard. His experiment did not work. Partisans of charioteers and players grew more tumultuous and lawless, the population more angrily divided, and "in terror of worse commotions," the old order was restored, and actors and their claques then and shortly later exiled from Italy, or imprisoned. They evidently returned, for someone whom Pliny in his *Panegyric* (§46) is too delicate to name (Domitian, it must be) suppressed the pantomime dancers, who were successfully demanded back from Nerva, and whom Trajan had again to suppress. Once more, Commodus exiled them; yet again, riots about charioteers are mentioned, in 356. Though Rome alone is the focus of almost all this evidence, the misbehavior of theater audiences in provincial cities is occasionally referred to, along with the need to take some dancer into custody "owing to the factions formed among the people."[11]

But what is important in the present subject is the connection that existed between the people as an audience and the people as an assembly in the constitutional sense—a connection made express in the use of theaters for mass meetings. Romans no longer had a voice of any significance in affairs of state, and cities Italian or provincial were run by rich oligarchies. The withering of democratic institutions could by no means cure people of the habit of holding opinions essential to the government to discover and, if possible, to conciliate. Emperors, their legates and procurators, and municipal magistrates still had to reach their fellow citizens, and for the purpose no place came so pat as the theater. Here announcements and religious sacrifices were made, political displays and anniversaries staged; to theater crowds the ruler could appear as a benefactor footing the cost of extravagant spectacles, granting popular requests, wooing the mob, and if absent himself from the reading of his own proclamations, receiving a copy of the applause recorded in the *acta populi* and forwarded to him by the urban prefect. The audience for their part responded in their behavior "as if holding an assembly," hiring themselves out to cheer for this or that demand or candidacy, feeling rightly that "in the circus and theaters there was the greatest license for the masses" (Tac., *Hist.* 1.72). They might riot. Under that crude threat, officials had to reason with them and sometimes give way to their insistence. Emperors, consuls, prefects, great noblemen and women, religious sects and leaders, popes and pretenders, the level of taxation or of the grain supply, all were attacked or applauded by the most ungovernable elements of the population in an atmosphere created by the obscenity of pantomine and the brutality of gladiation.[12]

The political effectiveness of disorders is more easily assumed than proved. They sufficed to send a praetorian prefect, Cleander, to his death, and to recall an urban prefect, Symmachus, from hiding. Shouts could clearly shake the throne itself—let anyone read of the last weeks of Nero, Julianus, or Maxentius. Away from Rome, imperial representatives feared anything that might reflect discredit on their term of office, yielded up a Barabbas to preserve peace and their careers, courted applause the record of which could be made known to their superiors in grandiloquent resolutions by provincial meetings, and without any doubt arranged, even purchased, demonstrations in their own favor. To control the devious and degenerate democracy still to be found in the empire required organizations ready at hand, nobody being able to guarantee the loyalty of each separate individual who might have a voice. Hence the importance of making contact with theatrical claques through whose practiced and infectious noisiness one got the most for one's money. The connection between claques and their presumed employers, or between their actions and their presumed motives, cannot be directly established, however, and beyond repeating that they existed, that their catch phrases, rhythm, and unison were applied to political cheers, and that popular demonstrations seem to have been taken more seriously by the government authorities in the later Empire than in the earlier period, there is little that can be said with confidence.[13]

One kind of organization which would, on the other hand, repay closer study is the *collegium*, known by a dozen synonyms in Greek and Latin, referred to several times already by the usual translation, "guild," but corresponding best with our word "society." In Pompeii, societies were implicated in the massacre of Nucerians in 59—Tacitus calls them *collegia* without further identification—and dyers and tavernkeepers along with a dozen other groups of the same kind campaigned on behalf of candidates to municipal office. Other societies in Alexandria originated and circulated the Acts of the Pagan Martyrs. The whole subject, then, has been touched on at the edges, so to speak, but now is the time to return to it in a more systematic fashion.

From the first naming of the Kerameikos in Athens down to our own days of Harley and Wall Street, men of some single profession have tended to set up shop next to each other. A location convenient to one has turned out to be convenient to all; and thus we have, in Roman times, Cobblers' Square in Apamea, and the Corn Quarter and Shepherds' Quarter in other cities. Men called themselves "The Workmen of" this or that address because they lived or worked more or less together, and sharpened the focus of their fellowship by renting or building some meeting place, perhaps a splendid hall like that presented to the Pompeian fullers or like that of the theater artists of Athens, big enough for a visiting sophist to use when he wanted to display his powers of eloquence. The city might provide a site. At Caere, a man "petitioned that a place be given him at public expense, under the portico of the Sulpician basilica, that he might erect a union-house for the Augustales in this place; where, by vote of the councilmen, the place that he desired was given." In this case, it was the worshipers of the imperial house that won their wish; but the urge to congregate and incorporate themselves inspired philosophers and palace cooks, and every conceivable trade, ethnic minority, religious sect, or social class in every city. Their objects were simple, summed up in the phrase "social security": to have a refuge from loneliness in a very big world, to meet once a month for dinner, to draw pride and strength from numbers, and at the end of life (if one's dues were paid up) to be remembered in a really respectable funeral. These were needs so commonly felt that societies at their height in the second century must have included something like a third of the urban male population. Consider the fourteen societies known from inscriptions of one single town, Vienne, the seventeen of Lyons, and the average size of memberships, apparently between one and two hundred.[14]

No one would have paid any attention to an individual cobbler or stonecutter. Fifty, a hundred, a thousand of them were another matter. The emperor himself listened to their requests; men of standing felt it an honor to list, in careers that reached to the Roman senate or higher still, the post of patron to the Tiber Bargees or Milanese Rag and Cloth Dealers. Such societies won for themselves an almost official status. They sent a deputation to meet the emperor on his travels and recorded his gracious reply to their welcome; their banners marched in his triumphal parades or at his funeral. They contributed to the pomp of shows and spectacles, and were accorded seats *en bloc* at the theater, where, to be sure, they sometimes caused or joined outbreaks of disorder. Largesses that were offered to the population of a city might specify the recipients: Councilmen, Hymners, Holy Square Association, Heracles Worshipers; or, Councilmen, Augustales, Wood Carriers; or, Councilmen, Knights, Augustales, Wine Merchants, "and all authorized societies"; beneath these, the undifferentiated plebs. At Philadelphia, the Wool- and Leatherworkers formed the basis for the official political division of the population; it consisted elsewhere of Councilmen, Elders, Assemblymen, *Vindictarii*, Freedmen. Societies were obviously a prominent and respected element in the urban scene.[15]

Yet such were the lurid memories of the Roman Republic in the days of Clodius and Milo, and such the reputation of political societies throughout Greek history from Alcibiades on, that people's attempts to organize themselves everywhere aroused an instant suspicion and were from the first moment of imperial power methodically controlled and discouraged. Suspicion would have died had it not fed on realities. Since it did not die, since legislation against societies did not cease, since Trajan warned of what might happen if their formation were allowed indiscriminately and Ulpian and other jurists linked them to sedition, it is clear that they must have constituted a perennial source of unrest. No doubt their meetings grew a little rowdy at times. The by-laws of a funerary association enjoined polite behavior, "that we may dine together on the appointed days quietly and cheerfully." Economic interests produced quarrels with the government or with some other society, requiring adjudication. Tradesmen and artisans could see when their livelihood was threatened and made this the excuse for hostility to Christians. Occasionally they went out on strike. The rarity of this recourse shows how wide a gulf separates ancient "trade associations" or "unions" from their modern equivalents. In Egypt, workers were reduced to parading the streets to protest their low wages, or to the pleading of pitiful circumstances that might oblige them to flee from home and property. Dissatisfied builders at Miletus asked an oracle if they should go back to work, and bakers, bankers, or shippers who suspended their services had to be disciplined by high authorities: procurators, prefects, proconsuls.[16] If anything can be said on the basis of the evidence—a dozen strikes scattered over four centuries—it is only this: that their potential as a weapon of aggression was never realized, in drawn-out campaigns, and that their defensive use, such as it was, appeared more clearly in the period when, by the government's own policy, the internal organization of societies had been more firmly articulated.

Perhaps, after all, there is some value in this latter conclusion. It fits exactly with the evidence of theater claques, from whom more was to be feared in the fourth century than earlier; and like them, trade and artisans' societies began to feel their political as well as their economic power late in their history, in a number of eastern cities. This power, as has been said, was attacked by Augustus and others after him in a succession of edicts, yet in the second century an emperor not given to imaginary anxieties was still warning his subordinates, "It is to be remembered that this sort of society (*factio*) has greatly disturbed the peace of [Bithynia] in general, and of those cities [Nicomedia and Nicaea] in particular. Whatever title we give them and whatever our object in giving it, men who are banded together for a common end will all the same become a political association (*hetairia*) before long." Trajan's opinion was understood by Tertullian: "For if I am not mistaken, the reason for prohibiting societies is to provide for public order, lest the state be split into factions, a thing that may easily disturb elections, meetings, senate, assemblies, and games by the collision of hostile partisans." Tarsus offers an illustration through "a group of no small size outside of the constitution, so to speak, whom some people generally call 'linenworkers,' and are irritated by them and consider them a useless rabble and the cause of uproar and disorder." Though reviled and viewed as outsiders, in fact they were mostly natives of the town, admitted to the popular assembly, and "in some sense citizens." In the next century, in Rome, occurred the rebellion of the mintworkers under a certain Felicissimus, crushed by Aurelian with the loss of seven thousand slain, and fear of "the mintworkers and public leatherworkers" in Cyzicus led Julian to forbid the Christians in his retinue from entering the town lest they join these societies in some sedition. Under the emperor Valens, to defend St. Basil against the harryings of the praetorian prefect, the whole city of Caesarea rose in wrath, "especially the armsworkers and imperial weavers . . . who draw boldness from their free way of speech," and surged into the streets brandishing the tools of their trade. Armsworkers were evidently prominent in demonstrations against the Arian council held in Hadrianople, and bakers and unspecified artisans in Antioch were blamed for many disturbances in Libanius' time. Church leaders popular in Alexandria could stir up the Constantinopolitan mob through the sailors of the grain fleet plying between the two cities. This happened three times that we know of within a half century.[17] Reviewing the whole collection of stories in which societies figured as villains, we can see why earlier emperors feared the promiscuous multiplication of *factiones* (or "whatever title we give them," in Trajan's words), while later emperors simply invited difficulties by their new policy. They had decided to supply the most essential needs of the state—the feeding of the capital, manufacture of military arms and uniforms, minting of coins to pay the troops—by means of existing associations, whose membership and obligations were gradually brought under imperial control. Precisely these groups of workers came handiest to the ambition of a demagogue, presumably because they were the best regimented and most responsible to their own leaders; while, in descending order of notoriety, weavers or builders or the poor peasants likewise compacted by law into hereditary professions to serve the public interest used their sense of solidarity to go out on strike.

In the fourth century, societies thus took a part in the public life of every large center—Rome, Constantinople, Alexandria, Antioch, Cyzicus, Hadrianople, Caesarea—and no doubt in every little town as well. To their strength exercised in support of their friends or patrons, add the strength of the Greens and Blues; add that of ecclesiastical parties, rallying around a bishop or a candidate for a see. Fourth century episcopal elections assigned to the lower classes a most significant role, and encouraged vigorous partisanship.[18] The sum of all this may very well be called "democratization," at a time when one would least expect to find the word justified, that is, under the Dominate of the late Empire. But it is in the nature of aloof and authoritarian governments to communicate with their subjects from some royal box or palace balcony, framed by embroidered hangings and flags, with bands and similar overwhelming humbug, and to respond not only to mass acclaim but to mass abuse. An authority resting on demonstrations must in logic succumb to them, too, whether it be the authority of the emperor, or of a prefect, bishop, pretender, or great general—all respected by their equals because so clamorously applauded by their inferiors, and in danger of being dismissed if their popularity diminished. Their way of looking at their own political power thus permitted the mass of the people to exercise considerable influence over them; and while the instruments of this influence were in themselves innocent—combinations of men, or the old client-patron relation, or the relation that developed more fully in the later Empire, binding the local magnate to an entire town, village, or society—the methods employed were increasingly violent and lawless. In the history of disorder, in fact, can be read more and more clearly the history of the *demos* itself, throughout the empire. The subject we are studying begins to assume a certain respectability.

In all periods, the weapons of the mob were the same: to shout, to insult, to burn down houses, to beat up and kill. Rulers suffered only in effigy. Their statues were attacked. Beyond doubt, however, these weapons came to be applied more freely in the third and fourth centuries than earlier. The incitement in Antioch in 387 was a new tax. More often religious passions were involved, among the Oxyrhynchites against the Cynopolites, for eating each other's sacred animals, "as a result of which they went to war and inflicted much harm on each other," or among the Alexandrians against themselves "on account of Apis, who, when he was discovered after many years, produced a tumult among the people over the question, where was he to be kept, everybody competing zealously." Pagans fought fiercely for their gods and temples, in a Christian empire, later; and internal clashes of the Church echoed through the fourth century, filling the streets with bedlam and bloodshed. The Arian controversy alone provided a score of lying accusations, inflammatory sermons, banishments, beatings, riots, and murders.[19]

Commonest cause of all, throughout the history of riots, was hunger, attested in almost every province and period (see Appendix A). So far as inadequacies of heavy transport and market supervision were to blame, small cities and rural areas were always vulnerable to famine, but supplies for large cities were evidently fairly well assured by Flavian times and did not give anxiety again until the fourth century. Scarcities, when they came, badly strained the social fabric. Though relief might be offered "to the whole people," πάνδημος, as inscriptions say, it was more common to specify degrees of generosity according to status, thereby arousing desperate resentment among slaves, freedmen, resident aliens, or the general plebs excluded. Whatever might be done, the poor always suffered worse than the rich, and expressed their sense of wrong by mob attacks on emperor, officials, or local grandees such as Dio Chrysostom or Symmachus. These were the men responsible, or else they had their own farms, their own private stores; they dealt in grain themselves, or could afford to buy what they needed, perhaps sell it again at a profit, since shortages raised prices. Extraordinary pressure was needed before they would release their surplus to the market, and when they yielded, the ample amounts they could indeed disgorge excited bitter comment. Hostility, however, though automatically directed at the rich in times of stress, thereafter relaxed. If famine proved the existence of class tensions, abundance proved how fleeting were their aims.[20] As a guest of Trimalchio summed it up (*Cena* 44), with no thought of revolution, the "big mouths" eat well, "the little people have a hard time of it."

Urban Unrest

Fourth century scarcities in the East (the western provinces being hidden from us) are reported quite fully. Libanius often speaks with sympathy of the suffering poor, urban or rural. He does not instinctively defend his fellows in the Council. Julian (*Misopogon* 368C) has something to say of "the insatiable greed of the rich." Reasoned and explicit criticism of their conduct, however, leading into general comments on social justice, is first heard in the empire from Christian writers: Clement of Alexandria, Basil, the two Gregories, Asterius, Ambrose, and Chrysostom. By their doctrine, the world belongs to all men, and inequalities of possessions, though according to divine dispensation, do not constitute unconditional ownership. Private property there is, but only if others' lives do not depend on the sharing of it. The really rich man is like someone who goes into a theater himself and then locks out everyone else; excessive wealth comes from sin—theft, deception, cruelty—and is of less value than moderate means: for the rich need the poor to build their houses, wait on them, and so forth, while the poor can get along without silver plate, gilded beds, jewels, and rare foods. "Are not such things responsible for making many robbers and thieves who dig through house walls? Is it not these things that make runaway slaves? Wherever they turn their eyes, they see the gleaming silver, and the disease of theft is nourished in them." The poor are not poor because God wishes them so, but rather by mischance and necessity, even by the wickedness of the rich, who, while tempting them to crime with displays of luxury and setting them an example of the immoral pursuit of gain, exploit them by the means most harshly to be condemned, usury. The rich, then, should lower their pride, acknowledge their obligations, and pity the less fortunate: in reminder, moving sermons on "love for paupers" or the like, and action, too. The story of Ephraim in Edessa is typical.

Famine strikes, he urges the rich to save the poor; his hearers answer, We are all so dishonest, we know no one who could administer our charity. Ephraim volunteers his services and saves the situation. On a smaller scale, take two letters from Constantinian Egypt directed to the rescue of one Pamonthius, a wine dealer first forced into debt by the exactions of the local magistrates, then obliged to sell all his property, his very clothes, and at last to yield up his children to be sold for slaves by his creditors. His Meletian brothers first go bail for him, and then appeal to the head of the community for further help. Perhaps he was taken into the monastery, like so many humble fugitives in fourth century Egypt. In any event, he would look on the Church as his friend.[21]

Though the Church had a special mission which inspired its spokesmen to defend the lowly, its doctrine just outlined had an urgency best explained by conditions of the time. This is not the place to discuss them in any detail, but everyone will agree that there was less comfort to go round in the fourth century, consequently keener competition for ease and wealth; that there was less help to be expected from the law, if the plaintiff lacked lands and dignity; that habits of benevolence strong in Pliny's day had retreated somewhat before habits of oppression, among the aristocracy. It is the fashion to reason further, that the later Empire suffered from a sharpened hostility between the "haves" and the "have nots," between citizens and government officials, that everything, in short, pointed "to a state of acute tension which on the least excuse turned into open rebellion of large sections of the people against established authority." I am inclined to distrust such views as no more than *a priori*, since I cannot find any citizen of the period saying, "We fear the poor" or "We hate the rich," and since the popular disorders that have been discussed, occasioned by pretenders, famines, or doctrinal disputes, fall into no pattern of the poor with their own leaders against the rich with theirs. The kind of evidence that would be needed comes instead from the wrong period. We are warned, for example, that "the masses are more hostile to a rich man who does not give them a share of his wealth than a poor man who steals from the public funds, for they think that the former's conduct is due to arrogance and contempt of them, but the latter's to necessity." There were indeed hard feelings, then, but the writer quoted is Plutarch, the contemptuous are men like Tacitus; and it is another writer of the *first* century who says, "In those days [of Caligula's early reign] the rich did not carry it over the poor, nor the well-known over the obscure, nor creditors over debtors, nor were masters above slaves, the times giving equality before the law, so you would think that life under Saturn, as the poets record it, was no mere fiction of myth."[22] What Philo here describes, and regrets, are just the themes that one might reasonably expect to be regretted in Libanius' time, when in fact vaguely similar Golden Age dreams did circulate (see above, Chap. IV at n. 30).

Wants and sufferings quite obvious in the later Empire should have produced divisions in the urban population. Perhaps they did so. But word of such warring groups comes chiefly from the first and second centuries: "the men of the upper town against those near the sea" in Smyrna, and the like situation in a dozen other cities. Division into the Councilmen, Elders, Augustales, societies, and so forth, was even made formal, with effects harmful, surely, to a sense of community. Add the common distinction between dwellers within the walls, and those outside in districts assigned to municipal oversight, "the registered" and "the inhabitants of the countryside," the latter looked on by the former with a certain scorn. Dio Chrysostom recommended to the Tarsians that they minister to peace by conciliating the workers' societies and by abolishing a regulation that excluded from the assembly those whose property fell below a certain level. He speaks also of the rhetors as a class of men who made trouble in the forum by pursuing political vendettas, taking bribes, and advocating land taxes, and we have seen what a bad reputation traveling Cynics enjoyed, for stirring up the masses. At Dio Chrysostom's own town of Prusa, tensions of a cause and nature unknown so disturbed the public assemblies that the governor suspended them indefinitely. All this political ferment, it should be noted again, belongs to the later first and second centuries.[23]

The truth seems to be this: that the East in the era of its greatest prosperity was not free from a certain amount of friction produced by inequalities of wealth. Famine naturally made this friction worse. Conditions of the fourth century would lead one to assume more class tension, but for this there is no evidence. At most, the methods of agitation changed, to make greater use of organized groups. Horizontal divisions of the population such as have appeared in modern industrial societies could hardly appear in the ancient city because of the vertical ties binding together opposite extremes, a cobbler being unlikely to join in attacks on some local magnate who turned out to be patron of the leatherworkers' association, a sailor loath to take part with longshoremen, let us say, in burning down a bishop's house, when the bishop was Athanasius. His power over the grain fleet has been mentioned. Sympathies of this sort cut across classes and existed in profusion: formal ties of mutual obligation, informal ones of something much more than condescension face to face with deference. If they served the purposes of political rivalries, at the same time they worked against revolution. At Thyatira, for example, the *strategos* was also president of the dyers' society, the vice president of the Council at the same time their *curator*.[24] The battle lines in gatherings of the populace, here or elsewhere, at all periods, must have been very blurred.

Our survey of disorders within the city, having begun with street-crossing gossip and tavern brawls, passing to the theaters, and then to artisan sections, squares, and market places where the societies had their origin, has now reached the forum. Here not only internal dissensions showed themselves, but angers of the whole city against outer enemies, such as erupted in Pompeii in 59. We turn next to these intercity rivalries.

The extraordinary aggressive value placed on the possession of an amphitheater bigger than anyone else's was explained earlier. Illustration was drawn from Placentia and Pompeii, but from Greek centers also, and indeed the habit of emulation was properly and originally theirs in the first place. The Greeks made a contest out of everything. To do so was as characteristic of their nature as to pursue restraint and moderation. Aristotle recommended the mean; "Nothing in excess," warned the oracle. But at Delphi, every fourth year in rivalry with Olympia, international games were held (as at scores of other centers, by the second century A.D.), where crowds applauded the most frenzied straining to be immoderately fleet of foot, strong of hand, or sweet of voice. Nero entered his talents not of course for the foot race (*there* is a picture!) but for chariot races, singing, and the lyre. The recitation of Homer at Athens is well known; but elsewhere prizes were awarded for sculpture as well, and painting, the trumpet, and ballplaying. Against this background of incessant competition, Pliny's discoveries in Bithynia become intelligible: city after city up to its neck in debt for vaunting, extravagant, needless, and ill-conceived building, chiefly of structures that would make a show. By some emperor unknown this was prohibited. A third century jurist quotes the law: building permits are not needed "unless it is a matter of rivalry with another city." Whether rivalry or public improvement was the aim could be disputed, project by project. Roman reason, in fact, made little headway in the Greek city, which retained its right to every citizen's love, even his life; but that last sacrifice of patriotism being denied by the *pax Romana*, men were obliged to contribute to the glory of their native state by a conspicuously expensive household and retinue, or, better yet, by putting up the money for theaters, archways, porticoes, and the other structures which were so often praised, and which today make such splendid ruins. "Buildings and games and independent jurisdiction and exemptions from standing trial away from home or from paying taxes jointly with others, just like some village—in all these things the repute of cities naturally consists, and the prestige of their peoples is increased, and they draw more honor from visitors and proconsuls alike." To be acknowledged as the first in rank—that was the universal ambition: first in the province, the claim occasioning continual disputes; first along with another city which also stubbornly claimed the primacy; if not first, then nearly first, perhaps Third City in Pamphylia (Aspendus) or at least Seventh in the Province of Asia (Magnesia). Bitter wrangling over titles drew criticisms from Greeks themselves, sometimes a letter of rebuke and adjudication from the emperor. How far disputes could be carried can be read in the tiny letters and cunning abbreviations crammed onto the coinage of a city by no means great or famous: "Anazarbus, Noble Metropolis, the First, the Greatest, the Fairest, Standard Bearer of Rome, Site of the Free Common Council of Cilicia." Neighboring Mopsuestia bristled, and asserted its own cause in an equal list of superlatives. The two were at some time reconciled. An inscription announces "The

Concord of Mopsuestia and Anazarbus." Concord: the word was stamped on many coin issues, and served as title to many speeches delivered throughout the eastern provinces. It was incessantly urged, often proclaimed, seldom lasting.[25]

Indirect costs of all such rivalry, through waste of money and energy, cannot be estimated. Arguments about who owned what territory led to litigation, official surveys, high courts, embassies, and occasionally little border wars. Economic effects are indicated, but may have involved only limited interruption of commerce. More serious consequences followed in the wake of pretenders' wars, if a chance offered for one city to exact as payment for its loyalty the lands and liberties of another, its own enemy. This almost happened in Gaul in 68 and 69, Lyons and Vienne at each other's throats "too savagely for mere partisanship of Nero or Galba." Vienne chose the winning side and rejoiced in the humiliation of its rival—too soon. Lyons got its revenge through roaming detachments of soldiers urged on to the destruction of Vienne. A similar nexus of events in the 190's brought about the assigning of Byzantium to Perinthus, which "treated it like a village and insulted it in every way possible," "just as Antioch was given to Laodicea." In the fourth century, attribution of one city to another was still enforced as a penalty, and a most drastic one, for offending the emperor. Its consequences are described in a petition to Constantine from Orcistus in Phrygia, a town then desolate, its buildings tumbling down, its water supply inoperative, all because of its status as a mere *vicus* of nearby Nacolia, whose chief citizens plundered it. The same fate was intended for the too-Christian Constantia, attached to Gaza by Julian, and for Antioch in 387, attached once again to "its rival from earliest times," Laodicea.[26]

Civic pride did not necessarily lead to anti-Roman sentiments. It had not done so when the Roman Republic drifted into the conquest of Greece, nor did it so in the second and third centuries A.D., when Sardis strung out its oddly mixed titles, "Autochthonous City, Sanctuary of the Gods, *First of Greece* and Metropolis of Asia and all Lydia . . . *Friend and Ally of the Roman People*."[27] In contacts with the Greeks, Rome had earlier exploited and later permitted their dissensions, so useful to conqueror and ruler alike—always provided that dissensions did not turn into police problems. If that happened, the government intervened, sometimes gently, sometimes harshly. So Plutarch urged municipal magistrates to behave moderately, to cultivate concord as the greatest blessing, not to invite punishment by stirring up popular ambitions. What was once a virtue had become a vice, as he pointed out, since "war . . . has been banished, and of liberty the peoples have as great a share as our rulers grant them, and perhaps more would not be better for them." Competitive patriotism, if not suppressed, must be at least diverted. Plutarch's contemporary, Dio Chrysostom (*Or.* 38.33), suggests that the cities of Bithynia, abandoning the struggle each one to be first, turn to the pursuit of the general good, in a sort of pan-Bithynianism, not so odd as it sounds, for local differences in eastern cities did abate somewhat in the second century. Contemporaries understood one aspect of the phenomenon, the constitutional. Rome, said Aelius Aristides, "assigned common laws for all, and put an end to the previous conditions which were amusing to describe but which, if one looked at them from the standpoint of reason, were intolerable." It is important to note such statements, all coming from citizens of Hellenic culture, all out of sympathy with one of the chief characteristics of that culture. Civic pride, so far as it was too fiercely separate and aggressive, made no sense in a world of peace.[28]

Urban Unrest

Pax Romana rested in large part on municipal aristocracies. The poor, then, must have looked on Romans as accomplices to the rich, and must at times have cursed them both in the same breath—must have, according to speculation, nothing more. Only one doubtful instance is known of poverty and anti-Romanism conjoined, to be set against a mountain of indirect proof of the popularity of the empire among the lower classes. Indeed, Aelius Aristides tells us that "all the masses have as a share in it the permission to take refuge with [the Roman government] from the power of the local magnates."[29] Though any meddling of the sort would be rare and contrary to the policy of letting local governments do the Romans' work for them, yet when oppression by the magnates had become extreme, after the mid-fourth century, the emperor did appoint special officials to defend the weak and lowly. The *defensores civitatum* came too late, and disappeared again too soon; and earlier evidence for imperial championing of the lower classes is lacking, except through general legislation on the rights of slaves and freedmen, and the establishment of relief systems for orphans, the imperial *alimenta* in Italy. But the whole tradition of rule prevented more. Compare the silence of the urban poor with the fairly numerous documents of the rural poor, asking the emperor or governor to come to their defense. On the countryside, imperial agents intervened more frequently because there was no danger of undermining some useful, existing, strong authority.

Rome's internal enemies were not the urban poor but rather members—a small minority—of the very group she specially favored: Greeks of the upper class, defending the purity of their cultural inheritance. They would never have been so vocal had that purity not been seriously threatened. The most typical of Roman enthusiasms, gladiation, for example, attracted an immense following in eastern cities. A few Romans, but more Greeks, protested its brutality. And just like senators of Republican times who outlawed the teaching of Greek rhetoric, so Greeks—a small minority—sought to stem the tide of bilingualism and Latin loan words among their fellows by an exaggerated scorn of "the barbaric tongue" of their rulers and by an ardent conservatism in language, the latter taste, however, being shared by men who combined an antique Hellenism with careers as imperial bureaucrats or consuls. It would be wrong, then, to see in literary movements of the second and early third centuries anything specially disloyal or nationalistic in the modern sense. Some Greek writers certainly spoke of Roman imperialism as being no better than robbery on a gigantic scale—but Romans used the same criticism against themselves; some criticized Roman rule and sneered at Rome's crude, fratricidal origins and present boorish wealth. When examined in context, however, the passages that are sometimes taken as separatist turn out to be really very inoffensive: critical of vice whether of the ruling people or of anyone else; if summons to a revival of vanished Hellenism, at least not summons to rebellion as well; in short, no source of danger to the peace of the empire.[30]

Nationalistic revolts, or the lack of them, will be discussed more fully in the next chapter. Here, only a word of summary. The end and aim of the Roman empire was urban civilization, to the support of which, if need arose, the rural population must be sacrificed. The cities got a great deal more than their fair share of whatever life had to offer, so long as prosperity lasted, and in the East, at least, they survived the shocks of the third century with considerable success. They could at all times look about them and see no one better off than they. What, then, could make their leading classes restive? Not invidious contrast, the very spring of revolution; not the clear conception of what their enemy or oppressor might be. Few Greeks could see the empire as an institution that might be overthrown; a condition, yes, and one that brought peace; a people, yes, whose uncultured ways aroused scorn, but whose worst representative could be endured in the likely hope of getting a better man as his successor. In the meantime, contentiousness could be directed at a more traditional and convenient target, the neighboring city.

✧ VI ✧

The Outsiders

THE brigand has always been (except to his victims) a romantic and half-attractive figure. To the dramatic possibilities of his life the Greeks and Romans were not blind. He made his appearance in their novels, perhaps also in their folk poetry, and often in the soberer pages of their histories. A certain Claudius troubling Judea under Septimius Severus, in the midst of the hue and cry after him, coolly accosted the emperor and conversed with him unrecognized. A decade earlier Bulla Felix, also disguised, promised a centurion to pursue himself vigorously and to arrest himself on sight. In the fourth century we meet with monks made over, or abbots reclaimed and elected, from a life of brigandage, and the leaders of the fierce Bagaudae, Amandus and Aelian, eventually received veneration as saints.[1]

For these stories, not false simply because they are entertaining, inspiration and heroes in every period were easy to find. In backward, wild, or mountainous parts of the Roman empire, robber bands were never wholly suppressed, despite the energy of private individuals in their own defense, in spite of municipal officials and imperial troops—all three methods of police tested in the cities (see Chapter V) but more difficult to operate on the rural scene (see Appendix B, 2). Certain areas naturally favored crime; certain forms of society resisted civilization. Moorish and Arab nomads, Quinquegentanei, Garamantes, Bessi, Maratocupreni, Brisei, Cietae, or whatever tribe it might be, retained their ancient constitution, their traditional lawlessness, their inexpugnable haunts, ready at the first sign of weakness on the part of the government to launch their raids against farmlands and cities. Only in the era of most settled rule could they be fenced off to themselves with reasonable success, while civil or foreign wars gave opportunity to sudden explosions of violence from out of wasteland fastnesses.

But a phenomenon much more interesting and important was the outlaw not born to the trade, so to speak, but drawn to it from among its proper enemies. Without such recruits, brigandage could never have challenged the massed authority of Roman laws and armies. Challenge them it did, in the later Empire, and supplied folk heroes—Bulla Felix, Claudius, Amandus, and Aelian—to its very victims. A widespread sympathy felt, or half-felt, for the lives and deeds of outlaws testifies to a loosening loyalty within civilized society, where to be poor, to be rejected, to scrape a living irregularly in the company of others clinging like oneself to the edge of the respectable world; to envy and then to hate the man of property, and to admire the style of his plunderers; to consort with them, then shield them, and at last join them, were the successive steps leading beyond the boundaries of the law.

A historian under Tiberius wrote, "The imperial peace keeps every corner of the earth safe from the fear of bandits' attacks." Under Trajan, Epictetus repeated the boast: "You see how profound a peace the emperor has achieved for us, how there are wars no longer, nor battles, nor brigandage on a large scale, nor piracy"; travel everywhere is safe;[2] whereas in the 250's Cyprian bids his readers, "Look at the roads barred by brigands, the seas beset by pillagers" (*Ad Donat.* 6). To this latter state, the point of transition can be fixed more exactly. In the known and dated records of kidnappings on the countryside, of murders lamented on gravestones of Spain or Dacia or Syria, of chance meetings with brigands in Italy, Greece, or Africa, there is a pause almost complete between the mid-first and mid-second centuries, proof of a genius for rule triumphant in every province; and indeed, to anyone who reviews in his mind the history of the Mediterranean world over the millennia preceding and succeeding, the Roman achievement in this one serene stretch of a hundred years seems nothing short of miraculous. Not that individual crime ceased, of course; to expect that would be too much; but organized groups of robbers on the land are simply not heard of. Then, as hint or warning, comes the order that "irenarchs, when they have arrested brigands, should question them about their associates and about those who shelter them" (*Dig.* 48.3.6.1)—an order issued in the early 130's by the then proconsul of Asia, Antoninus Pius, under whose rule as emperor the prefect of Egypt circulated a similar letter to his district officials (BGU 372): let every fugitive from debts, liturgies, or proscriptions now return to his home; let soldiers cease from their arrests; but after the period of grace offered, wanderers will be seized as brigands self-confessed. Some time between 210 and 214 another Egyptian prefect angrily renewed his earlier command for the arrest of bandits, and of their confederates, too, since "it is impossible to root out robbers apart from those who shelter them, some, partners to their plunderings, some innocent" (*P. Oxy.* 1408). The jurist Paul in the third century and many laws in the fourth protest this kind of complicity offered by villagers, by rural magnates, and notoriously by country hostels.[3]

What confronted the emperor was a sense—how widespread among his subjects, or how deeply felt and destructive, we cannot say—that someone who broke the law might be an ally, and officers who enforced it enemies. More will be said on the point later, but it is not hard to understand. Against brigands, the chief weapon was the army, and more and more soldiers were sent out—under Septimius Severus, "military guard posts . . . allotted to the pursuit of brigands in all the provinces" (Tert., *Apol.* 2.8)—with never a thought that they would not prove a blessing; instead of which, they were often a curse to the countryside. Complaints about their truculence and extortions, not unknown in earlier times, grow frequent in the third century. Not only did they take what was not theirs, in the name of taxes or "protection"; they protracted their "mopping-up operations" to serve their rapacity, especially in the wake of civil wars, and, as love of pillage grew upon them, abandoned the army entirely for an outlaw's life. A "deserters' war" required the concentration of special forces on Gaul in 187–88. Its origins no doubt reached back to the Marcomannic campaigns and to the border raids that had recently afflicted the northern parts of the province. It is reasonable to believe that the same causes later produced the same effects throughout the troubled years of the third and early fourth centuries, though specific measures against deserters as robbers are taken up again only in 365. Repeated laws thereafter, relating to Italy, Gaul, and Pontus, or more generally to "the provinces," threatened deserters as well as those who concealed them. Self-defense, for example, was officially encouraged against those who "enter fields as nocturnal ravagers or beset frequented roads by attacks from ambush . . . Let no one spare a soldier who should be resisted with arms as a brigand."[4]

While the emperor's loyal troops robbed and murdered his subjects, the real enemy broke in. Historians need not depend on their imaginations to picture the consequences, need not draw the obvious conclusions from blackened strata of conflagration in the remains of northern cities and farms, nor guess the meaning of hundreds and hundreds of coin hoards scattered along the paths of invasion. Written records survive, too. Treaties stipulated the return of captives, subscriptions were raised for their ransom, thanksgivings to the gods were inscribed on stone for their restoration to their family—if indeed any family remained. It might have happened that all were killed and buried under gravestones that told their names but did not know their ages; so a blank was left, to be filled in if some cousin should turn up later with the information. Friends and relatives not dead might have fled, perhaps to a more primitive safety. Caves along the Rhone Valley, unoccupied since the Stone Age, received in the mid-third century a population of fugitives some of whom thereafter never sought out their homes again. Those who neither fled nor died had problems of conscience to solve in the wake of the invasions. What of Christians carried off who offered sacrifice to the barbarians' gods? What of the deserted houses from which looters took what later owners demanded back, or stolen property which a man said he had found abandoned by the raiders? What of the slaves and wild youths who seized the chance of barbarian incursions to plunder and besiege the rich, or, most serious of all, those persons who were known to have joined the enemy, betraying to them the best routes and the hiding places of valuables—in short, persons who had taken up a bandit's life?[5] The Latin language made the transition easy. It offered the same word for "brigand" and for "raider"—*latrunculus*.

Outlawry thus drew recruits from deserters and from the victims of invasion. A source more prevalent was the growing body of the very poor. "Tell your masters that if they would put a stop to brigandage, they must feed their slaves," was Bulla Felix's message (Dio 77.10.2); or, as an anonymous commentator of the fourth century put it more fully, "the poor [under Constantine and later] were driven by their afflictions into various criminal enterprises, and, losing sight of all respect for law, all feeling of loyalty, they entrusted their revenge to crime. For they often inflicted the most severe injuries on the empire, laying waste the fields, breaking the peace with outbursts of brigandage, stirring up animosities; and, passing from one crime to another, supported usurpers (*tyranni*)." Statements like this are matched by the reasoning of the Egyptian prefect's edict of 154, already quoted; but, on the face of it, a connection so obvious to contemporary observers, between poverty and crime, cannot have gone unrecognized in the calculations of government officials. Relief of orphans, well-advertised destruction of public debt records in every century of the Empire, and administrative measures to tie men down to jobs, farms, and homes, must all have been inspired, at least in part, by the wish to strike at the roots of crime. From our vantage point today it is clearer still that lawbreaking on the countryside was attended and without doubt chiefly caused by economic, political, and social dislocation: witness the concentration of evidence for our present subject in the later Empire, with a continually increasing number of proofs and documents and, moreover, with a particular clustering around the reign of Septimius Severus. Thenceforward, the empire entered on more unsettled times, the effects of which—deserters, beggars, monks, and the merely desperate roaming loose from province to province—were inadequately combated by strings of laws going off like firecrackers into the gathering dusk of disorder.[6]

It has been the fashion of late to detect in brigandage an expression of class struggle and social revolution. Such terms, of course, introduce complex and polemical associations; but if they were taken in their bare, literal sense, they would still be very hard to justify. Legislation municipal and imperial did indeed mark off the city dweller from the peasant, town councilors or Roman senators from plebeians, *honestiores* from *humiliores*, and so on, in dozens of overlapping categories. The very number of these, however, seems to have worked against the formation of class feeling; and besides, they were defined by purposes of state, thereby accustoming people to think of the state as the tyrant—quite correctly, since rank as town councilor, shipowner, landowner, or whatever, determined what burdens of public service one had to support. Thus the much broader divisions that might seem natural to us—slaves, peasants, "owners of the means of production"—did not impose themselves on the consciousness of contemporaries. Quite the reverse. Turning from general argument to specific instance: there were certainly slaves in the later Empire, they certainly shared a common legal status, and they occasionally helped to make history. That their revolutions were very few and minor has been pointed out elsewhere, and if they broke loose against authority, it was sometimes under leaders of great wealth and free birth.[7] Naturally, they also plundered the rich. Their complicity with circumcellions and Bagaudae, whom we will turn to shortly, is well attested. The only caution offered here is against *general* statements about slaves, in default of evidence that they thought or acted as a class.

In the third century, African peasants armed themselves with clubs and axes at the orders of "certain young men of high birth and wealth in the country." In the 260's, "a band of rustics," of "Syrian farmers," fought for the prince of Palmyra. Asia, Syria, and Pisidia in the East and Italy in the West provide inscriptions recording country folk, tribes, and villages as clients of officials and local landowners. In the face of these facts it would be impossible to imagine the rural rich and poor as two compact armies confronting each other. For the fourth and fifth centuries there is a wider choice of information pointing, however, in the same direction. The weak are brought into ever closer contact with the strong from motives of the harshest self-interest, yielding up their loyalty, lands, selves, and labor in exchange for protection from the still more ruinous demands of the imperial government—protection ensured not only by influence and bribery but by armed force as well. If patrons held a military command, as many did, so much the better; they could use their official powers for their own ends; if not in so favored a position, they assembled private guards, among whom brigands and deserters could be found.[8] From the troubles of the late Empire peasants thus sought asylum not so often or so naturally with brothers of their own condition as with men of higher status, whose little realms united in a single interest clients and patrons, slaves, *coloni*, small proprietors, perhaps rural artisans, idle hangers-on, guards, bailiffs, and *domini*. The various forms assumed by these clusters of men, transitional to the medieval and Byzantine worlds, have often been discussed. They are mentioned here only because they are not easily forced into a framework of class struggle. The rural population in fact resembled the urban in its tendency to form vertical rather than horizontal relationships.

Turning from these refractory phenomena, Marxist historians emphasize the other side of the picture: discontent and unrest on the part of those unable to fit into any of the dominant social forms.[9] From a variety of evidence on the subject, much agreement may be drawn. In contrast with the earlier movement of people *toward* something desired, be it wider empire, new markets, reclaimed desert zones, more scattered landholdings, or higher rank through training at special centers of education, it is undeniable that movement *away from* something undesirable grew commoner after the Antonine age, and it seems likely, too, that social mobility in a broad sense not only took on a predominantly 'anti' character but also increased absolutely. Many who changed their place in life became brigands—just how many we cannot say, but peace in Isauria, for example, more or less vanished, and travel was made virtually impossible in Thrace and in parts of Italy in the last quarter of the fourth century. On all such matters there is agreement. Without disputing the great importance of these developments, however, we have nevertheless questioned whether they can be explained as class struggle. A second term of explanation should be rejected also: social revolution.

The African circumcellions have been called social revolutionaries. They appeared before the mid-fourth century, concentrated in Numidia, men with small properties or none at all, supplying seasonal labor to the olive plantations that stretched for endless miles across the High Plains. In the eyes of the law they were definable as an *ordo;* they had, at least sometimes, known leaders—Axido and Fasir in 347—and, according to their enemies, had organized themselves in *turbae*, *agmina*, *greges*, *cunei*, and *legiones*. In some ways they resembled a monastic order, though Augustine refuses such a title to men lacking spiritual supervisors, rules of conduct, and any settled habitation. They did indeed wander wide, frequenting especially the martyrs' shrines in the countryside, the *cellae*, from which it was thought they derived their name, and from the traditions of which they certainly derived their suicidal ardor for self-sacrifice. Were nothing further known of them, they might at this point be compared to other fanatic rigorists, Montanists or Meletians, that were split off from the main body of the faithful by the blows of the Great Persecution. Instead, circumcellions played a more vigorous and varied role. Brandishing the stout staffs that they employed to knock the harvest off the olive trees, and in the 390's with more formidable weapons, they stood forward as the shock troops of Donatism. Very rough customers they were. "They live like brigands," said Augustine. They sheltered runaway slaves and *coloni,* and with sporadic violence, in the 340's and 360's and often in the period when Augustine, our chief source, was presbyter and bishop, they broke into Catholic churches, beat, mutilated, or killed Catholic priests, and wrought or threatened the same violence to their secular enemies. Here, however, difficulties of interpretation arise. Was their ferocity aimed at the rich as such or at the rich as Catholics? On the one hand, their principal victims seem to have been men of property, *possessores.* They freed slaves, destroyed notes of indebtedness, frightened creditors from trying to collect, tossed men out of carriages and bade their servants to ride. "By their judgment and command the condition of master and slave was reversed." On the other hand they were expected, sometimes in vain, to respond to pressure from Donatist priests or from the wealthy men on whose estates they worked, suggesting neither irreconcilable hatred of the upper classes nor any social and economic program, but rather a religious orientation—suggesting, in short, that they were schismatics in the plain sense of the word. One thing at any rate is sure: they left no record of a revolutionary plan.[10]

The nature of circumcellionism might be discoverable in Donatism. One was a less extreme form of the other, sharing the same stronghold, Numidia. There, however, Donatists numbered in their ranks not only the poor and reckless but the rich, landed, educated, and influential, even high officials, whose ideas of justice and class relations reflected their position and sometimes inclined them to disown the deeds of their fanatical coreligionists. As far as one can see, the districts where Donatism flourished retained the social patterns that had prevailed on similar landscapes in provinces where Catholicism had never been opposed. The schism in Numidia changed nothing. That most powerful Donatist, Optatus of Timgad, for many years could do exactly as he wished within and well beyond the borders of his episcopal see. When his authority was questioned, he whistled for his circumcellions. Augustine tells us that this man, "with intolerable power, accompanied even by bodyguards not because he feared anyone himself but to inspire fear in everyone else, oppressed widows, evicted minors, distributed other people's patrimonies, broke up marriages, saw to the sale of innocent persons' properties and took a share of the proceeds while the owners wept." A horrible roll of crimes, no doubt about it, but nothing new in the Roman world; nothing, perhaps, that the emperor was not guilty of himself after the defeat of his enemy Gildo—we know, at least, that he rewarded his partisans with confiscated estates in Africa—and nothing that could not be duplicated a hundred times over in the civil strife of Roman Republican days; in sum, nothing that could be called social revolution. If a great deal of wealth changed hands in the decade or so around A.D. 400, as it certainly did, it came not from the rich per se but from Optatus' Catholic or pagan opponents, and much of it went to the costs of "one of the largest cathedrals ever erected in Christian Africa," of a size and glory suitable to the bishop of Timgad.[11]

The origins of Donatism reached back to Diocletian's persecutions and to the question whether a priest who has betrayed his church—a *traditor*—could administer a true sacrament? Simpler, poorer people said no (for simplicity and harshness are often found together), and they pointed to the better example of many, many of their own kind who had unyieldingly professed their faith, who had won the crown of martyrdom and, with martyrdom, fervent veneration. The persecutions had in fact been thorough enough to strike humble followers as well as leaders of the Church. But those leaders who survived, those who had mixed in the world, who had gained learning, and who felt the responsibility of wide cures and wider relations with other churches in other provinces, took a prudential view of things. For them, Christianity was more than a war cry. They did not favor the entire exclusion of every *traditor* or a radical change in the doctrine of baptism. At Carthage, as at Rome and Alexandria, rigorist schisms were driven off the field by toleration. Rural areas alone maintained the cause of the martyrs unrelentingly. Clear down to Augustine's day, a century removed from the origins of Donatism, its adherents threw in his face his descent from the betrayers of Christ.[12] The word they used was not "oppressor" but *traditor*.

Schism in Africa has been much studied. This is not the place to repeat what others have said more fully.[13] Let this short discussion suffice to throw doubt on the view that the circumcellions or the Donatists had enlisted in a class struggle or that they were social revolutionaries. A further question has been raised, however: Was not religious dissent in the fourth century only one chapter in a long history of African anti-Romanism?

From the reign of Antoninus Pius, the African provinces were disturbed by Moorish incursions of unusual depth and frequency, threatening, beyond the peace, the very civilization they attacked; for with them they brought a different culture—their own language, for one thing; for another, a sort of cult of their ancient kings. The native word for "king" was *aguellid*, translated *princeps* in the earlier centuries, sometimes by the more pretentious *rex* in the third. The implied promotion may have meant little to the Baquates, for example —they later submitted to the older term—but it does suggest a willingness on the part of Rome to honor and conciliate a certain independence in her neighbors at a time when her own strength was turned in upon herself.[14] The point is easily confirmed. In 238, to pay for northern campaigns, the emperor Maximinus had so squeezed his African subjects that they rose against him, young and old, rich and poor, ultimately placing their own candidate on the throne. It was by no means a national revolt since there was no sense of nation to be found in Africa, but it had the indirect effect of disrupting the province's defenses. In the 240's, again under Valerian and Gallienus, serious tribal wars broke out. More followed in the early years of Diocletian. Their whole pattern explains itself. Whenever Rome was divided and weak, her enemies to the south of Numidia and Mauretania descended on her like jackals. They were never fully incorporated into her empire nor fully pacified. Pillage and the Berber language, the breaking of treaties and the venerating of their kings, belonged equally and irremediably to their way of life. Ammianus repeats the same phrase twice, to describe the favorite activities of the Austoriani and Musones: "rapine and massacre." The latter tribe, incidentally, joined Firmus' revolt. So much for the "anti-Romans" in the third and fourth centuries. Their history really tells us nothing about the popularity or unpopularity of imperial rule except in the obvious sense that tribes so little civilized could gain strength only at the expense of the empire.[15]

Something further is claimed for events that mark the year 372. Taxes and irregular exactions drove Firmus to rebellion. He was chief of the Jubaleni. Tribesmen like himself formed his army, but he could also find welcome, or at least shelter, in the walled villages of the African plains, and the Donatists were not too proud to use him as a weapon in the harrying of their own schismatics. The latter thereupon accused the "orthodox" Donatists of being "Firmiani." Evidently it was not a respectable alliance even in Donatist country. Firmus at the height of his success controlled large areas of Mauretania and parts of Numidia. He held out for three years. The Romans, aided by his renegade younger brother, Gildo, ended his career in 375. Within a decade, that same Gildo had been made Count of Africa, his daughter (a Catholic) had married a nephew of the empress. The rewards bestowed on his house show how useful he appeared to his masters. But, after all, the tribes had changed very little since the days when Jugurtha killed his relatives, seized their lands, and unwillingly defied Rome, four hundred years earlier. Gildo's murders in the family drove a third brother to Rome in exile, only to return in 397 at the head of an army of invasion. Gildo was captured and executed, and along with him, accused of complicity, died Optatus, bishop of Timgad. The motives and relations of the pair have been often debated. One, taking advantage of divisions between East and West, had zigzagged upward to dangerous power. "There is nothing, however, to show that Gildo was ever in revolt against the Empire as such, or had conscious aims beyond gratification of the personal ambition of acquiring an enormous landed estate." He deserved no better than the name flung at him, "plunderer." As for the other, Optatus, it is probable that he had supported Gildo, and certain that he employed him against Donatist schismatics (just as Firmus had been employed earlier). For the same purpose, however, the Donatists officially invited the intervention also of the emperor. They saw in him a proper umpire of their difficulties. Augustine would surely have made them all out as traitors if he could have; whereas in fact he concentrates his charges only on Optatus. "One of your colleagues," he says, "was Gildo's closest friend."[16] These two chiefs, alike in their rise and fall, give a glimpse of complex alignments but not of any deep historical undercurrents. Claims that they represented a native populace aroused or that they were the armed forefront of a separatist heresy rest on a very weak basis.

The lifelines of the various groups in the African population, and such abstract forces as modern historians are used to calling nationalism, social revolution, and anti-imperialism, have been woven together in startling patterns by scholars of the last generation—patterns which it has been the aim of the preceding few pages to pick apart: Donatists from Berbers, Berbers from a nonexistent African nation, circumcellions from raiders and brigands, and all groups together from anachronistic theories of social justice. Better to take the past on its own terms. No sentence in the sources leads us to think that Augustine, or some other writer, had seen the exquisite complications inherent in Donatist doctrine, or had heard, in his travels through the rural towns, peasant orators calling for the poor to shake off their shackles. Perhaps, then, the complications did not exist, the orators did not orate; perhaps schismatic violence was just what everybody thought who could observe it at first hand, that is, basically religious, and tribal risings were not nationalist but merely what people called them, "rapine." This is not to deny all truth to the connections we have surveyed. We may well believe, for example, that Berber chiefs had what might be called a foreign policy, a relation with the neighbors most important to them. For Gildo, such neighbors were the Donatists under Optatus, whose friendship he bought by the loan of his troops. We may easily imagine, too, that circumcellions, themselves barely above the condition of serfs, took more pleasure in roughing up the owner of twenty olive groves than in oppressing his peasants, and sheltered those peasants as natural brothers if they were pressed for the payment of some grievous debt. So much the circumcellions might do without losing their essential character of fanaticism. None of this speculation carries us beyond the bounds of common experience into the realms of theory, where the flesh and blood of the past are somehow transformed into long words.

Parallels in support of more ambitious interpretations have sometimes been suggested between Donatism and heresies in other provinces. The entangling of motives cultural, religious, economic, social, and political has been discovered in Montanism; in Pelagianism; and in orthodoxy (against Arianism) and, later, in Monophysitism in Egypt.[17] These are among the most prominent heresies, whose full catalogue men like Epiphanius combated, or at least compiled. So many variant and deviant doctrines, so many scores of them. They testify to the extreme difficulty in agreeing not only on what was true belief but on what body of men should determine it. Since decisions were made in the great urban centers, heresies naturally took firmest root in remote parts of the empire where (coincidentally) Greek and Roman ways were little known.

The mixed, retarded culture prevailing in southern areas of the African provinces has left its trace in martyrs' chapels haunted by circumcellions. Montanism, born in Phrygia, similarly established itself in the backlands. It attracted its following in the second century, expanded across the West, and shrank slowly into its home again in the third century. Its adherents, like Donatists, were accused of drunkenness—possibly ritual drunkenness. Like Donatism, it numbered brigands in its ranks; like Donatism and Coptism, vestiges of pagan beliefs clung to and disfigured it. Its founder, Montanus himself, had apparently been a priest of Cybele. Her worship, popular in Phrygia, communicated to Christians of the area a taste for orgiastic mysticism and revelation; and Christian monuments there in the third century incorporated further peculiarities of an earlier paganism. The old gods more than flourished in this same period, the later second and third centuries. They seem even to have enjoyed a livelier veneration. We should add, too, that Montanists may well have spoken their own Phrygian. Records of that language, instead of diminishing steadily in number before the advance of Hellenism, became more plentiful in the later Empire, and the map of their find-spots coincides fairly well with the distribution of the heresy. The total picture of this corner of the world is, however, not a chain of cause and effect but a mosaic of coincidence. Language, religion, art: all differ from patterns dominant in more central areas, not because of a hostility to Hellenism, or to Rome, or later, to Christian orthodoxy —not because of any conscious nationalism, as is sometimes inferred—but simply because of isolation. There is no denying that this isolation produced some very curious innovations in Christianity: the branding of neophytes, the prophesying of priestesses, and the expectation of the New Jerusalem in that tiny city so ridiculously named Pepuza. Tertullian (though a Montanist) anticipates some of our own feelings when we consider these eccentricities. "It has been observed," he says, "that heretics have connections with very many magicians, itinerant charlatans, astrologers, and philosophers." He has in mind the heresies of the third century, excluding his own, naturally. The ferment continued later, new ideas bubbled up. A single Phrygian town at one time harbored the churches of Montanists, Novatianists, Encratites, and Apotactites or Saccophori. All four were illicit sects.[18]

Saccophori got their name from their way of life. They were Wallet Bearers, vagabonds or wandering saints each one according to his disposition. Many similar groups circulated. Chance mentions scattered over the third and especially the fourth century give the impression of an almost incessant stir of peoples along the many spiritual paths of dissent and schism, and along the dusty roads of the eastern and southern empire: of Montanists driven from the more urbanized districts into the country towns, of the Enthusiasts expelled from Syria into Pamphylia; of priest-deserters from their appointed sees in Cyrenaica, the *vacantivi;* of *catenati*, the long-haired, chained ascetics in Syria whom Jerome warns against, as Libanius against fanatic monks who, he alleges, go about in bands, robbing and pillaging. In Chapter IV we described also the eschatological pilgrimages of whole congregations, and the priests of Bithynia who led their flock in a raid against heretical Ophites; in the present chapter the circumcellions have appeared at market villages of the High Plains. Collisions between opposing doctrines were often tumultuous, especially if they involved what our invariably upper-class sources call "the mob," "neatherds, shepherds, and undisciplined young men, the rabble of the market place," quarrymen, peasants, and low women, and so on. Religious fervor added much to the flux and violence of the age.[19]

Tribesmen, deserters, fugitives from barbarian raids or from poverty; now, heretics and fanatics: our list of the unrooted is complete. To explain where they all came from would be to explain the crumbling of the empire, in which, when it still stood firm, these various elements had somehow been incorporated. That they constituted a source of serious danger was clear to the officials responsible for the security of the state. Each category of men was laid under a specific ban. Tribes were to stay where they belonged; soldiers absent without leave must return to the ranks; beggars and wanderers might be seized and enslaved by anyone who could catch them; and as for heretics, they received the particular compliment of over a hundred laws in the Theodosian Code, declaring illegal their beliefs, meetings, proselytizing, ownership of property, and very existence. Legislation of the 380's is typical. It deals with "those who contend about religion . . . to provoke any agitation against the regulation of Our Tranquillity, as authors of sedition and as disturbers of the peace of the Church . . . There shall be no opportunity for any man to go out to the public and to argue about religion or to discuss it or give any counsel."[20]

Finally, monks. Not a few of them had taken up an ascetic life as alternative to arrest; a vast number had turned to it instead of to the long-traditional recourse of the landless and bankrupt, *anachoresis*, "flight into the country," whence "anchorite." Monasticism was heavily indebted for its origin and growth to the fugitives whom the government tried so strictly to recall. The debt was repaid. As proof, imperial fulminations: let no cleric or monk shelter convicted criminals, let monks keep to their solitudes, away from cities—in spite of which the venerable Macedonius came down from his mountains to reason (in Syriac; he spoke no Greek) with the emperor's troops in 387, when Antioch was about to be punished, and the abbot Shenute, taking up the cause of the peasants against landowners and officials, passed from preaching to the point of open warfare. This was in early fifth century Egypt. His views on social justice, always sympathetic to the humble and driven, matched those of other Church leaders, which we have sketched in the preceding chapter. He would have found a very hostile audience, however, among the legislators of the age. They were rich men and feared innovation.[21]

From the many laws against these several unrooted groups, an unlooked-for effect followed: they made *out*laws. Roman rulers should have been careful to keep their subjects with*in* the law by withholding decisions and pronouncements that could not be enforced, that ran counter to received behavior or alienated too large a part of the population. Such self-restraint was beyond the emperors. Bewildered by conditions too complex for their understanding, they offered one response to every ill: legislation. They succeeded only in driving more thousands into the ranks of their enemies. Certain it is, in any case, that respect for law slowly gave way to every kind of corruption and complaint about the government's instruments and inefficiency, while at the same time the injustices that turned men into criminals grew more severe.

Against this larger background of social dislocation and alienation, we now return to the subject of brigandage. It was worst in Gaul. In 286 we first hear of Bagaudae, "the fighters," as the name may mean, described in our sources as irregularly armed rustics and brigands, serfs, farmers, and shepherds encouraged by their wide successes in the countryside to attack a number of cities also. Their movement took its rise in distress, not treason; so Maximian, for all his military resources, could not put an end to it until he had done something to improve the administration of the province; yet after a generation the Bagaudae raised their heads again, occupied the Alpine passes, and there extorted toll even from passing armies, spread into Spain, and challenged the attention of the greatest generals. Their hold was firmest on western Gaul from the Loire to Brittany (Armorica). "That's where men live by the laws of nature, where there's no rank, where capital sentences are posted up on an oak limb or marked on a man's bones, where peasants make the speeches and ordinary folk do the judging, where anything goes!" That was the life of the Loire brigands. Against Maximian, the Bagaudae had followed two acknowledged leaders, Aelianus and Amandus, whose coinage proclaimed their ambition to be emperors. As barbarians flooded into the West, the Bagaudae could envision a more drastic step. In 409, Armorica threw off Roman rule; reduced to allegiance, again in 435 the Bagaudic Tibatto and his Armorican followers "abandoned the Roman alliance."[22]

The history of brigandage in Gaul, beginning in alienation from the pattern of life officially encouraged or enforced, thus ended in separation. Before too much is attributed to the term, it should be asked what the Bagaudae wished to be separated from? The answer "Rome" is meaningless unless it be added that what passed for the *imperium Romanum* in the fifth century was the sorriest excuse for an empire, incapable of defending its subjects, oppressive to all, and made visible only in the person of some barbarian mercenary or rapacious tax collector; so Gallic peasants need have felt no positive impulse of independence, merely a negative revulsion from their rulers. The same reasoning even more clearly prevents the substitution of the term "nationalism" for "separatism." Consider the history of earlier centuries. If we work back in time to the period before 300 when the Bagaudae took their rise, we find local orators ignorant of the very idea of nation, using the word *patria* to describe, not the Gallic people as a whole, but some single city like Augustodunum (Autun) or some tribe, for example the Heduans, whose ancient devotion and suffering for Rome as long ago as Caesar's day are recalled with emphatic pride. They boast of their refusal to support the pretenders of the preceding few decades. Their capital, Augustodunum, "glorying in a name fraternal to the Roman people," that is, named for Augustus, had held firm though "besieged by the brigandage of the Batavian rebellion"; while at the same time Carausius, head of that rebellion, trafficking with Rome's enemies and wishing to be in fact his own master —even Carausius employed extravagant stratagems to remain at least nominally loyal and Roman. To have laid stress on the separate, special claims of his Batavians would have alienated all the other peoples whom he hoped to rule. Nationalism would have ruined his cause. A generation earlier there had been other rebels. These, like Carausius, arose from the vacuum of power. The central authorities seemed to have forgotten the West; barbarians were streaming in. Broader movements toward the so-called "Gallic empire" at this time, however, represented an effort to save and assert rather than to deny Roman rule against a general collapse.[23] Reviewing events in their proper sequence, from the Gallic emperors in the 260's to Tibatto and his Armorican Bagaudae in 435, we can see an increase in the readiness of the population to do for themselves what Rome was unable to do for them; we can see a steady loosening of loyalty in these areas; but we cannot see any explosive repudiation of an alien rule. What need, in the fifth century? It was as easy to be free as to step out from under a dark shadow.

It should follow (if our survey reaches back still farther) that Gaul in the first century A.D. was even less capable of a national rebellion than later, not because Rome then was weak but because Gaul was divided. Several first century movements have been called nationalistic; the evidence points in other directions. Florus and Sacrovir in the south appealed in 21 to debtors, beggars, criminals. The spurs to revolution were high taxes, high interest rates, and the arrogance of Roman representatives. The northern population under Vindex in 68, "being hostile first of all toward the Sequani and the Heduans, and then toward other states in proportion to their wealth," fought in order to pillage; Treviri and Lingones brooded over the better treatment accorded by Galba to their rivals. Hard on Galba's heels came Vitellius, whose ruthless recruiting proved unbearable to the Batavians. They drew their neighbors the Canninefates and Frisii into their revolt;

but each of these tribes went to war brigaded apart and, when they defeated Gallic levies, tried to win them over to war also by promising liberty such as they had enjoyed before there was tribute to pay. Treason spread, more converts joined: Bructeri, Tencteri, discrete in battle "in order that their separate bravery might be seen more clearly." To subsequent appeals for loyalty by the Romans, the answer came: No more recruitment, no more taxes. Bitterness repeated unvarying cries.[24]

The further course of events in 69 and 70 has been retraced a thousand times since Tacitus, but their main character is obvious. They were disunited efforts in reaction to administrative severity. When Tacitus fills the mouth of some insurgent chieftain with an angry speech, he does indeed introduce such topics as "our common gods," *libertas*, ancestral "customs and culture." These were sentiments not of the real speakers, whom Tacitus never heard, nor even wholly Tacitus' own invention, but borrowed by him from his reading in Greek sources; and when he lowers his account to a more historical level, the cause of unrest regularly cited is dislike of the burdens imposed by Rome: levying of soldiers and tribute, harsh judges.[25] So narrow a basis for rebellion should cause no surprise. In Africa it explains, without hint or need of other motives, the risings of 238, of Firmus, and of Gildo. The evidence has been presented above, with mention of why the Moors raided the province, and why the Musones joined Firmus: only for plunder; and in the preceding note, the motive of Queen Boadicea's followers has been told: hatred of taxes. Material discontent, hopes of material advantage, underlie the characterization of the Batavians (or equally the other Gallic or African or British rebellions) as "brigandage." Making all allowance for an orator's bias, the term was still justified.

A very simple kind of self-interest moved the unsettled elements in the empire. The explanation is evident in Tacitus' description of the Year of the Four Emperors. When he comes to the story of the Gallic rebellion, he must tell it in terms of tribes—a score of them, all at each other's throats. No scope, then, for grand coalitions, no possibility of appealing to mutual pride in a common history. To the present *pax Romana*, Greeks and Gauls alike compared their past.[26] They found in it memories only of squabbles and murders, rising to the dignity of an occasional armed adventure inserted between seedtime and harvest. When had there been a Greece, a Gaul, an Africa, a Spain, to undertake anything greater? Rome had never encountered such formidable unities nor were her conquests able or intended to create them. After as before Caesar's campaigns, "all Gaul was divided"—not into three, rather into thirty or a hundred clusters of kinsfolk, some large, some paltry. So also in the Greek world. Pliny (*Nat. hist.* 5.146f) could count 195 "peoples and tetrarchies" in Galatia alone. Every province was the same. Far from being a congregation of city-states, in the ecstatic vision of Aelius Aristides (to say nothing of descriptions to be found occasionally in modern writers), the empire was rather made up of thousands of tribes. Many and infinitely the more important ones had risen to an urban life. Others were only partly dissolved into an undifferentiated peasantry and others again arrested in a semibarbarous condition. They did not love their nation; there was none to love. They did not hate Rome. The horizons of Musones, Brisei, Garamantes, Bessi, Cietae, Mauri, Maratocupreni, Tencteri, and the rest whose strange names have appeared in this chapter surely reached no further than their neighbors' inviting fields, cattle, and houses. For a moment, in 68 to 70, and once more for good, when the Antonine peace had declined into general disorder, their foreign policy emerged. It was nothing but pillage. It has been mistaken for something more because, under the *pax Romana*, warlike energies were necessarily and by definition anti-Roman. But war may be only an expression of culture at a certain level, an expression of an indivisible way of life. As natural for circumcellions to fight with harvest staves as for the Bagaudae to use reaping hooks, or Arabs, bows; as natural for circumcellions to choose the weapons they did as it was inevitable that they should draw their name from the rural shrines they haunted, and the Bagaudae, *their* name from a Celtic root, and the sheiks of Palmyra, theirs in turn from Semitic: Odainat, Hairan, Vabalat. These figures will reappear shortly.

By declaring them enemies or outlaws, the government put into formal words the simpler wish that they would all go away, behave themselves, or die. No chance of that. The need for legislation only acknowledged how vigorous they had become, and their vigor continued unabated, ultimately transforming the world from which the insiders—the acquiescent or directing members of the dominant civilization—tried to exclude them. That is the whole point of the present chapter: to pick up the history of hostile institutions outside the Roman order as soon as it can be separately discerned, and to follow it further in its relations with that order. The hostility between the two lines of history is obvious. A group like Bulla Felix' 600 brigands, stealing into Italy in scattered bands bent on the assassination of the emperor, were as much his foes as the Marcomannic kingdom to the north. They were in the empire only physically; and Bagaudae who infested Gaul in the 280's, whose acknowledged chief laid cities under siege and minted his own coins proclaiming him IMP(ERATOR) C(AESAR) C. AMANDVS P(IVS) F(ELIX) AVG(VSTVS), constituted still more plainly a foreign power that happened also to be an internal one. In the end, their descendants broke loose from Rome entirely.

Beneath the level of political events, life of another sort went on more silently but no less fatefully. From this, too, sprang a line of descent. The Church is the supreme proof of what could develop among people who were in but not of the empire, that is, little Romanized or sunk in those classes from which nothing was expected or wanted beyond obedience. At a time when Tertullian angrily observed their names on police lists in the company of barkeeps and pickpockets, Christians had worked out their own system of government. At a time when they were officially under ban, imprisoned, beaten, tortured, and condemned to death, monasticism and vernacular literature, two inventions of extraordinary importance, had taken root in their community. And when the Church was merged in the state, its uncontrollable energies inspired more innovations, more reforms—more outlaws: heresies by the dozen, some destined to endure for centuries, even to direct the nascent independence of whole provinces in the fifth century. These were only the more obvious consequences of an origin and growth outside the Roman establishment. Others that we will call attention to as we go along, beyond what Christianity gave birth to, included the development of alien arts, alien rites of burial, and, of course, alien habits of war. Each group, sensing release, gave expression to whatever life stirred within it, whether creative or destructive, in any event characteristic.

What was characteristic of the outsiders was not necessarily opposed to Roman civilization in its entirety. Simultaneous conflict on all planes of life is rather an invention of the modern world, where warring peoples arm themselves at every point material and ideological, devise new salutes and flags, canonize new saints and scripture, exhume dead languages or bury living religions lest any taint or trace of the enemy remain among them. The fabric of Roman civilization was never ripped apart by such methodical hatreds, in part because the purpose of the rulers was more limited. They wanted taxes. They did not insist that they be imitated in every particular. For just this reason, the Anatolian farmer, who could be tithed only at the point of a sword, inscribed on his gravestone not Greek but a few crabbed phrases in Latin; the German warrior clinging to his ancestral German worships nevertheless enlisted in the emperor's armies. Anti- or un-Romanism was selective. Misfits could therefore be tolerated without serious consequences. Take for proof the attitude of contemporaries toward the hodgepodge nature of the empire's population. They recognized it, but they neither feared nor exploited it. They recognized also that classical civilization constituted a threat to minorities. The tension implied in that situation was not turned to the uses of rebellion even in the period when in fact the dominant culture had begun to break up, admitting light and freedom to the elements under its surface.

Those submerged elements responded to freedom each in its own way. No broad patterns of protest appear, no empire-wide movements; in particular, cultural energies and political energies generally operated on separate levels. The political have received principal emphasis so far, in our review of the groups that the Roman government gathered under the loose term "brigands." It was applied, we have seen, to pretenders, heretics, true bandits, and relatively backward peoples living remote from the center of the empire. The activities of all of these groups placed them beyond the reach of Roman toleration. What remain to be discussed are matters such as language and literature, arts and artifacts, costume and manners, deviating from the prevailing Roman standard. We turn next to these, using as transition the concept of nationality.

Nationes was the term applied to tribes swarming within, though most often near the edges of, the empire. It was applied also to much larger units. Men spoke of themselves as being of the Greek, Syrian, or Italic "nation," each with its stereotyped reputation: "frivolous by nature, always ready to overturn established things," "bloody-minded and ready for battle, but thick-witted," "by nature theater lovers and more willingly given to soft living than to serious undertakings." Ancient literature abounded in these crude, biased thumbnail sketches of the population of every land and of every considerable city. They are, however, less often met with in the first century than later. The same is true of the very word *natio* (ἔθνος), and of the recognition of the remarkable diversity of peoples that the Romans ruled. The explanation may lie in Stoicism. It was at its height in the early Empire, it sought to replace narrow loyalties with a sense of patriotism toward the whole universe. "The poet has said, 'Dear city of Cecrops.' Wilt thou not rather say, 'Dear city of Zeus?' " But when Marcus Aurelius wrote these lines, a change in thought had begun. The light of Stoicism was fading. His contemporary, the pagan Celsus, was reminding men to live according to their individual country's custom; Origen and Tertullian appealed to a far higher law. Battle was joined, pagan against Christian, one recalling the traditional native ways of life, the other defending a new obedience. Skirmishes continued into the fourth century. A man could be described then as being "of good character, not departing from the old. ancestral constitution." "It is right to respect the country where I was born, since this is the divine law, and to obey all her commands," added Julian. He rebuked Alexandrian converts to Christianity because, turning their backs on their glorious past, they had submitted to men "who have quite neglected their ancestral beliefs." His position, however, grows hopelessly confused. He must espouse Stoicism. It had been the creed of Marcus Aurelius whom he so much admired. But if its doctrine of universal citizenship in which the Christians would not share permitted Julian to sneer at them as mere Galileans, the same doctrine contradicted his defense of local ethnic differences. These were, he felt, divinely established. Syrians, for example, were somehow intended to be "unwarlike and soft, though at the same time intelligent, hot-tempered, vain and quick to learn." All peoples (ἔθνη) possess a distinct character; possess, moreover, their own language, their own laws. "If some presiding national god (ἐθνάρχης τις θεὸς), and under him an angel and a demon and a hero and a special class of spirits as subordinates and agents to greater powers, had not established the differences in laws and nations, tell me, whatever else has produced these?"[27]

There was no danger to the state to be feared from these differences. Julian's arguments make that perfectly clear. His contemporaries shared his sense of security. They knew what caused border raids: desire for booty; so they called raiders "brigands," and erected guard posts against them. The motives of an insurgent from inside the empire were obvious, too: him (like Gildo) they called "plunderer." Events in first century Gaul they attributed to the fault of governors in laying unbearable burdens on their subjects, and the analysis of the anonymous *De rebus bellicis* confirmed the response of Maximian to the Bagaudae. Maximian reformed the local administration; the anonymous author wrote that poverty lay at the root of both crime and sedition. In none of this reasoning (which was surely right, in its broad lines) is there the faintest recognition of nationalism. The meaning of that word, with its essential mixture of the political and the cultural, eluded Romans because it described nothing they had ever seen. Not that they were blind to the existence of different inheritances among their subject peoples. It was a commonplace of ancient thought that each *natio* had its own special character. Had *natio* meant "nation," however, in the modern sense, we would never be confronted with the incongruity of a Roman emperor defending cultural particularism. His thought, of course, carried no invitation to rebellion, nor would he have expressed it had he not sensed how harmless were its tendencies. No citizen in the realm, he knew, would advocate revolt or secession in order to worship Lug or Men or Ammon in more perfect isolation. There was no necessity. All cults were tolerated, all had their acknowledged place. Precisely Julian's argument against monotheism.

To the question of cultural diversity, Tertullian and Origen addressed themselves, as we have seen, and two other Christians besides: Tatian, around the year 175, and Bardesanes in the early third century. Both were born and became famous and active in Mesopotamia; both spoke and wrote in Greek and Syriac, and contributed enormously to the spread of their faith in the East. Tatian presented a bitter *Oration* to the Greeks, whose guest he had been for the space of some years. After reminding them that the best part of their civilization derived, by their own account, from other peoples, and that their literature, philosophy, and religion had declined into abominable corruption—this and his injunction, "Be not so hostile toward the barbarians," show some personal pique, it seems—he proceeds to a catalogue of contradictions among what various peoples believe: the Greeks, that incest is execrable, the Magi, that it is honorable, and so on. Pondering the moral disorder in the world, he inclines to the writings of the barbarians, meaning the Bible, so much older and more venerable than the oldest of Greek wisdom (*Or. ad Graecos* 1, 3f, 28f). Bardesanes, perhaps a generation later, emphasizes at greater length but in a similar catalogue how little agreement there is between Brahmins and Britons, Persians and

Medes, Jews and Gauls, on every question of right conduct. His object is to illustrate, in the first place, the ethical chaos that prevails; and in the second place, to show the power of free will in individual choice; for, he says, no matter where they live, no matter by what strange or wicked customs surrounded, Christians everywhere obey the same code.[28] Confronting a hundred forms of local worship, Julian finds them all good; confronting as many systems of law, as many views on burial, marriage, adultery, theft, and homicide, Tatian and Bardesanes reject them all for a religion rising above "nations." On only one matter are these several writers agreed, and their agreement fits naturally with their times: they take for granted the diversity unfolding among the peoples of the empire.

Though most of Tatian's dislike is reserved for the Greeks, he also met and hated "the Roman haughtiness." Bardesanes had little cause to mention his western neighbors, but in the list of things that each people does most characteristically he gives it as the Romans' particular nature "to conquer"; and their conquests, he saw, brought an end to their subjects' native laws. Still another Mesopotamian knew the Romans and had some scarifying comments to make on the life lived in their capital city: Lucian. The appearance of these three men in the latter half of the second century, from a country that had earlier lain quite outside the orbit of classical letters, matches the increasing contribution from Africa in the same period—Apuleius comes to mind, and Tertullian, Fronto, Minucius Felix, and Aulus Gellius—suggesting the stir of reaction to an alien genius in widening circles from the centers of the Greco-Roman world. The western provinces, however, whose arts and laws and ways of life lay on a lower level than that of their masters, reacted with imitation; Spain and Gaul as well as Africa bred Latin writers; whereas the eastern provinces possessed cultures of great antiquity, the value of which they sensed, and which they were occasionally moved to assert against any competition, not necessarily that of Rome. Sufficient to recall the confusion of enemies attacked in the *Sibylline Oracles* (Chapter IV, above) or the Acts of the Pagan Martyrs (Chapter II). Tatian's resentment focused on the Greeks; the Egyptians' on the Greeks; the Alexandrians' on Romans and Jews; the Jews' on Romans and Greeks. A rabbi quoted earlier rebuked an admiration for the material achievements of the Romans with the answer that they did indeed build "market places to place harlots in them; baths for their own pleasure; bridges to collect toll." So much for the blessings of the *pax Romana!* But when that peace was enforced with special cruelty, in the crushing of revolts in the diaspora, Jewish leaders responded by forbidding any man among their people "to teach his son *Greek*."[29]

In the East, the emperor's enemies thus fought chiefly with words, and often fought each other. Pretenders appeared, drawing no power, however, from cultural differences that divided Romans and, let us say, Egyptians. Egyptians were quite as divided from each other. We may imagine what fellahin thought of the smooth Hellenophiles that gabbled Greek in Alexandria. One revolt did break out against Marcus Aurelius, led by the Syrian Avidius Cassius, and his own race supported him. "A law was then passed that no one should hold command over the people from whom he sprang." Nothing else is known about this measure. It soon became a dead letter. It is a unique recognition of a danger more obvious to us than to the emperors. Perhaps they were not so obtuse as they seem. Postumus and the African pretender Celsus (if his revolt really occurred) and one or two others obtained their following in the land of their origin; yet Gordian and many more did not. There is no pattern, nothing except chance. The interest of the emperors in these figures was fixed not on the point from which they took their rise—their native country—but on the point to which they aspired—the throne; and they were, by that narrow view, all the same: "robbers," in the sense that they wished to seize what was not theirs. "Mighty rulers always use the term *latrones* in speaking of those whom they slay when attempting to seize the purple."[30]

Our discussion of *latrones*, *nationes*, and pretenders may end with Odenathus. As Persian fortunes rose and Roman strength declined, the eastern areas of the empire faced a difficult choice, whether to remain loyal, to attempt independence, or to desert to the side that seemed certain to win. In the mid-third century Emesa, for example, warded off attack with a scratch force of peasants and, in its isolation and exhilaration, hailed a local dignitary first as "Augustus and Imperator," loyal junior to the true emperors, then by more subordinate titles expressing his illustrious descent and his favor with the local deity, Sol Elagabalus.[31] He was called a pretender, to be crushed as such—how we are not told, though his coins cease in 255; yet his ambiguous ambitions held out no threat to Rome, only succor to his fellow citizens. A few years later, in Palmyra, under just the same pressures—invasion at the gates, relieving armies busy on other frontiers or engaged in civil strife—and using at times the same kind of irregular troops of ill-armed volunteers, Odenathus went to war. His family had long supplied the ruling sheiks. They bore almost entirely Semitic names and their crack troops, the mounted bowmen so highly valued by Roman generals, were a specialty developed for patrol of the deserts and protection of the caravans streaming in and out of the city. There the Archers formed a sort of public association and presided at feasts and festivals in honor of the god Bel. Despite these native elements, the aristocracy looked to the East or West for importations to set off their rank. They favored tunics and himations, more often Iranian costumes such as can be seen on a relief of the 260's showing Vorod wearing a riding caftan and loose trousers, richly decorated, with a sword belt round his waist. No less than six statues of this same man lined the colonnade down the main street. He was "Procurator, ducenarius, juridicus, president of the Banquets of Bel, and argapet"—a characteristic mingling of half-understood Roman offices, Palmyrene honors, and Parthian words, Vorod being a Parthian name and argapet denoting the highest military command under Sassanian kings. Like master, like man: Odenathus, too, faced in two directions, toward Rome yet away from Rome. His family boasted senatorial rank, he himself the right to call himself Imperator granted by the grateful emperor for his triumphs over Persia; yet he added the title "King of Kings," bestowed it unauthorized on his son, spread his hand over Syria, and transmitted to his widow, Zenobia, the strength to expand still further into Cappadocia and Egypt. The latter war may have been less popular with her proper subjects than the earlier blows against Persia. It carried a direct challenge to Rome. Zenobia hoped to soften the affront. Her son continued to be called Augustus. Such aping of Roman forms, such juggling of ambitions, was possible, of course, because there was nothing of nationalism in her movement; not only possible, it was necessary in order to provide a claim and to attract a loyalty in the Roman provinces around her.[32] Like Carausius a little later, at the opposite corner of the empire, she aimed at actual independence combined with nominal obedience. Had the conditions continued in which she began her career, that much she could have secured; but in 270 Aurelian ascended the throne bent on reclaiming the insurgent parts of his realm. Zenobia's official position was attacked, her capital besieged, and after the defeat of her main army, mopping-up operations took care of the remnants of her followers whom Aurelian would call only "Syrian brigands" (SHA *Trig. tyr.* 26.1).

The triumphant emperor was a native of Sirmium, a soldier with a soldier's ways. His men gave him the nickname Hand-on-Hilt. With Decius and Claudius before him, with Probus, Diocletian, Maximian, Galerius, Jovian, and the whole line and family of Constantine and Valentinian after him, he belonged to a peculiar group whose homes all lay within the area of modern Yugoslavia and Hungary; or, to introduce the ancient name, "Their fatherland was Illyricum; and although they had little concern with liberal culture, yet seasoned in the hardships of the farm and the camp, they proved best for the state." For a century and a half, until gradually replaced in the West by other emperors (and in both East and West by great generals and semi-independent feudatories) still less concerned with "liberal culture," the Illyrians bent their rude talents and tremendous physical vitality to the salvation of Rome. They mounted the throne hand-on-hilt, even (like Diocletian) gripping the sword newly driven into the breast of a rival candidate. They died hard: collapsing from a stroke in the midst of an explosion of rage, or from the blows of the enemy on the battlefield. And they surrounded themselves with others of their kind whose ways of thought they could understand. The high offices quickly filled with Pannonians and Dalmatians, with stranger men yet, named Fullofaudes, Charietto, Balchobaudes. Our literary sources, antipathetic to almost everything for which they stood, exaggerated their barbarism.[33] Still, there is no reason to doubt that the passage of power to less traditionally Romanized persons, already demonstrated in Severan times, became more marked and fateful after the mid-third century. "The farm and the camp" formed a character new to the summits of society.

We know very well what camp environment was like. A rising tide of irregulars recruited from remote corners of the empire and beyond, importing alien manners particularly to the border provinces, has left its trace, for instance, in northern British and German forts the garrisons of which formed a large market for provincial and barbarian pottery. For such evidence we depend on what archeologists can find, often little enough; but what emerges from the earth in the shape of a broken, dirty jug handle may imply a whole range of objects and customs either intangible in their original nature or destroyed by long burial. The soldier who bought his kitchenware molded in the patterns of the Picts or Chatti would surely pick up some words of their language, some hint of their accent, some taste for their food or manner of dress or for their religious cults, and become to that extent different from the parents that bore him—if indeed his parents were not Chatti or Picts themselves. The fact would not detract from the prestige he enjoyed nor lessen the rewards for his services. Even quite minor officers received gifts of value from the emperor on their enlistment or promotion, or on the anniversaries of his reign; simple centurions could afford a handsome gravestone. In this way they could be called, not too ridiculously, patrons of the arts of the stonecutter or silversmith whose works were meant for them, and could exercise a general influence through their own tastes. Their love of showy ornament penetrated the aristocracy; so did their bad manners and ungovernable behavior. In so many details, by such routes of promotion, travel, retirement, the army of the later second, third, and fourth centuries transmitted to the whole of the empire the culture typical of its more backward regions.[34]

After conquest Illyricum was exposed to the full effect of an overwhelming civilization advancing city by city to the banks of the Danube. Its triumphs have often been described;

its defeats, too, should be noted. In the first century, native arts continued to be practiced; in the later second, third, and fourth centuries they began actually to revive—that is, on cups and vases, and funerary stelae, and in the costumes displayed on the latter, styles that had prevailed before the Romans came but had then rapidly disappeared now re-emerged.[35] This is the society and the period that bore the savior dynasties of the later Empire. The evidence comes from rural areas, as we would expect, the urban centers like Sirmium and Aquincum being more thoroughly Romanized. In the native revival both the well-to-do and the poor took part. Thus we touch on the second aspect of the Illyrian emperors' environment, the farm.

There is some reason to think that Illyricum recalled its Celtic past under the stimulation of trade contacts with provinces farther west where, on a far wider scale, throughout modern Austria, Switzerland, France, and parts of Britain, the same stirrings of pre-Roman culture were felt. The renaissance began in the maturity of the Antonine age, gathering strength over the next two centuries, spreading into Spain in the fourth, and reinforcing and mingling with the effects of barbarian infiltrations. Knowledge of this movement is gained principally from archeology. The literary evidence by itself would not be enough. Though written sources in the later Empire recount more incidents about the Druids than can be found earlier and though they contain more references to the use of the Gallic language, which obviously continued in use, nevertheless any deductions from such scattered facts could easily be challenged. What counts is rather the material remains: metal harness parts bearing opposed pairs of animal heads distorted to a purely ornamental design; wedge-shaped incisions or belt buckles forming a pattern of chevrons and circles; brooches laced with openwork whorls and swinging arabesques; flat, frontally posed stone heads of gods, their features rendered in a geometrizing fashion, their hair combed back in straight deep lines or wavy rays; above all, pottery reverting to the narrower repertoire of shapes, the decoration in bands of chevrons or lozenges or concentric circles, even the polychromy and techniques, that had prevailed in centuries before the Roman conquest.[36]

In two ways the resurgence of native culture is notable: in timing and extent. Its first signs can be detected in the mid-second century, when one would have thought the ascendancy of Roman arts and artifacts assured; its extent, though never a match for that of the steadily spreading Latin language nor for that of classicizing sculpture and the favorite motifs of Arretine and Arretine-derived ceramics, was still sufficient to carry the Celtic spirit far and wide: clear down the Danube to Illyricum, for example, where Belgic brooches have been found. In architecture, in portraiture, in stone generally, relatively little success; in pottery, great popularity; in jewelry, by the fourth century, dominance; in works in glass or silver intended for buyers of the highest class, occasional triumphs. Arts once scorned returned, nomenclature of persons and places took on a more native sound, the old gods raised their shaggy heads.[37] Though parts of the picture are confused, and many details of origin and diffusion quite unknown, this much is certain: the Celtic renaissance represented a perceptible and highly significant shift of cultural energy to areas and classes formerly neglected or parasitical, now rising to independence. It represented a challenge to Rome.

To the question of cause we will return shortly. At this point only one factor needs emphasis, direct barbarian influence. In Marcus Aurelius' reign, for example, as if the raids had overthrown the barriers to communication, imports from free

Germany began to be seen in Cologne. Commerce quickened over the succeeding centuries. It looked in both directions. North of the Rhine and Danube, so far even as Scandinavia, Roman manufactures had always found a market. In the late Empire they began to show features not of technique but of spirit and motif purely barbarian. At the same time, pottery, clothing, and personal ornaments of northern inspiration were being produced inside the empire by and for the barbarians established as soldiers in frontier forts or with their families in large reservations, some as far south as Italy. No doubt these products also appealed to Roman provincials. Kilns in Gaul and elsewhere turned out the very type of cooking vessel that was being made in Sweden; the embellishments carved around inscriptions in the German provinces contained exactly the elements that had been favored among the unconquered Brittones; harness fastenings bearing the names of Roman regiments were indistinguishable in other respects from such objects produced in Denmark; and brooches originating in the neighborhood of legionary camps borrowed patterns from the enemy. Graves of Burgundians who had been transplanted to Pannonia contained the tools of cobblers, wainwrights, stonecutters, and weavers, whose work (had it survived) would no doubt reveal only a partial adaptation to Roman ways. And weapons, too, were buried with their owners. That was a wholly un-Roman custom largely displaced during the first and second centuries. In the third and fourth, at sites ranging from Dorchester to Budapest, it appears with ever greater frequency, a proof that it was as warriors that many of the alien tribes were admitted into the empire under the general name of *laeti*. They should not be pictured in a bare military context. They were, at least, different from earlier auxiliary troops in being not isolated in a fortress, not paired with regiments of good Italian stock nor commanded by young Roman nobles, but permitted instead to surround themselves with the whole of their native life. *Laeti* cemeteries offer a full spectrum of men, women, and children, the very poor, the middling rich, and chieftains (as really they remained) dressed up for eternity in gaudy gold.[38]

Besides the *laeti*, various victims of the northern European folk ferment or of the emperor's arms received asylum *en masse:* 50,000 Getae, 100,000 Transdanubians, 300,000 Sarmatians, our sources tell us, settled in abandoned lands. Roman ways penetrated their lives with diminishing force. What had once been sufficient to work the full conversion of some Batavian trooper immured in garrison duties could operate only with partial success on entire peoples whose womenfolk talked daily to each other, whose children were reared in the old beliefs, whose weapons and soup pots and trace buckles and cloaks were all made for them by their own kind in their own villages. Such semimilitary, semiagricultural enclaves in the course of time diffused their influence over the countryside to no inconsiderable degree, since they were numerous and sometimes extremely large. Under Constantine, it is a fair guess that the inhabitants of the northern provinces saw in every twentieth citizen around them the example or descendant of these migrations.

Quickening barbarization inside, continued though slackening Romanization outside, combined to blur the meaning of the frontier. In proof, archaeologists are not always sure on which side originated the objects they have discovered. What is true of a brooch must be true of its owner, whether he was immigrant or native, no one could tell; and as a further, far heavier consequence, he himself hardly knew his allegiance. He could not, of course, mistake the agents of the state, nor their purpose; hence the men "who prefer to endure an indigent liberty among the barbarians rather than the harried condition of a taxpayer among the Romans" (Oros., *Hist.* 7.41). But no one in the Antonine age would have called that a real choice. What had changed was something beyond measurement in terms of interest rates, taxes, fines, or even their ultimate effects: bankruptcy and flight. If people in the earlier Empire indeed fled, it was not across the border. Afterward, from the later second century on, matters began to change. Men could aid invaders, perhaps desert to them,[39] because they appeared no different in dress, language, or arms, because, in short, there was nothing alien about them. If they waylaid travelers, as even the *laeti* did (Amm. 16.11.4), why, so did Bagaudae. They were equally brigands, they shared an equal hatred for imperial representatives. Political loyalties needed yet lacked the support of cultural loyalties.

The story of how the emperor's subjects were gradually transformed into his enemies, and mingled with them, and ate and talked and dressed like them, has still to be written. Archeologists prefer to leave the responsibility to historians; and historians, at least those in the tradition of Gibbon, continue to ruminate on texts that are, in this as in so many other regards, quite useless. Here, not the story, but at any rate the chapter headings, can be strung together. We may begin with what seems to be the simplest statement, that classical civilization, by whatever secrets extended and for centuries preserved, at length receded from the periphery of its realm. Like rocks taking visible shape under the lightening waters of an ebb tide until they emerge first shiny with its colors, then dried and nakedly themselves, so native cultures to the south of the Rhine and Danube reappeared in the later Empire—and not only in these provinces but elsewhere also: in some slight degree among the rural peoples of North Africa and in those districts of Asia Minor which had not felt the full force of Greek influence: Caria, Phrygia, Bithynia, from the mid-second century on. "As the Hellenized layer of society gradually disappeared, the past reappeared, and with it the old gods in their old shape. Along with that most antique idol of [Leucusphryene at] Prusa, we find other archaic cult forms in Heraclea . . . Popular beliefs that had hardly ever changed, and had maintained the past in its most stubborn and unaltered fashion, penetrated, through these cult forms, into official worships." The results went beyond mere survival, for which all areas of the empire offer evidence touching religion, arts, language, or costume—evidence sufficiently surprising when set against the dynamic history of Greco-Roman civilization, yet far less significant than movements of actual resurgence that we have just surveyed. The demonstration of these growing powers, however, in such various surroundings, raises new problems. Causes that seemed adequate to explain what happened in Gaul or Illyricum—migrations, wars, and the rest—cannot be extended to Phrygia or Bithynia. We must cast a wider net.[40]

Preclassical cultures were revealed when classical culture retreated. The latter made its converts in cities whose eventual decline exposed what had remained little changed and little challenged in the rural parts. Thus far, nothing that is not obvious; and no need to extend the discussion to the causes of the urban decline. As to the survival of pre-Roman life, wherever it is found, its usual though not its only home is the countryside. That fact too rests on abundant evidence. We can go further. The return of political conditions like those that had prevailed before the extensive urbanization of the eastern provinces and before the pacification of the West favored the return also of other aspects of life. For example, the violent disturbances affecting third century Gaul brought an increase in prestige, wealth, and power to the man of war, in whose grave it was as natural to place his weapons as to enrich them with the traditional hatched or openwork designs. Customs of burial and metal decoration thus went together—and went further—that is, continued to develop. Rural civilizations possessed their own active principles. The point is best illustrated by Dacia, where occupation had never entirely eradicated the older styles of burial or tastes for pottery painting and where "the traditions were taken up again after the Roman withdrawal in 271, and emerged into the open";[41] but other proofs could be drawn from the history of the Batavians and Palmyrenes who responded to their abandonment (for such it was) with the most expansive ambitions; and, to say nothing of Goths and Alans, the Jubaleni and Blemmyes thrust themselves through the chinks of Roman weakness to a certain equality, or at least respectability, as instruments of the empire's internal feuds.[42] The names of the latter two should be added to our earlier lists of a dozen tribes that quarreled and pillaged whenever they got the chance. To do so was their way of life. It is only the inadequacy of our sources that obliges us to speak of a keener veneration for their native gods among one people, a keener taste for plunder among another. It would be closer to the truth to suppose that it was the whole of Roman culture—military strength, police power, commercial enterprise, manufactures, arts, and worships—that receded, and consequently the whole of hitherto darkened cultures that could advance into the light of history. Occasionally we learn enough to reconstruct the full picture: both the jewelry and brigandage of *laeti*, the grave reliefs and rebellions of the Moors. If only unconsciously, arts and actions were equally anti-Roman.

The period of the decline offered a kind of liberation. Freedom does not always bring progress. In several regions that have been surveyed, it rather lowered life to a coarser level. Tatian, on the other hand, shaking the dust of Rome and Athens from his garments and angrily turning back to Mesopotamia, there laid the chief foundation stone of Syriac literature and Christianity through his translation of the gospels. If his example be rejected as being confined in its effects to places beyond the empire, we may turn instead to Egypt, a province incompletely Hellenized, scarcely Romanized at all, and subject to a notoriously burdensome administration which, as its demands grew heavier, took from the upper classes the purchase price of their cultural loyalty and from the lower classes the very means of livelihood. Fewer men could pay a Greek sculptor for their tombstone or a Greek schoolmaster for their children, while their peasants became involved in stricter difficulties still, and abandoned their fields. Each in his own way, rich and poor, became what we would call displaced persons. And from both types together monasticism drew the majority of its recruits. That ancient recourse of desperation, *anachoresis*, turned into asceticism; brick construction traditional for houses of the poor was adapted to the ambition of abbots; deserted army posts, temples to emperors and gods, or Pharaonic tombs were made over into the dwellings of monks; and themes indigenously Egyptian as much as those from the Greco-Roman world decorated Christian graves. A simple alphabet was developed for the Egyptian language, an achievement of immense general importance though originally intended chiefly for the service of the Church. Early Coptic writers plundered immemorial myths and stories for details to embellish hermits' biographies, producing what is often called a kind of folk literature. All this tells a tale of triumph. From the fugitives, almost the rubbish, of society, from the abandoned monuments of a shrinking civilization, something new and excellent could be constructed. It is particularly remarkable how much Coptism owed to the remote past: how much its sculpture, architecture, literature, symbolism, and superstition testify to the long memories of the fellahin; for the upper classes had certainly looked to Greece for inspiration in such matters. It was a further proof of the humble origins of the Church in Egypt that, despite the honor accorded to its men of learning, others who knew no Greek whatsoever were chosen as its heroes, even as its representatives at some ecumenical council. The famous Shenute, abbot of the White Monastery, had a little schooling, but Coptic was the language he preferred—the speech of peasants—and their needs and rights were what he defended most naturally when he exerted his weight in the neighborhood. If it would be exaggerated to call Coptism atavistic and proletarian, at least those terms point in the right direction; at least they suggest how trifling was its debt to the Greco-Roman Establishment.[43]

Elsewhere less than in Egypt, but still significantly, Christianity spoke for the lower classes. A new doctrine of social justice was elaborated in sermons mitigating the harshness of Roman law. The theory of the just price entered legislation in the fourth century. "Everywhere [the Church] stood for *caritas*, *benignitas*, and *clementia*." A new language slowly evolved, too, departing from the strict traditions of rhetoric in order to reach a wider audience, and abbots and bishops acknowledged the wisdom and equal value of the lowly, even sought their support. Athanasius' appeals to sailors of the grain fleet may be recalled, and the somewhat unwilling efforts of Ephraim and Augustine to combat heresy by churning out dozens of orthodox hymns. Their object was confessedly "to catch the attention of the humblest masses and of the ignorant and obscure, and to fasten to their memory as much as we can" (Aug., *Retractio* 1.20). The Church was no democracy, neither were the men who led it levelers. Especially after its legitimation by Constantine it reflected in its upper ranks very much the same keen sense of high and low, very much the same structure of patron and client, that prevailed in secular society; but its origins lay among the despised, its recent past among the persecuted. When it rose to the heights of imperial favor in the fourth century, it elevated with it many men, ideas, practices, and preferences which had never before enjoyed any prominence and which still retained their former character. In this sense the Church can be fairly considered a democratic force. Without its triumph, no party of the rich and leisured would have traveled from Rome to Egypt to talk to a poor peasant—but he was a hermit, a true saint; that explains the matter—nor would men trained in the elaborate rules of literature, and so entitled to the highest rewards that an undereducated age could bestow, have troubled their heads about interpreters to translate their eloquence into the obscure tongues of the natives, whether Punic, Syriac, or Coptic.[44] A still better illustration can be found in ecclesiastical art. But first, a short digression into a related subject.

While it is true that the poor, the rural and backward, even the outlawed, won recognition and a certain power through the Church, yet these advantages were not in the exclusive gift of the Church but of much greater forces instead, the nature of which there is no need to discuss here. It is an obvious feature of the empire's history that, as time went on, it granted a larger role to races and classes that would have raised Tacitus' eyebrows. To touch on only two aspects of the question: the point of view of the poor found expression in Roman law partly because of ecclesiastical sponsorship; partly also, however, for reasons totally different, resulting in a simplifying and popularizing of terminology and procedure; and from the time of Tatian and Irenaeus, that is, from the second half of the second century, the claims of provincial languages were admitted for Christians' needs, but simultaneously also for the needs of ordinary secular litigants—a significant departure from the older prejudice that Roman law must not be corrupted by translation. The Church was evidently borne along by the same currents as any other institution.[45]

One of the crucial features of the third and fourth centuries is the contribution made by the mass of the people to the culture of the aristocracy. Prose style, for example, was in Tacitus' day a matter of rhythms, rules, and ornamentation, a highly artificial form of expression from which in a thousand ways the natural and plebeian were excluded. So, too, but less completely, for Ammianus. In his work as in that of many contemporary poets and rhetors, the search for images reaches beyond the handbooks of commonplaces to gladiation and circus hunts, military parades and imperial ceremonies—in short, to just the things that made the crowd shout;[46] and on the silver dishes and ivory diptychs presented by his friends to the circle of their acquaintance—consuls, great bureaucrats and Italian landowners—those very scenes reappear, rendered sometimes in the best tradition, with delicate shading, realism, technical perfection, sometimes in harsh relief, the figures facing straight forward, their features not so much carved as drawn with deep lines. Of the two tendencies here, one is classical or Hellenistic, the other "popular" or "Roman"; and it is the latter that interests us. It can be seen more clearly in stone relief sculpture such as the frieze of Constantine's arch, where the effect is frontal and linear, the people are arranged in blocks without proper perspective, often symmetrically, almost geometrically, their poses stiff and inorganic. They are made to stand out by coarse, abrupt chiaroscuro. Experts who a generation ago defended particular theories on the origins of late antique art, whether it came from Parthia or Greece or early Rome or the northern and western provinces, have now acknowledged the truth of the whole spectrum of explanations earlier advanced and contested one by one: frontality, linear presentation, two-dimensionality, hierarchical ranking of figures, and the transformation of the real into the abstract and ornamental, all these can be discovered renascent in the empire wherever one looks, from the Severan age on.[47] Their dominance is achieved under Diocletian, whose portrait in porphyry, distrustfully clasping his Augustus colleague with one hand, his sword hilt with the other, now adorns a corner of San Marco in Venice and typifies what is sonorously termed Tetrarchic neo-primitivism. For perhaps a generation official and private art coalesced. The emperor's visage on his coins and that of some retired centurion on his tombstone were equally informed with a quality of "the folk," of artisans as opposed to artists. And if the classical regained a certain favor by the end of the fourth century, it was never again strong enough to rebuild the barriers that had divided it from the popular. The foundations of medieval and Byzantine art thus rested on a unity created (after a long, long period of duality) in the later third century.

How was this unity achieved? Was it through the influence of the Church? That suggestion returns us to our recent starting point. It can be powerfully supported.[48] Christianity was the dynamic force of the times and brought with it an aesthetic developed in humility among the folk and small craftsmen. Its power meant wealth, and wealth, patronage, to be displayed in wall paintings and mosaics and sculpture and objects of gold and silver for its service. Moreover, men whose Savior was born in a manger could not feel so sharply as pagans the inappropriateness of depicting great subjects in an unassuming, even a crude, style. In so many ways could Christianity impose an artisan art on the empire.

But these arguments prove only the participation of the Church in larger movements with which it had no causal contact at all and which must be explained in some independent way. Since a painter or sculptor without customers cannot support himself, to say nothing of founding a school of followers, clearly half of art history must lie in the study of the patron classes. Their rise or fall in the world will heighten or diminish the general influence of their favorite artists. It follows even *a priori* that the social upheavals of the third century must have been attended by corresponding changes in tastes. Illyrians assumed the leadership of the state. The Celticizing revival in their homeland has been indicated, and we might rightly expect them to commission works of a kind familiar to them, though on a larger scale than was traditional. In general, too, the military enjoyed increased prestige and wealth; hence, more business for those working in the styles that had always pleased them—more business especially in heavily garrisoned provinces; and finally, with the decline of cities, more clients whose roots lay in the countryside. These several groups encouraged men who, if it would be too scornful to call them all mere artisans, at any rate lacked the training and theme books and subservient Hellenization of artists in the earlier Empire.[49] Synchronisms between the history of taste and of different classes have never been analyzed in detail, but in broad outline they satisfactorily explain what happened to public art in the third and fourth centuries.

When semibarbarian warriors commission jewelry from a Constantinopolitan goldsmith, or city dwellers move out to the country, there to patronize the local stonecutter turned sculptor; when a farmer's son commands a garrison fort and supervises the decoration of its chapel; when a peasant writes sermons in Coptic or attends a synod in the capital—then the task of this chapter is done. The outsiders have become insiders. Their lives are merged in the total history of Rome and must be described in bigger books than this. Only a footnote remains to be added. The later emperors, despite their own origins as outsiders, strenuously resisted the participation of their enemies in the destinies of the state, hurled them back from the frontiers or, admitting them as allies perforce, forbade them (doubtless without the least effect) to marry into the older citizen body. The corruption of custom was opposed by laws recalling men to the wearing of the toga. Diocletian encouraged legists in a return to the purity of classical law, and conservative tendencies appeared in the coinage and religious policies of his reign. The Great Persecutions were the chief result. His and his successors' insistent attempts to arrest social changes fill pages of the Codes, and at the shrunken heart of the empire, as late as the early fifth century, some sluggish pulse of life still circulated, among the aristocracy's salons, the memory of Alexander, even of Nero strangely heroized, and the worship of the Pantheon. By such puzzled and pointless measures the rear guard of imperial civilization endeavored to keep their enemies at bay.[50]

✧ VII ✧

Conclusion

THE purpose of this book is to show how energies both harmonious and hostile to the Roman order appeared in a given class at a given time. As the locus of these energies moved down the social scale in the course of the first four centuries of the Empire, so the enemies of the state were, to begin with, drawn from senatorial ranks and, in the end, from peasants and barbarians. The drift of directing power outward and downward from the Roman aristocracy is well known; its corollary is the simultaneous movement of anti-Establishment impulses in the same direction. I can see no significant struggle of slave against free or poor against rich. Protest originated within whatever classes were dominant at different periods. Perhaps this is what we should expect. The French Revolution, favorite cadaver for historical dissection, offers all the signs of a narrowly internal disease, the bourgeois fomenting reforms of a system they themselves controlled. The phenomenon is typical. History, as it is not one of the semiexact, or social, sciences, does not easily accommodate theories; people, *deo gratias*, retain the right to be puzzling; but the patterns detected here seem to fit times and peoples other than Roman.

At any rate, when the story of the empire begins, it is men like Brutus who crowd the councils of the monarch, and who murder monarchy, as they think, on the Ides of March. Had Caesar been able to tell friends from foes, he would have survived that day, but they appeared identical down to the smallest detail of family and origin, of earlier careers and training, of accent and dress, of enthusiasm for a good prose style that Caesar ardently shared. A century later the descendants of this group of pro- and anti-Caesarians, somewhat mixed now with a newer nobility, were still supplying both supporters and destroyers of the throne, the two so similar that in fact many members of one allegiance—Seneca or Lucan, let us say—passed over to the other without giving up any essential belief. There have always been men who switched sides, of course; they have often insisted that it was rather the rest of the world that changed, not themselves; still, it is striking how interchangeable and ambiguous were the attitudes of the different groups in the aristocracy, how Janus-faced they were, looking toward the past, *libertas*, and senate, and at the same time toward the future, stability, and the emperor. The emperor himself often cultivated the literature that nerved his subjects to speak out, the astrology that they pursued at the risk of capital punishment, and the rhetorical exercises that extolled tyrannicide. Literature, astrology, and rhetoric, like their practitioners, were sources of possible danger to the throne. They were also characteristic to the Roman establishment. Add the old families, political marriages, and Stoicism. The operation of these latter factors, too, in the circles of the emperor's enemies, is obvious.

In sources for the history of the opposition in the first century, that is, in Tacitus above all, and Seneca, and Pliny, the dominant figures are men of high birth whose home is Italy. The making of events belongs to them even if their dearest ambition sometimes seems to be the unmaking of events and the return to an age long past, whether Cato's or Zeno's or Aristogeiton's. Succeeding generations admitted an increasing admixture of recruits to the inner circle of influence. Tacitus' family may have come from southern Gaul, Seneca's was Spanish. In the second century the very emperors were no longer exclusively Italian. Their friends—Herodes Atticus, Avidius Cassius—might be Greek or Syrian. Opening opportunities for colonials by no means guaranteed their loyalty. Herodes participated in a movement, the so-called Second Sophistic, perfectly harmless on the surface but anti-Roman in its implications, since its intent was the reassertion of Hellenism. As for Avidius Cassius, he rebelled, getting help from his countrymen. For a time thereafter an attempt was made to assign officers to provinces other than those of their birth. Events proved the precaution pointless and it was abandoned. The list of revolts and pretenders over the next two hundred years reveals no pattern of "Syria for the Syrians" or of aid given only to native sons. Not separatism but power without definition found expression as much in Herodes Atticus as in Cassius; for the first benefit of power has always been to use it as one pleases. Once a share had passed from the more generous or slackening grasp of Tacitus' like to a wider circle, it was destined to appear embodied in a thousand shapes, some harmonious with the historic aims and character of Rome, some otherwise. The provincial elite under the Antonines played on a far wider stage the same ambiguous role as the older Roman elite had played in the capital a century earlier.

Developments that gave a chance to leaders in the provinces to assert themselves worked equally in favor of once-despised classes in Italy as everywhere else. They attained wealth and influence without wholly abandoning their inheritance. A love of gaudily colored clothes, for example, slowly grew upon the upper classes, though much of the style seems to have originated among circus habitués. In the Greek East, plebeian enthusiasms for gladiation in the end infected the aristocracy.

As medical science stagnated, a scum of superstition rose to the surface: the gods could reveal cures in dreams, hence the crowds of consulars thronging the shrines of Asclepius as never before, to talk to him, and no doubt ceaselessly to each other, about their stomach disorders and arthritic joints. The number and artistry of amulets rises in the third and fourth centuries. St. Basil assumes their popularity in his congregation. "Is your boy sick? Then you search out the incantation expert, or someone who will put a charm with curious characters on it around the necks of innocent children"—such a charm, perhaps, as the encyclopedic authority of Alexander of Tralles recommended for colic, to be worn as a necklace or a ring; while at the other extremity of the empire, a Gallic peasant who got something stuck in his throat invoked his ancestral gods in Celtic in a spell duly recorded by medical handbooks: "Rub out of the throat, out of the gullet, Aisus, remove thou thyself my evil out of the throat, out of the gorge."[1]

Testimony here to the rise of popular culture into the ruling classes; testimony also to the tenacious conservatism characterizing beliefs in the supernatural. As Celtic, a language living only among the poor and the isolated, found its way into books in the form of an incantation, so the last inscriptions in Phrygian, of the third century, are predominantly curse formulas; and of a similar nature, by the third century, the development of a usable alphabet for the Egyptian tongue answered the needs of religion and its literature embodied in various hagiologies and Last Judgment scenes a great deal of the fellahin's immemorial dreads, visions, and symbols. Archeologists working with a totally different kind of evidence report parallel findings. The dominant culture of the empire exerted its strongest influence on the material plane, while unmaterial aspects such as cults and superstitions remained least affected.[2] If Romanization worked least on the unmaterial plane, it follows that an un-Roman religion, Christianity, attaining riches and power, could elevate with it to official favor the beliefs and tastes that had lain hitherto hidden away among the masses. That conclusion can in fact be confirmed through the study of such scattered subjects as late antique art, literary metaphors, and ideas of social justice.

The life that Tacitus knew because he saw it among the tenant farmers who worked his fields, or among the troops that he must surely have commanded at some time in his career, had its own force of growth needing only the stimulation of opportunity to express itself through its risen heroes: peasants chosen as abbots, freedmen become municipal councilors, the sons of barbarian irregulars clothed with high government office by that loosening of society typical of the third century and still effective in the fourth. Tacitus, however, would have insisted that Roman civilization meant something higher and narrower: the capital; more, the great within it; eloquence and philology; the Ara Pacis and the Temple of Concord. It was from this world that rules reached down to give structure to the life of the masses.

With consensus very flattering to Tacitus' smugness, modern assessments of what Rome achieved emphasize much the same things; but the distortion here is evident. What is outstanding is by definition untypical; what rules forbid does not cease to exist. No doubt illegal resorts to magic were more important to the bulk of the population than visits to publicly acknowledged divinities, even though less obvious in our sources. Relative lack of evidence proves nothing. Consider, by way of analogy, how much of today's literature and how rich a selection of material remains might be known without ever hinting at the modern popularity of gambling. Equally true of many private associations, lacking even a name, simply friends and neighbors meeting every Monday afternoon, now as then hardly the concern of historians. Inhabitants of the Roman empire were continually forming clubs of every conceivable description, despite laws that might, for all their elasticity, be at any moment invoked against them. And again, despite legislation that forbade slander or treasonous publications, the ordinary citizen told his rulers what he thought of them in furtive doggerel posted on statues or, safe in a crowd, in rhythmic shouts at the theater. This was democracy, of a sort; clubs demonstrated sociability; and superstition demonstrated religiosity—all three, aspects of popular culture, and not a whit less Roman for being actually illegal. In the later Empire, all three were admitted to a public role. Membership in associations was positively enforced; whole cities bought amulets to ward off plagues and earthquakes; and leaders of Church and state had their cause noised abroad in polemical songs or in the unison chanting of some theatrical or senatorial audience: " 'Claudius Augustus, may the gods preserve you,' said sixty times; 'Claudius Augustus, you or your like we have always desired as emperor,' said forty times."[3]

Rostovtzeff ended his incomparable *Social and Economic History of the Roman Empire* with two famous questions: "Is it possible to extend a higher civilization to the lower classes without debasing its standard and diluting its quality to the vanishing point? Is not every civilization bound to decay as soon as it begins to penetrate the masses?" The assumption behind his despair is Tacitean: there is one drop of purple—let us take that, the color of the senatorial stripe and, for Epictetus, the blazon of moral eminence—one drop of purple in a pool of water. Dilution destroys it. But, as Rostovtzeff showed better than anyone else has done, civilization is the whole pool, and all its levels possess a distinctive color. Pursuits of the lower classes forbidden by the nobility or excluded by them from what they would have defined as Roman nevertheless had their own vital principle. The unlawful and un-Roman can be kept out of history only if it is written by people of the purple stripe.

Illyricum supplies a final illustration of what I am getting at. Here (less clearly than in the Rhine provinces, to be sure) archeologists have discovered traces of decorative arts driven off the field by the competition of classicizing tastes in the first and earlier second centuries, reclaiming a part of their popularity in the late second, third, and fourth centuries, and joining other local customs and beliefs which had never been much changed to form a cultural whole. This latter was certainly un-Roman, though not in any aggressive sense of the term. Yet the same area and the same population produced the savior dynasties of the later Empire. They appeared before the middle of the third century, tightened their grip on power right through the fourth century, and over that long, long duration of crisis succeeded in keeping far more hostile and un-Roman forces than themselves at bay. Was Illyricum un-Roman, then? No more than the senate of the first century, from which came the enemies of the state as well as its chief upholders. What had occurred in the interval was a shift in the locus of energy. Its causes do not concern us here. Its effects are detectable in the increasing prominence of actors barely participant in the drama of the earlier Empire, gradually coming forward to the center of the stage. Sometimes they appeared as aberrant or destructive to the civilization in which they originated; they have then supplied the chief focus for this book; at other times they spoke, as it were, for the majority; but in either case, the broad lines of Roman and un-Roman history trace the same course.

Appendix A

Famines

What scholars of ancient history choose to write about, and choose not to write about, is equally surprising. No large percentage of the people in the Roman empire can have lived their lives through without at least once wondering where the next meal was to come from. The circumstances in which this uncertainty could exist were of desperate interest to the people of the time, yet Rostovtzeff was obliged to write in 1926, "A full collection of the evidence about famines in the Roman Empire is highly desirable" (*The Social and Economic History of the Roman Empire*[2] [1957] 600, where he offers his own valuable findings). Forty more years have passed, now, and the need still exists. What follows does not pretend to be that full collection, but should be a sufficient basis for my conclusions (see above, Chapter V).

1. It should be said at the start that there are, in epigraphic sources especially, scores of mentions of the generosity of citizens holding the office of local market superintendent or the like, some of which, if we could understand them, recall times of short supply in the city; and we learn of other acts more explicitly, where someone made food available at a low price or free, implying emergency conditions, as in *Orientis graeci inscriptiones selectae* 511, ca. A.D. 165–170; *CIL* 11.379,

ca. A.D. 175 in Italy; 8. 1648, Cirta, n.d.; 9250, Rusguniae, n.d.; and other examples in Rostovtzeff 599; L. Robert, *Etudes anatoliennes* (1937) 346f; D. Magie, *Roman Rule in Asia Minor . . .* (1950) 618f; and B. V. Head, *Historia numorum*[2] (1911) 733, 782, and 798. Difficulties may be recognized more clearly, for example, in the very high prices of *CIL* 8.25703f, Thuburnica, for which Professor Broughton, *per litteris*, suggests a date in the first century B.C. or A.D., on the basis of *AE* 1951, no. 81. Some references to real famines cannot be dated, such as *Bulletin de correspondance hellénique* 51 (1927) 97, Hatzfeld, and Rostovtzeff later, offering no comment on a five-year shortage at Panamara; E. A. T. W. Budge, *The Paradise or Garden of the Holy Fathers . . .* (1907) 1.348, Egypt sometime in the fourth century; *IGRR* 3.796 (Perga) and 4.870 (Laodicea ad Lycum), perhaps, on the basis of the names and offices mentioned, datable to the first and second centuries respectively; and *IGRR* 4.791 (Apamea, n.d.) Shortages of wine in Rome (Amm. 14.6.1., A.D. 353–355) or of oil in Stratonicea (Robert 346, in the reign of Jovian) do not really concern us; others were artificial, or soon over when the grain fleet reached Rome (Dio 73.13 and Herodian 1.12.4, A.D. 189; Amm. 19.10, A.D. 359). But Rome and, later, Constantinople were particularly vulnerable to interruptions of the convoys bringing food, and the emperor's enemies—Antonius, Vespasian, Avidius Cassius, the Gordians, Athanasius, and Gildo, to name a few—were accused or suspected of intending to embarrass him by closing off the ports of Africa or Egypt. Shortages at Rome, for obvious reasons, are reported quite fully: Dio 55.26.1, A.D. 6–8; Tac., *Ann.* 6.13, A.D. 32; Dio 60.11.1, A.D. 42; Tac., *Ann.* 12.43, and Suet., *Claud.* 18.2, A.D. 51; then Claudius turns his attention to Ostia and the *navicularii*, and three centuries follow without crisis, so far as I can discover, until A.D. 353, 357, 375–76, and 383

(H. P. Kohns, *Versorgungskrisen und Hungerrevolten* . . . [1961] 89 and 164; J. R. Martindale, *Public Disorders in the Late Roman Empire* . . . [1960] 46; J.-R. Palanque, *REA* 33 [1931] 346f). What allowance should be made for the sudden illumination afforded by Ammianus and Symmachus I cannot guess, but I presume that the third century and Constantine's reign did not pass without trials that we know nothing about. These were times of recurrent war certain to interrupt farming and transport; and effects that we might presume can be documented at least for a later time, the early fifth century, with raids and consequent famines (Idatius, *Chron.* 16, *PL* 51.877; Jerome, *Ep.* 114.1).

2. Similar considerations contaminate the evidence for Antioch, in which Libanius, Julian, John Chrysostom, and others had a special interest, in the fourth century. So we learn of a famine in 45–47 affecting Syria, Egypt, and Palestine as well as Antioch specifically (G. Downey, *A History of Antioch in Syria* [1961] 195), and then nothing until 312 (Oriental provinces generally, *ibid.* 334), A.D. 324 and 333 (of the same extent, *ibid.* 336f and 354); and at Antioch specifically, in A.D. 354, 362, and 382–384, the last-mentioned also felt in many other areas (*ibid.* 383 and 419; P. Petit, *Libanius et la vie municipale à Antioche* . . . [1955] 107 and 109f; Martindale 13). A fairer picture may be drawn of Italy, where, with a dramatic date of Titus' reign, Petronius mentions a shortage (*Cena Trimalch.* 44). A century later Marcus Aurelius sent a representative to the north to deal with shortages (*CIL* 5.1874, Concordia, A.D. 175–180; 11.377, same date, hunger at Ariminum "and the neighboring cities"; 11.5635, "frequent shortages" in Camerinum in the third quarter of the second century); another crisis hit Cemenelum apparently in the 240's (*CIL* 5.7881), and other areas thereafter in 388 and 395 (Palanque 346f). The general famine of 383 and later af-

flicted Gaul, Rhaetia, and Pannonia as well as Syria and Egypt (Kohns 161f), and Africa suffered in 170 (*CIL* 8.26121), in the first third of the third century (*Inscriptions latines de l'Algérie* 1.2145, Madaurus; *CIL* 8.15497, A.D. 225) and in 368 (Carthage: Amm. 28.1.17 and *CIL* 6.1736; P. de Jonge, *Mnemosyne*[4] 1 [1948] 73, puts the date in 371–72).

3. In the East, besides details about Antioch, we know of difficulties, perhaps not a real famine, at Corinth under Claudius (*Corinth* . . . vol. 8 pt. 2 [1931] nos. 83 and possibly 86, cited by Rostovtzeff 599), and in Judea in the later 40's (Jos., *Ant. Jud.* 20.101); under Vespasian, in Prusa and Aspendus (Dio Chrysostom, *Or.* 46.10; Philostr., *Vit. Apoll.* 1.15), at Teos sometime in the first century (*IGRR* 4.1572) and all over the eastern provinces in ca. 93. See W. M. Ramsay, *JRS* 14 (1924) 180–184, an inscription of Antioch in Pisidia, and its date, which he puts at 91–92, advanced to 93 in F. F. Abbot and A. C. Johnson, *Municipal Administration in the Roman Empire* (1926) 381, with references. Other grave shortages afflicted Lete in Macedonia (M. N. Tod, *BSA* 23 [1918–19] 73 and 77, the situation worsened by passage of an army); Sparta in 125–128 (A. M. Woodward, *BSA* 27 [1925–26] 228 and 230); Koila in the Thracian Chersonese (*Forschungen in Ephesos* [1923] III 134); in Prusias in the second century (*IGRR* 3.69), Termessus in the late second century (*Tituli Asiae minoris* 3.4 and 62), and Phrygia and Ephesus under Marcus Aurelius (P. LeBas and W. H. Waddington, *Inscriptions grecques et latines* . . . [1870] 1192; *Forschungen in Ephesos* 3.117). In the third century, Philadelphia and Prusias suffered (*IGRR* 3.60, A.D. 215; 3.1423; 4.1631); in 368, Cappadocia (Basil, *Homil.* 8 *In famem*), in 372–73, Edessa (Soz., *Hist. eccl.* 3.16; Pallad., *Hist. Laus.* 101 [*PG* 34.1206]), in 409, Constantinople (Martindale 24).

4. At Lete, Antioch, and elsewhere, shortages were created

by the sudden appearance of large numbers of troops (above, on Lete; Rostovtzeff 600f; Petit 107 and 115; on the general effect of armies in passages, R. MacMullen, *Soldier and Civilian in the Later Roman Empire* [1963] 85f, with references), who not only consumed reserves but forced up prices for miles around. The point emerges most clearly from the preface to Diocletian's price edict. More often, the cause of short supply was bad weather, specified in the evidence for Pisidian Antioch, Antioch in Syria, and such: a severe winter, excessive rains, or drought—the last forming an image of the end of the world in people's minds (above, Chap. IV at n. 24). Descriptions survive: by Philostratus, for one (*Vit. Apoll.* 1.15), telling us how Apollonius at Aspendus "found nothing but vetch on sale in the market, and the citizens were feeding on this and on anything else they could get; for the rich (οἱ δυνατοί) had shut up all the grain and were holding it for export from the country." Galen (ed. Kühn) 6.749f, cited by F. Millar, *A Study of Cassius Dio* [1964] 174n2), referring to recent prolonged shortages "among many of the peoples subject to the Romans," and the diseases resulting therefrom, records how "those who lived in cities, according to their habit of storing up in the summer sufficient food to last through the whole next year, took all the wheat from the fields, along with the barley, beans, and lentils, and left the peasants the other leguminous crops which they call 'pulses,' though they also took a good deal of those too to the city. The country folk, finishing what was left over the winter, had to make do with an unwholesome diet throughout the summer, eating shoots and suckers of trees and bushes, and bulbs and roots of unwholesome plants." By the end of the spring, many, and by the end of the summer, almost all had developed various diseases, and many died. The connection between poor diet and disease is clear in the description of the famine at Edessa (see references above), where the ascetic Ephraim, persuading the rich to give him money, spent it on a 300-bed hospital set up with partitions in the public porticoes. Here for a year he cared for the casualties of starvation.

Appendix B

Brigandage

1. Bands of robbers living on the countryside were usually referred to as *latrones* (ληϛταί), sometimes by other names. See A. Alföldi, *Archeologiai ertesitö*[3] 2 (1941) 41, and R. MacMullen, *Revue internationale des droits de l'antiquite*[3] 10 (1963) 223. But the word *latro* was applied also to types of men not discussed here: pretenders to the throne (*ibid.* 221–224 and *Dizionario epigrafico di antichita romane*, ed. E. de Ruggiero [1895] s.v. *Latrones*—the valuable article of 1946 by R. de Ruggiero and G. Barbieri, cited below as De R.-B, pp. 464f). It applied also to individuals, as opposed to groups, who broke into buildings and stole (*Ephemeris epigraphica* 5.623, Sicca Veneris in the early fourth century; SHA *Max. et Balb.* 10.8, riots in Rome giving opportunity to plundering by *latrones; Cod. Just.* 4.65.1, A.D. 213, and 4.34.1, A.D. 234, laws against housebreakers), and to barbarian raiders across the Rhine and Danube. Pausanias (10.34.5), for example, mentions "an army of bandits called the Costoboci" who entered Greece under Marcus Aurelius; Ammianus (16.10.20) tells of the plundering of Moesia and Pannonia in 357 by Sarmatians, *latrocinandi peritissimum genus* (cf. De R.–B. 464 and Alföldi 40f, on Commodus' forts built to repel *latrunculi*, and J. Fitz, *Klio* 39 [1961] 199f, on the date and area of these attacks).

Brigands, being endemic in the ancient world, naturally made a place for themselves in its culture, giving their name to a kind of chess game (Martial 7.72.8; cf. 14.7), and supplying incidents to several books of Apuleius' *Metamorphoses.* They were favorite figures of the Hellenistic novel, as P. A. Mackay points out, *Greece and Rome* 10 (1963) 148f, and offered to Cyprian (*Ep.* 68.3.3) an easily intelligible analogy: imagine, he says, "if some hostel on the road began to be occupied and held by brigands, so that anyone who came in would be caught in any enemy ambush."

2. Continual efforts were made to keep brigandage in check. Not long after the conquest of a province, arms and armor were rounded up and confiscated—this, at any rate, was done in Egypt under Tiberius, and yielded an enormous haul (Philo, *In Flacc.* 92f, saying that the rural Egyptians "had often revolted and were suspected of revolutionary aims"; cf. partial disarming of Gaul by Tiberius, *Cambridge Ancient History* 10 (1952) 645n1, and of Britain in 47, Tac., *Ann.* 12.31). To some *lex Iulia* (Augustan?) forbidding people to keep other than weapons of defense or of the chase in their homes (*Dig.* 48.6.1 and 11) other laws were added, prohibiting the arming of one's servants (*Dig.* 48.6.3.1, Marcian), or generally forbidding civilians to make or bear arms. See Synesius, *Ep.* 107, and C. Lécrivain, *Mél.Rome* 10 (1890) 268. Because rural crime often consisted of the theft of cattle, laws were directed generally at "rustlers," *abiegi* or *abactores* (Dig. 47.8.2.21; 47.14.1 and 3—texts of Ulpian and Callistratus referring to edicts of Trajan and Hadrian), those terms sometimes used synonymously with *latrones* (*Cod. Theod.* 9.30.2), who, in the fourth century, were to be suppressed by measures to deprive them of their means of swift attack. Persons below the rank of decurion, and who were not swine

collectors, were forbidden to ride or own horses in southern Italy (*Cod. Theod.* 9.30.1–5, A.D. 364–399). *Latrones* were thus demobilized and disarmed—at least, in theory.

3. Permission to bear arms in self-defense took account of individual efforts such as those of the slaves and farmers of Pamphylia "who were experienced in constant fighting against the neighboring brigands" (Zos. 5.15.8, A.D. 399), or of the future emperor Maximinus in Thrace who headed a band of youths to ambush brigands and to rescue their captives (SHA *Maximini* 2.1). In the same province, σαλτυάριοι were found, private guards of *saltus* (large estates), as also in Italy, Africa, and Noricum. See M. Rostovtzeff, *Philologus* 64 (1905) 301. The laws accepted their existence and aid (for *Digest* texts, *ibid.* 298). Eastern and presumably also western townships sent guards on the round of their territory, which might include publicly owned estates—hence municipal *saltuarii* as well as private ones—but the more common titles for rural constables were irenarchs (as within cities, too; see App. A), mountain, country, and night wardens, or the like. For irenarchs patrolling the country, see D. Magie, *Roman Rule in Asia Minor* . . . (1950) 647, 1514f; I. Lévy, *REG* 12 (1899) 287f; L. Robert, *Etudes anatoliennes* (1937) 105, an irenarch τῶν ἄνω κωμῶν τοῦ Δρομοῦ of Termessus; *Dig.* 48.3.6.1, telling us that Antoninus Pius when proconsul of Asia "declared by edict that irenarchs, when they captured brigands, should question them about their associates and about those who sheltered them." On *paraphylakes*, specified as standing guard in the villages or rural areas, accompanied by little squads of young men, διωγμῖται, ἱπποκόμοι, νεανίσκοι, ὀροφυλακήσαντες, and παραφυλακῖται, even "killed by brigands," as one second or third century inscription of Hadrianopolis says, see De R.-B. 462; Magie 1515f; Lévy 284 and 288; and Robert 102–108. The

orophylakes, apparently mountain, and not border, guards (L. and J. Robert, *La Carie* 2 [1954] 42n8) seem to have differed from the *saltuarii* in their duties (Magie 1516, vs. Rostovtzeff 302f). One of them, too, was "killed by brigands" (Rostovtzeff 302f, ca. A.D. 201). A third municipal magistrate who fell victim of his duties was a fourth century decurion in Syria (R. Mouterde, *Syria* 6 [1925] 243f) and other similar deaths are recorded from elsewhere in both eastern and western provinces (Robert, *Etudes anatoliennes* 96f, 102; De R.-B. 461f, with inscriptions of Spain, Dacia, Dalmatia, Moesia, Gaul, and Germany, where datable, belonging to the second and third centuries). Danger was greater or less according to the times or place. An outbreak of crime would require the organization of posses—the λῃστοπιασταί of third century Egypt (BGU 325; *Papyri fiorentini: Documenti pubblici e privati dell'età romana e bizantina*, ed. D. Comparetti and G. Vitelli [1905–1915] 2), the "brigand searches" of Libanius' day (*Or.* 18.104; 25.43), the "country commanders" of various inscriptions from Asia Minor (Lévy 283; Magie 1510). John Chrysostom remarks on precautions taken along the road east from Palestine, for the protection of which the magistrates of the cities drew strong men from the countryside to serve with slings, arrows, and armor, under appointed officers, even including night guards as well, "a check upon the attacks of malefactors" (*Ad Stagirium* 6=*PG* 47.458, A.D. 380; cf. *Homil. in Act.* 26.4, Constantinople, referring to times "when we are obliged to go out into the country or to an all-night watch"; on equipment and arms of such police, see the description of those carried by a mountain guard in Robert, *Etudes anatoliennes* 102). In Egypt, irenarchs of Oxyrhynchus reported their findings on "the assault of certain people of the village of Tychinphagi against those of the hamlet of Ptol . . ." (P. Oxy. 2233, A.D. 350), and other officials of Antinoopolis on a criminal charge of "complicity with brigands," the defendant speaking only Coptic and needing the aid of an interpreter. A *stationarius* figures in the investigation (P. Ant. 87, late third century). Rural police in the late Empire abused their power and fell under the control of big landowners (Robert, *Etudes anatoliennes* 104; R. MacMullen, *Soldier and Civilian in the Later Roman Empire* [1963] 139). Till then, they had been subject to the authority of municipal senates or of nome-*strategi* in Egypt, in turn under the prefect (P. Oxy. 1408), or under the governors of other provinces, shown acting in Tiberius' reign, "rounding up brigands" (Dio 54.12.1), or directed generally to suppress brigandage (*Dig.* 1.18.13 pr., Ulpian). A special order went out for this purpose to the *defensores* of cities in 392 (*Cod. Theod.* 1.29.8 = *Cod. Just.* 1.55.6).

4. Governors could draw on the military resources of their provinces for help, and no doubt local troop commanders often acted on their own initiative. The most usual way in which soldiers were employed to discourage or combat brigandage was through the posting of a *statio*, a small detachment of *stationarii.* In Italy, in the wake of civil wars, "numerous highwaymen went about openly with swords at their belts, ostensibly for self-defense . . . Augustus therefore stationed guard posts in the worst places to check highwaymen" (Suet., *Aug.* 32.1; their number increased by Tiberius, Suet., *Tib.* 37.1). After more civil wars of the 190's, "military guard posts were allotted to the pursuit of brigands in all provinces" (Tert., *Apol.* 2.8; on the passage, see G. Charles Picard, *La Civilisation de l'Afrique romaine* [1959] 385). *Stationarii* are known to us from many inscriptions. See above, Chap. V n. 3; and to MacMullen, *Soldier and Civilian* 55f, add Lévy, *REG* 12 (1899) 286; T. R. S. Broughton in *An Economic Survey of Ancient Rome*, ed. T. Frank, 4 (1938)

868; S. J. De Laet, *Portorium* (1949) 139, discussing *CIL* 13.5010 and 6211, the *praef. latrociniis arcendis*, *praef. Bin . . . praef. stationibus*, De Laet and De R.-B. 463 taking the post to be a municipal one, though I incline to doubt that. And further, we have a picture of a *stationarius* in a third century Lycian relief. See De R.-B. 462 and L. Robert, *Villes d'Asie Mineure*[2] (1962) 323. The person there shown is honored for "having killed many brigands with his own hand." Soldiers assigned to patrol rural areas, *regiones*, sometimes took their title from that duty: *regionarii*. See MacMullen, *Soldier and Civilian* 55; Lévy 286; A. Betz, *JOAI* 35 (1943) Beiblatt col. 137, a *regionarius* at Brigetio in A.D. 210, and other mentions from the time of Septimius Severus on. H. Vetters, *JOAI* 39 (1952) Beiblatt cols. 103f, cites another at Augsburg under Aurelian. Other rural police duties fell to subofficers (*beneficiarii*) posted at crossroads, as A. von Domaszewski described them in the *Westdeutsche Zeitschrift* 21 (1902) 159 and 210f, dating them to the reign of Commodus and later. *Stationarii*, *regionarii*, and *beneficiarii* were by no means restricted to the special tasks that interest us; they attended to such other things as pursuit of runaway slaves or collection of tolls; but the arrest of brigands undoubtedly occupied them, as can be shown through scattered bits of evidence. Nothing, of course, points so surely to an encounter with brigands as to be killed or kidnapped by them, like the soldiers in Moesia under Trajan, or in Gaul in the second or third century (De R.-B. 462), or like the ἔπαρχος = prefect who "died for his country in an engagement with brigands" (Robert, *Etudes anatoliennes* 97—if the man was not rather a municipal magistrate of some sort; cf. some civilian who, near Viminacium, "died a horrible death at the hands of brigands," *AE* 1934 no. 209; the various other victims mentioned above; St. Martin captured by a band in northern Italy in the 360's, Sulp. Sev., *Vita Martin.* 5.4f; and the man *abducto a latronibus* of *CIL* 3.2544). We hear of detachments of the praetorian guard joined with sailors of the Ravenna fleet striking back against brigandage, *CIL* 11.6107, A.D. 264; more troops again sent by the emperor against the Brisei on the borders of Upper Moesia on the 170's, in H.-G. Pflaum, *Libyca* 3 (1955) 135–149. A curious title from third century Thrace records "the rounding up" of brigands—the capture, probably, though the enrolling or recruiting, as an emergency force, may possibly be meant: ὠρδινάριος ληστολογήσας in D. Zontschew, *JOAI* 32 (1940) Beiblatt cols. 89f; G. Mihailov, in *Inscr. graecae in Bulgaria* 1126, comparing SHA *Marcus Aurelius* 21.7, *latrones etiam Dalmatiae atque Dardaniae milites fecit.* Troops were used against rural criminals in various incidents of the third and fourth centuries. See Zos. 1.69.2f; under Valerian, the Termessus inscription, A. von Domaszewski, *RhM* 58 (1903) 389, and Magie 712; Oros., *Hist.* 7.25; *Paneg. vet.* 9 [12].21.3, on the Rhine and Danube under Constantine; Count Lauricius present in Isauria to suppress brigandage, in Amm. 19.13, A.D. 359, with *CIL* 3.6733, A.D. 359–361, from Cilician Antioch, telling us how "a fort for a long time previously held by brigands, and hurtful to the province, Bassidius Lauricius, *vir clarissimus,* count and governor, occupied and fortified with a garrison of soldiers, for enduring peace." Other examples of the activity of regular soldiers will appear below.

5. Cilicia, before it was taken directly under Roman rule, was the scene of a tax rebellion launched by the tribe of the Cietae, for the suppression of which Roman troops were invited in. This was in A.D. 36. By 52 the Cietae had reverted to brigandage against peasants, townspeople, merchants, and

ship masters, daring even to besiege a city and succeeding in routing the cavalry sent against them. Their forces were ultimately dissolved by the oily diplomacy of Antiochus (Tac., *Ann.* 6.41; 12.55). Several aspects of the story are characteristic: rural disorders rife before the authority of Rome was fully felt (as also in Pannonia in A.D. 8, Dio 55.34.7); rife among tribes traditionally fierce and lawless, like those in whose neighborhood brigandage later appeared (see above, for the Brisei in Moesia, and the Bessi in Thrace, noted as brigands by Strabo 7.318). In Cilicia, moreover, where the mountains come right down to the sea, robbers might easily strike at maritime towns. Hence the mention in the Termessus inscription, above, of the suppression of lawlessness "on the sea and on the land," and, in similar countryside in Thrace and Sardinia, a double history of brigandage and piracy. See the decree of a date "no doubt before Caracalla" honoring the struggle of the *strategos* of the Chersonese against "piratical banditry," in *AE* 1948 no. 201 (cf. *IGRR* 4.219, "the banditry in the Hellespont"), and the police patrol in Sardinian waters under Alexander Severus, Domaszewski, *RhM* 58 (1903) 384, with mention by Dio 55.28.1, A.D. 6, that the whole island was overrun by robbers, and governorless for some years. But Cilicia, Sardinia, and Thrace resembled each other in another essential, being all mountainous and offering safe shelter to outlaws. We find the same topography and the same social disease in Mauretania, Dalmatia, and throughout what is now southern Turkey. Robert, *Etudes anatoliennes* 96, Lévy, *REG* 12 (1899) 285, and Broughton, in *Economic Survey* 4.868, all notice the particular susceptibility of the last-mentioned area to crime.

6. The wildest tales came out of Isauria after the mid-third century. Until then, peace could be preserved there by *stati-*

ones such as the one appearing in *IGRR* 3.812. Then, under Probus, two famous outlaw bands emerged, one headed by Palfuerius, "most powerful" throughout the province, killed by the emperor; the other headed by Lydius "the Isaurian, reared in brigandage," who oppressed all Pamphylia and stood a formal siege in the captured city of Cremna until superior force overcame him (SHA *Probus* 16.4f; Zos 1.69.2f; but the pretender and "archbrigand" in the 260's, Trebellianus of Isauria, may be only an invention of SHA *Trig. tyr.* 26). By the mid-fourth century the coast cities were engaged in a regular constant war with the bandits of the inland and received support from regular imperial armies. The bandits often defeated them and maintained a hold on the roads. When pressed, they moved into Pamphylia, long immune because heavily garrisoned. Count Castricius, in one incident of the campaigns, did not trust his three legions to face the enemy, preferring to stand a siege in Seleucia until reinforcements reached him (Amm. 14.2.1–20, A.D. 353–54). Our sources fail us at this point, till the early fifth century, when Isaurians made an eruption against Phoenicia, Galilee, Palestine, and especially Jerusalem (Jerome, *Ep.* 114.1; 126.2; cf. *Cod. Just.* 3.12.8 [10] of A.D. 408, concerning interrogation of *latrones*, "especially Isaurians.").

7. In the area between Isauria and Egypt, bandits never established themselves so dangerously. Josephus, to be sure, repeatedly stresses the lawless state of Judea in the first half of the first century. In Jos., *Ant. Jud.* 16.8.347, we find brigands of Trachonitis under Augustus driven out to Arabia; in 17.5.271, a prominent rebel of the same reign is son of "an archbrigand," and, 17.8.285, "Judea then was filled with bands of robbers." A brigand arrested in 54 had been active for 20 years, (Jos., *Bell. Jud.* 2.253). Under Claudius, the

same conditions prevailed in Idumaea and Arabia, until Judea was for a while cleared of the scourge (Jos., *Ant. Jud.* 20.1.5), though it shortly recurred (*ibid.* 20.6.124; cf. 20.8.160 and 185). Further troubles do not seem to have arisen till the tumultuous 190's, when a famous outlaw, Claudius, overran Judea and Syria, and on one occasion, in the midst of the hue and cry after him, had the impudence to accost Septimius Severus himself without being recognized (Dio 75.2.4). It is possible, as M. Platnauer suggests, in his *Life and Reign of . . . Septimius Severus* (1908) 206n6, that Claudius' followers represented in some way the human flotsam of a Jewish-Samaritan feud of the preceding years. The father of the future emperor Philip about this time headed a company of brigands, presumably in Arabia (Aurel. Vict., *Epit.* 28.4), and in 369 "the Maratocupreni, a fierce race of brigands" near Apamea, circulating in the disguise of traders and soldiers, ravaged their neighborhood (Amm. 28.2.11f).

8. Fronto expected to find a bandit problem in the province of Asia in the 150's (*Ep. ad Marcum* 8 [Loeb ed. vol. 1 p. 237]; the text proves nothing about brigandage in Mauretania, despite some commentators), and the roughly contemporary *Metamorphoses* of Apuleius present a picture of widespread danger in the country around Boeotia, for example, *Metam.* 8.17, and Mackay 150. Gregory of Nyssa (*PG* 46.452) refers generally to "those who lie in wait, and robbers who trouble both land and sea" in his own day. In the period of the Gothic disturbances in 377, Thracian roads were "infested with robbers and deserters" (Basil, *Ep.* 268); runaway slaves and deserters beset the country again at the beginning of the fifth century, passing themselves off as Huns (Zos. 5.22). Other references to the Greek East, so far as they are datable, begin in the mid-second century (SHA *Marcus Aurelius* 21.7; *Inscriptions graecae in Bulgaria* 686;

De R.-B. 461; 462, on *Sylloge inscriptionum graecarum*[3] 900; and *CIL* 3.8242).

9. But the fullest information, because of papyri, comes as always from Egypt, beginning with the prefect's edict of 154 (BGU 372). He alludes to prevalent poverty and disorder, to "recent disturbances," proscriptions, and soldiers attacking the innocent. His people have wandered off from their homes in flight from liturgies or arrest; some have turned to new sources of livelihood but others are consorting with brigands. To all, amnesty is offered for a certain period after which, if they have not returned to their homes, they will be seized as brigands on sight. Similar conditions under Caracalla induced a similar response: a prefect's circular to the *strategi* of Heptanomia and the Arsinoite nome, reminding them of his previous letter on the same subject and now repeating, that they must "search out robbers with every care" (P. Oxy. 1408). The dislocations of the time, the crimes and police measures, appear again in *Griechische Papyri im Museum des Oberhessischen Geschichtsvereins zu Giessen*, ed. E. Kornemann, O. Eger, and P. M. Meyer (1910–1912) 40 II, and better still in BGU 159 (A.D. 216), the lament of a bankrupt fugitive from debts and liturgies who, going home in obedience to the prefect's orders, fell victim to the extortions of his old creditors. Similar situations over the next few generations must account for the brigand hunts of BGU 325, *Papiri fiorentini* 2, and P. Ant. 87, all of which have been cited above. In the fourth century, Church writers contribute information on a subject dear to their hearts, the reformed criminal, the abbot ἀπὸ λῃστῶν or the like (*PG* 21.105; MacMullen, *Aegyptus* 44 [1964] 198; *Hist. Laus.* 73, *PL* 73.1170f; cf. Sulp. Sev., *Vita Martin.* 5.6). Palladius recounts the story of two villages quarreling over the possession of lands lying between them, one village "relying on a certain arch-brigand

as a famous fighter." A monk makes peace between them, and the brigand captain leaves his band to enter a monastery (*Hist. Laus.* 52, *PG* 34.1145).

10. In western provinces, the best known outbreaks of disorder on the countryside are associated with the Bagaudae and circumcellions, discussed in Chapter VI above; and a good part of the remaining evidence has been already cited in this appendix, especially in sections 2–4. Troubles with bandits in Africa are rarely mentioned. An inscription (*CIL* 8.2728) supplies an example: the place, near Saldae, the date, about the middle of the second century. And Tac., *Hist.* 2.58, speaks of the Moors of Mauretania as "practiced in war through brigandage and pillage," and of the Garamantes as "the rich source of rapine among their neighbors" (*Hist.* 4.50). A fort erected by Commodus "between two highways, for the safety of travelers" in Numidia, *CIL* 8.2495, obviously points to our subject, too. For Germany, we have only bare mentions of *latrones* (*CIL* 13.6429; De R.-B. 462), and no more for Spain (*ibid.* 461). In Gaul, funerary inscriptions to the victims of bandits were set up (*ibid.* 462, second and third centuries, in Aquitania and Lyons), and the Alps sheltered bandits in the third century, some growing very rich on their spoils. Their descendant (like Philip the Arabian), Proculus, aspired to the throne in the 270's (SHA *Firmus, Saturninus, and Proculus* 12.1f; cf. the third century brigand victim in the Alps, *RE s.v. Legio col.* 1721). A major outbreak throughout all Gaul is recorded by Ammianus (28.2.10) for the year 369, making travel unsafe.

11. For Italy, we have Marcus Aurelius' story to his friend Fronto (*Ep.* 2.12, Loeb. ed. vol. 1 p. 150) of a ride in the country, when, "right in the road, there were a lot of sheep which were jammed in a narrow stretch, as they always are, and just four dogs and two shepherds; and one shepherd,

when he sees quite a few horsemen coming up, says to the other, 'Look at those horsemen. They're the ones who always commit the worst robberies.' " Marcus' son Commodus was plagued by a famous figure, Maternus, a deserter from the army who shortly gathered a large band together, consisting mostly of other deserters like himself (cf. *bellum desertorum*, SHA *Commodus* 16.2; "deserters who were then [187–88] in great numbers ravaging Gaul," SHA *Pescennius Niger* 3.4), but some recruited through the breaking open of jails; and this leader beset Gaul and Spain, especially Gaul, attacking even the largest cities. In answer to the formidable measures taken against him, he split up his followers into small units who infiltrated Italy, aiming at the assassination of the emperor. Disguised in the uniform of a guardsman, however, Maternus was betrayed and killed (Herodian 1.10.1–6). A few years later, Commodus was indeed assassinated, and unrest increased in the peninsula, attributed by Dio 75.2.5 to the disbanding of the praetorian guard, so that the youth of Italy "turned to brigandage and gladiation instead of the army, as before." Septimius Severus, "the enemy of brigands everywhere" (SHA *Sept. Sev.* 18.6), confronted the outcome about 206–07: Bulla Felix, an Italian with a band of 600, who plundered far and wide for two years, baffled the most vigorous attempts to end his activities, and became the center of marvelous stories of cleverness and evasion: dressing as an official to free some of his followers from jail, or sending an insolent message through a captured soldier to his masters, " 'to feed their slaves lest they turn brigand,' for he had many imperial freedmen who had been paid little or nothing at all" (Dio 77.10.1f). His mistress at length betrayed him and he died in the arena. An inscription that records "the annihilation of most savage brigands" may possibly refer to him (De R.-B. 466, on *CIL* 6.234), or perhaps to somewhat later incidents.

Appendix B

In southern Italy, pursuit of bandits is known from two other third century inscriptions (De R.-B. 463; cf. the gladiators turned brigands under Probus, Zos. 1.71.3), and, beyond the obvious implications of the evidence cited above in section 2, for mounted brigandage in the south of the peninsula in the decade after 364, we have the statement of Symmachus (*Ep.* 2.22, A.D. 382–83) that he feared to move out of the city into the countryside. *Intuta est latrociniis suburbanitas, atque ideo praestat macerari otio civitatis, quam pericula ruris incidere.*

Bibliography

Abbot, F. F., "The Theater as a Factor in Roman Politics under the Republic," *Transactions of the American Philological Association* 38 (1907) 49–56.

——— and A. C. Johnson, *Municipal Administration in the Roman Empire*, Princeton, 1926.

Aigrain, R., *L'Hagiographie: Ses sources, ses méthodes, son histoire*, Paris, 1953.

Albertario, E., "Oriente e Occidente nel diritto romano del Basso Impero," *Scritti di diritto romano in onore di Contardo Ferrini*, ed. G. G. Archi, Milan, 1946, pp. 119–137.

Alexander, P. J., "The Strength of Empire and Capital as Seen through Byzantine Eyes," *Speculum* 37 (1962) 339–357.

Alföldi, A., "The Numbering of the Victories of the Emperor Gallienus and of the Loyalty of His Legions," *Numismatic Chronicle*[5] 9 (1929) 218–279.

——— "Die Ausgestaltung des monarchischen Zeremoniells am römischen Kaiserhofe," *Mitteilungen des deutschen archäologischen Instituts*, Römische Abteilung 49 (1934) 1–118.

——— "Epigraphica IV," *Archeologiai ertesitö*[3] 2 (1941) 30–59.

——— "Rhein und Donau in der Römerzeit," *Jahresbericht der Gesellschaft Pro Vindonissa* 1948–49, pp. 5–21.

——— *A Conflict of Ideas in the Late Roman Empire: The Clash between the Senate and Valentinian I*, trans. H. Mattingly, Oxford, 1952.

——— "Der Philosoph als Zeuge der Wahrheit und sein Gegenspieler der Tyrann," *Scientiis artibusque* 1 (1958) 7–19.

Alföldy, G., "Pannoniciani augures," *Acta antiqua academiae scientiarum Hungaricae* 8 (1960) 145–164.

Allen, W., "A Minor Type of Opposition to Tiberius," *Classical Journal* 44 (1948) 203–206.

Bibliography

Amand, M., "Objets en jais d'époque romaine découverts à Tournai," *Latomus* 11 (1952) 477–483.

Anderson, J. C. G., "Paganism and Christianity in the Upper Tembris Valley," *Studies in the History and Art of the Eastern Provinces of the Roman Empire*, ed. W. M. Ramsay, Aberdeen, 1906, pp. 183–227.

Arnold, E. V., *Roman Stoicism*,[2] London, 1958.

Audollent, A., *Defixionum tabellae quotquot innotuerunt tam in Graecis Orientis quam in totius Occidentis partibus praeter Atticas in 'Corpore Inscriptionum Atticarum' editas*, Paris, 1904.

Bachelier, E., "Les Druides en Gaule romaine, II: Les Druides après la conquête," *Ogam* 11 (1959) 173–184.

Baldwin, B., "Executions under Claudius: Seneca's *Ludus de morte Claudii*," *Phoenix* 18 (1964) 39–48.

Ballanti, A., "Documenti sull'opposizione degli intellettuali a Domiziano," *Annali della Facoltà di Lettere e Filosofia della Università di Napoli* 4 (1954) 75–95.

Balsdon, J. P. V. D., "The Ides of March," *Historia* 7 (1958) 80–94.

Bardon, H., *La Littérature latine inconnue*, 2 vols., Paris, 1952 and 1956.

Bardy, G., " 'Philosophie' et 'philosophe' dans le vocabulaire chrétien des premiers siècles," *Revue d'ascétique et de mystique* 25 (1949) 97–108.

Barigazzi, A., "Note al 'De Exilio' de Telete e di Musonio," *Studi italiani di filologia classica* 34 (1962) 70–82.

Barkoczi, L., "The Population of Pannonia from Marcus Aurelius to Diocletian," *Acta archaeologica academiae scientiarum Hungaricae* 16 (1964) 257–356.

Bartelink, G. J. M., " 'Philosophie' et 'philosophe' dans quelques oeuvres de Jean Chrysostome," *Revue d'ascétique et de mystique* 36 (1960) 486–492.

Baur, P. V. C., and M. I. Rostovtzeff, *Excavations at Dura-Europus . . . Preliminary Report of the First Season of Work, Spring 1928*, New Haven, 1929.

Bayet, Jean, "Le Suicide mutuel dans la mentalité des Romains," *L'Année sociologique* 3 (1951) 35–89.

Baynes, N. H., "The Supernatural Defenders of Constantinople," *Analecta Bollandiana* 67 (1949) 165–177.

Beaujeu, J., "La Religion de la classe sénatoriale à l'époque des Antonins," *Hommages à Jean Bayet*, Collection Latomus 70, Brussels, 1964, pp. 54–75.

Behn, F., "Ein vorfränkisches Gräberfeld bei Lampertheim am Rhein," *Mainzer Zeitschrift* 30 (1935) 56–65.

Bibliography

Bell, H. I., *Jews and Christians in Egypt: The Jewish Troubles in Alexandria and the Athanasian Controversy*, London, 1924.

Beninger, E., "Spätkeltisches Schwert aus Mihovo (Krain)," *Wiener Beiträge zur Kunst- und Kulturgeschichte Asiens* 9 (1935) 35–44.

Benz, E., *Das Todesproblem in der stoïschen Philosophie*, Stuttgart, 1929.

Béranger, J., "*Tyrannus:* Notes sur la notion de tyrannie chez les Romains, particulièrement à l'époque de César et de Cicéron," *Revue des études latines* 13 (1935) 85–94.

Betz, A., "Zum Sicherheitsdienst in den Provinzen," *Jahreshefte des oesterreichischen archäologischen Instituts* 35 (1943) Beiblatt cols. 137f.

Bianchi Bandinelli, R., *Hellenistic-Byzantine Miniatures of the Iliad (Ilias Ambrosiana)*, Olten, 1955.

——— *Archeologia e cultura*, Milan, 1961.

Bickel, E., "Seneca und der Seneca-Mythos," *Das Altertum* 5 (1959) 90–100.

Bidez, J., *Vie de Porphyre, le philosophe néo-platonicien*, Ghent-Leipzig, 1913.

Birley, A. R., "The Origins of Gordian I," *Britain and Rome*, ed. M. A. Jarret and B. Dobson, Kendal, 1966.

Bloch, H., "The Pagan Revival in the West at the End of the Fourth Century," *The Conflict between Paganism and Christianity in the Fourth Century*, ed. A. Momigliano, Oxford, 1963, pp. 193–218.

Boissier, G., *L'Opposition sous les Césars*,[5] Paris, 1905.

Bonicatti, M., "Industria artistica classica e tradizioni popolari nella cultura del basso impero," *Scritti di storia dell'arte in onore di M. Salmi*, Rome, 1961, 1.35–86.

Bonner, "Magical Amulets," *Harvard Theological Review* 39 (1946) 25–53.

——— *Studies in Magical Amulets, Chiefly Graeco-Egyptian*, Univerversity of Michigan Studies 49, Ann Arbor, 1950.

Bosch, C., *Die kleinasiatischen Münzen der römischen Kaiserzeit*, vol. II pt. 1: *Einzeluntersuchungen: Bithynien*, Stuttgart, 1935.

Bouché-Leclercq, A., *L'Astrologie grecque*, Paris, 1899.

Boulanger, A., *Aelius Aristide et la sophistique dans la province d'Asie au IIe siècle de notre ère*, Bibliothèque des Ecoles françaises d'Athènes et de Rome 126, Paris, 1923.

Bousset, W., *Der Antichrist in der Ueberlieferung des Judentums, des neuen Testaments und in der alten Kirche: Ein Beitrag zur Auslesung der Apocalypse*, Göttingen, 1895.

——— "Zur Dämonologie der späteren Antike," *Archiv für Religionswissenschaft* 18 (1915) 134–173.

Brezzi, P., "L'Idea d'impero nel IV secolo," *Studi romani* 11 (1963) 265–279.

Brisset, J., *Les Idées politiques de Lucain*, Paris, 1964.

Brisson, J.-P., *Autonomisme et christianisme dans l'Afrique romaine de Septime Sévère à l'invasion vandale*, Paris, 1958.

Brown, P. R. L., "Religious Dissent in the Later Roman Empire: The Case of North Africa," *History* 46 (1961) 83–101.

Browning, R., "The Riot of A.D. 387 in Antioch: The Role of the Theatrical Claques in the Later Empire," *Journal of Roman Studies* 42 (1952) 13–20.

Bruck, E. F., "Political Ideology, Propaganda, and Public Law of the Romans: *Ius imaginum* and *consecratio imperatorum*," *Seminar* 7 (1949) 1–25.

Brunt, P. A., "The Revolt of Vindex and the Fall of Nero," *Latomus* 18 (1959) 531–559.

Buckler, W. H., "Labour Disputes in the Province of Asia," *Anatolian Studies Presented to Sir William Mitchell Ramsay*, Manchester, 1923, pp. 27–50.

Budge, E. A. T. W., *The Paradise or Garden of the Holy Fathers, being histories of the anchorites, recluses, monks, Coenobites, and ascetic fathers of the deserts of Egypt . . .*, 2 vols., London, 1907.

Buecheler, F., "Prosopographica," *Rheinisches Museum für Philologie* 63 (1908) 190–196.

Burian, J., "Zur Geschichte der nordafrikanischen einheimischen Bevölkerung in den ersten zwei Jahrhunderten u. Z.," *Studii clasice* 3 (1961) 163–174.

Burkitt, F. C., *Jewish and Christian Apocalypses*, The Schweich Lectures, 1913, London, 1914.

Busch, G., "*Fortunae resistere* in der Moral des Philosophen Seneca," *Antike und Abendland* 10 (1961) 131–154.

Cagnat, R., *L'Armée romaine d'Afrique et l'occupation militaire de l'Afrique sous les empereurs*, Paris, 1912.

Calder, W. M., "Corpus inscriptionum neo-phrygiarum," *Journal of Hellenic Studies* 31 (1911) 161–215.

——— "Philadelphia and Montanism," *Bulletin of the John Rylands Library* 7 (1922–23) 309–354.

——— "The Epigraphy of the Anatolian Heresies," *Anatolian Studies Presented to Sir William Mitchell Ramsay*, Manchester, 1923, pp. 59–91.

——— "Some Monuments of the Great Persecution," *Bulletin of the John Rylands Library* 8 (1924) 345–364.

——— "Leaves from an Anatolian Notebook," *Bulletin of the John Rylands Library* 13 (1929) 254–271.

Bibliography

Calderini, A., *I Severi: La Crisi dell'impero nel III secolo,* Storia di Roma 7, Bologna, 1949.

——— " Οἱ ἐπὶ ξένης ," *Journal of Egyptian Archaeology* 40 (1954) 19–22.

Carcopino, J., *Le Maroc antique,*[10] Paris, 1943.

——— Review of L. R. Taylor, *Party Politics in the Age of Caesar,* in *Revue des études anciennes* 53 (1951) 148–155.

——— "Un Procurateur méconnu de Néron," *Bulletin de la Société nationale des antiquaires de France* 1960, pp. 150–158.

Carter, R. E., "Saint John Chrysostom's Rhetorical Use of the Socratic Distinction between Kingship and Tyranny," *Traditio* 14 (1958) 367–371.

Caster, M., *Lucien et la pensée religieuse de son temps,* Paris, 1937.

——— *Etudes sur Alexandre ou Le Faux Prophète de Lucien,* Paris, 1938.

Castiglioni, L., "Lattanzio e le storie di Seneca padre," *Rivista di filologia e di istruzione classica*[2] 6 (1928) 454–475.

Chadwick, H., trans., *Origen, Contra Celsum,* Cambridge, Eng., 1953.

Charles Picard, G., *La Civilisation de l'Afrique romaine,* Paris, 1959.

——— "Influences étrangères et originalité dans l'art de l'Afrique romaine sous les Antonins et les Sévères," *Antike Kunst* 5 (1962) 30–41.

Chastagnol, A., *La Préfecture urbaine à Rome sous le Bas-Empire,* Paris, 1960.

Chevallier, R., "Rome et la Germanie au Ier siecle de notre ère: Problèmes de colonisation," *Latomus* 20 (1961) 35–51 and 266–280.

Chilver, G. E. F., "The Army in Politics, A.D. 68–70," *Journal of Roman Studies* 47 (1957) 29–35.

Christ, F., *Die römische Weltherrschaft in der antiken Dichtung,* Tübinger Beiträge zur Altertumswissenschaft 31, Stuttgart-Berlin, 1938.

Christ, W. von, *Geschichte der griechischen Litteratur,*[6] rev. W. Schmid and O. Stählin (I. von Müller, *Handbuch der Altertumswissenschaft,* Abt. 7), 2 vols., Munich, 1920 and 1924.

Cilento, V., "Mito e poesia nelle Enneadi di Plotino," *Les Sources de Plotin,* Fondation Hardt 5, Geneva, 1960, pp. 243–310.

Coffey, M., "Juvenal 1941–1961," *Lustrum* 8 (1963) 239–271.

Cohn, N., *The Pursuit of the Millennium,* Fairlawn, N.J., 1957.

Comfort, H., "Roman Ceramics in Spain: An Exploratory Visit," *Archivo español di arqueologia* 34 (1961) 3–17.

Corinth: Results of Excavations Conducted by the American School of Classical Studies at Athens vol. 8 pt. 2: *Latin Inscriptions,* ed. A. B. West, Cambridge, Mass., 1931.

Cramer, F. H., "Bookburning and Censorship in Ancient Rome: A Chapter from the History of Freedom of Speech," *Journal of the History of Ideas* 6 (1945) 157–196.

——— *Astrology in Roman Law and Politics*, Memoirs of the American Philosophical Society 37, Philadelphia, 1954.

Cremosnik, I., "Céramique coloriée de l'époque romaine découverte sur le territoire de Bosnie-Herzegovine," *Glasnik*[2] 15–16 (1960–61) 200–202.

Crook, J., Consilium principis: *Imperial Councils and Counsellors from Augustus to Diocletian*, Cambridge, Eng., 1955.

Cumont, F., *Alexandre d'Abonoteichos: Un Episode de l'histoire du paganisme au II*[e] *siècle de notre ère*, Mémoires couronnées de l'Académie royale de Belgique 40, Brussels, 1887.

——— "Ecrits hermétiques, II: Le Médecin Thessalus et les plantes astrales," *Revue de philologie* 42 (1918) 85–108.

——— "Astrologues romains et byzantins, I: Balbillus," *Mélanges d'archéologie et d'histoire de l'Ecole française de Rome* 37 (1918–19) 33–54.

——— "Alexandre d'Abonotichos et le néo-pythagorisme," *Revue de l'histoire des religions* 86 (1922) 202–210.

——— "La Fin du monde selon les mages occidentaux," *Revue de l'histoire des religions* 103 (1931) 29–96.

——— "L'Iniziazione di Nerone da parte di Tiridate d'Armenia," *Rivista di filologia*[2] 11 (1933) 145–154.

——— *Lux perpetua*, Paris, 1949.

Currie, H. MacL., "The Purpose of the *Apocolocyntosis*," *L'Antiquité classique* 31 (1962) 91–97.

Daicoviciu, C., and I. Nestor, "Die menschliche Gesellschaft an der Unteren Donau in vor- und nachrömischer Zeit," *Rapports du Congrès international des sciences historiques*, Stockholm, 1960, 2.117–142.

Degrassi, A., *I Fasti consolari dell'impero romano dal 30 avanti Cristo al 613 dopo Cristo*, Sussidi eruditi 3, Rome, 1952.

De Laet, S. J., *Portorium: Etude sur l'organisation douanière chez les Romains, surtout à l'époque du Haut-Empire*, Bruges, 1949.

———, J. Dhondt, and J. Nenquin, "Les *laeti* du Namurois et l'origine de la civilisation mérovingienne," *Etudes d'histoire et d'archéologie dédiées à Ferdinand Courtoy*, Namur, 1952, 1.149–172.

——— and A. Van Doorselaer, "Gräber der römischen Kaiserzeit mit Waffenbeigaben aus Belgien, den Niederlanden und dem Grossherzogtum Luxembourg," *Saalburg Jahrbuch* 20 (1962) 54–61.

——— "Romains, Celtes et Germains en Gaule septentrionale," *Diogène* 47 (1964) 89–108.

Bibliography

Delbrueck, R., "Uranius of Emesa," *Numismatic Chronicle*[6] 8 (1948) 11–29.

Delehaye, H., *Les Passions des martyrs et les genres littéraires*, Brussels, 1921.

Della Corte, M., *Case ed abitanti di Pompei*,[2] Rome, 1954.

——— "Le Iscrizione di Ercolano," *Rendiconti della Accademia di archeologia, Napoli*[2] 33 (1958) 239–308.

Diesner, H. J., "Konservative Kolonen, Sklaven und Landarbeiter im Donatistenstreit," *Forschungen und Fortschritte* 36 (1962) 214–219.

——— *Kirche und Staat im spätrömischen Reich: Aufsätze zur Spätantike und zur Geschichte der alten Kirche*, Berlin, 1964.

Diez, E., "Der provinziale Charakter der römischen Skulptur im Norikum," *Huitième Congrès international d'archéologie classique (Paris 1963): Le Rayonnement des civilisations grecque et romaine sur les cultures périphériques*, Paris, 1965, pp. 207–212.

Dmitriev, A. D., "Movement of the *latrones* as One of the Forms of the Class Struggle in the Roman Empire," *Vestnik drevnei istorii* 1951, no. 4, pp. 61–72 (in Russian).

Dodds, E. R., "Theurgy and Its Relationship to Neoplatonism," *Journal of Roman Studies* 37 (1947) 55–69.

——— "Numenius and Ammonius," *Les Sources de Plotin*, Fondation Hardt 5, Geneva, 1960, pp. 1–32.

Domaszewski, A. von, "Die Beneficiarierposten und die römischen Strassennetze," *Westdeutsche Zeitschrift* 21 (1902) 158–212.

——— "Untersuchung zur römischen Kaisergeschichte, IV: Die Piraterie im Mittelmeere unter Severus Alexander," *Rheinisches Museum für Philologie* 58 (1903) 382–390.

Dornseiff, F., "Der Märtyrer: Name und Bewertung," *Archiv für Religionswissenschaft* 22 (1923–24) 133–153.

Dörrie, H., "Ammonios, der Lehrer Plotins," *Hermes* 83 (1955) 439–477.

Downey, G., *A History of Antioch in Syria from Seleucus to the Arab Conquest*, Princeton, 1961.

Dudley, D. R., *A History of Cynicism from Diogenes to the Sixth Century A.D.*, London, 1937.

Dupont-Sommer, A., *Le Quatrième Livre des Macchabées*, Paris, 1939.

Düring, I., *Chion of Heraclea: A Novel in Letters*, Göteborg, 1951.

Dutoit, E., "Le Thème de 'la force qui se détruit elle-même' et ses variations chez quelques auteurs latins," *Revue des études latines* 14 (1936) 365–373.

Dyroff, A., "Cäsars *Anticato* und Ciceros *Cato*," *Rheinisches Museum für Philologie* 63 (1908) 587–604.

Economic Survey of Ancient Rome, An, ed. T. Frank, 6 vols., Baltimore, 1933–1940.

Eitrem, S., "Der Skorpion in Mythologie und Religionsgeschichte," *Symbolae Osloenses* 7 (1928) 53–82.

——— "Die magischen Gemmen und ihre Weihe," *Symbolae Osloenses* 19 (1939) 57–85.

——— "La Magie comme motif littéraire chez les Grecs et les Romains," *Symbolae Osloenses* 21 (1941) 39–83.

——— "La Théurgie chez les néo-platoniciens et dans les papyrus magiques," *Symbolae Osloenses* 22 (1942) 49–79.

——— *Orakel und Mysterien am Ausgang der Antike*, Albae Vigiliae, ser. II, no. 5, Zürich, 1947.

——— and L. Amundsen, "Complaint of an Assault, with Petition to the Police," *Journal of Egyptian Archaeology* 40 (1954) 30–33.

Ermoni, V., "Les Phases successives de l'erreur millénariste," *Revue des questiones historiques* 36 (1901) 353–388.

Fantecchi, E., "Monete di Carausio e Alletto del Gabinetto Numismatico di Milano," *Rivista italiana di numismatica* 61 (1959) 133–145.

Fascher, E., ΠΡΟΦΗΤΗΣ: *Ein sprach- und religionsgeschichtliche Untersuchung*, Giessen, 1927.

Festugière, A.-J., "L'Expérience religieuse du médecin Thessalos," *Revue biblique* 48 (1939) 45–77.

——— "Trois rencontres entre la Grèce et l'Inde," *Revue de l'histoire des religions* 125 (1943) 32–57.

——— *La Révélation d'Hermès Trismégiste*, 4 vols., Paris, 1944–1954.

——— *Corpus Hermeticarum*, 4 vols., Paris, 1945–1954.

——— trans., *Hermes Trismegistus: Corpus Hermeticum*, ed. A. D. Nock, 4 vols., Paris, 1945–1954.

Fitz, J., "Massnahmen zur militärischen Sicherheit von Pannonia inferior unter Commodus," *Klio* 39 (1961) 199–214.

Floriani-Squarciapino, M., "Le Sculture severiane di Leptis Magna," *Huitième Congrès international d'archéologie classique (Paris 1963): Le Rayonnement des civilisations grecque et romaine sur les cultures périphériques*, Paris, 1965, pp. 229–233.

Forschungen in Ephesos, vol. 3, Oesterreichisches archäologisches Institut, Vienna, 1923.

Fox, M. M., *The Life and Times of St. Basil the Great as Revealed in His Works*, Catholic University of America, Patristic Studies 57, Washington, 1939.

France-Lanord, A., "Une Cimetière de Lètes à Cortrat (Loiret)," *Revue archéologique* 1963, pp. 15–36.

Franchi, L., *Ricerche sull'arte di età severiana in Roma,* Seminario di Archeologia e Storia dell'Arte Greca e Romana dell'Università di Roma, Studi Miscellanei 4, Rome, 1964.

Frank, T., "Curiatius Maternus and His Tragedies," *American Journal of Philology* 58 (1937) 225–229.

Frazer, A., "The Cologne Circus Bowl: Basileus Helios and the Cosmic Hippodrome," *Essays in Memory of Karl Lehmann,* New York, 1964, pp. 105–113.

Frend, W. H. C., "The Revival of Berber Art," *Antiquity* 16 (1942) 342–352.

——— "Religion and Social Change in the Late Roman Empire," *Cambridge Journal* 2 (1949) 487–497.

——— *The Donatist Church: A Movement of Protest in Roman North Africa,* Oxford, 1952.

Friedländer, L., *Darstellungen aus der Sittengeschichte Roms in der Zeit von Augustus bis zum Ausgang der Antonine,*[10] 4 vols., Leipzig, 1922.

Fuchs, H., *Der geistige Widerstand gegen Rom in der antiken Welt,* Berlin, 1938.

Fuhrmann, M., "Die Alleinherrschaft und das Problem der Gerechtigkeit," *Gymnasium* 70 (1963) 481–514.

Fumarola, V., "Conversione e satira antiromana nel *Nigrino* di Luciano," *Parola del passato* 6 (1951) 182–207.

Gagé, J., "Le 'templum urbis' et les origines de l'idée de 'Renovatio,'" *Annuaire de l'Institut de philologie et d'histoire orientales et slaves* 4 (1936) 151–187.

——— "*Saeculum novum:* Le Millénaire de Rome et le 'templum urbis' sur les monnaies du IIIe siècle ap. J.C.," *Transactions of the International Numismatic Congress . . . London . . . 1936,* London, 1938, pp. 179–186.

——— "Commodien et le mouvement millénariste du IIIe siècle (258–262 ap. J.C.)," *Revue d'histoire et de philosophie religieuses* 41 (1961) 355–378.

Gagnière, S., and J. Granier, "L'Occupation des grottes du IIIe au Ve siècle et les invasions germaniques dans la basse vallée du Rhône," *Provence historique* 13 (1963) 225–239.

Gauckler, P., *Nécropoles puniques de Carthage,* 2 vols., Paris, 1915.

Gebhardt, O. von, *Ausgewählte Märtyreracten und andere Urkunden aus der Verfolgenzeit der christlichen Kirche,* Berlin, 1902.

Geffcken, J., "Die christlichen Martyrien," *Hermes* 45 (1910) 481–505.

——— *Der Ausgang des griechisch-römischen Heidentums,* Religionswissenschaftliche Bibliothek 6, Heidelberg, 1920.

Giancotti, F., *L'Octavia attribuita a Seneca*, Turin, 1954.
Giet, S., *Les Idées et l'action sociales de saint Basile*, Paris, 1941.
——— *L'Apocalypse et l'histoire: Etude historique sur l'Apocalypse Johannique*, Paris, 1957.
Giordano, O., "Il Millenarismo orientale alla fine del II secolo," *Helikon* 3 (1963) 328–352.
Goossens, R., "Note sur les factions du cirque à Rome," *Byzantion* 14 (1939) 205–209.
Grbic, M., "Römische Kunstschätze aus dem serbischen Donaugebiet," *Carnuntina: Vorträge beim internationalen Kongress der Altertumsforscher, Carnuntum 1955*, Graz-Cologne, 1956, pp. 78–84.
Gresseth, G. K., "The Quarrel between Lucan and Nero," *Classical Philology* 52 (1957) 24–27.
Grimal, P., "Auguste et Athénodore," *Revue des études anciennes* 47 (1945) 261–273; 48 (1946) 62–79.
——— "L'Eloge de Néron au début de la *Pharsalie* est-il ironique?" *Revue des etudes latines* 38 (1960) 296–305.
Griset, E., "Lucanea, III: L'Anticesarismo," *Rivista di studi classici 3* (1955) 56–61.
——— "Lucanea, IV: L'Elogio Neroniano," *Rivista di studi classici* 3 (1955) 134–138.
Grosse, R., *Römische Militärgeschichte von Gallienus bis zum Beginn der byzantinischen Themenverfassung*, Berlin, 1920.
Grosso, F., "La 'Vita di Apollonio di Tiana' come fonte storica," *Acme* 7 (1954) 333–532.
Grueber, H., *Coins of the Roman Republic in the British Museum*, 3 vols., London, 1910.
Grünhagen, W., *Der Schatzfund von Gross-Bodungen*, Berlin, 1954.
Hadas, M., "Roman Allusions in Rabbinic Literature," *Philological Quarterly* 8 (1929) 369–387.
——— *The Third and Fourth Books of Maccabees*, New York, 1953.
Hahn, I., "Die soziale Utopie der Spätantike," *Wissenschaftliche Zeitschrift der Martin-Luther-Universität* 11 (1962) 1357–1362.
Halkin, F., "L'*Apologie* du martyr Philéas de Thmuis (papyrus Bodmer XX) et les *Actes latins* de Philéas et Philoromus," *Analecta Bollandiana* 81 (1963) 5–27.
——— "Une Nouvelle Passion des martyrs de Pergame," *Mullus: Festschrift Theodor Klauser*, Münster, 1964, pp. 149–154.
Hammond, M., *The Augustan Principate in Theory and Practice during the Julio-Claudian Period*, Cambridge, Mass., 1933.
——— *The Antonine Monarchy*, Papers and Monographs of the American Academy in Rome 19, Rome, 1959.

Bibliography

Hammond, M., "*Res olim dissociabiles: Principatus ac libertas.* Liberty under the Early Roman Empire," *Harvard Studies in Classical Philology* 67 (1963) 93–113.

Hardie, M. H., "The Shrine of Men Askaenos at Pisidian Antioch," *Journal of Hellenic Studies* 32 (1912) 111–150.

Hardy, E. R., *Christian Egypt. Church and People: Christianity and Nationalism in the Patriarchate of Alexandria*, New York, 1952.

Harmand, L., *Un Aspect social et politique du monde romain: Le Patronat sur les collectivités publiques des origines au Bas-Empire*, Paris, 1957.

Hartke, W., *Römische Kinderkaiser: Eine Strukturanalyse römischen Denkens und Daseins*, Berlin, 1951.

Häsler, B., *Favorin, Ueber die Verbannung*, Berlin, 1935.

Hatt, J. J., *La Tombe gallo-romaine: Recherches sur les inscriptions et les monuments funéraires gallo-romains des trois premiers siècles de notre ère*, Paris, 1951.

——— *Histoire de la Gaule romaine (120 avant J.-C.–451 après J.-C.): Colonisation ou colonialisme?* Paris, 1959.

Havet, L., "La Fable du loup et du chien," *Revue des études anciennes* 23 (1921) 95–102.

Haywood, R. M., "The African Policy of Septimius Severus," *Transactions of the American Philological Association* 71 (1940) 175–185.

Head, B. V., *Historia numorum: A Manual of Greek Numismatics*,[2] Oxford, 1911.

Hendrickson, G. L., "Cicero's Correspondence with Brutus and Calvus on Oratorical Style," *American Journal of Philology* 47 (1926) 234–258.

Henry, P., "La Dernière Parole de Plotin," *Studi classici e orientali* 2 (1953) 113–130.

Herrmann, L., *Querolus (Grognon)*, Paris, 1937.

——— "Claudius Antoninus et la crise religieuse de 394 ap. J.C.," *Annuaire de l'Institut de philologie et d'histoire orientales et slaves* 10 (1950) 329–342.

——— "Néron et la mort de Perse," *Latomus* 22 (1963) 236–239.

Hirschfeld, O., *Die kaiserlichen Verwaltungsbeamten bis auf Diocletian*,[2] Berlin, 1905.

——— *Kleine Schriften*, Berlin, 1913.

Hirzl, R., "Der Selbstmord," *Archiv für Religionswissenschaft* 11 (1908) 75–104, 243–284, and 417–476.

Holl, K., "Das Fortleben der Volkssprachen in Kleinasien in nachchristlicher Zeit," *Hermes* 43 (1908) 240–254.

Holl, K., "Die Vorstellung vom Märtyrer und die Märtyrerakte in ihrer geschichtlichen Entwicklung," *Neue Jahrbücher für das klassische Altertum* 33 (1914) 521–546.

Hölscher, G., *Die Quellen des Josephus für die Zeit vom Exil bis zum jüdischen Kriege*, Leipzig, 1904.

Homo, L., *Essai sur le règne de l'empereur Aurélien (270–275)*, Bibliothèque des Ecoles françaises d'Athènes et de Rome 89, Paris, 1904.

Hopfner, T., *Griechisch-ägyptischer Offenbarungszauber*, Studien zur Paleographie und Papyruskunde 21 and 23, 2 vols., Leipzig, 1921 and 1924.

——— *Ueber die Geheimlehren von Jamblichus*, Leipzig, 1922.

——— "Apollonios von Tyana und Philostratos," *Seminar Kondakov* 4 (1931) 135–164.

Hornsby, H. M., "The Cynicism of Peregrinus Proteus," *Hermathena* 48 (1933) 65–84.

Hubeaux, J., "La Crise de la trois-cent-soixante-cinquième année," *L'Antiquité classique* 17 (1948) 343–354.

——— "L'Enfant d'un an," *Hommages à Joseph Bidez et à Franz Cumont*, Collection Latomus 2, Brussels, 1949, pp. 143–158.

——— "Saint Augustin et la crise eschatologique de la fin du IVe siècle," *Bulletin de la classe des lettres, Académie royale de Belgique* 40 (1954) 658–673.

Hubert, H., *Les Celtes depuis l'époque de la Tène*, Paris, 1932.

Ingholt, H., "Inscriptions and Sculptures from Palmyra," *Berytus* 3 (1936) 83–125.

Jal, P., "Images d'Auguste chez Sénèque," *Revue des études latines* 35 (1957) 242–264.

——— *La Guerre civile à Rome: Etude littéraire et morale*, Paris, 1963.

Jonge, P. de, "A Curious Place in Ammianus Marcellinus Dealing with Scarcity of Corn and Cornprices," *Mnemosyne*^{4} 1 (1948) 73–80 and 238–245.

Kantorowicz, E. H., "*Puer exoriens:* On the Hypapante in the Mosaics of S. Maria Maggiore," *Perennitas . . . P. Thomas Michels OSB zum 70. Geburtstag*, Münster, 1963, pp. 118–135.

Kazhdan, A. P., "On Disputed Questions in the History of the Establishment of Feudal Relationships in the Roman Empire," *Vestnik drevnei istorii* 1953, no. 3, pp. 77–106 (in Russian).

Kiechle, F., "Das Giessener Gräberfeld und die Rolle der *Regio translimitana* in der römischen Grenzpolitik," *Historia* 11 (1962) 171–191.

Kiefer, A., *Aretalogische Studien*, Leipzig, 1929.

Bibliography

Klauser, T., "Studien zur Entstehungsgeschichte der christlichen Kunst," *Jahrbuch für Antike und Christentum* 1 (1958) 20–51.

Kleberg, T., *Hôtels, restaurants et cabarets dans l'antiquité romaine: Etude historique et philologique*, Uppsala, 1957.

Klemenc, J., "Die keltischen Elemente auf den Grabdenkmälern von St. Peter im Sanntale," *Omagiu liu Constantin Daicoviciu*, Bucharest, 1960, pp. 303–310.

Klingner, F., "Tacitus und die Geschichtsschreiber des 1. Jahrhunderts," *Museum Helveticum* 15 (1958) 194–206.

Kohns, H. P., *Versorgungskrisen und Hungerrevolten im spätantiken Rom*, Antiquitas 6, Bonn, 1961.

Kollwitz, J., *Oströmische Plastik der theodosianischen Zeit*, Studien zur spätantiken Kunstgeschichte 12, Berlin, 1941.

Korver, J., "Néron et Musonius," *Mnemosyne*[4] 3 (1950) 319–329.

Kotula, T., "L'Insurrection des Gordiens et l'Afrique romaine," *Eos* 50 (1959–60) 197–211.

——— "Sources du séparatisme africain au IIIe siècle de notre ère," *Travaux de la Société des sciences et des lettres de Wroclaw*, ser. A, no. 74 (1961) 1–34.

Kovalev, S. I., "Thoughts on the Problem of the Character of the Social Revolution of the Third to the Fifth Centuries in the Western Roman Empire," *Vestnik drevnei istorii* 1954, no. 3, pp. 33–44 (in Russian).

Köves, T., "Les *vates* des Celtes," *Acta ethnographica academiae scientiarum Hungaricae* 4 (1955) 171–272.

Labriolle, P. de, *La Crise montaniste*, Paris, 1913.

Laffranchi, L., "Su alcuni problemi storico-numismatici riferentesi agli imperatori gallo-romani," *Rivista italiana di numismatica* 43 (1941) 130–140.

Lane, E. N., "A Re-study of the God Men," *Berytus* 15 (1964) 5–58.

Last, H., "Rome and the Druids," *Journal of Roman Studies* 39 (1949) 1–5.

Latte, K., *Römische Religionsgeschichte*, Handbuch der klassischen Altertumswissenschaft vol. 5, pt. 4, Munich, 1960.

Laumonier, A., *Les Cultes indigènes en Carie*, Bibliothèque des Ecoles françaises d'Athènes et de Rome 188, Paris, 1958.

Laur-Belart, R., "Keltische Elemente in der Kunst der römischen Schweiz," *Huitième Congrès international d'archéologie classique (Paris 1963): Le Rayonnement des civilisations grecque et romaine sur les cultures périphériques*, Paris, 1965, pp. 165–176.

LeBas, P., and W. H. Waddington, *Voyage archéologique en Grèce et en Asie Mineure . . . 1843 et 1844*, 7 vols., Paris, 1847–1877 (which includes the three-volume work of LeBas and Waddington, *Inscriptions grecques et latines recueillies en Grèce et en Asie Mineure*, Paris, 1870).

Lécrivain, C., "Etudes sur le Bas-Empire, III: Les Soldats privés au Bas-Empire," *Mélanges d'archéologie et d'histoire de l'Ecole française de Rome* 10 (1890) 267–283.

Leglay, M., "La Déesse Afrique à Timgad," *Hommages à Jean Bayet*, Collection Latomus 70, Brussels, 1964, pp. 374–382.

Levi, M. A., *Ottaviano capoparte: Storia politica di Roma durante le ultime lotte di supremazia*, 2 vols., Florence, 1933.

——— *Nerone e i suoi tempi*, Biblioteca storico universitaria, ser. II, no. 1, Milan, 1949.

——— "Iscrizioni relative a collegia dell'età imperiale," *Athenaeum* 41 (1963) 384–405.

Lévy, I., "Etudes sur la vie municipale de l'Asie Mineure," *Revue des études grecques* 12 (1899) 255–289.

——— *Recherches sur les sources de la légende de Pythagore*, Bibliothèque de l'Ecole des hautes études, Sciences religieuses 42, Paris, 1926.

——— *La Légende de Pythagore de Grèce en Palestine*, Bibliothèque de l'Ecole des hautes études 250, Paris, 1927.

Lewy, H., *Chaldaean Oracles and Theurgy: Mysticism, Magic, and Platonism in the Later Roman Empire*, Publications de l'Institut français d'archéologie orientale, Recherches d'archéologie, de philologie et d'histoire 13, Cairo, 1956.

Lieberman, S., "The Martyrs of Caesarea," *Annuaire de l'Institut de philologie et d'histoire orientales et slaves* 7 (1939–1944) 395–446.

Liebeschuetz, W., "Did the Pelagian Movement Have Social Aims?" *Historia* 12 (1963) 227–241.

Lopuszanski, G., "La Police romaine et les chrétiens," *L'Antiquité classique* 20 (1951) 5–46.

L'Orange, H. P., and A. von Gerkan, *Der spätantike Bildschmuck des Konstantinsbogen*, Berlin, 1939.

Luck, G., "Die Form der suetonischen Biographie und die frühen Heiligenviten," *Mullus: Festschrift Theodor Klauser*, Münster, 1964, pp. 230–241.

Lutz, C. E., "Musonius Rufus, 'The Roman Socrates,'" *Yale Classical Studies* 10 (1947) 3–147.

McAlindon, D., "Senatorial Opposition to Claudius and Nero," *American Journal of Philology* 77 (1956) 113–132.

Mackay, P. A., "KLEPHTIKA: The Tradition of the Tales of Bandits in Apuleius," *Greece and Rome*[2] 10 (1963) 147–152.

MacMullen, R., "The Emperor's Largesses," *Latomus* 21 (1962) 159–166.

Bibliography

MacMullen, R., "Barbarian Enclaves in the Northern Roman Empire," *L'Antiquité classique* 32 (1963) 552–561.

——— "A Note on Roman Strikes," *Classical Journal* 58 (1963) 269–271.

——— "The Roman Concept Robber = Pretender," *Revue internationale des droits de l'antiquité*[3] 10 (1963) 221–225.

——— *Soldier and Civilian in the Later Roman Empire*, Cambridge, Mass., 1963.

——— "Nationalism in Roman Egypt," *Aegyptus* 44 (1964) 179–199.

——— "Some Pictures in Ammianus Marcellinus," *Art Bulletin* 46 (1964) 435–455.

——— "Social Mobility and the Theodosian Code," *Journal of Roman Studies* 54 (1964) 49–53.

——— "The Celtic Renaissance," *Historia* 14 (1965) 93–104.

——— "Provincial Languages in the Roman Empire," *American Journal of Philology* 87 (1966) 1–17.

——— "A Note on *sermo humilis*," *Journal of Theological Studies* 17 (1966) 108–112.

Macrea, M., "Les Daces à l'époque romaine à la lumière des récentes fouilles archéologiques," *Dacia*[2] 1 (1957) 205–220.

Magie, D., *Roman Rule in Asia Minor to the End of the Third Century after Christ*, Princeton, 1950.

Maiuri, A., *Roman Painting*, Geneva, 1953.

——— "Pompei e Nocera," *Rendiconti della Accademia di archeologia, Napoli*[2] 33 (1958) 35–40.

Manteuffel, G. von, "Zur Prophetie in P.S.I., VIII.982," *Mélanges Maspero, 2: Orient grec, romain et byzantin*, Mémoires de l'Institut français d'archéologie orientale du Caire 67, Cairo, 1934–1937, pp. 119–124.

Marchesi, C., *Apuleio di Madaura, Della Magia*, Rome-Bologna, 1955.

Maricq, A., "Factions du cirque et partis populaires," *Bulletin de l'Académie royale de Belgique*[5] 36 (1950) 396–421.

Marti, B. M., "Seneca's *Apocolocyntosis* and *Octavia:* A Diptych," *American Journal of Philology* 73 (1952) 24–36.

Martindale, J. R., *Public Disorders in the Late Roman Empire, Their Causes and Character*, Oxford, 1960.

Martroye, F., "La Répression de la magie et le culte des gentils au IVe siècle," *Revue historique de droit français et étranger* 9 (1930) 669–701.

Marx, F. A., "Tacitus und die Literatur des 'exitus illustrium virorum,'" *Philologus* 92 (1937) 83–103.

Mattingly, H., *Coins of the Roman Empire in the British Museum*, 5 vols., London, 1923–1950.

Mattingly, H., and E. A. Sydenham, *The Roman Imperial Coinage*, London, 1923—.

——— "Fel. Temp. Reparatio," *Numismatic Chronicle*[5] 13 (1933) 182–202.

——— "EID. MAR.," *L'Antiquité classiqué* 17 (1948) 445–451.

Maurice, J., "La Terreur de la magie au IVe siècle," *Revue historique de droit français et étranger* 6 (1927) 108–120.

Mazzarino, S., "La Democratizzazione della cultura nel 'Basso Impero,'" *Rapports du XIe Congrès international des sciences historiques*, Stockholm, 1960, 2.35–54.

Mesnil du Buisson, Comte du, *Les Tesserès et les monnaies de Palmyre: Un Art, une culture et une philosophie grecs dans les moules d'une cité et d'une religion sémitiques*, Paris, 1962.

Meyer, E., "Apollonios von Tyana und die Biographie des Philostratos," *Hermes* 52 (1917) 371–424.

Millar, F., *A Study of Cassius Dio*, Oxford, 1964.

Mitteis, L., "Zur Berliner Papyruspublication," *Hermes* 30 (1895) 564–618.

Möbius, H., "M. Junius Brutus," Ἀρχαιολογικὴ ἐφημερίς 1953–54 [1961] 207–211.

Mocsy, A., "Zu den Verwüstungen der Markomannenkriege in Savaria," *Archaeologiai ertesitö* 1963, pp. 17–20.

Mogenet, J., "La Conjuration de Clemens," *L'Antiquité classique* 23 (1954) 321–330.

Momigliano, A., "Pagan and Christian Historiography in the Fourth Century A.D.," *The Conflict between Paganism and Christianity in the Fourth Century*, Oxford, 1963, pp. 79–99.

Mommsen, T., *Römisches Strafrecht*, Leipzig, 1899.

Morehart, M., "Early Sculpture at Palmyra," *Berytus* 12 (1956–57) 53–83.

Mouterde, R., "Inscriptions grecques et latines du Musée d'Adana," *Syria* 2 (1921) 280–294.

——— "Inscriptions grecques conservées à l'Institut français de Damas," *Syria* 6 (1925) 215–252.

Münzer, F., *Römische Adelsparteien und Adelsfamilien*,[2] Stuttgart, 1963.

Musurillo, H., *The Acts of the Pagan Martyrs, Acta Alexandrinorum*, Oxford, 1954.

Must, G., "A Gaulish Incantation in Marcellus of Bordeaux," *Language* 36 (1960) 193–197.

Myres, J. N. L., "Pelagius and the End of Roman Rule in Britain," *Journal of Roman Studies* 50 (1960) 21–36.

Nagy, T., "Quelques aspects de la romanisation dans la Pannonie orientale," *Huitième Congrès international d'archéologie classique*

(*Paris 1963*): *Le Rayonnement des civilisations grecque et romaine sur les cultures périphériques*, Paris, 1965, pp. 375–381.

Neill, S. C., and A. D. Nock, "Two Notes on the *Asclepius*," *Journal of Theological Studies* 26 (1925) 173–177.

Neugebauer, O., "The Chronology of Vettius Valens' *Anthologiae*," *Harvard Theological Review* 47 (1954) 65–67.

——— and H. B. Van Hoesen, "Astrological Papyri and Ostraca: Bibliographical Notes," *Proceedings of the American Philosophical Society* 108 (1964) 57–72.

Niedermeyer, H., *Ueber antike Protokoll-Literatur*, Göttingen, 1918.

Nock, A. D., "Alexander of Abonuteichos," *Classical Quarterly* 22 (1928) 160–162.

——— "Greek Magical Papyri," *Journal of Egyptian Archaeology* 15 (1929) 219–235.

——— "*A diis electa:* A Chapter in the Religious History of the Third Century," *Harvard Theological Review* 23 (1930) 251–269.

Norsa, M., and G. Vitelli, eds., *Il Papiro vaticano greco . . .*, Rome, 1931.

Nutting, H. C., "The Hero of the *Pharsalia*," *American Journal of Philology* 53 (1932) 41–52.

Oliva, P., *Pannonia and the Onset of Crisis in the Roman Empire*, Prague, 1962.

Oliver, J. H., "The Ruling Power: A Study of the Roman Empire in the Second Century after Christ through the Roman Oration of Aelius Aristides," *Transactions of the American Philosophical Society* 43 (1953) 871–1003.

Oltramare, A., *Les Origines de la diatribe romaine*, Geneva, 1926.

O'Meara, J. J., *Porphyry's Philosophy from Oracles in Augustine*, Paris, 1959.

Onorato, G. O., ed., *Iscrizioni pompeiane: La Vita pubblica*, Florence, 1957.

Oppenheim, P., *Das Mönchskleid im christlichen Altertum*, Freiburg im Breisgau, 1931.

Pack, R., "The Volatilization of Peregrinus Proteus," *American Journal of Philology* 67 (1946) 334–345.

Palanque, J.-R., "Famines à Rome à la fin du IVe siècle," *Revue des études anciennes* 33 (1931) 346–356.

Palm, J., *Rom, Römertum und Imperium in der griechischen Literatur der Kaiserzeit*, Acta regalis societatis humaniorum litterarum Lundinensis 57, Lund, 1959.

Palol de Salellas, P., "Esencia del arte hispánico de epoca visigoda: Romanismo y germanismo," Settimane di Studio del Centro Italiano di Studi sull'alto Medioeveo 3, *I Goti in Occidente*, Spoleto, 1955 [1956], pp. 65–126.

Paratore, E., *Tacito*,[2] Rome, 1962.

Pedicini, C., "Il Significato politico della escatologia di Ippolito di Roma," *Annali della Facoltà di Lettere e Filosofia della Università di Napoli* 4 (1954) 97–122.

Pekary, T., "Spätrömische Gräber in Fenekpuszta," *Archeologiai ertesitö* 82 (1955) 19–29. (German resumé, p. 29).

Pellegrino, M., *Ponzio: Vita e martirio di San Cipriano*, Alba, 1955.

Peretti, A., *La Sibilla babilonese nella propaganda ellenistica*, Biblioteca di Cultura 21, Florence, 1943.

——— *Luciano: Un Intelettuale greco contro Roma*, Florence, 1946.

Petit, P., *Libanius et la vie municipale à Antioche au IVe siècle après J.-C.*, Paris, 1955.

Pettazzoni, R., "The Gaulish Three-Faced God on Planetary Vases," *Journal of Celtic Studies* 1 (1949) 35–46.

Pflaum, H.-G., "Deux carrières équestres de Lambèse et de Zama," *Libyca* 3 (1955) 123–154.

Pfligersdorfer, G., "Lucan als Dichter des geistigen Widerstandes," *Hermes* 87 (1959) 344–377.

Picard, G. C., "L'Art religieux populaire dans l'empire romain," *L'Information d'histoire de l'art* 7 (1962) 135–142.

Pilloy, J., *Etudes sur d'anciens sépultures dans l'Aisne*, 2 vols., St. Quentin, 1895.

Platnauer, M., *The Life and Reign of the Emperor Lucius Septimius Severus*, Oxford, 1918.

Plinval, G. de, "Une Insolence de Lucain," *Latomus* 15 (1956) 512–520.

Popescu, E., "The Histrian Decree for Aba (Second Century of Our Era)," *Dacia*[2] 4 (1960) 273–296.

Preisendanz, K., et al., *Papyri graecae magicae: Die griechischen Zauberpapyri*, 2 vols., Leipzig-Berlin, 1928 and 1931.

——— "Zur synkretischen Magie im römischen Aegypten," *Akten des VIII. internationalen Kongresses für Papyrologie, Wien 1955*, Mitteilungen aus der Papyrussammlung der oesterreichischen Nationalbibliothek[2] 5, Vienna, 1956, pp. 111–125.

Protase, D., "Considérations sur la continuité des Daco-Romains en Dacie post-aurélienne à la lumière des recherches archéologiques et numismatiques," *Dacia*[2] 7 (1964) 177–193.

Questa, C., *Studi sulle fonti degli Annales di Tacito*,[2] Rome, 1963.

Rambaud, M., "L'Apologie de Pompée par Lucain au livre VII de la *Pharsalie*," *Revue des études latines* 33 (1955) 258–296.

Ramsay, A. M., "Isaurian and East-Phrygian Art in the Third and Fourth Centuries after Christ," *Studies in the History and Art of the Eastern Provinces of the Roman Empire*, ed. W. M. Ramsay, Aberdeen, 1906, pp. 3–92.

Bibliography

Ramsay, A. M., "Examples of Isaurian Art: The Screen in Isaurian Monuments," *Anatolian Studies Presented to Sir William Mitchell Ramsay*, Manchester, 1923, pp. 322–338.

Ramsay, W. M., "The Tekmoreian Guest-Friends: An Anti-Christian Society on the Imperial Estates at Pisidian Antioch," *Studies in the History and Art of the Eastern Provinces of the Roman Empire*, Aberdeen, 1906, pp. 305–377.

——— "The Tekmoreian Guest-Friends," *Journal of Hellenic Studies* 32 (1912) 151–170.

——— "Studies in the Roman Province Galatia, VI: Some Inscriptions of colonia Caesarea Antiochea," *Journal of Roman Studies* 14 (1924) 172–205.

Rees, B. R., "Popular Religion in Graeco-Roman Egypt, II: The Transition to Christianity," *Journal of Egyptian Archaeology* 36 (1950) 86–100.

Reitzenstein, R., *Hellenistische Wundererzählungen*, Leipzig, 1906.

Riccobono, S., et al., *Fontes iuris Romani antejustiniani in usum scholarum*,[2] 3 vols., Florence, 1940–1943.

Richmond, I. A., and C. E. Stevens, "The Land-Register of Arausio," *Journal of Roman Studies* 32 (1942) 65–77.

Richter, W., "Römische Zeitgeschichte und innere Emigration," *Gymnasium* 68 (1961) 286–315.

Robert, L., "Etudes d'épigraphie grecque," *Revue de philologie* 56 (1930) 25–60.

——— *Etudes anatoliennes*, Paris, 1937.

——— *Les Gladiateurs dans l'Orient grec*, Bibliothèque de l'Ecole des hautes études 278, Paris, 1940.

——— and J. Robert, *La Carie: Histoire et géographie historique, avec le recueil des inscriptions antiques, II: Le Plateau de Tabai et ses environs*, Paris, 1954.

——— *Villes d'Asie Mineure: Etudes de géographie ancienne*,[2] Paris, 1962.

Roberts, C. H., "Literature and Society in the Papyri," *Museum Helveticum* 10 (1953) 264–270.

Rodenwaldt, G., "Zeus Bronton," *Jahrbuch des deutschen archäologischen Instituts* 34 (1919) 77–86.

——— "Zur Kunstgeschichte der Jahre 220 bis 270," *Jahrbuch des deutschen archäologischen Instituts* 51 (1936) 82–113.

Rogers, R. S., "A Group of Domitianic Treason-Trials," *Classical Philology* 55 (1960) 19–23.

Romanelli, P., "Le Iscrizioni volubilitane dei Baquati e i rapporti di Roma con le tribù indigene dell'Africa," *Hommages à Albert Grenier*, Collection Latomus 58, Brussels, 1962, pp. 1347–1366.

Ronconi, A., *Da Lucrezio a Tacito*, Messina, 1950.

Rostovtzeff, M., "Die Domänenpolizei in dem römischen Kaiserreiche," *Philologus* 64 (1905) 297–307.

——— *The Social and Economic History of the Roman Empire*,[2] rev. P. M. Frazer, 2 vols., Oxford, 1957.

Roussel, P., and F. de Visscher, "Les Inscriptions du temple de Dmeir," *Syria* 23 (1942–43) 173–200.

Rowley, H. H., *The Relevance of Apocalyptic: A Study of Jewish and Christian Apocalypses from Daniel to the Revelation*,[2] New York, [1955].

Sági, K., "Die spätrömische Bevölkerung der Umgebung von Keszthely," *Acta archaeologica academiae scientiarum Hungaricae* 12 (1960) 187–256.

Ste. Croix, G. E. M. de, "Why Were the Early Christians Persecuted?" *Past and Present* 26 (1963) 6–38.

Sander, E., "Die Germanisierung des römischen Heeres," *Historische Zeitschrift* 160 (1939) 1–34.

Sanford, E. M., "Contrasting Views of the Roman Empire," *American Journal of Philology* 58 (1937) 437–456.

Saumagne, C., "La 'Passion' de Thrasea," *Revue des études latines* 33 (1955) 241–257.

Scarpat, G., *Parrhesia: Storia del termine e delle sue traduzioni in Latino*, Brescia, 1964.

Schede, M., "Inschriften aus Kleinasien," *Mitteilungen des deutschen archäologischen Instituts*, Athenische Abteilung 36 (1911) 97–104.

Schefold, K., *Die Bildnisse der antiken Dichter, Redner und Denker*, Basel, 1943.

Schepelern, W., *Der Montanismus und die phrygischen Kulte*, trans. W. Baur, Tübingen, 1929.

Schlumberger, G., "Amulettes byzantines anciennes destinées à combattre les maléfices et maladies," *Revue des études grecques* 5 (1892) 73–93.

Schmidt, W., *De ultimis morientium verbis*, Marburg, 1914.

Schnayder, G., "De infenso alienigenarum in Romanos animo, I," *Eos* 30 (1927) 113–149.

Schober, A., "Zur Entstehung und Bedeutung der provinzial-römischen Kunst," *Jahreshefte des oesterreichischen archäologischen Instituts* 26 (1930) 9–52.

Schönberger, O., "Zu Lucan: Ein Nachtrag," *Hermes* 86 (1958) 230–239.

Schoppa, H., *Die Kunst der Romerzeit in Gallien, Germanien und Brittanien*, Munich, 1957.

Schulz, F., *History of Roman Legal Science*, Oxford, 1946.

Schwarte, K. H., "Das angebliche Christengesetz des Septimius Severus," *Historia* 12 (1963) 185–208.

Schweitzer, B., *Die spätantiken Grundlagen der mittelalterlichen Kunst*, Leipziger Universitätsreden 16, Leipzig, 1949.

Schwinge, E.-R., "*Festinata mors:* Zum Ende des taciteischen *Agricola,*" *Rheinisches Museum* 106 (1963) 363–378.

Scott, W., "The Last Sibylline Oracle of Alexandria," *Classical Quarterly* 9 (1915) 144–166 and 207–228; 10 (1916) 7–16.

——— *Hermetica, the Ancient Greek and Latin Writings which contain religious or philosophic teachings ascribed to Hermes Trismegistus*, 4 vols., Oxford, 1924–1936.

Scramuzza, V. M., *The Emperor Claudius,* Harvard Historical Studies 44, Cambridge, Mass., 1940.

Sedlmayr, H., "*Ars humilis* in der Spätantike," *Perennitas . . . P. Thomas Michels OSB zum 70. Geburtstag,* Münster, 1963, pp. 105–117.

Seel, O., *Römertum und Latinität,* Stuttgart, 1964.

Seston, W., *Dioclétien et la Tétrarchie,* Bibliothèque des Ecoles françaises d'Athènes et de Rome 162, Paris, 1946.

Seyrig, H., "Antiquités syriennes 20: Armes et costumes iraniens de Palmyre," *Syria* 18 (1937) 4–31.

——— "Note sur Hérodien, prince de Palmyre," *Syria* 18 (1937) 1–4.

——— "Palmyra and the East," *Journal of Roman Studies* 40 (1950) 1–7.

—— "Antiquités syriennes 58: Inscriptions grecques," *Syria* 31 (1954) 212–218.

——— "Némésis et le temple de Maqâm er-Rabb," *Mélanges de l'Université St. Joseph* 37 (1961) 261–270.

——— "Les Fils du roi Odainat," *Annales archéologiques de Syrie* 13 (1963) 159–172.

Sherwin-White, A. N., *The Roman Citizenship,* Oxford, 1939.

Simonetti, M., *Studi agiografici,* Rome, 1955.

——— "Qualche osservazione a proposito degli Atti dei martiri," *Revue des études augustiniennes* 2 (1956) 39–58.

——— "Qualche osservazione sui luoghi comuni negli atti dei martiri," *Giornale italiano di filologia* 10 (1957) 147–155.

Sinnigen, W. G., *The Officium of the Urban Prefecture during the Later Roman Empire,* Rome, 1957.

——— "The Roman Secret Service," *Classical Journal* 57 (1961) 65–72.

Sirago, V. A., *Gallia Placidia e la trasformazione politica dell'Occidente,* Université de Louvain, Recueil de Travaux d'histoire et philologie,[4] 25, Louvain, 1961.

Sirinelli, J., *Les Vues historiques d'Eusèbe de Césarée durant la période prénicéenne*, Paris, 1961.
Sizoo, A., "Paetus Thrasea et le stoïcisme," *Revue des études latines* 4 (1926) 229–237; 5 (1927) 41–52.
Smallwood, E. M., "Some Notes on the Jews under Tiberius," *Latomus* 15 (1956) 314–329.
——— "Palestine c. A.D. 115–118," *Historia* 11 (1962) 500–510.
Smith, R. E., "The Greek Letters of M. Junius Brutus," *Classical Quarterly* 30 (1936) 194–203.
Smith, W., and S. Cheetham, *A Dictionary of Christian Antiquities*, 2 vols., London, 1875.
Sodano, A. R., *Porfirio, Lettera ad Anebo*, Naples, 1958.
Söder, R., *Die apokryphen Apostelgeschichten und die romanhafte Literatur der Antike*, Würzburger Studien zur Altertumswissenschaft 3, Stuttgart, 1932.
Solari, A., "La Politica orientale del principato palmireno," *Philologus* 92 (1937–38) 239–243.
Starr, C. G., "Epictetus and the Tyrant," *Classical Philology* 44 (1949) 20–29.
Stein, A., "Zu Lukians Alexandros," *Strena Buliciana: Commentationes gratulatoriae Francisco Bulić*, Zagreb, 1924, pp. 257–266.
Stjernqvist, B., "Runde Beschlagplatten mit Befestingungsöse," *Saalburg Jahrbuch* 13 (1954) 59–68.
Straub, J., *Heidnische Geschichtsapologetik in der christlichen Spätantike: Untersuchungen über Zeit und Tendenz der Historia Augusta*, Antiquitas vol. 4 pt. 1, Bonn, 1963.
Stroux, J., "Vier Zeugnisse zur römischen Literaturgeschichte der Kaiserzeit," *Philologus* 86 (1931) 338–368.
Swift, E. H., *Roman Sources of Christian Art*, New York, 1951.
Swoboda, E., *Carnuntum: Seine Geschichte und seine Denkmäler*,[3] Graz-Cologne, 1958.
Syme, R., *The Roman Revolution*, Oxford, 1939.
——— *Tacitus*, 2 vols., Oxford, 1958.
——— "Tacitus und seine politische Einstellung," *Gymnasium* 69 (1962) 241–263.
Tadic-Gilloteaux, N., "Sénèque face au suicide," *L'Antiquité classique* 32 (1963) 541–551.
Tambornino, J., *De antiquorum daemonismo*, Giessen, 1909.
Tengström, E., *Donatisten und Katholiken: Soziale, wirtschaftliche und politische Aspekte einer nordafrikanischen Kirchenspaltung*, Studia graeca et latina Gothoburgensia 18, Göteborg, 1964.
Terzaghi, N., *Per la storia della satira*, Turin, n.d. [1932?].
Thompson, E. A., "Peasant Revolts in Late Roman Gaul and Spain," *Past and Present* 2 (1952) 11–23.

Thompson, E. A., *A Roman Reformer and Inventor, being a new text of the treatise De rubus bellicis*, Oxford, 1952.

Thompson, L., "Lucan's Apotheosis of Nero," *Classical Philology* 59 (1964) 147–153.

Timpe, D., "Römische Geschichte bei Flavius Josephus," *Historia* 9 (1960) 474–502.

Tod, M. N., "Teams of Ball-Players at Sparta," *Annual of the British School at Athens* 10 (1903–04) 63–77.

——— "Macedonia, VI: Inscriptions," *Annual of the British School at Athens* 23 (1918–19) 67–97.

——— "Sidelights on Greek Philosophers," *Journal of Hellenic Studies* 77 (1957) 132–141.

Torraca, L., *Marco Giunio Bruto, Epistole greche*, Naples, 1959.

Touilleux, P., *L'Apocalypse et les cultes de Domitien et de Cybèle*, Paris, 1935.

Toynbee, J. M. C., "Dictators and Philosophers in the First Century A.D.," *Greece and Rome* 13 (1944) 43–58.

Trowbridge, M. L., "Folklore in the 'Scriptores Historiae Augustae,'" *Classical Philology* 33 (1938) 69–88.

Uslar, R. von, "Römisch-germanische Keramik in Saalburg-Museum," *Saalburg Jahrbuch* 8 (1934) 61–182.

——— "Germanische Keramik vom Kastell Zugmantel in Taunus als Zeugnis germanischer Siedler," *Klio* 28 (1935) 294–296.

Vallette, P., L'Apologie *d'Apulée*, Paris, 1908.

——— *De Oenomao Cynico*, Paris, 1908.

Vandenbossche, A., "Recherches sur le suicide en droit romain," *Annuaire de l'Institut de philologie et d'histoire orientales et slaves* 12 (1952) 471–516.

Van Loy, R., "Le 'Pro Templis' de Libanius," *Byzantion* 8 (1933) 7–39, 389–404.

Verdière, R., "Notes critiques sur Perse," *Hommages à Max Niedermann*, Collection Latomus 23, Brussels, 1956, 339–350.

Vetters, H., "Ein neues Denkmal des Sicherheitsdienstes in den Provinzen?" *Jahreshefte des oesterreichischen archäologischen Instituts* 39 (1952) Beiblatt cols. 103–106.

Veyne, P., "*Contributio:* Benevent, Capoue, Cirta," *Latomus* 18 (1959) 568–592.

Vittinghoff, F., "Zum geschichtlichen Selbstverständnis der Spätantike," *Historische Zeitschrift* 198 (1964) 529–574.

Walker, B., *The Annals of Tacitus: A Study in the Writing of History*, Manchester, 1952.

Waltzing, J. P., *Etude historique sur les corporations professionnelles chez les Romains depuis les origines jusqu'à la chute de l'empire d'Occident*, 4 vols., Louvain, 1895–1900.

Weinreich, O., "Alexandros der Lügenprophet und seine Stellung in der Religiosität des IIe Jahrhunderts nach Chr.," *Neue Jahrbücher für das klassischen Altertum* 47 (1921) 129–151.

Werner, H., "Zum Λούκιος ἤ Ὄνος," *Hermes* 53 (1918) 225–261.

Werner, J., "Kriegergräber aus der ersten Hälfte des 5. Jahrhunderts zwischen Schelde und Weser," *Bonner Jahrbücher* 158 (1958) 372–413.

Whittaker, C. R., "The Revolt of Papirius Dionysius, A.D. 190," *Historia* 13 (1964) 348–369.

Wieacker, F., "Vulgarismus und Klassizimus im Recht der Spätantike," *Sitzungsbericht der Heidelberger Akademie der Wissenschaften* 1955, no. 3, pp. 1–64.

Will, E., "Art parthe et art grec," *Etudes d'archéologie classique* 2 (1959) 123–135.

Windisch, H., *Die Orakel des Hystaspes,* Verhandelingen der Koninklijke Akademie van Wetenschappen te Amsterdam vol. 28 pt. 3, Amsterdam, 1929.

Wirszubski, C., Libertas *as a Political Idea at Rome during the Late Republic and Early Principate,* Cambridge, Eng., 1950.

Woodward, A. M., "Excavations at Sparta, 1924–25, 3: The Inscriptions," *Annual of the British School at Athens* 26 (1923–25) 159–239.

——— "Excavations at Sparta, 1926, 3: The Inscriptions," *Annual of the British School at Athens* 27 (1925–26) 210–254.

Woodward, E. L., *Christianity and Nationalism in the Later Roman Empire,* New York, 1916.

Wuilleumier, P., "Cirque et astrologie," *Mélanges d'archéologie et d'histoire de l'Ecole française de Rome* 44 (1927) 184–209.

——— *L'Administration de la Lyonnaise sous le Haut-Empire,* Annales de l'Université de Lyon[3] 16, Paris, 1948.

Zinserling, G., "Altrömische Traditionselemente in Porträtkunst und Historienmalerei der ersten Hälfte des dritten Jahrhunderts u. Z.," *Klio* 41 (1963) 196–220.

Zontschew, D., "Das thrakische Heiligtum von Batkun," *Jahreshefte des oesterreichischen archäologischen Instituts* 32 (1940) Beiblatt cols. 81–106.

Abbreviations

AC	*L'Antiquité classique*
AE	*L'Année épigraphique* (yearly supplement to *Revue Archéologique*)
AI	*Annuaire de l'Institut de philologie et d'histoire orientales et slaves*
AJP	*American Journal of Philology*
BGU	*Berliner griechische Urkunden*, Aegyptischen Urkunden aus den königlichen Museen zu Berlin, 9 vols., Berlin, 1892–1937
BSA	*Annual of the British School at Athens*
CIL	*Corpus inscriptionum latinarum*
CJ	*Classical Journal*
CP	*Classical Philology*
IGRR	*Inscriptiones graecae ad res Romanas pertinentes*, ed. R. Cagnat *et al.*, vols. 1, 3, 4, Paris, 1911–1927
JEA	*Journal of Egyptian Archaeology*
JOAI	*Jahreshefte des oesterreichischen archäologischen Instituts*
JRS	*Journal of Roman Studies*
Mél. Rome	*Mélanges d'archéologie et d'histoire de l'Ecole française de Rome*
P. Ant.	*The Antinoopolis Papyri*, ed. C. H. Roberts, J. W. B. Barns, and H. Zilliacus, London, 1950–
PG	*Patrologia graeca*, ed. J. P. Migne
PGM	*Papyri graecae magicae*, ed. K. Preisendanz
PL	*Patrologia latina*, ed. J. P. Migne
P. Oxy.	*The Oxyrhynchus Papyri*, ed. B. P. Grenfell, A. S. Hunt, *et al.*, London, 1898– .
RE	*Real-Encyclopädie der klassischen Altertumswissenschaft*,[2] ed. A. Pauly, G. Wisowa, *et al.*, 1894–
REA	*Revue des études anciennes*
REG	*Revue des études grecques*
REL	*Revue des études latines*
RhM	*Rheinisches Museum für Philologie*

SEG	*Supplementum epigraphicum graecum*
SHA	Scriptores historiae Augustae
Symb. Oslo	*Symbolae Osloensis*
YCS	*Yale Classical Studies*

Notes

Chapter I. Cato, Brutus, and Their Succession

1. On Brutus' being Caesar's son, see App., *B.C.* 2.112; J. P. V. D. Balsdon, *Historia* 7 (1958) 87, dismisses the rumor on the basis of dates. Cato's chaplains and character appear in Plut., *Cato min.* 4.1 and 20.1, and are discussed by P. Grimal, *REA* 47 (1945) 264. Cicero's ridicule is found especially in *Pro Murena* 30f, and Cato's characterization as a Stoic in Cic., *Paradoxa Stoic.* 2. The quotation is from Cicero's *De fin.* 3.5.17, and should be compared with a number of similar passages in Cicero's own writings, such as *De rep.* 2.2.1.

2. The imagined conversations with Cato take place in Sen., *Ep.* 14.13, and Lucan, *Phars.* 2.288; the description of Cato's death is in Plut., *Cato min.* 67–70.

3. R. Hirzl, *Archiv für Religionswissenschaft* 11 (1908) 75f, 243f, 417f, and especially 433–475, subjects the Greek and Roman view of suicide to a rather rambling treatment. E. Benz, *Das Todesproblem in der stoïschen Philosophie* (1929) 54–59, considers the Stoic views, bringing out the concept of suicide as a road to freedom (pp. 78f). Seneca's views are discussed by Benz, pp. 57–59, and by N. Tadic-Gilloteaux, *AC* 32 (1963) 543f, and the history of popular views on the subject by J. Bayet, *Année sociologique* 3 (1951) 42–56. For further discussion focused on attitudes expressed in legislation, see A. Vandenbossche, *AI* 12 (1952) 471–516 *passim*, especially 486, Principal texts referring to Cato and suicide are Cic., *Tusc. disp.* 1.30.74, *ut tunc Socrati, nunc Catoni;* Sen., *De prov.* 3.14; and Mart. 1.78.8–10: "A nobler death, that fame might prize above Cato's end." For the invention of Catonian speeches, see Sen., *Ep.* 24.6; yet, at the time, the death was cartooned (App., *B.C.* 2.101) in the expectation of exciting ridicule, as is pointed out by P. Jal, *La Guerre civile à Rome* (1963) 173, "suicide having been long considered in Rome as a disgraceful act."

4. These versions of *Cato* and *Anti-Cato* and Metellus Scipio's earlier anti-Cato pamphlet, in the first round of propaganda warfare, have all perished. For their dates and nature, see A. Dyroff, *RhM* 63 (1908) 586f; H. Bardon, *La Littérature latine inconnue*, 1 (1952) 276f; and Balsdon 92. Augustus' work was titled *Rescripta Bruto de Catone* (Suet., *Aug.* 85.1). J. Carcopino,

REA 53 (1951) 155, attributes the need of more anti-Catonism to the propaganda of the Stoics. Typical passages attesting Cato's later repute can be seen in Sen., *Ep.* 11.10; 95.70f; Sen., *De const. sap.* 2.2; Verg., *Aen.* 8.670; Tac., *Hist.* 4.8; Marcus Aurel., *Medit.* 1.14; Lucan, *Phars.* passim; Mart. 1.8.lf; 9.27; and Hor., *Od.* 1.12.35; 2.1.21f.

5. Balsdon and Bardon (above, nn. 1 and 4) suggest the effect of the pamphlet warfare on Brutus' attachments. To marry Porcia, he divorced his first wife, daughter of Appius Claudius, against his mother's wishes. His second wife was the widow of Bibulus, consul in 59 B.C. with (or against) Caesar. Her kin could be traced to Cinna, and were to reach forward to Nero. Brutus' motives can be guessed at from scattered surmises—his love of Cato (Plut., *Brut.* 2.1; Dio 44.13.1), his shame at his mother's adultery (App., *b.c.* 2.112), his love of fame (*ibid.* 2.114; Cic., *Ad Att.* 15.1, *cum ille suae inmortalitati melius quam nostro otio consuluerit*). Sources for Brutus' personal appearance are less satisfactory. No bust seems to survive (I do not accept the identification offered by H. Möbius, Ἀρχαιολογικὴ ἐφημερίς 1953–54 [1961] 207f), but the coins offer a characteristic profile. The best photographs of coins are in Möbius, pl. I, 2f; in H. Mattingly, *AC* 17 (1948) 448f and pl. I, ii, 3; and in H. A. Grueber, *Coins of the Roman Republic in the British Museum* (1910) 2.477f and pl. cxi, 12 and 14. On the collection of Brutus' letters, see R. E. Smith, *Classical Quarterly* 30 (1936) 202f, and L. Torraca, *Marco Giunio Bruto, Epistole greche* (1959) pp. xxviii–xxix. For Brutus' smile, *ibid.*, *Ep.* 13. His other qualities emerge in asides of his contemporaries: his *suavissimos mores* (Cic., *Ad fam.* 9.14.5) and his charm, συνόντα κεχαρισμένως (Plut., *Brut.* 6.7). Brutus' tact is illustrated by his writing to Cicero (*Ad Brut.* 1.4a.2), "Everything is there to ensure that your virtue may stand comparison with those of any man among our forebears" (note the typical standard of reference, Rome's honored past); and on his own immunity to flattery, see Plut., *Brut.* 6.5. Other phrases are revealing: on his *singularem probitatem*, see Cic., *Ad fam.* 9.14.5, and on his *incredibilis virtus*, Cic., *Ad Att.* 14.15, which is clear also in Plut., *Brut.* 29.1, and in Brutus' own letters. For his hesitation, see Plut., *Brut.* 6.4; 29.1; and Cic., *Ad Att.* 16.5, μετεωρότερος.

6. A summary of a familiar subject, with bibliography, is given by E. F. Bruck, *Seminar* 7 (1949) 1f, discussing funerals. The quotation on Cicero's laudatio is from Jal, *La Guerre civile* 207n7.

7. Juv. 8.55, *tua vivit imago*, of a man with nothing but ancestors, reminds one of Pope's "tenth transmitter of a foolish face." The description of Cato as a *viva imago* is Seneca's (*De tranq.* 16.1). The device to show Brutus' lineage was a φιλοτέχνημα *illud tuum, quod vidi in Parthenone, Ahalam et Brutum* (Cic., *Ad Att.* 13.40; cf. Nepos, *Att.* 18.3). The "Parthenon" was some room in the house. Doubts about the line of descent are mentioned by Dio 44.12.1f, but the derivation from L. Junius Brutus was already made in

the second century. See F. Münzer, *Römische Adelsparteien und Adelsfamilien*[2] (1963) 336n1. Gelzer collects the references to Brutus' ancestors in Cicero and later writers (*re* s.v. Iunius [Brutus] col. 988).

8. Cato's offer of tyrannicide was known to Plutarch (*Cato min.* 3.3; cf. Val. Max. 3.1.2). On Ahala, see Cic., *In Cat.* 1.3; Cic., *Pro Milone* 3.8; Cic., *Cato* 16.55; and Plut., *Brut.* 1.3; on the line of the Junii Bruti, see Gelzer, *RE* s.v. Iunius [Brutus] col. 988. Cicero's rhetorical question is asked in *Philip.* 2.11.

9. Dio 43.45.3f speaks of the statues, as does Plut., *Brut.* 1.1. For the various graffiti and comments addressed to Brutus, see Plut., *Brut.* 9.3; Dio 44.12.2; App., *B.C.* 2.112; and Suet., *Caes.* 80.3. For the common practice of pasquinades on statues, see Jal, *La Guerre civile* 174. Gelzer (*RE* s.v. Iunius [Brutus] col. 990) believes that the squibs on both statues were directed against Caesar, not Brutus. This acute suggestion applies to some of the graffiti, but not to those mentioned in Plut., *Brut.* 9.3; App., *B.C.* 2.112; and Dio 44.12.3. In a letter, quoted in the text, Cicero urged Brutus to action (*Brut.* 96.331). Compare also the pamphlets (γράμματα) circulated in support of action by Brutus, stressing his name and lineage (Dio 44.12.2). On the coins, dated only approximately, see Grueber 1.479f, with the legend LIBERTAS, r. BRVTVS, and L. Junius Brutus as consul with lictors; or BRVTVS, r. AHALA. On the plot of 59 B.C., see Cic., *Ad Att.* 2.24. Another member in it was Porcia's first husband, Bibulus. For L. Junius Brutus alone on coins, see Mattingly, *AC* 17 (1948) 450, and Grueber 2.474 and 477.

10.The statue of Brutus' ancestor had, at least, a drawn sword in its hand (Plut., *Brut.* 1.1). Brutus' words, *recuperatam libertatem,* are given by Cicero, *Philip.* 2.12.28, perhaps inexactly. The words of Dio 47.20.4, quoted in the text, tell us of the statues dedicated to Brutus in Athens. Compare a philosopher's answer to a tyrant asking what is the best bronze: "The kind from which they made the statues of Harmodius and Aristogeiton" (Plut., *Mor.* 68A; for the same tale, with a different cast, see Diog. Laert. 6.50).

11. Latin equivalents of "tyrant" are *rex* and *dominus,* but of course *tyrannus* was early naturalized. For these words and their sometimes inconsistent usage in the late Republic, see J. Béranger, *REL* 13 (1935) 87–91. Cicero uses both Greek and Latin terms for tyrants (*Ad Att.* 14.6; *Ad fam.* 12.22.2). Opposition of Solon to Pisistratus is detected, in seven letters preserved in Diog. Laert., by A. Ballanti, *Annali della Facoltà di Lettere e Philosophia della Università di Napoli* 4 (1954) 91. On Hellenistic tyrannicides, see Cic., *Tusc. disp.* 2.52, and Val. Max. 3.3.2–5 and 6.2.3. On the commonplace of tyrannicides, see W. von Christ, *Geschichte der griechischen Litteratur*[6] 2 (1924) 717n1.

12. I. Düring, *Chion of Heraclea* (1951), has edited the letters. Quotations are from *Ep.* 3.5f (cf. *Ep.* 5, τὴν φιλοσοφίαν οὐκ ἀπολίτευτον ἔργῳ τοῖς γνωρίμοις ποιεῖ) and 14.3f.

13. Düring (p. 20) points to the mixture of Stoicism and Platonism in Chion's letters. For a similar confusion in Brutus' philosophy, see Cic., *Ad Att.* 13.17f and 25; Cic., *Acad.* 1.3.12; Cic., *De fin.* 1.3.8; and Plut., *Brut.* 2.2. Περὶ καθήκοντος is the Greek title of Brutus' work given by Sen., *Ep.* 95.45. It offers, he says, "many precepts to parents, children, and brothers." Priscian gives the Latin title, as Bardon, *La Littérature latine inconnue* 1.209, points out. Bardon (1.209) also supplies the opinion on the reconciliation of the two philosophic schools, which is quoted in the text. As to Stoic elements in Brutus, G. L. Hendrickson, *AJP* 47 (1926) 240, goes so far as to say that Brutus was "essentially Stoic in his character and in his philosophical point of view. Indeed, Antiochus himself [one of Brutus' teachers] is accounted by Cicero a true Stoic (*germanissimus Stoicus*) masking in the disguise of the Academic name." A second quotation in the text, on Brutus' sincerity, is from Quint., *Inst. orat.* 10.1.123; a third, stressing his consistency in aiming his attack only at Caesar, is drawn from App., *B.C.* 2.114 (cf. Dio 44.19.1f); and a fourth, that citizens should seek the blood of none but a tyrant, comes from Vell. Pat., *Hist. Rom.* 2.58; cf. Brutus' calling the Triumvirate τυράννους (Plut., *Brut.* 28.2f). His abstract idealism in the assassination is attested by Tac., *Dial.* 25, and by Plut., *Brut.* 8.3, distinguishing between μισοκαῖσαρ and μισοτύραννος.

14. Brutus' love of freedom appears in Dio 44.1.2 and 44.19.1f; Plut., *Brut.* 29.6; and Nic. Dam., *Vit. Caes.* 25. The words that recur are (κοινὴ) ἐλευθερία, *communis libertas, libera res publica*, matched by LIBERTAS on the coins. The meaning of that word, however, requires the explanation offered by R. Syme, *The Roman Revolution* (1939) 155; by C. Wirszubski, *Libertas . . .* (1950) *passim;* and by a review of the latter by A. Momigliano, *JRS* 41 (1951) 146f.

15. Plutarch (*Brut.* 4.4) and Cicero (*Ad Att.* 12.5b; 13.8) refer to Brutus' literary activity. On his style, see Quint., *Inst. orat.* 9.4.76; 10.1.123; Tac., *Dial.* 21; Cic., *Brut.* 90.309; 97.331; Plut., *Brut.* 2.3; and Hendrickson 235–242. Literature as the typical pursuit of the nobility is shown in the remarks of Cicero (*Brut.* 72.253; *Ad Q. frat.* 3.5.7) on his brother and on Caesar.

16. Stoicism countenanced literature. See Quint., *Inst. orat.* 2.15.20, and Cic., *De orat.* 3.18.65.

17. The lack of free speech under Caesar was the subject of complaints in Dio 44.10.2. When a degree of παρρησία was restored, it was safe for Cicero to say that he "could not endure to exist under a monarchy or tyranny where [he] could neither live rightly μήτε παρρησιάσθαι" (Dio 45.18.2). Plutarch says Cassius was not a "tyrant hater" but a "Caesar hater" (*Brut.* 8.5), but compare Cassius' remark to Antony (Dio 44.34.7) and the tale of his earlier plot against Caesar (Cic., *Philip.* 2.11.26, rejected by Balsdon, *Historia* 7 [1958] 82). The saying "So love as if destined to hate" was attributed to both Bias (Aul. Gell., *N.A.* 1.3.30) and Chilon (Cic., *De amicitia* 16.59).

18. On the choice of a site for the attack on Caesar, see M. A. Levi, *Ottaviano capoparte* (1933) 1.3; on the gladiators before and after the slaying, see Nic. Dam., *Vit. Caes.* 26A; Dio 44.16.2; and App., *B.C.* 2.120. For details of the day, Nicolaus is the most useful. App., *B.C.* 2.147, supplies the account of Caesar's funeral quoted in the text, and of Herophilus, alias Amatius, alias Marius (*B.C.* 3.2f). Accius' patron was D. Brutus Callaicus. On the play, see Münzer, *Römische Adelsparteien* 336nl, and Jal, *La Guerre civile* 155. Cicero (*Ad Att.* 16.4) tells us of Brutus' reaction to the change of program.

19. Plut., *Brut.* 51f and Dio 47.49 give details on Brutus' end. Suet., *Aug.* 13.1, describes the fate of his body. Plut., *Brut.* 2.3 and 48.1, is quoted in the text as our source for Volumnius and Empylus, and Tac., *Ann.* 4.34, and Dio 53.32.4 for the two other later admirers of Brutus.

20. Statements showing the veneration of Cato (in addition to those cited above in note 5) include Sen., *De ira* 2.32; Sen., *Ad Marc.* 20.6; Sen., *De prov.* 2.9f; Sen., *De tranq.* 7.5; Sen., *De const.* 2.3; Sen., *De benef.* 5.17; Sen., *Ep.* 95.69; 104.29; Petron., *Satyr.* 119 lines 45f; and Pliny, *Ep.* 4.27. After Cato's death, even so recently as the reign of Augustus, an open Republicanism was tolerated, as emphasized by Syme, *The Roman Revolution* 317; by W. Richter, *Gymnasium* 68 (1961) 293; and by F. Klingner, *Museum Helveticum* 15 (1958) 196–201, who carries the account farther. Innocent schoolboys recalled Cato's martyrdom without reproof (Pers., *Sat.* 3.44f).

21. There is much information on Cremutius Cordus in Tac., *Ann.* 4.34; Dio 57.24.2f; Suet., *Tib.* 61.3; Suet., *Calig.* 16.1; Sen., *Ad Marc.* 1.2–4; Quint., *Inst. orat.* 10.1.104; for modern commentary, Klingner 197f; Richter 99f; J. M. C. Toynbee, *Greece and Rome* 13 (1944) 44f; and F. H. Cramer, *Journal of the History of Ideas* 6 (1945) 191f. Val. Max. 6.4.5 illustrates the kind of servile abuse of Brutus that Cremutius refers to. *Parricida* was a much-used word after Caesar's death (Jal, *La Guerre civile* 470). Later writers praised Cremutius, such as Sen., *Ad Marc.* 1.4, referring to his *eloquentia* and *libertas.* To show the natural union of the two words, Klingner 197f compares Tac., *Hist.* 1.1.1, where it is said, *dum res populi Romani memorabantur, pari eloquentia ac libertate.* Such freedom of speech was feared by the emperors, especially in high circles—as Tiberius put it, *in conviviis et in circulis* (Tac., *Ann.* 3.54). G. Boissier, *L'Opposition sous les Césars*[5] (1905) 70f, collects references to the phrase in other writers.

22. Longinus was suspect for his veneration of Cassius' *imago,* for his ancient wealth, and *gravitas morum* (Tac., *Ann.* 16.7)—not less for his connection with the Junii, one of whom was linked with him in his indictment. The Junii were joined to the imperial house also. For their dangers and trials, from Augustus on, see D. McAlindon, *AJP* 77 (1956) 119f. For more on Longinus, see Suet., *Nero* 37.1, and Dio 62.27.1.

23. Suetonius (*Nero* 37.1) traces Thrasea's connection with Longinus; for his essay, *Cato,* see Plut., *Cato min.* 25.1; 37.2; and H. Bardon, *La Littérature*

latine inconnue, 2 (1956) 170; on his trial, Tac., *Ann.* 13.49; 14.48f; 15.20–23; 16.19–27; Dio 62.20.1; A. Sizoo, *REL* 4 (1926) 230f; Sizoo, *REL* 5 (1927) 42f; Toynbee 50f; R. Syme, *Gymnasium* 69 (1962) 246f; R. Syme, *Tacitus* (1958) 1.298f; C. Saumagne, *REL* 33 (1955) 241f (not reliable). Plutarch (*Mor.* 810A) and Tacitus (*Ann.* 15.23) mention conciliation with the emperor. His friends after his death painted him as a harmless victim, martyr to his own prominent virtue (Dio 62.26.1; Suet., *Nero* 37.1). Yet his accusers charged him with a more dangerous character, as Tac., *Ann.* 16.22, shows.

24. Tac., *Ann.* 16.34f, and Dio 62.15.4 record Thrasea's dying words, and the libation recalled Socrates.

25. On the aspects of Lucan's work that matter for us, see J. Brisset, *Les Idées politiques de Lucain* (1964), with bibliography, 231–234. On his old-fashioned grandfather, see Sen., *Ad Helv.* 17.4, *maiorum consuetudini deditus;* on his father, Tac., *Ann.* 16.17; and on the tolerant atmosphere of the court in Lucan's day, see Suet., *Nero* 39.1, supplying the quotation in the text.

26. In interpreting Lucan's break with Nero, I follow the ingenious emendations of G. de Plinval, *Latomus* 15 (1956) 513f; the date is discussed by de Plinval 517 and by Brisset 12f; further, on the rupture, see G. K. Gresseth, *CP* 52 (1957) 24f, and G. Pfligersdorfer, *Hermes* 87 (1959) 370f. For the actions of Lucan thereafter, leading to disloyalty and to his death, see Suet., *Vita Lucani,* for Lucan's talk about tyrannicides, and Tac., *Ann.* 15.56f and 70.

27. P. Grimal, *REL* 38 (1960) 297, traces the debate on Lucan through centuries of scholars—so many men, for so many hundreds of years, with nothing better to do!

28. In passages such as *Phars.* 2.439f, 3.303f, 5.237–373 *passim* (especially 310f), and 7.168f, 240, and 551, Lucan attacks or criticizes Caesar. For modern commentary, see Brisset 161f; E. Griset, *Rivista di studi classici* 3 (1955) 58f; O. Schönberger, *Hermes* 86 (1958) 231f; and H. C. Nutting, *AJP* 53 (1932) 44f. Veneration of Brutus speaks in *Phars.* 2.234f, 7.587f, and 9.15f; Stoic coloring is analyzed by Brisset 44, 51, 151, and by M. Rambaud, *REL* 33 (1955) 282f, 286, and 290. Note especially the stock picture of Stoic morality ascribed to Cato in *Phars.* 2.380–391. M. A. Levi, *Nerone e i suoi tempi* (1949) 62f, deals with the reactionary social views of the *Pharsalia*, with considerable exaggeration. Other writers, such as Brisset 180 and 204f and Pfligersdorfer 348, have pointed to the treasonous jibes in the epic. Lucan went so far as to say that liberty was dead (*Phars.* 1.670f; 4.823; 6.807; and 7.640f).

29. Lucan, *Phars.* 133f, contains the adulation mentioned in the text; and on Nero's apotheosis foretold, see 1.45f. L. Thompson, *CP* 59 (1964) 148, argues for Lucan's borrowing from a play of Seneca. For the conflict in

Lucan shown typically, compare the two views of emperor worship in *Phars.* 1.45f and 7.457. Griset 134–148 suggests that the adulation of Nero is ironic, a suggestion rightly rejected by Grimal 305 and by Pfligersdorfer 368. For the organic development of the epic, see Schönberger 231f and Brisset 179–185.

30. Tac., *Dial.* 2f, reveals the offense of Curiatius. His friends at the scene suggested a second edition, "not better but safer." He also wrote a *Domitius*, concerning which one of Nero's ancestors, and whether for or against the throne (more likely against), is not known. A possible third work, play or speech, was the *Nero*. On a corrupt passage referring to these, see Bardon 2.215 in preference to J. Stroux, *Philologus* 86 (1931) 341–347, and T. Frank, *AJP* 58 (1937) 225f. There is no record of his being harmed by any one of these productions. A σοφιστής Maternus, killed under Domitian for a practice declamation on tyrants (Dio 67.12.5), is probably a different man (Syme, *Tacitus* 2.799). For Curiatius' cultivation of martyrs' busts "with wonderful veneration," see Pliny, *Ep.* 1.17. The description of the man, in the text, is from Syme, *Tacitus* 1.92.

31. For charges of rabble rousing against the opposition, see Dio 65.12.2, describing Helvidius Priscus as ταραχώδης, τῷ ὄχλῳ προσέκειτο, and so on; further, Philostr., *Vit. Apoll.* 7.4, Apollonius τὰ Ῥωμαίων πάτρια, ὡς κ'ακεῖνοι δῆμος τὸ ἀρχαῖον ὄντες τὰς τυραννίδας ἐώθουν ὅπλοις. But these are special examples, and belong to Domitian's reign. See below, p. 57. The opposition appealed less naturally to democratic principles than to sympathy for the nobility, to *magni nominis miseratio* (Tac., *Ann.* 14.58). On Lucan's and Seneca's anti-democratic bias, see Brisset 44; on Thrasea Paetus' hostility to provincials, Tac., *Ann.* 15.21. On the careers of such figures, see text at notes 24f; and *RE* regarding Annaeus Serenus, who was *praef. vigilum* about 55. He died in 62–63 and was mourned by Seneca (*Ep.* 63.14). Another such, Herennius Senecio (Dio 67.13.1f), was criticized for not advancing farther in his career.

32. Tac., *Ann.* 16.17, *petitione honorum abstinuerat*, reveals the check in the career of Seneca's brother.

33. Dio 54.12.3; 58.17.3–18; 58.18.5; 60.3.2; and Suet., *Aug.* 35.1, indicate how much emperors feared attack, in the very *curia*.

34. The text of Jos., *Ant. Jud.*, is corrupt at 19.17f, but from the emendations of Dindorf and Hudson in B. Niese's edition (1890) the meaning can be reconstructed. I read, for the end of the passage, τὴν Γαίου τελευτὴν οὐκ ἀνελεύθερον ὑπολαμβάνων.

35. Modern discussion of Josephus' source for these passages can be found in G. Hölscher, *Die Quellen des Josephus . . .* (1904) 67; D. Timpe, *Historia* 9 (1960) 474f; M. Hammond, *Harvard Studies in Classical Philology* 67 (1963) 98; and Syme, *Tacitus* 1.287. Investigating the source, one early commentator even imagined some fundamental "Chaerea-Roman" (Timpe

474n3). For that Greek touch in the drama, the ascent to the Capitol, see Jos., *Bell. Jud.* 2.204f; for the Greek parallels to the lament for the lost spirit of freedom, see Ballanti 89, who collects some typical passages: Chion, *Ep.* 14.lf, νὺν τε γάρ, ὡς πυνθάνομαι, σφαγάς τ'ἀνδρῶν καὶ φυγάς ὑπομένει [ἡ πόλις] στερομένη μὲν τῶν ἀρίστων πολιτῶν, τοῖς δ'ἀσεβεστάτοις δουλεύσα . . . ἐπειδὰν δ'ἅπαξ ὑπερισχύσῃ τὸ κακὸν καὶ μηκέτι ᾖ τοῖς ἀνθρώποις λόγος, ὅπως ἀπαλλάξωσιν ἑαυτῶν, ἀλλ' ὅπως ἄν ῥᾷστα ἐν αὑτῷ διάγοιεν, τότε ὁ παντελὴς ὄλεθρος γίνεται; cf. Tac., *Agr.* 2, *dedimus profecto grande patientiae documentum;* Pliny, *Ep.* 8.14, *inertia in pretio, otium summum;* and Pliny, *Paneg.* 66, *neque enim adhuc ignavia quadam et insito torpore cessavimus.* The nobility's *torpor* was no doubt shameful, but they lived in fear. For the sources of descriptions of the Roman terror, reaching from Tacitus (and of course later writers) back to Hellenistic times, see Ballanti 89 and B. Walker, *The Annals of Tacitus* (1952) 204–214.

36. The words are ἐλευθερία and ἀρετή, that is, *libertas* and *virtus.* See Timpe 485. For rejoicing at the return of freedom of speech, see Jos., *Ant. Jud.* 19.2.178, and Ballanti 76, who compares Tac., *Agr.* 2, on the loss of *loquendi audiendique commercio,* and Tac., *Hist.* 1.1, *rara temporum felicitate ubi sentire quae velis et quae sentias dicere licet.* Tiberius himself believed, genuinely, that *in civitate libera linguam mentemque liberas esse debere* (Suet., *Tib.* 28). Yet, at Caligula's death, freedom of speech proved a meaningless possession, as Josephus' source seems to realize (Timpe 478, 486–488, and 492), and contemporaries or somewhat later writers even doubted if the other old Republican ideals held much of value for their own imperial times. See Pliny, *Paneg.* 6.3; 44.4; Brisset 171; Walker 200f; and Sen., *De benef.* 2.20.2, and often elsewhere.

37. On these familiar points in the opposition's program, see, for example, Wirszubski 129–133 and 136f. On changes in the meaning of *libertas,* see Wirszubski 125 and Syme, *Gymnasium* 69 (1962) 260. Hammond, *Harvard Studies in Classical Philology* 67 (1963) 98–103, gives a good discussion of the coin legends and their meaning, but it is doubtful how sincerely Galba offered himself as a mere tool of senatorial restoration. See further, on the coins, Wirszubski 159 and Toynbee 45, though I disagree with Toynbee's interpretation of Trajan's coins.

38. 'Αρχαῖος and πάτριος are words of praise in the opposition's vocabulary. Compare Pliny's friend Cornutus Tertullus, *exemplar antiquitatis* (Pliny, *Ep.* 5.14.3), or his approval of an orator, *sonantia verba et antiqua* (*Ep.* 1.16; cf. 2.9; 3.1). For Tacitus' loving use of *vetus, priscus, antiquus,* and the like, see Walker 200 and Syme, *Gymnasium* 69 (1962) 253. Yet men of Pliny's generation had no first-hand knowledge of the world they praised, as he admits (*Ep.* 1.16), speaking on the orator: *An, si inter eos, quos nunquam vidimus, floruisset, non solum libros eius, verum etiam imagines conquireremus.* Doubts about the later Republic appear even

among its admirers, such as Sen., *De const.* 2.2, compared to Sen., *De benef.* 2.20.2; Sen., *Ep.* 14.13; and Sen., *De clem.* 2.2. On Lucan's doubts, see the text at note 29. The resultant "historical pessimism," in the quotation in the text, is noted by Richter (303), summing up an interesting discussion of early historians (297f). For illustration, see Seneca's views on Augustus, discussed by P. Jal, *REL* 35 (1957) 255f. The elder Seneca's phrase for the principate as a support to the state, *nisi adminiculo regentium niteretur*, has been quoted in the text from Lactantius' resumé, *Inst. div.* 7.15.15f. For commentary, see Richter 302 and, more fully, L. Castiglioni, *Rivista di filologia e di istruzione classica*[2] 6 (1928) 458f. On the question of authorship, whether Seneca the elder or younger, see W. Hartke, *Römische Kinderkaiser* (1951) 354n2. Views similar to the elder Seneca's were held by Horace, Livy, Manlius, Propertius, and Petronius, the passages gathered by E. Dutoit, *REL* 14 (1936) 366–371. Lucan belonged in the list, too. See Brisset 41f.

39. Pro-imperial historiography is rare (Richter 306), in this period. To the more obvious anti-imperial accounts minor ones can be added (*ibid.* 308; Klingner 199f). But Suet., *Domit.* 10.1, supplies the quotation showing how anti-imperial history might be punished.

40. Dio 67.12.4, explained by Suet., *Domit.* 10.3, records the punishment for "excerpting and reading aloud" the speeches in Livy, and two further instances are known: of Maternus (Dio 67.12.5; above, n. 30) and of Carrinas Secundus in A.D. 39 (Dio 59.20.6). Emperors sometimes encouraged rhetorical studies—Vespasian gave the money for Quintilian's chair—but such studies nevertheless contained such offensive features as the antityrannical *topoi* known from Quintilian's *Inst. orat.* 7.1.28, 7.2.25, 7.3.7, 7.4.22f; 7.7.5; 7.8.3; 12.1.40; and from Seneca's *Controversiae* 1.7; 2.5; 3.5; 4.7; and 9.4. For an example of what whole orations were like, see Lucian's *Tyrannicide.* Tacitus saw the absurdity of these topics. His *Dial.* 35 is quoted in the text; and compare Juv. 7.150 "troops of scholars murdering savage tyrants" with volleys of clichés.

41. An example of punishment for a declamation may be found in Suet., *De rhetor.* 6 (Albucius Silus' invocation to a statue of Brutus). Stroux 344f detects an anti-imperial *Nero* by Curiatius Maternus in a passage of Tacitus. The reading is disputed and the speech probably imaginary. See above, n. 30. W. Allen, *CJ* 44 (1948) 203f, discusses hostile misconstruction of innocent remarks, but stretches the evidence.

42. Seneca's *Thyestes* 32–43 and 205f shows what anti-imperial hints could be drawn from drama. On other possible allusions, see Boissier 84–88. On the history of the Thyestes plot in Roman drama, see Jal, *La Guerre civile* 403. Martial at last asks (5.53.1), "Why, my friend, write a Thyestes?" For an innocent *Atreus*, see Juv. 7.73; for a fatal one under Tiberius, see Dio 58.24.3f; for an *Agamemnon* (or the same incident), see Suet., *Tib.*

61.3; for Paris and Oenone, see Suet., *Domit.* 10.3. Anti-imperial reactions of the audience are mentioned by F. F. Abbot, *Transactions of the American Philological Association* 38 (1907) 52–56, and below, p. 172f, for Rome; for an incident at Ephesus, see the reference in Philostr., *Vit. Apoll.* 7.5, mentioning applause of an allusion to tyranny.

43. B. M. Marti, *AJP* 73 (1952) 24, and F. Giancotti, *L'Octavia attribuita a Seneca* (1954), are among those who ascribe the *Octavia* to Seneca, but I follow the majority of scholars (such as Richter 306n45, with references), without wishing to join a fruitless debate.

44. M. Coffey, *Lustrum* 8 (1963) 256f, gives access to earlier literature on the *Apocolocyntosis,* and most recently B. Baldwin, *Phoenix* 18 (1964) 39f, though his arguments for rejecting Senecan authorship seem flimsy. For different views on the purpose of the piece, see Baldwin 43–45; H. MacL. Currie, *AC* 31 (1962) 91–93; and Coffey 261f.

45. For laws of censorship, see Suet., *Aug.* 55; Dio 57.22.5 (in the reign of Tiberius); and the discussion in F. H. Cramer, *Astrology in Roman Law and Politics* (1954) 49. Instances of book burning are recorded under Augustus, Tiberius, and Domitian (Cramer, *Journal of the History of Ideas* 6 [1945] 172–177 and 191f; Tac., *Agr.* 2). But the Torah suffered the same fate (S. Lieberman, *AI* 7 [1939–1944] 418). Tacitus (*Ann.* 4.31; 14.48f; 16.14) recounts the fate of anti-imperial poets. On Phaedrus' difficulties, see his *Fabulae* 3 pr. 38f. L. Havet, *REA* 23 (1921) 96, suspects that "Phaedrus perhaps wrote nothing but *fables à clé,*" but fails to prove his case. Persius' verses on Arria are known from [Suet.], *Vit. Persi.* L. Hermann, *Latomus* 22 (1963) 237–239, and R. Verdière, *Hommages à Max Niedermann* (1956) 347–349, try to interpret different passages in Persius as being hostile to the throne. Nothing can be proven—some of Herrmann's arguments are quite unfair—but I agree to the possibility that what they think *they* can detect, some enemy of Persius might have pointed out to Nero. For the possibility that the poet was murdered, see Herrmann 239, offering no solid evidence but some undeniable parallels.

46. For treasonous literature in circulation, see Suet., *Calig.* 16.1. Much, however, was censored by the author himself (Dio 62.25.2) or by his friends (Tac., *Dial.* 3), and Tacitus, for one, chose to play safe altogether (*Hist.* 1.1.6), under Domitian relapsing into total silence (*Agr.* 2; cf. Pliny, *Ep.* 3.5). Others, like Martial, even prostituted their talents to flattery of the tyrant, though (*Epigrams* 7.21 and 44) he could in safety vilify Nero and, later, Domitian (10.72: "I am not about to address anyone 'Master and God.' ").

47. For minor forms of literary attack, generally anonymous, see Dio 57.14.1; Suet., *Vesp.* 19–2; and Suet., *Domit.* 8.3 (remarks directed against "leading men and women"; see above, n. 45). The inscription in Pompeii, *Restitutus Neronis* (*CIL* 4.2337), is explained by *quater Nerone u(s)us*

Restitutus cinedus (*CIL* 4.2338), both cited by J. Carcopino, *Bulletin de la Société nationale des antiquaires de France* 1960, p. 155. Another inscription, *Cicuta ab rationibus Neronis Augusti,* is very acutely explained by Carcopino 151f and 155–158. Lists of matricides were posted against Nero, also. To Dio, quoted in the text, add [Lucian], *Nero* 10; Philostr., *Vit. Apoll.* 4.38; and Suet., *Nero* 39.2).

48. *Hausit libertatem,* says Tacitus (*Hist.* 4.5) of Helvidius' education; compare Marcia's indoctrination by her father (Sen., *Ad Marc.* 26). For the ties of political conviction uniting Pliny's friends, see Syme, *Tacitus* 1.58–89 and *passim.*

49. On the solidarity and real threat presented by opposition families, see the remarks of Syme, *Tacitus* 2.560f; R. S. Rogers, *CP* 55 (1960) 22f; and McAlindon 131. The anxieties prevalent among the opposition are clear in passages of Epictetus, for example, Τί δόξει τῷ Καίσαρι (*Diss.* 2.13.11; cf. 2.19.17).

Chapter II. Philosophers

1. Tacitus (*Agr.* 4), supplying the quotation on the young Agricola, and Quintilian (*Inst. orat.* 11.1.35, *vir civilis vereque sapiens*), express doubts about too much philosophy, the latter especially in his statement (*ibid.* 12.2.7), *Romanum quendam velim esse sapientem, qui non secretis disputationibus, sed rerum experimentis atque vere civilem virum exhibeat;* cf. 1 pr. 14.

2. For confusion of the doctrine of the several schools, see above, Chap. I n. 13, on Brutus; I. Düring, *Chion of Heraclea* (1951) 21, treating especially the dilution of Platonism; D. R. Dudley, *A History of Cynicism . . .* (1937) 137 and 148; and E. V. Arnold, *Roman Stoicism*² (1958) 121, on the blending of Cynicism and Stoicism "practically indistinguishable, alike in their rationale and their propaganda"—disputed by J. M. C. Toynbee, *Greece and Rome* 13 (1944) 56, with arguments that will be answered below; C. E. Lutz, *YCS* 10 (1947) 28, on Musonius; H. Bardon, *La Littérature latine inconnue,* 2 (1956) 173, on Seneca; and generally, on all the schools, their commixture dating from the first century B.C., A. Oltramare, *Les Origines de la diatribe romaine* (1926) 10.

3. P. Grimal, *REA* 47 (1945) 262f, identifies the Stoic Athenodorus. But other court philosophers of the time were Arius Didymus, also a Stoic (Dio 51.16.4; Plut., *Vit. Ant.* 80f; Sen., *Ad Marc.* 4f), and under Domitian, Publius Celer (Tac., *Hist.* 4.10 and 40; Dio 62.26.1), and Seras and Flavius Archippus, *philosophi* (Pliny, *Ep.* 10.58).

4. Despite their doctrines, Stoics scorned aliens (see Thrasea's views in Tac., *Ann.* 15.20f) and slaves (Sen., *Ep.* 88.2, using an old cliché), as well

as the lower classes and the uneducated. See Epict., *Diss.* 2.1.21f, and Musonius in Favorinus, Περὶ φυγῆς, in M. Norsa and G. Vitelli, eds., *Il papiro vaticano greco . . .* (1931) 5.43–46. As one moved closer to Cynic and "popular" doctrine, emphasis on study disappeared; but emphasis on *effort* remained. See G. Busch, *Antike und Abendland* 10 (1961) 133f.

5. Though Seneca enjoined an active role, he agreed (*Ep.* 4.11 and 14) with Epictetus (*Encheiridion* 46) that it need not be ostentatiously active. Here as elsewhere in this section, I need not give lots of references to illustrate the same common idea. Fuller references on several topics can be found in Oltramare, *Les Origines de la diatribe romaine.*

6. Seneca advocates that the wise man "will not struggle uselessly," in *De otio* 3.3, and in *Ep.* 14.8: "The wise man shuns a force that can hurt him." Chrysippus (Diog. Laert. 7.21) acknowledges limits to that role set by ill-health or the like, and Seneca (*Ep.* 22.8) acquits the wise man of participation if he cannot be truly effective. In the latter case, he may retire (*Ep.* 19.1; 22; 68.2), though here again, "A part of safety lies in not seeking it openly" (*Ep.* 14.8). "Let him who would be righteous leave court life," added Lucan (*Phars.* 8.493f); and, says Seneca (*De otio* 5.1), nature has begotten us for both contemplation and action. Earlier Stoics such as Zeno and Cleanthes had retired, thus canonizing that choice (Sen., *De tranq.* 1.10); and (Epict., *Diss.* 3.22.83) it offers genuine rewards, especially if devoted to the development of doctrine for all mankind (Sen., *Ep.* 14.14; 68.1f). "The work of a good citizen is never in vain" (Sen., *De tranq.* 4.6) by serving as an example. It is a proof of the power of that example, that retirement could be used as a charge against men. See Tac., *Ann.* 16.22; Dio 62.26.3; 65.12.2; 67.13.2; and W. Allen, *CJ* 44 (1948) 205, collecting earlier demonstrations of opposition by retirement, of uncertain nature: Epicurean(?), Stoic(?), or simply Roman.

7. The final goal of retirement is action (Epict., *Diss.* 3.2.15; Dio Chrysos., *Or.* 20.9f and 26), through the increase in solitude of one's inner powers (Sen., *Ep.* 74.19), developed by constant solitary exercise. "To live is to serve in arms" (*Ep.* 96.5; compare 74.19, *intus instruamur*) or as "athletes" (78.16; compare Sen., *De tranq.* 3.1, and Aul. Gell, *N.A.* 13.28, urging that men be always ready "like athletes for the pancration").

8. Inner exercise leads equally to action or contemplation (Diog. Laert. 7.130), some men preferring the former, the character of ὁ σπουδαῖος (*ibid.* 7.123, quoted as general Stoic doctrine) who responds to the call for help (Sen., *Ep.* 39.2f; 66.21). Such is the role recommended by various Stoics. See Sen., *De tranq.* 3.1. Grimal's attempt, *REA* 48 (1946) 76f, to deny the passage seems weak. Another proponent of action is Dio Chrysostom—if a dream may be trusted (Philostr., *Vit. soph.* 490); still another is Euphrates, in Pliny, *Ep.* 1.10, *esse hanc philosophiae et quidem pulcherrimam partem, agere negotium publicum.* Others are quoted generally for this view: "My

teachers," says Seneca's friend Serenus (Sen., *De tranq.* 1.10), though Seneca tries to rebut their testimony. Chion's letters urge the claims of patriotism (*Epp.* 12 and 13, and above, Chap. I); but the calls of one's country are recognized also by others (Diog. Laert. 7.130), and are exemplarily answered by Xenophon, Socrates, and Plato (Ael., *Variae hist.* 3.17; 7.14).

9. Seneca bequeathed to his friends only his example (Tac., *Ann.* 15.62, whence the quotation)—only that, in addition to his fortune of 300 million sesterces (Tac., *Ann.* 13.42).

10. Origen, *Contra Celsum* 3.66, matches Musonius to Socrates as a παράδειγμα τοῦ ἀρίστου βίου; Pliny, *Ep.* 9.13, responds to *exempla* to record the life of Helvidius; and (*ibid.* 6.29) Thrasea often said, *suscipiendas causas aut amicorum aut destitutas aut ad exemplum pertinentes.* Aul. Gell., *N.A.* 16.1.2, quotes the saying of Musonius on the immortality of good deeds, which Epictetus (*Diss.* 1.2.12–18 and 22) refers to, by metaphor, as the purple stripe.

11. Tacitus (*Hist.* 4.6; cf. *Ann.* 14.49 and 16; *Agr.* 42 and *passim*) sneers at the greed for glory.

12. Tacitus (*Ann.* 16.27) gives the relation between Thrasea and Helvidius. The latter's enmity to the Flavii is explained by Toynbee 52f. His exchanges with Vespasian, imagined by Epictetus (*Diss.* 1.2.19–22), are quoted in the text. On his later fame, cultivated by an admirer, Suetonius (*Domit.* 10.3) is wrong; Tacitus (*Agr.* 2), Pliny (*Ep.* 1.19.5), and Dio (67.13.2) are right: the admirer was Herennius Senecio, not Arulenus Rusticus. But the latter was killed for writing a life of Thrasea Paetus. The Flavian exiling of philosophers is reported in Aul. Gell., *N.A.* 15.11.4.

13. Thrasea Paetus was an acknowledged defender of the senate (Tac., *Ann.* 13.49; 14.12 and 48), as was Helvidius Priscus (Tac., *Hist.* 4.5f). On their relations with the aristocracy, see D. McAlindon, *AJP* 77 (1956) 113f; R. S. Rogers, *CP* 55 (1960) 19f; and Toynbee 51f.

14. Thrasea's alleged ambitions for *nova* [*instituta*] and *libertas* (Tac., *Ann.* 16.22) and his and Helvidius' championing of *vocem populi Romani et libertatem senatus* (Tac., *Agr.* 2) aim at nothing more than the old Republican constitution. The people's *vox* would have been very small. And I am suspicious of Dio's much wider statement (65.12.2) that Helvidius was turbulent, ταραχώδης, τῷ ὄχλῳ προσέκειτο, denounced monarchy, praised democracy, and acted "as if it were the business of philosophy . . . to stir up the masses, overthrow established affairs, and introduce innovations."

15. The virtuous character of the Stoic opposition is often attested (Dio 62.20.1 and Tac., *Ann.* 16.21, on Thrasea; Tac., *Hist.* 4.5, on Helvidius). They paid for their reputation (Dio 62.26.1; Suet., *Nero* 37.1; Tac., *Ann.* 14.22; 16.22). "Stoicizing" was called treasonous (see Dio 67.13.2 on Arulenus in trouble ὅτι ἐφιλοσόφει, like Musonius earlier, as given in Tac., *Ann.* 15.71, and Dio 62.27), and accused men were specified as Stoics, like Helvidius

(Tac., *Hist.* 4.5), Thrasea (Tac., *Ann.* 16.22), Rubellius Plautus (Tac., *Ann.* 14.59), or Arulenus (Pliny, *Ep.* 1.5). Their puritanism produced irritated comments cited in the text (Dio 65.13.1–1a; cf. Lucian, *Philosophies for Sale* 10f, and the scene also quoted at length, from Epict., *Diss.* 2.12.17–25, comparing 3.3.15 and 3.8.7 for further clashes between high rank and philosophy).

16. See Sen., *Ep.* 14.14 and 73.1, rebutting charges that Stoics are revolutionaries; more common prejudices are reflected in the quotations drawn from Dio 65.13.1; Tert., *Ad nat.* 1.4, on the philosophers howling against prevalent customs; Dio Chrysos., *Or.* 34.52, on their relaxing everything; and Aul. Gell., *N.A.* 1.2.1f, on their quibbling. Tac., *Ann.* 14.16, describes Nero's ridicule of philosophers, and Juv. 2 *passim,* with more on the *Stoicidae,* derides their hypocrisy. A picture of their bad character is most fully developed in Lucian, in many of his short works, goes back to the fourth century B.C. with Dio Chrysostom's description of Corinth (*Or.* 8.10, as he imagined that city scene), but seems to concentrate on the later first and second century A.D., throughout Italy and the Greek-speaking lands. The title used is most often just "philosopher." See Mart. 4.53.3f (calling them Cynics); Quint., *Inst. orat.* 1 pr. 15; 12.3.12; Sen., *Ep.* 5.2; Epict., *Diss.* 3.22.10 (Cynics); 4.8.5; Dio Chrysos., *Or.* 32.9; 34.2 (Cynics); 77–78.34; App., *Mithr.* 5.28; Aul. Gell., *N.A.* 9.2.1–6 and 8f; 13.8.5; 17.19.1–6; Dio 65.13.1a; Tat., *Ad Graecos* 25; Ael. Arist., *Or.* 46; Philostr., *Vit. soph.* 567; Julian, *Or.* 6.190D-E; 7.223B-C; and Dio Chrysostom's lost *κατὰ τῶν φιλοσόφων,* resumed by Synesius (*PG* 66.1116D). Note the warnings to the true philosophers (Sen., *Ep.* 19.1; 22; 68.2; Marcus Aurel., *Medit.* 1.7) not to sully the name of philosophy by bad conduct. Much of the ill-repute of Stoics was unfairly transferred from Cynics. See Dudley 199. For Stoics fitting just the same picture as Cynics, see Sen., *Ep.* 5.2, and P. Oppenheim, *Das Mönchskleid im christlichen Altertum* (1931) 218.

17. Oltramare 44f collects many references to the anti-intellectualism of Cynics. As N. Terzaghi says, *Per la storia della satira* (1932?) 12, "Stoicism [was] the Cynicism of the rich and lucky, while Cynicism was the Stoicism of the poor and unlucky, one meant for the salon and meeting rooms of the cultured, addressed to the higher problems of the spirit, the other to the market places and to men who wished to hear only some word of comfort and, if possible, of hope." For a good summary of the diatribe style, see Oltramare 12–16. Terzaghi, 17–42 *passim,* shows the debt owed by Roman poets to Cynic preachers.

18. Seneca (*De benef.* 7.11.1) recounts the tale of Caligula's bribing of Demetrius. Yet Seneca (*ibid.* 7.1.3; 7.8.2f; *Ep.* 62.3) admired him. He betrayed Musonius later (Tac., *Hist.* 4.10 and 40). He had been expelled from Rome twice. See Dio 65.13.3 and Dudley 126. With Demetrius, a certain Hostilianus was exiled. The association, and his ranting against monarchy,

seem to identify him as a Cynic (Dio 65.13.3), yet a case can be made out for his identification with C. Tutilius Hostilianus *philosophicus Stoicus* of *CIL* 6.9785. See F. Buecheler, *RhM* 63 (1908) 194, rejected too quickly in *RE* s.v. Tutilius (1). Other exiled philosophers are known from Dio 65.15.5 (one flogged, another killed). Dio Chrysostom was a victim, barred from his native Bithynia, apparently in 84, according to C. G. Starr, *CP* 44 (1949) 21. General expulsion orders were repeated in 93. See Suet., *Domit.* 10.3, and Dio 67.13.3: "Banished again," αὖθις, says Dio, but he may refer to an expulsion decree of Vespasian, not some putative first order of Domitian (contra, see Dudley 137 and below, n. 33).

19. For Stoic endorsement of retirement, see Epict., *Diss.* 3.3.15; Starr 27; and above, n. 8. For endorsement of a mixed constitution, see Diog. Laert. 7.131. But Stoics might also approve of monarcy, even, it seems, tyranny. Seneca's courtly letters, *Ad Polyb.* (esp. 1.2f and 12.3f) and *De clementia*, are the despair of his admirers. He loves Nero. He offers a defense of monarchy explicitly in *De benef.* 2.20.2 and *Ep.* 73.1f; and, by implication, in his views on the ruler's mercy and so forth, discussed by M. Fuhrmann, *Gymnasium* 70 (1963) 481 and 485. For similar opinions in other authors, see, for example, Epict., *Diss.* 1.29.9f, and Dio Chrysostom's three orations on kingship. For the Greek origins and development of the Roman views on monarchy, see Lutz, *YCS* 10 (1947) 60f; R. E. Carter, *Traditio* 14 (1958) 367f; Starr 21 and 27; A. Sizoo, *REL* 4 (1926) 230f and 234; C. Wirszubski, *Libertas* (1950) 134f, 145f, and esp. 149f, on Helvidius Priscus; and Dudley 129.

20. On the opposition's tolerance of the emperor's position, see Wirszubski 161 and Starr 21. Yet he must not extort adulation or betrayal of friends (Wirszubski 164; Starr 24), nor must his powers destroy virtue. See Sizoo 234f, with some possible support in Musonius' sayings (Lutz 131) and in Sentius Saturninus' speech, above, Chap. I. The inviolability of inner virtue is insisted on by Epictetus (*Diss.* 1.29.10f, quoted in the text), contrasted with external force by (among others) Themistius, quoted in J. Korver, *Mnemosyne*[4] 3 (1950) 319.

21. For vices as tyrants and vicious men as slaves, see Sen., *De ira* 3.15.3; Sen., *De clem.* 1.8.1; Diog. Laert. 7.121; Dio Chrysos., *Or.* 6 *passim.* On the types of resistance to be offered to force, the most important contemporary sources are Seneca, especially *Epp.* 22, 28, 66f, 70f, 80, and 104; *Ad Gall.;* and *De tranq.;* Lucian, especially *Demonax;* Diogenes Laertius; Dio Chrysostom, especially *Or.* 6 and 14; Epictetus; Musonius; and what survives of Favorinus. Particular emphasis is placed on the exercise of free speech in Dio Chrysos., *Or.* 6.58; Marcus Aurel., *Medit.* 1.6; and Diog. Laert. 6.69, supplying the quotation on "the best thing of all." It was linked with liberty in general (Lucian, *Nigrinus* 15; Lucian, *Demonax* 3 and 11; Lucian, *Peregrinus* 18; and above, Chap. I n. 21), and with Cynic free speech especially,

as in Epict., *Diss.* 1 pr. 3, where Arrian notes how he tries to preserve his master's διανοία καὶ παρρησία. The latter word, however, I cannot find in Epictetus, I suppose because he avoided the key term of another school. Cf. Lucian, *Demonax* 50, κατὰ τινα πάτριον τοῖς Κυνικοῖς παρρησίαν, along with much other ancient testimony. Free speech had its heroes—Thrasea or Helvidius (Dio 65.12.1)—but the ideal had degenerated by Pliny's day (*Paneg.* 66.4f), as is clear in the passage quoted in the text.

22. Pliny (*Ep.* 3.11) visited Artemidorus in exile. For a like loyalty to an exile, see Lutz, *YCS* 10 (1947) 7f, on Musonius' student Lucius, who compiled his master's lectures. Musonius himself had stuck by Rubellius Plautus (Lutz 14; Tac., *Ann.* 14.59). In exile, one might still gather a school (Lutz 16n56, on Demetrius; Norsa and Vitelli—cited above, n. 4—p. x, on Favorinus) or speak out boldly, as did Musonius (Korver 322f), Peregrinus (Lucian, *Peregrinus* 18f), Dio Chrysostom (Dudley 148 and 152), and Demetrius (Suet., *Vesp.* 13.1). Defending this last right, Musonius in his treatise *On Exile* quoted Euripides (Lutz 68–76), and others like him wrote on the right role of an exile. See B. Häsler, *Favorin, Ueber die Verbannung* (1935) 3f, 28–41, and A. Barigazzi, *Studi italiani di filologia classica* 34 (1962) 70f.

23. On strength under torture, see Sen., *Ep.* 67.3f and 6; cf. 66.21 and 37. Distinction between attacks on the flesh and on the spirit is drawn *ibid.* 71.27; 77.6–15; 78.19; 85.29; Aul. Gell., *N.A.* 12.5.1f; Epict., *Diss.* 1.1.21–27 and often elsewhere. On suicide as an escape from force, see Musonius in Tac., *Ann.* 14.59; Epict., *Diss.* 1.24.20 and *passim;* Starr 27; Sen., *De ira* 3.15.4; Sen., *Ad Marc.* 26.3; Sen., *Phoenissae* 151f; Sen., *Herc. furens* 426; as an escape from illness, see Dio 69.8.3 and Sen., *Ep.* 70.12. But suicide was looked at askance, to be attempted only after much deliberation, as is done, for example, in Tac., *Ann.* 16.25f, and as is recommended by Pliny, *Ep.* 1.22. That it might be resorted to for bad reasons is pointed out *ibid.* and by Martial 1.8.5; for suicide as a shortcut to fame, see Mart. 1.8.5 and *Dig.* 28.3.6f, *iactatione ut quidam philosophi;* cf. Lucian's *Nigrinus.* B. Walker, *The Annals of Tacitus* (1952) 268, lists 18 cases of suicide in Tiberius' reign alone, Cremutius Cordus being the only philosopher. He chose starvation, as did one of Pliny's friends, in extremity of illness (*Ep.* 3.7, *Silus Italicus inedia vitam finisse*); Euphrates the philosopher, old and sick, took hemlock (Dio 69.8.3); and earlier philosophers also had sanctioned suicide (Diog. Laert. 2.143; 7.167 and 176).

24. See Philostr., *Vit. Apoll.* 7.4, where Apollonius' calls to arms are described, whether or not historically, in passages that neatly illustrate the fusion of Roman and Greek tradition, Harmodius and Aristogeiton next to τὰ Ῥωμαίων πάτρια; further appeals to the memory of the two Athenians are made *ibid.* 8.16 and 25.

25. On acta of hearings, see F. A. Marx, *Philologus* 92 (1937) 96; R. Syme, *Tacitus* (1958) 1.188, 278, and 283, on the scope of the *acta senatus* and

their evidence in the accounts of Tacitus, especially *Ann.* 14 and 16. For the addition of color by Tacitus, see *Ann.* 16.29. On the literature of trial scenes available to Tacitus, see C. Questa, *Studi sulle fonti degli Annales di Tacito*[2] (1963) 245. Some of the conversation in such scenes, quoted in the text, is imagined in Sen., *Ep.* 78.19; in Epict., *Diss.* 1.1.22 (cf. 1.18.17f; 1.29.5 and 16f), and in Seneca the elder, *Controversiae* 2.5. It was a commonplace not only in rhetoric but in the typical dialogue form of Cynic diatribes, on which see Oltramare (cited above, n. 2) 11. For the cliché of giving one's torturer the slip, see Suet., *Tib.* 61.5, *me evasit.* Questa 247n27 cites this text and others from Senecan dramas: *Agamemnon* 994f and *Thyestes* 245f. Add Polyaenus, *Strat.* 8.62, the tyrant being greatly angered to have been "conquered by a woman," Epicharis. The story found there, that she was the mistress of Annaeus Mela, Lucan's father, strikes me as the invention of a late and unreliable source. Various martyrs indulged in repartee, for instance, the retort of the fourth century B.C. Theodorus to Lysimachus, that the latter's power extended only to a half pint of blood (Sen., *De tranq.*, 14.3; a different version in Val. Max. 6.2.3; and similar tales in Theodoret, *Graec. affect. curat.* 8.57f). Another example is Demetrius' retort to Nero, that nature threatened the emperor (Epict., *Diss.* 1.25.22). Stories of hurting or baffling one's torturer occur in Val. Max. 3.3.2–5; Clem., *Stromat.* 4.56.2; Plut., *Mor.* 505E; and Polyaenus, *Strat.* 8.45. Some were collected in a work *On the Courage of Philosophers,* by Timothy of Pergamum, quoted in Clem., *Stromat.* 4.56.2.

26. For a trial dialogue before Caracalla, see P. Roussel and F. de Visscher, *Syria* 23 (1942–43) 178f; for the staff that kept court records, see O. Hirschfeld, *Die kaiserlichen Verwaltungsbeamten bis auf Diocletian*[2] (1905) 329f, with notes, and *RE* s.v. *exceptor* and *commentarii,* cols. 738 and 743f, adding Sen., *Apocol.* 9.2 and 15. The titles are *commentarii, notarii, exceptores,* and variants of *a cognitionibus;* in Greek, γραμματεύς (τῶν βασιλικῶν δικῶν. Philostr., *Vit. Apoll.* 8.3). Dialogue reported in trial records is mentioned in *RE* Suppl. 7, s.v. *gesta,* col. 207, and its informality in J. Crook, *Consilium principis* (1955) 142–147.

27. Philostr., *Vit. Apoll.* 8.5 and 9, supplies the final details of the scene. Note similarities with the Acts of the Apostles 24.25: Paul "reasoned of righteousness, temperance, and judgment to come. Felix trembled," and dismissed Paul till a later time. This should be added to the numerous parallels, some strikingly close, between the Life of Apollonius and of Christ, strongly suggesting the dependence of Philostratus, for dramatic detail, on the synoptic gospels. See T. Hopfner, *Seminar Kondakov* 4 (1931) 160f.

28. F. Grosso, *Acme* 7 (1954) 333–353 (with copious references, but not aware of Hopfner's work), tries to rescue the whole of Philostratus' *Vita Apollonii* from almost unanimous skepticism. His treatment is curiously uncritical, considering the nature of the problem he addresses, and he makes no particular study of the trials. Without having anything new to con-

tribute, I am still inclined to accept the two hearings and acquittal as fact, based on the account of a companion of Apollonius, one Damis. The historicity of the Damis account is accepted by most though not all scholars, and at least the bare fact of the trial before Domitian is singled out for belief by that thorough doubter, E. Meyer, *Hermes* 52 (1917) 403 and 417f.

29. Philostr., *Vit. Apoll.* 8.2 and 7, and Grosso 484f point the parallels between Apollonius and Socrates; but Socrates was linked also to Musonius, in the writings of Origen and Julian later (Lutz, *YCS* 10 [1947] 3); was recalled by Epictetus in many passages, for instance, *Diss.* 1.29.16f (and, as Starr, *CP* 44 [1949] 28, points out, Socrates is "mentioned [by Epictetus] more than twice as frequently as any other person, and usually as a martyr executed by the state for his beliefs"). Reference to him is intended by Seneca also (*Ep.* 28.8), and by Thrasea Paetus. On the last, see Questa 248f, who is, I think, unnecessarily hesitant in suggesting that details in Thrasea's and Seneca's death scenes which recall Socrates' last hours were not later inventions but parts of a deliberate pose.

30. For Seneca's contempt for death, and for related views on suicide, see *Ep.* 77.6, comparing Epict., *Diss.* 1.24.20; on suicide, see Chap. I n. 3 and II n. 23. On deathbed discussions of the afterlife, see Sen., *De tranq.* 14.8f; above, Chap. I at notes 21 and 24, and Chap. II at note 18, on Demetrius; on Petronius, see Tac., *Ann.* 16.19, quoted in the text; for Seneca's vainglory, *ibid.* 15.63, and above, Chap. II at notes 9 and 11 for the description of the anonymous death scene (*ibid.* 5.6f).

31. On Seneca's deathbed discourse, see Tac., *Ann.* 15.63, and Dio 62.25.1f. Musonius' memory was preserved by Annius Pollio (Lutz 10), Helvidius' by Herennius Senecio (Pliny, *Ep.* 7.19; cf. *Ep.* 3.16, describing Fannia as full of tales of her grandmother's courage, devotion, and suffering under Claudius). For anniversary memorials, see Mart. 7.21–23, and Stat., *Silvae* 2.7.1f. It was Lucan's widow, Polla Argentaria, who commissioned these works, to be displayed with the subject's *imago*. A hint of the practice can be found in Mart. 7.44, referring to a man "whose face is captured in the living wax. Nero condemned him; but [he] dared to condemn Nero." Cf. the *carmina* of Titinius Capito (Questa 242).

32. Tacitus (*Hist.* 1.3) speaks of the period covered in the *Histories: laudatis antiquorum mortibus pares exitus;* in Tac., *Agr.* 42, Agricola resists the temptation to attain both fame and fate; cf. Pliny, *Ep.* 7.19, an *exemplum simile antiquis.*

33. On the dangers of retirement, see Sen., *Ep.* 14.8; cf. the exaltation of *otium* as a means of resistance, in Tacitus' *Agricola*, noted by E. Paratore, *Tacito*[2] (1962) 91. Loyalty was expected to show itself in applause, actively (Suet., *Vesp.* 4.4), in the proper facial expression (Tac., *Agr.* 45), without frowns (as in Suet., *Nero* 37.1) or philosopher's costume (Philostr.,

Vit. Apoll. 7.4 and 15). Philosophers were periodically banned, apparently in A.D. 66; in 71 (above, text at n. 15); probably in 89; and certainly in 93—according to F. H. Cramer, *Astrology in Roman Law and Politics* (1954) 242 and 245. And even in exile, they feared for their lives. For the atmosphere, see Plut., *Mor.* 606A-B; Philostr., *Vit. soph.* 488; Philostr., *Vit. Apoll.* 7.4 and 11; Epict., *Diss.* 2.12.17f. Hence the commonplace "There is παρρησία in exile" (above, n. 22). The quotation in the text is from Starr (cited above, n. 18) 20, with his italics.

34. The commemoration of Thrasea Paetus and Helvidius Priscus the elder is treated by Tac., *Agr.* 2; Suet., *Domit.* 10.3; by Dudley (cited above, n. 2) 139; Questa 235; and W. Richter, *Gymnasium* 68 (1961) 304; that of the younger Helvidius in *libri de Helvidii ultione* (Pliny, *Ep.* 9.13). For other memorial biographies, see Richter 304 and Bardon (cited above, n. 2) 2.170. And see Pliny, *Ep.* 5.5, describing Fannius' work as *inter sermonem historiamque*, and 8.12, on Titinius Capito's book.

35. Memorial pamphlets were written, says Pliny (*Ep.* 8.12), *pio munere;* cf. Tac., *Agr.* 3, Tacitus writing for *pietas.* The relation between the *Agricola* and memorial pamphlets is noted by Münzer, cited in Marx (cited above, n. 25) 85; by Questa 234; and by Paratore 41f. For the hint of foul play in Agricola's death, see E.-R. Schwinge, *RhM* 106 (1963) 363f and 370f. Marx 83–98 and Questa 235f point to Tacitus' factual debt to memorial literature. On the latter as a genre on the Roman scene, see Marx 84 and W. Schmidt, *De ultimis morientium verbis* (1914). The additional influence of funeral orations is noted by Paratore 42 and by A. Ronconi, *Da Lucrezio a Tacito* (1950) 211.

36. On the linking of Socrates' fame to Cato's, see Ronconi 213; the link to Seneca's fame also, in a double herm of the second century, is described by E. Bickel, *Das Altertum* 5 (1959) 91. In the end, "Seneca killed by Nero" appears in the company of Peter and Paul (Jerome, *De viris ill.* 12), at about the time when a moribund paganism was raising against Christians, in propaganda form on contorniates, the ghost of the Philosopher fearless in the face of Alexander (for which read "the pagan Roman senate challenging Christian emperors"; see A. Alföldi, *Scientiis artibusque* 1 [1958] 8).

37. M. Hadas, *The Third and Fourth Books of Maccabees* (1953) 96f, dates the work to Caligula's reign; A. Dupont-Sommer, *Le Quatrième Livre des Machabées* (1939) 76f and 81n45, supports a date (117–118?) under Hadrian. In fact neither offers solid evidence for such adventures in exactitude. For Eleazar, see 4 Maccabees 5.4. His devotion to philosophy, and his title of philosopher, are repeatedly referred to in 5.7, 10, 22, and so on —as often as Antiochus is called the tyrant in such passages as 5.1 and 22; 6.23; 8.1; and 9.1. The "prone yet erect" turn of phrase is in the tradition of the diatribe. For discussion of that element in the work, see Hadas 101 and Dupont-Sommer 22. The opposition between ἐγκρατεία or ὑπομονή, and

ἀνάγκη or *βία*, occurs in many passages. For Eleazar's challenging taunts and endurance quoted in the text, see 4 Maccabees 5.32; 6.23; 6.6f; and compare the tales of a famous Jewish martyr, a rabbi of the second century who, in successive interviews with the governor, always outargued him (S. Lieberman, *AI* 7 [1939–1944] 421; cf. above, n. 25). The athlete metaphor recurs often, as in 4 Maccabees 9.1; 12.14; and 17.12f. So does the conquest-of-tyranny theme: 7.10; 8.1; 8.15; 9.1. Hadas 126 draws the parallel between the torture scenes here and those of Christian martyr acts, and (101) points out the Socrates elements. On Stoicism in 4 Maccabees, see Hadas 117 and Dupont-Sommer 50f and 56.

38. The genre of pagan martyr acts was centered in Alexandria. Texts survive from elsewhere in Egypt: tiny bits, and about a dozen useful fragments, gathered by H. Musurillo, *Acta Alexandrinorum* (1961); but references hereafter will be to his *Acts of the Pagan Martyrs* (1954), to which his later book adds little, and which supplies texts, partial translations, and extensive, careful commentary. For the trial scene before Commodus, see Musurillo 66f, with further references on the same theme of the martyr's cultural heritage (254f). On Isidore's remarks to Agrippa, see Musurillo 23f; on the conversation with Trajan, 45f. He deals (10 and 53) with tortures and the stake. On the special reliability of one of the texts involved, see Musurillo 251; references to *παρρησία* are gathered *ibid.* 255. On pp. 267f, Musurillo rightly rejects an exclusively Cynic derivation for the martyr acts, but (272) admits "that the Acta came within the general tradition of martyr literature, which was fed largely—though not exclusively—by tales of Stoic heroes." For a passage in the pagan acts that has a proletarian sound see Musurillo 27: *οὐκ ἐμέμψατο Καίσαρα, ἔχων δικαστὴν ὀργιζομενον ἡδέως, εὐφυῆ κατὰ πλουσίων.* He discusses the debt of the acts to real trial minutes and to Greek fiction with perhaps too much ingenuity and tolerance of faint parallels (236–258).

39. For the choice of early, "pure" martyr acts, a list of roughly a dozen, see, among scores of titles, the selection of O. von Gebhardt, *Ausgewählte Märtyreracten . . .* (1902); R. Aigrain, *L'Hagiographie* (1953), especially 209f; and M. Simonetti, *Revue des études augustiniennes* 2 (1956) 40–54. For the extent to which martyr acts drew on court minutes, see Musurillo 249f and 261f; F. Halkin, in *Mullus: Festschrift Klauser* (1964) 153; Aigrain 133 and *passim;* H. Niedermeyer, *Ueber antike Protokoll-Literatur* (1918) 18, 29, 38f, and 58f; M. Simonetti, *Studi agiografici* (1955) 74; Simonetti, *Revue des études augustiniennes* 2 (1956) 40; and H. Delehaye, *Les Passions des martyrs . . .* (1921) 174–179. Christian acta emphasize their reliance on other true documents, too, wherever possible. See Aigrain 138 and 209, and Simonetti, *Studi* 9. Some evidence suggests the influence of Cynic diatribes, the use of words like *σωμάτιον* and *μάρτυς*, found also in Epictetus, and discussed by J. Geffcken, *Hermes* 45 (1910) 488n1 and 496. The dependence

is rejected or minimized by Delehaye 158 for *σωμάτιον*, and by F. Dornseiff, *Archiv für Religionswissenschaft* 22 (1923–24) 136f, and K. Holl, *Neue Jahrbücher für das klassiche Altertum* 33 (1914) 523 and 532f, for the second term (*martys*). As for similarities of celestial citizenship, Cynic *κοσμοπολιτεία*, and Christian visions of *ἡ ἄνω Ἱερουσαλήμ* (referred to in the Eusebius passage quoted in the text, p. 91), see Delehaye 157n1. The relation of Christian martyr acts to pagan acta and *exitus* is discussed by M. Pellegrino, *Ponzio: Vita e martirio di San Cipriano* (1955) 78; Niedermeyer 33; Musurillo 261; Simonetti, *Revue des études augustiniennes* 2 (1956) 40f and 52f; and below, on philosopher-*τελευταί* literature.

40. M. Simonetti, *Giornale italiano di filologia* 10 (1957) 148f and 154, deals with the sophistic quickness of exchanges from Christian martyrs, a feature of style rapidly popularized later. See also G. Luck, in *Mullus: Festschrift Klauser* (1964) 230f. An example is quoted in the text, drawn from *Mart. S. Pionii* 17; cf. *Mart. S. Apollonii* 33, Κυνικὸς δέ τις φιλόσοφος εἶπεν (spoke to the martyr—only to be discomfited by the answer he received); and a further invocation of Socrates' name, *ibid.* 41. For the Christians' interrogator as a "tyrant," see *Mart. S. Cononis* 4 and 5; *Passio S. Irenaei episcopi Sirm.* 1; and *Mart. SS. XL mart. Sebast.* 8.

41. The tale of the Egyptian martyrs is told by Eusebius, *Mart. Pal.* 11.7–19; on Christian *παρρησία*, see G. Scarpat, *Parrhesia* (1964) 82f, and Euseb., *Mart. Pal.* 11.2, speaking of a martyr "distinguished . . . by the regimen of philosophy and asceticism." Note also Sophocles, *Greek Lexicon* s.v. *φιλοσοφέω*, for entries demonstrating how commonly the word was used to denote strenuous Christian asceticism, especially monastic life. Christianity had its female philosophers, too. See *PG* 40.336 and M. Schede, *Mitteilungen des deutschen archäologischen Instituts*, Ath. Abt. 36 (1911) 103. With the same meaning, *philosophus* goes into medieval Latin. For martyrs as *ἀθληταί* in *ἀγῶνες*, the most familiar of metaphors, see, for example, Delehaye 211f. Eusebius' words in our passage, "struggled with in these contests," are *ἐγγυμνάσας τοῖς ἄθλοις*.

42. Simonetti, *Giornale italiano di filologia* 10 (1957) 152, speaks of the martyr's joyful face and smile; on the tyrant defeated, compare above, n. 25, and *Mart. SS. XL mart. Sebast.* 10, "But Satan, defeated . . . said in front of all, 'Alas, I am conquered by these holy men.'" Many like passages could be added from scenes of the fleshly temptations of Egyptian ascetics. For the martyr's miraculous gifts and acts, see Simonetti, *Giornale* 150, and Holl 523–527. Holl (538f) detects two different stages in the treatment of the martyr's prophetic and visionary powers, which are harder to accept. Simonetti, *Giornale* 147, is sceptical about the connection between aretalogy and martyrology, but unwilling to dismiss it. Holl (544) deals with some later miracles of martyrs; but the powers of martyr relics cannot be discussed here. One common strand is the sense of direct communication

between the hero and the heavens, as he "raises his eyes" (or a like phrase). Compare Philostr., *Vit. Apoll.* 8.4, and *Mart. S. Cononis* 5. As to martyrs clothed in traditional philosopher's garb, see Oppenheim, *Das Mönchskleid* 220f. Resemblances were not coincidental. Contemporaries called these Christian ascetics "philosophers," and efforts were made to draw a sharp distinction between theirs and pagan asceticism (*ibid.* 222).

Chapter III. Magicians

1. Seneca's experiments in Pythagoreanism are described in his *Ep.* 108.17–22, quoted in the text, and his desisting from them is explained by Tac., *Ann.* 2.85, *actum de sacris Aegyptiis Iudaicisque pellendis.*

2. Seneca (*De tranq.* 14.4–9) speaks of Canus with admiration; Plutarch, in Syncellus, *Chron.* p. 625 (*a.* 37), calls him a Stoic.

3. I. Lévy, *Recherches sur les sources de la légende de Pythagore* (1926) 102f and *passim*, studies the stories about Pythagoras. Those cited in the text come from Iamb., *Vit. Pyth.* 136, and Lévy 13 and 19. On Pythagoras' sources of enlightenment, see Lévy 27, 81, 127, and 131f; Iamb., *Vit. Pyth.* 151 and 158; on his conduct before Phalaris, *ibid.* 212–220 and Lévy 134. Here and throughout a long list of other details Lévy (131–135) traces parallels to Apollonius' own life according to Philostratus.

4. The passage quoted in the text is from Porphyry, quoted in Euseb., *Praep. ev.* 9.10.3; cf. Porphyry's admiration for the Brahmans, *De abst.* 4.17. The Greeks' willing dependence on eastern peoples for magic and the more adventurous side of philosophy is treated compendiously by A.-J. Festugière, *La Révélation d'Hermès Trismégiste* 1 (1944) 10–37 *passim.* Pythagoras' own debt to the Brahmans appears in Clem. Alex., *Strom.* 1.15.66, 69, and 72, and their general reputation in A.-J. Festugière, *Revue de l'histoire des religions* 125 (1943) 32f, where he deals with the commonplace of Greek wise men meeting eastern sages, being treated like children, and retiring discomfited. The theme goes back to Alexander's day, and the repute of the Brahmans still stood marvelously high throughout the empire. See Clem. Alex., *Strom.* 1.15; Porphyry, in J. Bidez, *Vie de Porphyre . . .* (1913) 10; Numenius, cited by E. R. Dodds, *Les Sources de Plotin* (1960) 5; Theodoret, *Graec. affect. curatio* (ed. Canivet) 1.25 and 5.58; and Apul., *Flor.* 6.7f. According to Porphyry, *Vit. Plot.* 3, study under Ammonius had made Plotinus eager to investigate the Persian and Indian systems; hence his adventure into the East. Saints Thomas, Andrew, and others also traveled to the East for instruction. See R. Söder, *Die apokryphen Apostelgeschichten . . .* (1932) 12 and 25, and Niceph. Call., *Hist. eccl.* 2.40 (*PG* 145.864), the tales starting at least as early as A.D. 200. Andrew reached China!

5. On the mixture of Peregrinus' beliefs, see R. Pack, *AJP* 67 (1946) 334–342; H. M. Hornsby, *Hermathena* 48 (1933) 65–84; and *RE* s.v. Peregrinus (K. von Fritz, 1937). Philostratus the elder wrote a life of Peregrinus (now lost), and Aulus Gellius (*N.A.* 12.11) attended his lectures and admired him. He may have been a good deal more than a fraud. The source of his inspiration is clear in Lucian, *De morte Peregrini* 27 and 39, containing comparisons to the Indian bird, the phoenix, and to Brahmans; *ibid.* 25 recalls Calanus (= Kalyâna), whose immolation was first described by Alexander's admiral, Onesicritus, and then by Strabo, Plutarch, Arrian, Aelian, and others. For Zarmanochegas, see Pack 335n1. Peregrinus' posthumous appearance, quoted in the text, is described in Lucian, *De morte Peregrini* 40.

6. See Lévy, *La Légende de Pythagore de Grèce en Palestine* (1927) on Pythagoras' double nature (8–15); on his being raised to the heavens corporeally (67); on the stories of his reappearance to his disciples (78); and on the influence of these miracles on wonder stories of Egypt (175 and 197).

7. I interpret as Plotinus' soul the snake seen by a reliable witness to disappear into the wall of his bedroom when Plotinus was "trying to give back, to what is divine in all, the divine part in himself" (Porph., *Vit. Plot.* 2). On his words, see P. Henry, *Studi classici e orientali* 2 (1953) 114–130 (date, A.D. 270, p. 113). For the invocation of his spirit, see Porph., *Vit. Plot.* 10, with comments on the scene by A. R. Sodano, *Porfirio, Lettera ad Anebo* (1958) pp. xxix–xxxi, and by E. R. Dodds, *JRS* 37 (1947) 60, noting the directions for the summoning of one's own soul, σύστασις ἰδίου δαίμονος, in a magical papyrus—*PGM* 2 (1931) 23. Note also the distinction between δαίμων (soul), the πάρεδρος ("familiar," or demon servant—both in Dodds, *JRS* 37 [1947] 60), and the *genius*, or tutelary spirit. The last also might be made visible, as to the emperor Constantius on the eve of his death (Amm. 21.14.2). Quotations in the text regarding the war of magic between Plotinus and a rival are drawn from Porph., *Vit. Plot.* 10. On the presence of several Egyptians in Plotinus' circle at Rome, see Sodano p. xxix; and on his invulnerability, see the opinion of a contemporary of Celsus, in Origen, *Contra Cels.* 6.41, "Magic is effective among the uneducated and corrupt, but can have no force among philosophers, because of their provisions for a pure regimen." Plotinus expresses just the same views, especially in the passages gathered by H. Chadwick, *Origen, Contra Celsum* (1953) 6.41n1.

8. For Serapis on Hadrianic coins, see C. Bosch, *Die kleinasiatischen Münzen der römischen Kaiserzeit* vol. 2 pt. 1 (1935) pp. 150 and 170: Alexandrine issues of 132–133. Serapis types increase in popularity up to the very end of the mint. More generally, on the second century popularity of Isis and Serapis, see J. Beaujeu, *Hommages à Jean Bayet* (1964) 65f, and

J. Geffcken, *Der Ausgang des griechisch-römischen Heidentums* (1920) 15f. The quotation in the text dealing with Pachrates and Hadrian comes from *PGM* 1.148; the other, on riding crocodiles, comes from *RE* s.v. Pachrates (K. Preisendanz, 1942) cols. 2071f. His pupil, Arignotus, is known from Lucian, *Philops.* 32.

9. How much Plotinus himself owed to this Egyptian background for the genesis of his philosophy is disputed, for instance, by S. Eitrem, *Symb. Oslo.* 22 (1942) 52–64 *passim*, and by Dodds, *Les Sources de Plotin* 5f. It must be remembered, of course, that at Alexandria one could pursue the purest Hellenic studies. Egypt was also the home of lower charlatans, as seen in Celsus quoted from Origen, *Contra Cels.* 1.68 (trans. Chadwick). In the text, the quotation of the curse is from A. Audollent, *Defixionum tabellae* . . . (1904) 415, the tablet from Cirta. Compare a tablet invoking a dead man's soul to come to the writer's aid, in C. Bonner, *Studies in Magical Amulets, Chiefly Graeco-Egyptian* (1950) 104. For a maleficent invocation in a papyrus, see *PGM* 2.14 and 26 (third century), and A. D. Nock, *JEA* 15 (1929) 220f. The range of evidence, in time and type, can be illustrated by the first century Cyranides 1.5.9 (17.8, ed. de Mely), a recipe for an amulet giving power over all men; Cyranides 1.3.10 (13.25, ed. de Mely), prescribing a plant effective for expelling demons; and the fourth century Vegetius, *De mulomedicina* 3.12, giving a recipe "to clean an animal, put devils to flight, or remove disease"—all quoted from J. Tambornino, *De antiquorum daemonismo* (1909) 17–24. Besides magic on tablets and papyri, a third source is gem stones. To his *Studies in Magical Amulets,* Bonner offers a fine introduction in *Harvard Theological Review* 39 (1946) 25f. See also S. Eitrem, *Symb. Oslo.* 7 (1928) 73f, and Eitrem, *ibid.* 19 (1939) 58–65. The several examples in the text are all drawn from Bonner, *Studies* 108–110, 115, and 118.

10. On exorcism, see an example in the preceding note, and *PGM* 2.15, an ἀπόλυσις spell in the form, "Anubis, be gone, for my health and salvation; off to your thrones"; also Justin, *Apol.* 2.6, and Tert., *Apol.* 37, who show that Christian exorcism was common in the 160's in Rome and in the early third century elsewhere; further, Damascius, *Vit. Isid.* 56; Eunap., *Vit. soph.* 457, where Porphyry expels a demon of the type locally called "Casautha" from a public bath. Exorcism was regularly attributed to fourth century Egyptian monks, as in E. A. T. W. Budge, *The Paradise or Garden of the Holy Fathers* (1907) 1.127f; Pallad., *Hist. Laus.* 52; Athanas., *Vit. S. Anton.* 48, 63, and 71; and Soz., *Hist. eccl.* 5.15. Lucian, *Philops.* 16, tells us that "everyone knows the Syrian from Palestine, adept (σοφιστής) in it," that is, in exorcism, who gets the devils to answer from human bodies they have invaded, and who finds out how they got in, and makes them go away. For the theory of demonic causation, see Porph., *De abst.* 2.40; for an exchange of accusations of unluckiness or contamination, as a cause of a long

drought in late fourth century Palestine, see Marc. Diac., *Vit. Porph.* 19f; 22f (contamination); 56 (Arians). Cyprian (*Ep.* 75.10.1f) blames a series of earthquakes for the outbreak of anti-Christian persecutions in the late 230's in Cappadocia and Pontus, and a host of similar passages to prove the connection between the persecutions and natural disasters are gathered by G. E. M. de Ste. Croix, *Past and Present* 26 (1963) 37n136. Earthquakes, however, also brought the rise of the madwoman mentioned in the text, *quaedam mulier quae in exstasin constituta propheten se praeferret.* For the miracle worker in Marcus Aurelius' army, Christians put up their own candidates. On the incident, see H. Lewy, *Chaldaean Oracles and Theurgy* (1956) 4f, and Dio 72.8.2 (attribution to "Arnuphis, an Egyptian *magus*"). If one philosopher could bring on a storm, another (under Constantine) could chain the winds. For that incident, see Eunap., *Vit soph.* 463. On Julianus' saving of Rome, see Dodds, *JRS* 37 (1947) 57. He failed, however, in competition with a Christian, in this tale of much later invention. The description, quoted in the text, of his routing of the Dacians, is by Psellus, in Lewy 248n72. Cf. SHA *Aurelian* 18.5, "sacrifices in certain places" to check barbarian invasion of Italy in 270, and a similar miracle of Eugenius, described by Aug., *Civ. dei* 5.26. For apotrapaic magic against later barbarian invaders, see Phot., *Bibl.* 60A-B (ed. Henry vol. 1 p. 177), supplying the quotation about the three silver statues. The feat of Nestorius is reported by "the philosopher Syrianus," in Zos. 4.18, A.D. 375; but Christians performed similar acts for the salvation of cities, as Constantinople was defended by martyrs' relics, in the fifth century. See N. H. Baynes, *Analecta Bollandiana* 67 (1949) 170 and 174.

11. Eunap., *Vit. soph.* 475, describes the invocation of Hecate. Other methods of communication are discussed by Dodds, JRS 37 (1947) 62f, and by Bonner, *Studies* 15f. On necromancy, see S. Eitrem, *Symb. Oslo.* 21 (1941) 74f; F. Cumont, *Lux perpetua* (1949) 87; on the birds to summon Plotinus' spirit, see Dodds, JRS 37 (1947) 61, and Eitrem, *Symb. Oslo.* 22 (1942) 64; on animals and animal noises, *ibid.* 70–72, and Euseb., *Praep. ev.* 4.23.2; for invocation formulas in papyri, see *PGM* 2.14f; and finally, on mediumistic trances, see Dodds, *JRS* 37 (1947) 66f; Eitrem, *Symb. Oslo.* 22 (1942) 55 and 59; Iamb., *De myst.* 3.14f; and *PGM* 2.16.

12. The researches of a certain Thessalus into astral plants are traced by A.-J. Festugière, *Revue biblique* 48 (1939) 52–63, and F. Cumont, *Revue de philologie* 42 (1918) 85f and 93f. The author was known in Nero's day as a self-advertising ignoramus whose extravagant claims included the boast that his prescriptions could overthrow armies or check floods (*ibid.* 98 and 105). Maximus of Tyre (*Philos.* 9.7) also had seen Asclepius face to face.

13. The words describing the elder Julianus' provisions for his son are those of Proclus, quoted by Psellus; see Lewy 224n195; Dodds, *JRS* 37 (1947) 55f; and, on the *Oracles*, *ibid.* 56 and Lewy *passim.* Eunapius' *Vitae*

sophistarum is the principal source. From many further illustrations of the mystic-philosopher, I mention here only Julian's teacher, Maximus (*ibid.* 473–481), and Sosipatra (*ibid.* 467–471), who founded a sort of dynasty, including the famous Antoninus, her son.

14. Hippolytus (*Refutatio* 9.17 [*PG* 16.3394]) quotes the invocation of Elkesai (see Chap. IV n. 25) to secrecy, and Eunapius (*Vit. soph.* 471) exalts the divine wisdom of Antoninus (see the preceding note) and (*ibid.* 499) of a certain Ionicus; see further references in *RE* s.v. Mageia (T. Hopfner, 1928) col. 372, and Festugière, on Thessalus, *Revue biblique* 48 (1939) 56. Neoplatonists talked the same way, to raise themselves above mere wonder workers. A gulf separated the true philosopher from common people with their cruder beliefs (Bidez, *Vie de Porphyre* 98; Dodds, *JRS* 37 [1947] 57; and Lucan, *Phars.* 10.195). Neoplatonist debts to other doctrines, for example, to Neopythagoreanism, are defended by H. Dörrie, *Hermes* 83 (1955) 439–477 *passim*, disputed by Dodds, *Les Sources de Plotin* 24–31: see also Cumont, *Lux perpetua* 153f. Iamblichus' views (*De myst.* 96.13, quoted in the text from the translation of Dodds, *JRS* 37 [1947] 59) at least show how far Neoplatonism had moved from Platonism.

15. In Chap. II nn. 1 and 16, references have been gathered on the deliberately unscholarly character of many Roman philosophers. See also A. Oltramare, *Les Origines de la diatribe romaine* (1926) 44f. For Cynic antipathy to liberal studies, see Diog. Laert. 4.53; 6.27 and 103f, cited by Oltramare; but Sextus Empiricus is a specially good illustration, as stressed in the quotation from F. H. Cramer, *Astrology in Roman Law and Politics* (1954) 203–205, on Book V of Sextus' *Adv. mathematicos.* His views are echoed by Hermes Thrice-Greatest, quoted from the *Asclepius* 1.12B.

16. The great variety of words denoting all kinds of philosophers is clear from Dio 49.43.4; Aug., *Civ. dei* 10.9; Min. Fel., *Octav.* 27.1; *Cat. cod. astrol.* 8.4; Ulp., *Mos. et Rom. legum coll.* 15.2.1; Paul, *Sent.* 5.21.3; *Cod. Theod.* 9.16.4; R. Reitzenstein, *Hellenistische Wundererzählungen* (1906) 37. For pejorative terms meaning "charlatan," see various lexicons, s.v. *ariolus* and the others; Jos., *Ant. Jud.* 20.5.1; Zos. 4.13; Philostr., *Vit. soph.* 590; Philostr., *Vit. Apoll.* 8.7.2; Dio 78.17.2; Marcus Aurel., *Medit.* 1.6; and Aug., *Civ. dei* 10.9. These texts illustrate the contamination of terminology. For equivalence between *philosophus* and *magus*, see Apul., *Apol.* 2.7; Min. Fel., *Octav.* 27, *magi et philosophi;* Firm. Matern., *Math.* 3.2.18, *magi . . . vel philosophi;* for *magus* in the sense of dabbler in the occult, or impostor, from the first century on, see *Thesaurus linguae latinae* s.v. *magus* and Liddell, Scott, and Jones, *Greek-English Lexicon* s.v. μάγος (Euripides and later authors). Suet., frg. 81 p. 94, links *Pythagoricus et magus* also; by the next century the word "sophist" had begun to appear in strange company. See above, n. 10; Tert., *De idol.* 9, *sophistas aut Chaldaeos aut . . . magos;* and Eunap., *Vit. soph.* passim. One equivalence (*astrologus* = *mathematicus*) occurs in a host of writers (*Thesaurus linguae latinae* s.v. *mathematicus*); another

(*mathematicus* = *philosophus*) in Jerome, *Chron. a.* 89–90 (*PL* 27.459). For the many synonyms meaning "astrologer," see Tac., *Ann.* 2.27; 12.22; *PGM* 2.35 (ὀνειρόμαντις μαθηματικός, third century); Juv. 6.553; and P. Vallette, *L'Apologie d' Apulée* (1908) 299. "Philosopher" was a title usurped by martyrs, pagan or Christian. See above, Chap. II nn. 37 and 40f; A. Dupont-Sommer, *Le Quatrième Livre des Machabées* (1939) 13 and 33f; *ibid.* 34, on Philo, *Leg. ad Gaium* 156 and 245. The borrowing of the prestige of philosophy for Christian purposes is more fully discussed by G. Bardy, *Revue d'ascétique et de mystique* 25 (1949) 97–108, on Justin, Melito, Clement, and later authors, and by G. J. M. Bartelink, *ibid.* 36 (1960) 482–487, on Chrysostom. From Bardy 102 I quote in the text Justin's description of Christianity as "the sole profitable philosophy." Even Christian asceticism was called "philosophy" by Eusebius and later authors (Bartelink 490f; Bardy 107; and the lexicons of later Greek, Du Cange and Sophocles, s.v. φιλοσοφία, φιλοσοφεῖν, φιλόσοφος).

17. Pictures and busts of philosophers can be studied in A. Maiuri, *Roman Painting* (1953) 65–66; K. Schefold, *Die Bildnisse der antiken Dichter, Redner und Denker* (1943) 179 fig. 3; and J. Kollwitz, *Oströmische Plastik der theodosianischen Zeit* (1941) pl. 40. Julian, *Or.* 6.190D, refers to the type of the philosopher "with a staff and long hair, as in the pictures of the men," still the Cynic type. A word-picture is quoted in the text from Eunap., *Vit. soph.* 473. Eunapius goes on, "Whoever was with [him] could hardly bear the swift glances of his eyes." Compare Damascius, *Vit. Isid.* 32, declaring that eyes cannot be used rightly without divine light, and Marinus, *Vit. Procli* 22, "His eyes were filled with brilliance and his face shared the radiance of divinity."

18. Dodds, *JRS* 37 (1947) 68n124, cites references (Lucian and later) to levitation—popularly attributed to Christian wonder workers also, as in *PL* 73.1001; for Pythagoras' talks with animals, see above, Chap. III at n. 4, and Porph., *De abst.* 3.3, mentioning the slave of a friend of his who could understand the noises of birds "and who said that all of them were prophetic." In Athanasius, *Vit. Anton.* 50, and Söder, *Die apokryphen Apostelgeschichten* 63, we learn of Christian heroes speaking to animals—a fine trick, though little enough compared to the North African lions that could speak to people, in Moorish! (Ael., *De nat. animal.* 3.1). Aretalogies as a literary genre have been studied by A. Kiefer, *Aretalogische Studien* (1929) 1–23; Reitzenstein 1–83; Söder 1–95; and H. Werner, *Hermes* 53 (1918) 236–247—all *passim.* I use the term "aretalogy" here in its widest possible sense. Jerome's account of *aretai* was aimed at a lowly audience, as his own words indicate, quoted in Reitzenstein 63. The vulgar quality of aretalogies is noted *ibid.* (*volkstümlich*), and by Werner 241 and 244.

19. Apollonius' good repute appears in Dio's tone (67.18.1f, Apollonius' telepathic knowledge of Domitian's death) and in Caracalla's and Alexander Severus' veneration of him (Dio 77.18.4; SHA *Alex. Sev.* 29.2; cf. H. Dessau,

ed., *Inscriptiones latinae selectae* 2918). Porpyry, *De abst.* 3.3, speaks of his knowledge of bird talk. *PGM* 2.54 (fourth-fifth century) speaks of his magical πάρεδρος, "The old woman of Apollonius of Tyana as servant." Cedrenus, Tzetzes, and other Byzantine writers give detailed attention to the means by which Apollonius averted floods and earthquakes or cleansed or protected Byzantium and Antioch from plagues of serpents, scorpions, and stinging insects. See T. Hopfner, *Seminar Kondakov* 4 (1931) 158f, and E. Meyer, *Hermes* 52 (1917) 390f. References to him in later literature include also Origen, *Contra Cels.* 6.41; Eunap., *Vit. soph.* 454 and 500; and a lost life, in the early fourth century, by Hierocles, answered by Euseb., *Contra Hieroclem*, and by Bishop Macarius at the end of the century (Hopfner 160n104). "Vopiscus" meant to write a life, and Virius Nicomachus Flavianus *did* write one, as did another fifth century writer (Hopfner 163).

20. The historicity of the two alleged biographers of Apollonius, Moiragenes and Damis, is generally accepted. On the source problems, see Hopfner and Meyer, and above, Chap. II n. 28. Iamblichus' debt to a life of Pythagoras by Apollonius is asserted by Lévy (cited above, n. 3) 102 and 110; another work by Apollonius, on prayer, is known also (Philostr., *Vit. Apoll.* 3.41; 4.19). His friendship with Dio Chrysostom appears in Philostr., *Vit. soph.* 488. Despite these literary claims, he was called γόης. The word has no English equivalent, and perhaps "fakir" is closest, meaning "juggler with magic," both as fraud and as black magician. This was the term against which he (like Pythagoras) contended (Philostr., *Vit. Apoll.* 5.7; 7.17; 8.7.2; 8.19; Origen, *Contra Cels.* 6.41; Iamb., *Vit. Pyth.* 216).

21. M. Caster, *Etudes sur Alexandre* (1938) 21, explains Alexander's descent from Perseus by reference to the ancient cult of Perseus in the area, and (49) identifies the legate of Cappadocia, Severianus. For discussion of Rutilianus, see Caster 53f; A. Stein, *Strena Buliciana* (1924) 260f; and F. Cumont, *Alexandre d'Abonotichos* (1887) 16f. I owe to Professor Broughton the reference to A. Degrassi, *I Fasti consolari dell'impero romano . . .* (1952) 41, dating Rutilianus' consulship.

22. O. Weinreich, *Neue Jahrbücher für das klassische Altertum* 47 (1921) 138; Cumont, *Alexandre* 18f; and Caster, *Etudes* 29, discuss elements of Asclepianism in Alexander's innovations. On snake elements, see Cumont, *Alexandre* 22, 25, 38, 42f, and 44 (the carved emerald); Weinreich 142; Bonner, *Studies* 162; Caster 26–29 and 97; Epiph., *Haer.* 37.5; Praedestinatus 1.17 (*PL* 53.592), quoted in the text; *Encyclopedia of Religion and Ethics* s.v. Ophitism (E. F. Scott, 1917) 499f; and *Dictionnaire d'archéologie chrétienne* s.v. Ophites (H. Leclercq, 1936) 2157. Outside of Lucian's pages, Alexander is known from other sources. See Cumont, *Alexandre* 25 and 43, and Weinreich 149f; but A. D. Nock, *CQ* 22 (1928) 160n7, sets aside part of the evidence, and one of the inscriptions, from Rome and Danube prov-

inces, mentioning Glycon, is disputed by Stein 259n2, against Cumont, *Alexandre* 37f.

23. On Alexander's Pythagoreanism, see Nock, *Classical Quarterly* 22 (1928) 161; Caster, *Etudes* 9; Weinreich 132f; S. Eitrem, *Orakel und Mysterien am Ausgang der Antike* (1947) 78 and 81; and Cumont, *Revue de l'histoire des religions* 86 (1922) 206f. Still other elements, Eleusinian and Apollonian, are detected by Weinreich 146f; Eitrem, *Orakel* 82f; Cumont, *Alexandre* 31f; and Cumont, *Revue de l'histoire des religions* 86 (1922) 208f.

24. The second century popularity of oracles is noted by Eitrem, *Orakel* 78; by Beaujeu, *Hommages à J. Bayet* 61f; A. Boulanger, *Aelius Aristide . . .* (1923) 129; Bosch (cited above, n. 8) 170 and 272; M. Caster, *Lucien et la pensée religieuse de son temps* (1937) 26 and 225f; and by Geffcken (cited above, n. 8) 6f. The orientalization of beliefs, illustrated at several points in this chapter, cannot be explored systematically; but note its influence on aretalogies (Reitzenstein 4n2), on Origen's and Clement's views of spirits (W. Bousset, *Archiv für Religionswissenschaft* 18 [1915] 162), on the spread of eastern cults to Rome (Geffcken 13f), on the Chaldean Oracles (Lewy 399–441), and on Porphyry's religious lore (Bidez, *Vie de Porphyre* 10f and 17). But Dodds, *Sources de Plotin* 5, seeks to correct older tendencies to find too much orientalism in Neoplatonism. Much of the superstition drawn on by Alexander—necromancy, for example—shows up in other, sometimes far earlier, settings. See Eitrem, *Symb. Oslo.* 21 (1941) 68–78, also discussing magic in general, as a theme. On witches in literature, see *RE* s.v. Lamia (Schwenn, 1924) col. 545. But belief in demons did not prevail among the educated before Alexander's century. See *RE* s.v. Lamia col. 545 and Cumont, *Lux perpetua* 89. Then it entered educated circles, along with the greater use of amulets. See Cumont, *ibid.;* Pliny, *Ep.* 7.27; and Eitrem, *Symb. Oslo.* 19 (1939) 59. For Dio's superstitions, see his story of a demon (79.7.4) quoted in the text and, more generally, F. Millar, *A Study of Cassius Dio* (1964) 77. Credulity in other writers is clear in Phlegon (C. Müller, ed., *Fragmenta historicorum graecorum* 2.1169f) *π.θ.* 6–10, 14, 23f; further, M. L. Trowbridge, *CP* 33 (1938) 69–88, offering a perfectly uncritical catalogue of miracles in the SHA, useful as a collection. By Plotinus' time, the upper classes were clearly superstitious. For illustrations from these ranks, see Porph., *Vit. Plot.* 7 and 9f, and Bidez 99 and 104.

25. Testimony to second and third century superstition includes the *defixiones* of Hadrumetum in Audollent, *Defixionum tabellae* 360–414; papyri such as *PGM* 2.18; and the *Book of Secrets,* read by Jews, as is now noted in the *New York Times,* Dec. 29, 1964, p. 29. Compare Acts of the Apostles 19.19, attesting the extremely common possession of books of magic among relatively simple folk, in Ephesus under Claudius. Pliny the elder was more skeptical (*N.H.* 17.267; 28.17, 19f, and 47). Yet Nero believed (Suet., *Nero* 34.4), and so did Lucan. On Lucan, see Lucan, *Phars.* 6.430–830, and

K. Preisendanz, *Akten des VIII. internationalen Kongresses für Papyrologie, Wien, 1955* (1956) 124, agreeing with the surmises of Eitrem and others that Lucan may have been an actual practitioner of magic. Doubters gradually disappeared—so I suppose, in an *argumentum ex silentio*. But there are plenty of believers to offer positive confirmation of the point: Tacitus (see below, n. 31); Juv. 6.610f, 615f, 638f, and 659; Dio 52.36.2f; Zon., *Epit.* 13.16; SHA *Did. Julianus* 7.10f; and Amm. 16.8.2; 19.12.14. If the Church thundered against magic beliefs, that was because they were wicked, not untrue. J. Straub, *Heidnische Geschichtsapologetik in der christlichen Spätantike* (1964) 59–61, collects interesting references, as does J. Maurice, *Revue historique de droit français et étranger* 6 (1927) 118f.

26. *Homo rusticanus et decrepitus senex*, Apuleius calls the third brother (*Apol.* 70.3).

27. See M. N. Tod, *Journal of Hellenic Studies* 77 (1957) 138f, on the "close association of philosophy and medicine."

28. In *Apol.* 27.1, Apuleius shows his contempt of the ignorant. Compare his use of the words *rusticus, rusticanus, agrestis . . . et barbarus, incultus et agrestis*, always contemptuously (9.1; 10.6; 16.10; 23.5; 70.3). On his reaction to the intellectual voyages of earlier philosophers, see the description quoted in the text from Vallette, *L'Apologie d'Apulée* 288. On Apuleius' philosophy, see Vallette's excellent discussion, 185–325 *passim*, especially 268, 289f, and 299. The second century *rapprochement* of philosophy and magic (see Chap. III at n. 16) is illustrated also by Philostr., *Vit. soph.* 590, describing Apuleius' contemporary, a rhetor "so famous that many thought him a γόης . . . By telling of marvels in his declamations about the customs of μάγοι, he drew on himself this name."

29. On the legal basis of the accusations against Apuleius (those of poisoning being dropped) see C. Marchesi, *Apuleio di Madaura, Della Magia* (1955) pp. x–xii, and Vallette 35f, pointing out that it was (hostile or maleficent) magic per se that was charged, not poisoning. The word *maleficus* (*ibid.* 36n2) is specified. True, Apuleius seems to have been charged also with the preparation of *amatoria pocula*. This underlay all the talk about his fishy interests, and received vague support by misinterpretation of his love poems. Love philters did fall under the *lex Cornelia* (Marchesi p. x; Vallette 35; T. Mommsen, *Römisches Strafrecht* [1899] 639); but the gravamen is clearly the general practice of magic. "Magic arts" are outlawed in Paul, *Sent.* 5.23.18, perhaps explaining references in Vettius Valens, *Anthol.* 4.24 and 5.10 (pp. 199 and 230, ed. Kroll) to "fines and judgements brought about because of mysterious writings," μυστικὰ γραπτά, or by "the law on writings."

30. *Cod. Theod.* 9.16.13 = *Cod. Just.* 9.18.4 (321). Compare Augustine (Vallette 73n2) distinguishing between good and bad medication, and Mommsen 640, on the importance in law of the specifying term *maleficus*.

Constantius' law is recorded in *Cod. Theod.* 9.16.5 (357), followed by later confirmation: *Cod. Theod.* 9.16.7 (364) and *Cod. Just.* 9.18.9 (389).

31. To references in Vallette 71, on amulet legislation, add Amm. 29.2.26, where "a simple-minded old woman" is executed for curing by spells. J. J. O'Meara, *Porphyry's Philosophy from Oracles in Augustine* (1959) 98, points out that Porphyry recognized theurgy and magic as prohibited; Eunap., *Vit. soph.* 471, speaks of a theurgist "keeping a wary eye on the opposing views of the emperor" in the 370's or 380's; and Amm. 28.1.14, 26, and 50 supplies still further instances of magical practices punished. In spite of all this T. Hopfner, *Ueber die Geheimlehren von Jamblichus* (1922) 231, reminds us that more than a third of magical papyri are taken up with less criminal love spells. For spells used against Germanicus, see Tac., *Ann.* 269, quoted in the text, comparing Libo's necromancy at 2.28; but (2.30) the evidence that told most against Libo was a paper with names of the imperial family and senators, marked with mysterious marks. Another man (6.29) had to defend himself against charges of practicing "rites of *magi*"; and in the third century, a punishment of exile was imposed for being a *φαρμακεὺς καὶ γόης* (Dio 78.17.2).

Chapter IV. Astrologers, Diviners, and Prophets

1. For confusion between prediction and geometry or philosophy, see Strabo 16.1.6 (philosophers = Chaldeans); Jerome, *In Dan.* 2 and *Chron. a.* 89–90, describing Domitian's ban on astrologers and philosophers (cf. Suidas s.v. Δομετιανός: φιλόσοφους καὶ μαθηματικοὺς); *Cod. Just.* 9.18.2 (294), thinking it necessary to point out the distinction between *geometria* and *mathematica.*

2. The Augustan law on divination (Dio. 56.25.5) is "the permanent basis of Roman law on the subject" according to F. H. Cramer, *Astrology in Roman Law and Politics* (1954) 232; and see 250f. Since Cramer's book is often referred to hereafter, as being the most comprehensive and accessible authority on astrology, it might be well to enter a warning here against his occasional tendency to treat his sources uncritically; but I have not indicated my misgivings on minor points, in the notes that follow. As to Tiberius' law on divination, see Suet., *Tib.* 63.1, comparing Ulpian's reference to a *senatusconsultum* of 17 "banning *mathematici*, Chaldeans, seers, and the like" (*Mos. et Rom. legum coll.* 15.2.1), evidently empire-wide, since Ulpian is handling the proconsular office. Antoninus Pius concerned himself with the matter (Ulpian, (*ibid.* § 4), and the quotation from Ulpian in the text (*ibid.* § 2) shows the extent of legislation. Compare Paul, *Sent.* 5.21.1, "*Vaticinatores* who pretend to be inspired of god are to be expelled from the city lest public manners, in hope of anything, be corrupted by

human gullibility, or the minds of the people be thereby disturbed; § 3, Whoever consults *mathematici, arioli, haruspices*, or *vaticinatores* concerning the health of the emperor or the destiny of the state, shall be executed together with him who responded; § 4, Not only will everyone be advised to abstain from divination, but from the art and its books as well" (cf. *ibid.* § 2). Aurelian's law, addressed to soldiers, is known from SHA *Aurel.* 7.8—though it is probably not historical. Diocletian renewed the prohibitions, seen in *Cod. Just.* 9.18.2 (cf. 9.18.8, A.D. 370); so also did Constantine and Constantius, *ibid.* 9.18.3 (319) and 9.18.5 (357), both quoted in the text. Compare 9.18.7 (358), penalties "regardless of rank" against those "who are in our court, in *comitatu meo vel Caesaris*," and *Cod. Theod.* 9.16.10 (371), accusing senators of practicing magic. On further laws of 341, 353, and 356, interpreted as antidivination, see F. Martroye, *Revue historique de droit français et étranger* 9 (1930) 673–676. Exile or conversion were in the end the only alternatives offered to *mathematici*, as in *Cod. Theod.* 9.16.12 (409); for further bans, *ibid.* 9.16.9 (371) and *Cod. Just.* 1.11.2 (385).

3. For strict control of the corpus of recognized pagan Sibyllines, see Dio 57.18.4f and Tac., *Ann.* 6.12 (A.D. 32); for the disturbance created by a false Sibylline in A.D. 19, foretelling civil war in Rome, see Dio 57.18.4f. Justin, *Apol.* 1.44.12, is quoted in the text on a law forbidding reading of prophetic books, though he adds that the books are read anyway. H. Windisch, *Die Orakel des Hystaspes* (1929) 31f, speculates whether the law, like an *Index prohibitorum*, specified titles or spoke more generally. Reference by Paul, *Sent.* 5.29.3, to books of diviners need not refer to such oracles. Marcus Aurelius exiled an inflammatory prophet (Ulpian, in *Mos. et Rom. legum coll.* 15.2.6, quoted in the text). Perhaps this is the measure referred to by Melito, but Montanism is another possible explanation. On the appearance of the heresy in the capital, see below. Diocletian passed similar laws, also quoted in the text, against Manichaeism (*ibid.* 15.3, Gregorianus).

4. Magic by itself might suffice for a treason charge from A.D. 49, as Cramer argues (*Astrology* 252 and 253f). Magic and divination even remotely touching the emperor or his family were still seen as *maiestas laesa* or *minuta* in Ammianus' day (Amm. 14.7.7; 16.8.1; and 19.12.1).

5. A. Bouché-Leclercq, *L'Astrologie grecque* (1899) 567, gives the evidence for secrecy about official consultations. For secrecy on Augustus' horoscope, see Suet., *Aug.* 31.1; 94.5; and Dio 45.1.3. It was known to Manilius (Cramer, *Astrology* 97). Imperial horoscopes known to us include those of Hadrian (*ibid.* 164f) and Septimius Severus and Constantine (O. Neugebauer and H. B. Van Hoesen, *Proceedings of the American Philosophical Society* 108 [1964] 66f—with my thanks to Professor Neugebauer for the reference). Ambitious horoscopes might prove dangerous to their owners (Cramer 168; SHA *Aelius* 3.8; and other instances of horoscopes

being divulged only to friends: Juv. 14.248; Hor., *Od.* 2.17.21f; Suet., *Tit.* 9.1). Septimius Severus, according to Dio 77.11.1, concealed his own. Diviners pretended inability to speak on imperial horoscopes—witness the disclaimer in Manilius, and then again in Firmicus Maternus (Bouché-Leclercq 567). The quotation in the text is from the latter's *Astronomica* 2.30.3f, of the second quarter of the fourth century (cited by Bouché-Leclercq).

6. Cramer, *Astrology* 233–248, with references, and K. Latte, *Römische Religionsgeschichte* (1960) 328f, give the history of expulsions of astrologers. Some individuals were exempted, at least under Tiberius' law (Suet., *Tib.* 36; Dio 57.15.8). Others were punished by ancient ceremonies (Ulpian, *Mos. et Rom. legum coll.* 15.2.1, on a law of A.D. 117; Tac., *Ann.* 2.32). The impudent response of the "Chaldeans" is quoted in the text, drawn from Suet., *Vitel.* 14.4; cf. Dio 64 [65].1.4; and the same story in a tenth century source, for a doubtful edict of Nero's (Cramer 242). Trouble with predictions varied according to the strength of the reign: witness, for example, incessant predictions of Claudius' death (Sen., *Apocol.* 3) and incessant doubts of Nero's rule (Tac., *Ann.* 14.22; 16.14f; Suet., *Nero* 40.2).

7. Cramer, *Astrology* 254–275, collects the evidence of trials for predictions. Add, not as astrology but as forbidden inquiries, Philostr., *Vit. Apoll.* 7.11; 7.20; and for the second century and later, Dio 79.22; Amm. 14.7.7; 16.8.2; 19.12.9 and 15; 29.2.6; and 29.2.26–28. Eusebius, *Praep. ev.* 4.2.10, notes the current practice of arresting and interrogating impostors prophesying by "divine powers." On Septimius Severus and astrology, see SHA *Sept. Sev.* 4.3, quoted in the text. For his general savagery against astrologers, see SHA *Sept. Sev.* 15.5f. The trial in his reign is known and quoted from Dio 77.8.1f. Naturally Dio took seriously the accusation he describes. He had begun his own literary career with a *Treatise on Dreams* (73[72].23.1f).

8. Amm. 29.1.29–32 gives a full picture of a prediction trial, discussed by T. Hopfner, *Griechisch-ägyptischer Offenbarungszauber* 2 (1924) 144. Zos. 4.13f adds details of Theodorus' consorting with ἀγύρται and γόητες, after he had heard of the prediction, and of Valens raging at "all men far-famed for philosophy or otherwise bred up in literature." The fate of some philosophers involved we learn from Amm. 29.1.39, and voluntary book burning from Amm. 29.1.41 and 29.2.4.

9. For a full, sympathetic account of Maximus' role in the Theodorus plot, see Eunap., *Vit. soph.* 480; on Iamblichus' crimes, Zon., *Epit.* 13.16, is wrong in the detail that the investigation led to Iamblichus' suicide. Libanius' friend Parnasius was caught in a charge of inquiring into matters "which it is forbidden to know," through astrology (Liban., *Or.* 14.16, A.D. 362). For another philosopher accused of high treason for oracular consultations, see Amm. 19.12.12. The quotation from Servilia's trial is in Tac., *Ann.* 16.30f. Acceptance of the reality of the charges of prediction in these times can be found *ibid.* 12.52.

10. For the hippodrome as the universe in miniature, see P. Wuilleumier, *Mél.Rome* 44 (1927) 193; the related quotations in the text are derived from Wuilleumier 184, and are discussed *ibid.* 187f. The mode of interpretation is traceable as far back as the second century (pp. 190–194). For Vettius Valens' customers, see his *Anthol.* 2.41 (ed. Kroll, p. 130); 2.26 (p. 94); 5.11 (p. 232); 7.2 (p. 268). On his date, see O. Neugebauer, *Harvard Theological Review* 47 (1954) 66f. On the high rank of his clientele, see *Anthol.* 2.21 (pp. 84f); 7.2 (p. 269). For his school, see Cramer, *Astrology* 191. Vettius Valens' complaints about the low repute of astrology come from his *Anthol.*, ed. Kroll p. 241 line 4, though its fortunes soon rose. See SHA *Alex. Sev.* 27.5 (quoted in the text) and 44.4, mentioning salaries and lecture rooms for astrologers. However, the whole account may not be historical.

11. On attitudes toward astrology under the Empire, see Cramer, *Astrology* passim, especially 83–90, 117–126, 140f, 145f, 155–162, 193–218, and 223f; Bouché-Leclercq 546–560; on doubters, *ibid.* 570–593, and Cramer 89 and 140. Hadrian's reign is perhaps the turning point, with the skepticism of figures like Favorinus, Diogenianus, and Oenomaus. See Aul. Gell., *N.A.* 14.1; Theodoret, *Graec. affect. curatio* (ed. Canivet) 6.8; 10.19; and P. Vallette, *De Oenomao Cynico* (1908) 1f. For purveyors of foreknowledge to the poor, see the quotations in the text drawn from Max. Tyr., *Philos.* 13.3c, and Origen, *Contra Cels.* 350. For customers and experts among the upper classes, see Bouché-Leclercq 570n1, and the example of Firmicus Maternus and others in the fourth century (Cramer 191).

12. The history of Thrasyllus' family is recounted in Cramer, *Astrology* 82, 92f, 104–115, 127–131, 136–139, and 172f; F. Cumont, *Mél.Rome* 37 (1918–19) 33–36; R. Syme, *Tacitus* (1958) 2.508, 525; H. A. Musurillo, *The Acts of the Pagan Martyrs* (1954) 130f; and D. Magie, *Roman Rule in Asia Minor . . .* (1950) 1399. The identity of some of the people involved is disputed, but I follow the majority opinion.

13. Seneca praises Balbillus in *Quaest. nat.* 4.2.13, *profectus in omni litterarum genere rarissime*. On Chaeremon, see Cramer, *Astrology* 116f.

14. On the destruction of the Capitol, see Tac., *Hist.* 4.54, quoted in the text; cf. his own feelings, 3.71f; for German prophets of the time, see 2.61 (Mariccus captured and executed) and 4.61 (Veleda of the Bructeri).

15. On Clemens alias Agrippa, see J. Mogenet, *AC* 23 (1954) 321–325, with references; on Marcus Silanus alias Drusus, Tac., *Ann.* 5.10, and Dio 58.25.1. For a false Caesar, see above, Chap. I n. 18. As to Nero's popularity, P. A. Brunt, *Latomus* 18 (1959) 558n3, unconvincingly contests the scholarly consensus. The anti-Nero texts from Greek writers are Dio Chrysos., *Or.* 31.150 (Nero's avarice), and Plut., *Mor.* 567f (early 80's), offering a vision of Nero's tortures in hell interrupted by a voice enjoining mercy on one "who had freed the best and most heaven-loved of his subjects." We have also Dio Chrysos., *Or.* 21.10, recounting how all Nero's subjects but his

immediate retinue hoped for his indefinite rule, and "even now everyone wishes he were alive—though most believe he *is,* despite the fact that, so to speak, he has died not once but many times, along with those who had been firmly convinced that he lived." Add that his grave in Rome was decorated with flowers (Suet., *Nero* 57). On the first false Nero, see Tac., *Hist.* 2.8f; Dio epitomized, Loeb ed. vol. 8 p. 210; on the second impostor, supplying a quotation in the text, *ibid.* p. 301 (Terentius Maximus). John of Antioch (*ibid.* n. 1) tells us "he soon perished." The history of the third is given in Suet., *Nero* 57, and Tac., *Hist.* 1.2, who says that he "almost roused the Parthians to arms." A false Alexander is reported only by Dio 79[80].18.1–3, quoted in the text. F. Millar, *A Study of Cassius Dio* (1964) 214f, thinks the δαίμων was actually imitating Caracalla, who imitated Alexander. For this possibility there is no direct evidence. Imitations of Alexander or claims to be his avatar were not unusual. Examples can be found in Livy 26.19.7 (Scipio); Suet., *Aug.* 94.5; *Nero* 19.2; SHA *Alex. Sev.* 13.3; and Soc., *Hist. eccl.* 3.21 (Julian).

16. On Nero and Tiridates, see F. Cumont, *Rivista di filologia*[2] 11 (1933) 146f and 151f.

17. Nero's return is quoted from *Asc. Isaiae* 4.2 (ed. R. H. Charles [1900] 24f). F. C. Burkitt, *Jewish and Christian Apocalypses* (1914) 46, is in the minority in dating the text to the early second century. For Nero in Revelation, date and identification, see H. H. Rowley, *The Relevance of Apocalyptic* (1955) 130f; S. Giet, *L'Apocalypse et l'histoire* (1957) 46–57, Nero as the sixth king, intended by John (pp. 77–79); and P. Touilleux, *L'Apocalypse et les cultes de Domitien et de Cybèle* (1935) 38. Nero also appears in the fourth book of the *Sibylline Oracles.* On the date, see *RE* s.v. Sibyllen and Sibyllinische Orakel (A. Rzach, 1923) cols. 2132f. The relevant passages on the return of Nero are *Or. Sibyl.* 4.119f, 137–139; 5.1–51, 100–110, 123, 215–246, 361f; 8.38–106; on the chronological problems, see *RE* s.v. Sibyllen cols. 2119f, 2132–2137, and 2143; *Or. Sibyl.,* ed. A. Kurfess (1951) 306 and 317. Lactantius refers to the myth in *De mort. persecut.* 2.7–9, quoted in the text. Commodian, *Carm. apol.* 823f and 933f, also recurs to the return of Nero. On the poet's dates, probably around 260, see J. Moreau, in his edition of Lactantius, *De mort. persecut.* vol. 2 p. 202; W. Bousset, *Der Antichrist . . .* (1895) 50, giving a date under Decius; and J. Gagé, *Revue de l'histoire et de philosophie religieuses* 41 (1961) 355 and 358f.

18. On prophets in Judea, details and quotations are drawn from Jos., *Ant. Jud.* 20.5.1; 20.8.5f and 10. The background and meaning of still others are discussed by E. Fascher, ΠΡΟΦΗΤΗΣ . . . (1927) 184, 190f, and *passim.*

19. The quotation concerning oracles that aroused the Jews is from Jos., *Bell. Jud.* 6.312, almost identically worded in Suet., *Vesp.* 4.5, and Tac., *Hist.* 5.13. That it was the Hystaspes oracle to which Josephus refers is

asserted by Windisch, *Die Orakel* 67f. On its sources, see Windisch 6–13, 25f, and 96f; E. M. Sanford, *AJP* 58 (1937) 439; and Cumont, *Revue de l'histoire des religions* 103 (1931) 64f, 68, and 93–95; on the stages of history foreseen, but very confused in extant references, see Windisch 6, 26f, and 52; Cumont 73–75; Lact., *Div. inst.* 7.15f; and on Hystaspes' date, Windisch 70; Cumont 65; A. Peretti, *La Sibilla babilonese . . .* (1943) 378, arguing inconclusively for a date before Augustus.

20. Rabbi Gamaliel (first-second century) is quoted from H. Fuchs, *Der geistige Widerstand gegen Rom in der antiken Welt* (1938) 70. Exactly similar statements are known from rabbis of the next three centuries (*ibid.* 71).

21. Anti-Egyptian prophecies appear in *Or. Sibyl.* 5.484f, 492; and 7.20f. For the Egyptian origins of Books 3–5 and 11–14 of the *Sybillines*, see the Kurfess edition, p. 306; *RE* s.v. Sibyllen cols. 2136 and 2139; and W. Scott, *Classical Quarterly* 9 (1915) 144. Anti-Jewish oracles preserved include *Papiri greci e latini* (1912–) 982, a part of which is quoted in the text. G. von Manteuffel, *Mélanges Maspero* 2 (1934–1937) 119–124, tries to fill the lacunae and make sense of the whole. He rightly compares *Papiri greci e latini* 760, the utopia scene, and P. Oxy. 2332, the restoration of worships to Egypt, and he rightly connects the text with Pharaonic oracular traditions; but I disagree with his interpretation of the prophecy as originating among the Greeks of Egypt. For the *Oracle of the Potter*, see the resumé quoted from C. H. Roberts, *Museum Helveticum* 10(1953) 272, of P. Oxy. 2332 (late third century; further commentary in P. Oxy. vol. 22 pp. 89f). Roberts thinks the *Oracle* is written by and for (non-Alexandrian) Greeks, which conflicts with the general tone (such as the mention of Memphis) and with the origin of the imagery lying in Hellenistic Egyptian oracles. Finally, there exists an Egyptian anti-Christian oracle, of which I quote a part from the text of A. D. Nock, in A.-J. Festugière, *Corpus Hermeticum* 2 (1945) 326f, *Asclepius* 24. The bulk of the work belongs to the third century, in its prophetic part embroidering a Jewish Sibylline text with Stoic and Platonic eschatology (Nock, in Festugière 2.288f; W. Scott, *Hermetica . . .* I [1924] 57f; A. S. Ferguson in Scott, *Hermetica* 4 [1936] xii, xv); but the prophecy contains interpolations from the second half of the fourth century (Nock, in Festugière 2.288f; S. C. Neill and A. D. Nock, *Journal of Theological Studies* 26 [1925] 174f). Scott, *Hermetica* 1. 54 and 76, and Ferguson in Scott, *Hermetica* 4.xv, acknowledge the writer's Egyptian nationality. I omit sections dealing with invasions of Egypt, mere clichés of eschatology. Its tone recalls Eunap., *Vit. soph.* 471, quoted in the text for comparison. On the prophet, Antoninus son of Sosipatra, see Chap. III n. 13. An exactly similar prediction of the triumph of Christianity over the gods and shrines in Greece in the 380's (?) is found in Eunap., *Vit. soph.* 475f. For our knowledge of Constantine's reading of the Sibyllines, the sources

can be consulted conveniently in the Kurfess' edition of *Or. Sibyl.* pp. 208–223.

22. Ephraim and Hippolytus are sources for the Assyrians, and for the king with a fleet, here quoted from Cumont, *Revue de l'histoire des religions* 103 (1931) 72n3 (cf. Lact., *Div. inst.* 7.17.2). The "king of another race" is foretold in *Liber Clementis* 81.15f, in Bousset, *Der Antichrist* 52; the date is A.D. 250–300 (*ibid.* p. 53).

23. Fuchs 63–66 and Sanford 448 discuss Baruch, Ezra, and Revelation. Hippolytus recorded his predictions in *In Dan.* 4.23.2f; cf. 4.5.1, regarding the stability of Rome. By Christ's coming is meant God's resting on the seventh day, a day in his sight being as a thousand years (Hippol., *De antichristo* 43; Psalms 90.4; II Peter 3.8). The Sabbath is taken by Lact., *Div. inst.* 7.14.8, as lasting for a day = millennium of utter peace, that is, the *pax Romana*, during which (7.25.6) there is no cause for apprehension. On earlier terrestrial powers, see Hippol., *In Dan.* 3.31.2, somewhat too sweepingly summed up in C. Pedicini, *Annali della Facoltà di Lettere e Filosofia della Università di Napoli* 4 (1954) 107. Rome is called the part of iron, following Daniel's allegory, in Hippol., *De antichristo* 33; cf. *Or. Sibyl.* 8.126f: "No longer shall Syrian, or Greek, or barbarian, nor any other race submit its neck to your yoke of slavery [O Rome]." But Rome is also compared to a serpent (Hippol., *De antichristo* 14, a piece of stock imagery; cf. Bousset, *Der Antichrist* 89 and 93f) and to the Beast of Revelation, and the number 666 is equaled to the letters in LATEINOS (Hippol., *De antichristo* 50, an equivalence suggested also by Irenaeus, *Adv. haereses* 5.30.3). Ultimately the empire's break-up into "democracies" was foretold by Hippolytus (*De antichristo* 27, and *In Dan.* 2.12.7). On this fragmentation, see Hippol., *In Dan.* 4.5.6; 4.24.7; and Lact., *Div. inst.* 7.16.1. S. Mazzarino, *Rapports du XIe Congrès international des sciences historiques* (1960) 2.38f, draws some extravagant conclusions from the image.

24. Bousset, *Der Antichrist* 16, 120, and *passim*, emphasizes the two streams of thought in Jewish-Christian apocalyptic, seeing Rome as the Antichrist (the Johannine view) or as his precursor and, to a point, his preventer. Pedicini 98f emphasizes the split in the tradition between those who saw all temporal powers as being of the Devil, and those who offered allegiance or tolerance to temporal powers, as in Clem. Alex., *Ep. to Corinthians* 37.1–3 (cited by Pedicini, p. 106); Irenaeus, *Adv. haereses* 5.24 (cited by Pedicini, p. 108); and Ps.-Ephraim 1 and 5 (cited by Bousset, p. 79). Tertullian rather saw the empire as a bulwark against the world's end, in a passage (*Apol.* 32) in the text; compare Tert., *De resurr. carnis* 25, and Tert., *Ad Scap.* 2, and, equally explicit, Lact., *Div. inst.* 7.25.8, *illa est civitas quae adhuc sustentat omnia* . . . What the world's end might be like is sketched in the quotation from an apocalyptic vision in Bousset 129; for more similar pictures, see Bousset 130f.

25. Seers in Rome are described in Dio 55.31.2f. (A.D. 7), and 57.18.4 (A.D. 19), and others in Syria are quoted in the text from Hippol., *Ref.* 9.16 (*PG* 16.3387), with the remarks of G. Strecker (1959) in the *Reallexikon für Antike und Christentum* s.v. Elkesai, especially cols. 1172f, dating the apostle Alcibiades' Roman visit to the early third century. Hippol., *Ref.* 9.13 and 15, often refers to his powers ταράσσειν. Another Roman seer is known from SHA *Marcus* 13.6 (A.D. 166).

26. In *Dig.* 21.1.1.9f, the questions of Vivianus (first century) are answered by Ulpian, on "fanatic" or inspired slaves; cf. above, Chap. III n. 18; on mendicant visionaries in Palestine and Phoenicia in the 170's, foretelling the end of the world or claiming to be God, see Origen, *Contra Cels.* 8.9.

27. P. de Labriolle, *La Crise montaniste* (1913) 279, 281, and 282n3, describes the reaction to Montanism by Gaius, who dates to between 199 and 217. For other details on Montanism mentioned in the text, see Labriolle, 13, 17, 29, 35f, 68, and 518. There is no way to settle the chronological problem, nor space to discuss it. I follow Eusebius, Labriolle (569–589), Bardy, Pincherle, and others. Montanist prophetesses are attested by Epiph., *Panarion* 50.2 (*PG* 41.881), quoted in the text; cf. the tomb of a Phrygian woman announcing her title, "Christian pneumatic," filled, that is, with the divine breath (*Dictionnaire d'archéologie chrétienne* s.v. Montaniste [H. Leclercq, 1934] col. 2539), and compare also the origins of the Marcionite heresy, "devoted to astrology" and tied in with prophecy and magic. It sprang up in nearby Pontus under Antoninus Pius, and a seceder published the *Oracles* or *Revelations* of a certain prophetess (Tert., *Liber de praescript.* 6 and 30; Tert., *Ad Marc.* 1.18f; 3.11).

28. Mentions of later Druidism are from SHA *Sev. Alex.* 60.6 and *Aurel.* 44.4. For commentary, see E. Bachelier, *Ogam* 11 (1959) 174–184 and 295f, and T. Köves, *Acta ethnographica academiae scientiarum Hungaricae* 4 (1955) 255; on the survival of Druidism in Pannonia, see G. Alföldy, *Acta antiqua academiae scientiarum Hungaricae* 8 (1960) 145f and 158f.

29. On early hostility to Jews and Isis worshipers, see E. M. Smallwood, *Latomus* 15 (1956) 319 and 322, and Jos., *Ant. Jud.* 18.4.73f. As the successful proselytizing, and not the religion or existence, of the Jews aroused Tiberius' displeasure, so it is argued that new missionary and baptismal institutions of the Christians aroused the persecutions of A.D. 202. See the interesting views of K. H. Schwarte, *Historia* 12 (1963) 185–208. Persecution of Christians I cannot, of course, discuss properly, but for the connection of clamorous riots and administrative severity, see (besides the New Testament) Tert., *Ad Scap.* 4.3f; *Mart. S. Polycarpi* 3, 8, 9, 11f; *Mart. SS. Carpi et soc.* 42; Euseb., *Hist. eccl.* 5.1.38—the *demos* shouting or the like; and generally, the excellent article of G. E. M. de Ste. Croix, *Past and Present* 26 (1963) 15f. Quoted in the text are the interesting views of Dio

(52.36.2f) on un-Roman religions, which, though they are put into the mouth of Maecenas, apply to Severan ideals.

30. For "renewal" propaganda on coins, see J. Gagé, *Transactions of the International Numismatic Congress . . . London . . . 1936* (1938) 180–185, and H. Mattingly, *Numismatic Chronicle*[5] 13 (1933) 188, Mattingly being unconvincing in his interpretation of the abbreviation *Fel. Temp.* Progress toward the millennium of Rome had been celebrated with a different, retrospective emphasis in A.D. 148 ("founding" motifs discussed *ibid.* 186). For *Reparatio temporum*, see J. Gagé, *AI* 4 (1936) 181, and H. Mattingly and E. A. Sydenham, *The Roman Imperial Coinage* (1923–   ) 9.xi and 25, mentioning the phoenix and *Perpetuetas* (sic), as well as *Gloria novi saeculi* (ibid. 45 and 65). *Renovatio Romanorum* and *Roma aeterna* are discussed by Gagé, *AI* 4 (1936) 161–163 and 169–175, citing *Paneg. vet.* 10.1. *Roma aeterna* is found on coins of every period, a fact that Gagé rather suppresses; but it is a legend more often met with, as he says, among pretenders and Illyrian emperors of the third and fourth centuries. They especially needed to hold out offers of better things, as did pretenders in the 190's (Albinus, Niger, Severus). By the same token, *Roma aeterna* is rare in a reign like Antoninus Pius'. See H. Mattingly, *Coins of the Roman Empire in the British Museum* (1923–1950) 4.34 (Pius); 5.26, 80, 84, 87, 97, 138f (Severus). The emphasis on the immortality of Rome is in harmony with another complex of desires, for a return to Romanness, to older traditions of the people and of the city. This has been detected by A. D. Nock, *Harvard Theological Review* 23 (1930) 256–260, in the third century fervor for the worship of Vesta, and in other contemporary popular or official enthusiasms, which incidentally sharpened angers against the challenge of Christianity. *Perpetuitas* (*Aug.* or *Augg.*) comes in the third century, so far as I can discover, with Alexander Severus, then Florian(!), Probus, Valentinian, and Gratian. See Mattingly and Sydenham 5.357; 9.159; R. A. G. Carson, in Mattingly, *Coins* 6.159, 161f; wrongly, Gagé, *AI* 4 (1936) 175. *Aeternitas Aug.* or *Augg.* is also late (Valerian, Gallienus, Claudius II). For other notes of renewal, see R. MacMullen, *Soldier and Civilian in the Later Roman Empire* (1963) 177n53, mentioning *Restitutor saeculorum* or the like, and Gagé, *AI* 4 (1936) 175 and 181. For the revival of the myth of the Golden Age, see A. Alföldi, *Numismatic Chronicle*[5] 9 (1929) 271 and 273; E. H. Kantorowicz, *Perennitas . . .* (1963) 125–129; and F. Christ, *Die römische Weltherrschaft . . .* (1938) 98–102. The symbolism is Jupiter as a babe, *Jupiter crescens* or *exoriens*, being suckled by the goat Amalthea, riding on her back, or reaching to the seven stars (the universe); to him a prince of the imperial house may be compared. The last previous reference to the *Saecula aurea* had been Hadrian's (Mattingly, *Coins* 3.278). Other references, in literature—Claudian, Symmachus, the SHA—are

gathered by I. Hahn, *Wissenschaftliche Zeitschrift der Martin-Luther-Universität* 11 (1962) 1357f, who finds in them the reflection of "social revolutionary," "propagandistic," "radical," or "communist Utopian" ideology. The texts will not bear this interpretation. For an example of how far one can be carried by a stubborn ambition to make bricks without straw: Hahn (1358) sees in Themistius' words, that the pretender Procopius in 365 promised *γῆς ἀναδασμοὺς, χρεῶν ἀποκοπὰς, τὴν ἐπὶ* Κρόνου *καὶ* 'Ρέας *εὐδαιμονίαν*, "the concept of the Golden Age as a vehicle for a wholly concrete, radical economic program"; whereas in fact the exact same phrase, "redistribution of land and abolition of debts," occurs in Isocrates, *Panath.* 259, Plato, *Rep.* 566A, and Demosthenes 17.15 and 24.149. Themistius was simply using ancient rhetorical clichés. For renovation by government projects, see the typical and highly interesting anonymous *De rebus bellicis* (ed. E. A. Thompson, 1952); for the end of wars, see SHA *Probus* 20.3 and 23.2, where Probus "truly promised a Golden Age," by which he must surely have meant (contemporaries believed) a world of no taxes and universal peace; and for the utopia, see Porph., *Vit. Plot.* 12: "A city was said once to have stood in Campania, now a ruin, which Plotinus, using his favor with [Gallienus and Salonina], begged to have resurrected and endowed with the countryside round about like a foundation; and its inhabitants should use the laws of Plato, and to it should be given the name Platonopolis; and Plotinus undertook to go there with his associates." The scheme was blocked by jealous courtiers. For comment, see the spoken remarks of several scholars *à propos* the paper by V. Cilento, in *Les Sources de Plotin* (1960) 320–323.

31. For allegorizing in scriptural interpretation — a large subject — see, for example, V. Ermoni, *Revue des questions historiques* 36 (1901) 372f; O. Giordano, *Helikon* 3 (1963) 329–343; P. Brezzi, *Studi romani* 11 (1963) 265 and 270; F. Vittinghoff, *Historische Zeitschrift* 198 (1964) 536–539 and 554; and N. Cohn, *The Pursuit of the Millennium* (1957) 13f. Eusebius' attacks on chiliastic number juggling are treated in J. Sirinelli, *Les Vues historiques d'Eusèbe de Césarée . . .* (1961) 40f, and Nepos' attacks on the allegorists in Euseb., *Hist. eccl.* 7.24, supplying the quotations in the text, and in Dionysius, *De promiss.* (*PG* 10.1210).

32. Basilidians deified Abrasax (Praedestinatus 1.3, in *PL* 53.589). The name, or Abraxas, is one of the most commonly invoked in magical papyri. On calculations of the exact year of the downfall of Rome, see Ermoni 374 and Sirinelli 38f. Fascination with the mystic meaning of numbers is clear in many writers—Augustine, in parts of his *City of God*, to name one—but Irenaeus is the supreme example, in his later second century *Adv. haereses* (especially Bks. 1 and 2). Pagan writers in the fourth century speculated on the end of the world. See SHA *Ant. Diadumen.* 1 (attributed to the third

century, but reflecting interests of the compiler), and J. Bidez, *Vie de Porphyre . . .* (1913) 45, describing Neoplatonist exposures of sham prophecies. Christian writers, in the same period, indulged in similar millenniar speculation. See Lact., *Div. inst.* 7.16; Bousset, *Der Antichrist* 79, on Cyril; and A. Momigliano, *The Conflict between Paganism and Christianity in the Fourth Century* (1963) 85; cf. Church opposition to belief in astrology discussed in Bouché-Leclercq, *L'Astrologie grecque* 571, and Tert., *De idol.* 9. On the prediction ending with the defeat of Gog and Magog, see Cohn 15f and P. J. Alexander, *Speculum* 37 (1962) 343f. This is the so-called Tiburtine Sibyl. Augustine, *Civ. dei* 20.11, refers to "certain people who suppose that the Goths and the Massagetae, because of the first letters of their names," are intended by the prophecies relating to Gog and Magog. He tells us also of the supposed magical acts of St. Peter. See J. Hubeaux, *Hommages à Joseph Bidez et à Franz Cumont* (1949) 144–158, discussing possible dates, before 365 or 398, and L. Herrman, *AI* 10 (1950) 330f, who is positive, on inadequate grounds, that the oracle was composed by a certain Pollentianus in 394 and was advertised and described by Virius Nicomachus Flavianus. H. Bloch, in A. Momigliano, ed., *The Conflct between Paganism and Christianity in the Fourth Century* (1963) 201, prefers A.D. 394 and says that the story originated with Flavianus. He refers to texts that do not mention that name. Augustine, *Civ. dei* 18.53, rather attributes the oracle to sources nameless and plural, but Rome of the 390's does offer a likely setting. The sacrifice of a baby or (less often) an adult for religion's sake was a commonplace of accusation. It was aimed against Montanists (Labriolle 523); against African Saturn worship (Tert., *Apol.* 9.2f); against Druids (H. Last, *JRS* 39 [1949] 1–4); against Christians (to say nothing of the charge that they ritually *ate* babies; see for example, Tert., *Apol.* 2.5; 4.11; and Min. Fel., *Oct.* 30.2–4); and against other groups and individuals (Dio 74.16.5; Juv. 6.552; Philostr., *Vit. Apoll.* 7.11; and SHA *Elagabalus* 8.2). For appeals to the supernatural to save the state, see SHA *Trig. tyr.* 22.13; Rufin., *Hist. eccl.* 2.23; and above, Chap. III n. 29.

33. On historical pessimism in the early Empire, see P. Jal, *La Guerre civile à Rome* (1963) 244f, and above, Chap. I n. 38; for the later Empire, see Amm. 14.6.4; Aug., *Sermo* 81.8; cf. *Asclepius* 25 and Liban., *Or.* 18.281, οἰκουμένην ὥσπερ λειποψυχοῦσαν in Julian's time. Vittinghoff 558f discusses the Ammianus passage, which he thinks relies on Florus, *Epit.* 1 pr. 4f (contra, W. Hartke, *Römische Kinderkaiser* [1951] 396). The biological metaphor need not have been more than a commonplace, in earlier imperial authors. Witness Florus, whom Vittinghoff dates to Trajan's reign (I would prefer a date near 140), but who yet sees the Roman people "grown old and losing its potency"—at the very height of the empire! In later times, the recurrence of references to decline seems more significant.

34. On the panic at Constantinople, see Aug., *Sermo de urbis excidio* 7 (*PL* 40.718f), and J. Hubeaux, *AC* 17 (1948) 345f, largely repeating his views in *Bulletin de la classe des lettres, Academie royale de Belgique* 40 (1954) 658f.

Chapter V. Urban Unrest

1. The praetorian guard was disbanded in 312, the seven cohorts of the *vigiles* perhaps in 317, the three urban cohorts by 357(?). The urban prefects, in this century responsible for good order, had to make do, most often ineffectively, with members of various civil offices helped by certain guilds and, later, by *maiores regionum.* See A. Chastagnol, *La préfecture urbaine à Rome* . . . (1960) 254f and 260; H. P. Kohns, *Versorgungskrisen und Hungerrevolten* . . . (1961) 104f and 106n156; and W. G. Sinnigen, *The Officium of the Urban Prefecture* . . . (1957) 89–98.

2. Various types of police are described by O. Hirschfeld, *Kleine Schriften* (1913) 586f; T. Mommsen, *Römisches Strafrecht* (1955) 318f; and W. G. Sinnigen, *CJ* 57 (1961) 68 and 72. Their titles, like those of their twentieth century equivalents, are the more terrifying for their blandness: *curiosi, frumentarii, agentes in rebus.*

3. Urban cohorts safeguarded the imperial mint at Lyons and the *annona* at Carthage (Hirschfeld, *Kleine Schriften* 593; P. Wuilleumier, *L'Administration de la Lyonnaise* . . . [1948] 23 and 28; Chastagnol 255; G. Lopuszanski, *AC* 20 [1951] 12) and *stationarii* occur in several African cities (*ibid.* 19f; Hirschfeld 597f). Other soldiers played a part in the persecutions (Euseb., *Hist. eccl.* 5.1.8; *Acta S. Cypriani* 2; Lopuszanski 19, 21, and 28), helped by municipal magistrates. On the few mentions of town officials doing police work, see Hirschfeld 609, a *praef. vigilum et armorum* at Nîmes (with apparently no subordinates, perhaps organizing volunteer posses, or *corporati*); Lopuszanski 25; and W. H. C. Frend, *The Donatist Church* (1952) 14 and 159f. For troops suppressing a riot, see Frend 179.

4. G. Downey, *A History of Antioch in Syria* (1961) 429, describes the role of soldiers in Antioch in 387. They were used in other police duties, for example (from a wide selection of documents), cooperating with town constables in Egypt: *The Archive of Aurelius Isidorus*, ed. A. E. R. Boak and H. C. Youtie (1960) 129; P. Oxy. 64f; *Papyrus de Théadelphie*, ed. P. Jouguet (1911) 8 and 22; *Fayûm Towns and Their Papyri*, ed. B. P. Grenfell, A. S. Hunt, *et al.* (1900) 38; BGU 321f; *Les Papyrus de Genève*, ed. J. Nicole (1896–1906) 3 and 47; *Papyri and Ostraca from Karanis*, ed. H. C. Youtie, O. M. Pearl, *et al*, 1944–) 425; L. Mitteis, *Hermes* 30 (1895) 568f; and R. MacMullen, *Soldier and Civilian in the Later Roman Empire* (1963) 53f. The same relationship is seen in other eastern provinces (Euseb., *Hist. eccl.* 6.40.2; *CIL* 3.7136; Justin, II *Apol.* 2; D. Magie, *Roman Rule in Asia*

Minor . . . [1950] 603). For governors' aides acting as police in Caesarea, see S. Lieberman, *AI* 7 (1939–1944) 397n12; also, *stationarii* in Thrace (Lopuszanski 20f) and Phrygia (*SEG* 16 [1959] 754 lines 30f). More amateurish agents are seen in operation against the Church (*Mart. S. Cononis* 2; *Mart. S. Polycarpi* 7, *diogmitai* in the same duties as irenarchs; and *Mart. S. Pionii* 18). For irenarchs, see *Mart. S. Cononis* 2; P. Oxy. 2233; I. Lévy, *REG* 12 (1899) 283 and 288; Hirschfeld, *Kleine Schriften* 602f; L. Robert, *Études anatoliennes* (1937) 99f; L. and J. Robert, *La Carie* 2 (1954) 42; Magie 647 and 1514–1516; S. Eitrem and L. Amundsen, *JEA* 40 (1954) 31. Pictures of rural police can be seen in Robert, *Etudes anatoliennes* pl. II, 2 (cf. pp. 102f), and of military police in M. Rostovtzeff, *The Social and Economic History of the Roman Empire*[2] (1957) pl. LXXIV, 1. Some 30 approximately dated references in inscriptions to irenarchs, *paraphylakes*, *archiphylakes*, or the like (*IGRR* passim; *SEG* 16 no. 761; 17 nos. 505, 509, 586; 19 nos. 718, 830) are especially concentrated in the century A.D. 150–250. Lévy (p. 288) cites Nysa in 220, equipped with an irenarch and a *paraphylax*, both mere children (their property, of course, liable to the cost of their substitutes), and P. Oxy. 43 (reign of Diocletian) records the occupations of *phylakes* under a *nyktostrategos*, being leatherworkers, potters, and the like, or their substitutes. The two bits of evidence typify the difficulties in finding candidates as time went on. Further difficulties were the small numbers of troops available as police and their violent behavior when assigned. See Pliny, *Ep.* 10.19–22, 27f; *SEG* 19 no. 718; MacMullen 84–89.

5. For proof of extensive litigation, see *CIL* 3.14191; 9.5420; and 6.266–268, an affair of 18 years. References to a rash of third century complaints in eastern provinces are gathered in MacMullen, *Soldier and Civilian* 86f.

6. On slaves in rural disturbances, see Chapter VI; Tac., *Ann.* 4.27 (A.D. 24), a plot to overthrow Tiberius beginning in southern Italy with appeals for a slave rising, quickly suppressed; *ibid.* 12.65 (A.D. 54), charges against a wealthy woman *quodque parum coercitis per Calabriam servorum agminibus pacem Italiae turbaret;* and rural slave barracks in Italy used as prisons for the kidnapped (Suet., *Aug.* 32.1; *Tib.* 8). *In Sicilia quasi quoddam servile bellum exstitit latronibus evagantibus, qui vix oppressi sunt* (SHA *Gallien.* 4.9). Gladiators and slaves on sale were banished 100 miles from Rome, in a time of general unrest, as possible sources of danger (Dio 55.26.1, A.D. 6–8); gladiatorial schools were closely watched by the government (I. A. Richmond and C. E. Stevens, *JRS* 32 [1942] 68; Pliny, *Traiani paneg.* 54.4, where the senate debates *de ampliando numero gladiatorum*, under Domitian, probably a sumptuary and not a police question), and a limit was set to the number of gladiators that could be shown at any one time in Syracuse (Tac., *Ann.* 13.49). An outbreak of gladiators at Praeneste was put down "by a military guard stationed there to watch them" (*ibid.*

15.45, A.D. 64), another was suppressed by Probus (Zos. 1.71.6). Gladiators were occasionally drafted for emergencies (Tac., *Hist.* 2.35f; 3.76; cf. Herodian 7.11.7, for the use of them in 238), and used in the fourth century in Rome, by Damasus (*Coll. Avellana* 1.7) and Nepotianus (Aur. Vict., *De Caes.* 42; Eutrop., *Brev.* 10.11). Student riots are known from Eunap., *Vit. soph.* 483, with note ad loc., Loeb edition; 487, where the students are divided not only by loyalty to their masters but according to the countries of their origin, and set the city in an uproar. Cf. Himerius, *Or.* 16 (Colonna). In Rome, professors of rhetoric had to be registered with the prefect, and foreign students also (Chastagnol 285 and 287f). Troubles of various kinds frequently centered in public houses. For the number of taverns in Pompeii, see T. Kleberg, *Hôtels, restaurants et cabarets dans l'antiquité romaine* (1957) 50. His arguments, pp. 46f and 55f, that the much smaller number in Ostia proves the effectiveness of legislation against taverns, is answered by H. T. Rowell in a review in *American Journal of Archaeology* 62 (1958) 124, who points to such factors as the larger number of Ostian guildhouses as an alternative to taverns for the poorer classes. For prostitution in taverns, and their evil repute generally, see Tert., *De fuga* 13; Paul, *Sent.* 2.26.11; *Dig.* 3.2.4.2; 23.2.43.1 and 9 (all Ulpian); *Cod. Just.* 4.56.3 (225); 9.9.28 (326); 5.27.1 (336); M. Della Corte, *Rendiconti della Accademia di archeologia, Napoli*[2] 33 (1958) 306f; and Kleberg 120 and *passim.* The edicts and the motives for edicts appear in Suet., *Tib.* 34.1; Suet., *Claud.* 38.2; Suet., *Nero* 16.2; Dio 60.6.7; 62.14.2; 65.10.3. The first of the Dio texts has been taken by Kleberg (p. 103) and by V. M. Scramuzza, *The Emperor Claudius* (1940) 30 and n. 100 (among wrong or pointless references, citing Suetonius when he evidently means Dio) as showing that Claudius suppressed clubs to dampen political activities. But Dio says, "He ordered [the Jews] not to hold meetings. He dissolved the ἑταιρεῖαι that Gaius had restored and, seeing that it was no use for anyone to forbid the masses to anything unless he changed the patterns of their daily life, he closed the shops where people gathered to drink." Sumptuary laws like this only return later in Amm. 28.4.4; *CIL* 6.1766 (A.D. 375–76) and 6.9920.

7. *CIL* 4.7919 names the Paridiani, on whom, and on their idol, Paris, see G. O. Onorato, ed., *Iscrizioni pompeiane* (1957) 92 and 166, and M. Della Corte, *Case ed abitanti di Pompei*[2] (1954) 269. *Prosopographia imperii Romani*[1] supplies references to Paris in Suetonius, Martial, Dio, and others. For theater clubs in politics, see also *CIL* 4.7585 (Della Corte, *Case* 336), "the *spectaculi spectantes* demand X for *duovir,*" written in an archway near the amphitheater. A good candidate would pay for good *ludi,* hence the political activities of fan clubs.

8. Lucian, *Demonax* 57, tells us of the rivalry between Athens and Corinth; cf. Philostr., *Vit. soph.* 529, relating how the Megarians in the

same period refused to admit Athenians to the Lesser Pythian games, being angry "as if the [Megarian] decree had just been passed." Amphitheatric rivalry breaks forth between Pompeii and Nuceria (Della Corte, *Case* 223f; A. Maiuri, *Rendiconti della Accademia di archeologia, Napoli*[2] 33 [1958] 35–40), and between Capua and Puteoli, determining their role in the Year of the Four Emperors. In Campania as a whole, local rivalries bulked larger than imperial rivalries (Tac., *Hist.* 3.57; 4.3). For the graffiti, see Maiuri 35n5. Cf. Dio Chrysos., *Or.* 40.28f, where rivalry between Apamea and Prusa is exacerbated by insulting shouts "at the shows." City antagonisms of this kind might be punished by the emperors; for example, Byzantium was stripped of its games and shows in about 197, Alexandria in 212, and Antioch in about 176 and in 387 (Herodian 3.6.9; Dio 78.23.3; SHA *Marcus Aurel.* 25.9; and Liban., *Or.* 20.6).

9. For the "Vedius fans" see L. Robert, *Les Gladiateurs dans l'Orient grec* (1940) 27 and 196, φιλοβήδιοι φίλοπλοι. Malalas, ed. Bonn p. 244, describes Antioch's factions; for Constantinople's, see Greg. Naz., *Or.* 37.18 (*PG* 36.301). It is often said that the Greens were democratic, the Blues aristocratic—true, perhaps, in the period after about 400; but what was especially democratic about Domitian or Elagabalus, and what was aristocratic about the pro-Blue slave of *CIL* 6.9719? On the whole point, I agree with L. Friedländer, *Darstellungen aus der Sittengeschichte Roms* . . .[10] (1922) 2.35, against A. Maricq, *Bulletin de l'Académie royale de Belgique* 36 (1950) 419n1, who follows R. Goossens, *Byzantion* 14 (1939) 207. Faction was roused at provincial cities, too. Horse racing inspired murderous brawls in Alexandria (Philostr., *Vit. Apoll.* 5.26). The emperors, for pleasure or policy, regularly attended the spectacles (Friedländer 2.4; Dio 57.14.10; Tac., *Ann.* 13.25; later, Julian (and his family), *Misopogon* 340A).

10. Unison cheering, accompanied by music or led by claques or in set phrases, is described by A. Alföldi, *Mitteilungen des deutschen archäologischen Instituts,* Römische Abteilung 49 (1934) 79–83. In Antioch of the 260's the supporters of Paul of Samosata had been taught to shout, jump about, clap, and wave handkerchiefs in the church assemblies "as if in the theater" (Euseb., *Hist. eccl.* 7.30.9). As to claques seated en masse, see Daremberg-Saglio, *Dictionnaire* s.v. Histrio, p. 230, and Chastagnol 82, on texts of A.D. 358 and 381 dealing with Constantinople. For claque leaders, called *capita factionum* or *duces,* see Suet., *Tib.* 37, and Suet., *Nero* 20.3; for guild participation in cheering and circus pomp, see Tert., *De spect.* 7 and 11, and L. Robert, *Gladiateurs* 41 (on leatherworkers in Philadelphia).

11. On the police problem at spectacles, as it developed in A.D. 15 and 23, see Dio 57.14.10 and Tac., *Ann.* 1.77, both quoted in the text. Drusus' indulgent enthusiasm encouraged the license that led to trouble. The riot was discussed in the senate, and the subject of possible scourging of the actors; later (Suet., *Tib.* 37) claque chiefs and actors, "causes of the trouble," were

banished. Under Nero, disorders were traced to dancers (Dio 57.21.3, on ὀρχηστάς = *pantomimi*, but called *histriones* in Tac., *Ann.* 4.14), or, at other times, to race crowds, controlled by troops. See Tac., *Ann.* 13.24, *statio cohortis adsidere ludis solita; Dig.* 1.12.1.12 (Ulpian), *quies quoque popularium et disciplina spectaculorum ad praefecti urbi curam pertinere videtur; et sane debet etiam dispositos milites stationarios habere ad tuendam popularium quietem et ad referendum sibi quid ubi agatur . . . interdicere poterit et spectaculis;* cf. P. Oxy. 43, guards in Oxyrhynchus, καὶ ἐν τῷ θεάτρῳ φύλακες γ'. Police controls at the Roman spectacles, briefly abandoned, had to be reimposed. See Tac., *Ann.* 13.24f; Suet., *Nero* 26; Dio 61.8.1–3. For trouble caused by *pantomimi*, see Suet., *Nero* 16.2; Tac., *Ann.* 13.25 and 28; 14.21, A.D. 60, *pantomimi*, the chief cause of riotous partisanship, are restricted to certain appearances only, and are later exiled, by a ban mentioned in SHA *Commod.* 3.4 (though the *mimi* there are not quite the same thing as *pantomimi*). Amm. 15.7.2 shows charioteers also as a focus of unrest. Vettius Valens, *Anthol.* 5.10 (ed. Kroll p. 231), A.D. 148, describes the release of a dancer demanded from the governor by the crowd, the description supplying the quotation on factions in the text. Philostr., *Vit. Apoll.* 1.5, tells of "many cities" in Pamphylia and Lycia split into factions over dancers and horses, "worthless shows"; cf. 5.26, on an incident in Alexandria.

12. In Jos., *Ant. Jud.* 19.24, the mob expects its petitions to be granted "as usual"; Vettius Valens, *Anthol.* 5.10, and Friedländer 2.6 refer to petitions to grant the life of a favorite actor or charioteer. For the *acta populi* of the fourth century, on the model of the *acta senatus*, see *Cod. Theod.* 1.16.6 (331) and 8.15.32 (371), and Chastagnol 81. It is likely that the emperors, in promoting various kinds of games, consciously tried to divert popular enthusiasms into nonpolitical channels. See Kohns, *Versorgungskrisen* 83f, on Dio 54.17.5. Hints of a political flavor to theater crowds are offered by Suet., *Nero* 20.3; Herodian 8.6.8, ὥσπερ ἐκκλησιάζοντες; Jos., *Bell. Jud.* 7.47, the Antiochenes ἐκκλησιάζοντες in the theater. On paid claques, see Suet., *Nero* 20.3; 46.5; Philo, *In Flaccum* 138; and Liban., *Or.* 41.7; on their license, Tac., *Hist.* 1.72, and Dio 79.20.1. To calm them, officials had to take action. *Acta apost.* 19.29f shows a *grammateus* speaking to a crowd in Ephesus; cf. similar incidents in Herodian 1.12.5; 1.13.3f; and Dio 72[73].13.3f where Commodus sacrifices Cleander to mob hatred, and Galba (Plut., *Galba* 17) stands firm to spare Tigellinus, while Symmachus' return from exile (Kohns 86) must be approved by the populace before it is possible. The populace shouts for Niger, Constantine, and Stilicho (SHA *Julianus* 4.7; Chastagnol 81; Lact., *De mort. persecut.* 44.7f), or against Julianus, Severus, Macrinus, or Pope Liberius (Dio 74.13.3f; 76.4.4f; SHA *Macrin.* 12.9; Chastagnol 81); protests taxes (Jos., *Ant. Jud.* 19.24; Dio 59.28.11) or famine conditions (Julian, *Misopogon* 368C; Sidon., *Ep.* 10.2,

A.D. 468; Tac., *Ann.* 6.13, A.D. 32; Herodian 1.12.5; Liban., *Or.* 18.195; 29.2; Philostr., *Vit. Apoll.* 1.15); the crowds' tumultuous behavior in theaters is a commonplace with historians as with novelists (Tert., *De spect.* 16; Tert., *Ad nat.* 1.17; Tac., *Ann.* 11.13; Amm. 16.10.13; R. Söder, *Die apokryphen Apostelgeschichten* . . . [1932] 161, with many references), and only the eloquence of a trained rhetor could deal with it (Philostr., *Vit. Apoll.* 1.15; 4.1; 4.8; Lucian, *Demonax* 9); it was sometimes incited by the wit of actors (Sen., *De ira* 2.11.3; Suet., *Nero* 39.3; Suet., *Galba* 13; SHA *Commod.* 3.4; SHA *Maximini* 9.3), and lines of plays are turned against an emperor or his ministers (Suet., *Aug.* 68.1; Dio 60.29.3). Race riots started in theaters (H. I. Bell, *Jews and Christians in Egypt* [1924] 25, and I. D. Amussin, quoted in *Bibliotheca Classica orientalis* 2 [1957] 146, on P. Oxy. 1912 and Malalas, ed. Bonn pp. 244–245C; Philo, *In Flaccum* 34, 37, 41, and 139f, on the troubles begun in the Alexandrian gymnasia and theaters; Jos., *Bell. Jud.* 7.47f, riots in Antioch in A.D. 70; Soc., *Hist. eccl.* 7.13, race troubles again in Alexandria springing from popular rivalries over dancers). Sometimes angers in the theater were appeased by summary executions of scapegoats (Jos., *Bell. Jud.* 7.47; Herodian 1.9.5; Philo, *In Flaccum* 75f).

13. The essential sources are Philo, *In Flaccum*, and Libanius (especially *Or.* 41), in passages emphasized by R. Browning, *JRS* 42 (1952) 16f. C. R. Whittaker, *Historia* 13 (1964) 358f, offers stimulating conjectures based upon texts handled—as it seems to me, after having checked some scores of them—in a misleading and unreliable fashion. Since Demosthenes' day, it has always been common, and comforting, to picture one's opponents in the assembly as only few and venal; and remarks by Libanius that the claques that cheered on the other side were composed of men of the theater —of the lowest tastes, that is—and foreign agitators to boot, may be mere abuse, without basis in fact. On the whole question of the real significance of claques, see P. Petit, in his nonpareil study, *Libanius et la vie municipale à Antioche* . . . (1955) 223–230.

14. Examples of trades locally concentrated are drawn from Robert, *Etudes anatoliennes* 533, 534n1, 535n3; *IGRR* 4.790; *SEG* 8 no. 43; and P. Oxy. 75; for "the workmen of" such-and-such an address, see *IGRR* 4.791 and J. P. Waltzing, *Etude historique sur les corporations professionnelles chez les Romains* . . . (1895–1900) 3.31 and 54. Philostr., *Vit. soph.* 580, provides the detail about the size of guildhalls, one of which is known and quoted in the text from *CIL* 11.3614 (*phretrium = fratrium*). On meeting places, most often called *scholae* (as in Mart. 4.61.3, *schola poetarum*), see Waltzing 1.210f. Societies even of philosophers and cooks are known from Strabo 17.1.8 and *CIL* 6.7458. The number of societies in individual towns can be deduced from Waltzing 3.536 and 558–564—some of the inscriptions being of different dates, to be sure, but no doubt the existence of some societies is totally unknown to us; for the size of enrollments, see *CIL*

2.5812; 3.633, 870, 4150, 5196, 6150; 5.2603; 6.631, 647, 1052, 1060, 1766, 7459, 9920, 10046, 13402, 1060, with 9405 and 10300; 9.3188; 11.1449; 14.150, 246, 250–252, 255–257, 2408; Waltzing 1.351; 4.191, 213, 253, 272; *Ephemeris epigraphica* 8.125; S. Riccobono et al., *Fontes iuris Romani antejustiniani* . . .[2] (1940–1943) 1.445; and M. A. Levi, *Athenaeum* 41 (1963) 384. Some of the figures would be larger if the inscriptions were not fragmentary. The societies range from the *fabri* of Rome (about 1500) and the *fabri et centonarii* of Milan (at least 1200, according to Waltzing 1.351) down to the 12 *acceptores* at Ostia; but the average is just about 150. Smaller guilds may not have wanted to specify their numbers; on the other hand, for many guilds known to have been divided into *centuriae* and *decuriae* (Waltzing 1.359) and probably numbering in the thousands, we have no statistics. Pliny, *Ep.* 10.33, refers to a projected society of 150 *fabri* as *tam paucos.*

15. On guild patrons, see Waltzing 1.415–446. For a deputation to Hadrian, see *IGRR* 4.349, the *iuvenes* of Ankara greeting the emperor; SHA *Gallieni* 8.6; *Aurel.* 34.4; Dio 75.4.5f; cf. societies contributing incense to a notable's funeral in *CIL* 5.337. The presence of societies in theater audiences is referred to by Tert., *De spect.* 7, and by Waltzing 4.574 (seats at theaters at Rome, Nîmes, Arles, Lyons, Trèves, and Smyrna). For disorders involving societies, see *Dig.* 48.19.28.3 and Tac., *Ann.* 14.17. Societies are also mentioned in inscriptions as separate parts of the town population. See E. Popescu, *Dacia*[2] 4 (1960) 291; *CIL* 9.3842; 13.1921; and Waltzing 4.570 and 572f; and they sometimes rose to the status of official, political divisions (Waltzing 1.174; Popescu 276 and 285, on *IGRR* 3802).

16. The laws of one guild (*CIL* 14.2112 II 23f), quoted in the text, deprecated rowdy meetings. Disturbances between, not within, guilds also took place, as in *CIL* 6.1759, a long quarrel between *mensores* and *caudicarii* in Portus in A.D. 389, and other instances in *CIL* 6.1016 (A.D. 175) and Waltzing 4.616–623, dealing with an inscription of A.D. 202. And guild members sometimes rioted against such threats to their interests as Christians. In *Acta apost.* 19.23–39, the silversmiths at Ephesus saw danger to the market for Diana icons if Christianity prevailed; in Tert., *Apol.* 42.1f, Christians were accused of "contributing nothing to commerce," Tertullian answering that they bought and sold like everyone else, and frequented the same places of business. How could they then be called *infructuosi?* A last resort of the laboring classes was the protest parade of P. Bremer 63 (ca. 116?). "Our folk," says a writer of Heptakomia, "have been marching all around the town demanding more pay," probably owing to economic straits connected with the Jewish war. For declarations to officials that "I shall have to abandon my land and flee," or like words—not threats but tears—see, for example, P. Oxy. 488, 2235, and 2410; *The Tebtunis Papyri*, ed. B. P. Grenfell, A. S. Hunt, *et al.* (1902) 327 (examples of the second century or later). For threats of flight from farms, see R. MacMullen, *CJ* 58 (1963)

270n3; and on rare strikes, *ibid.* 269 and W. H. Buckler, in *Anatolian Studies Presented to Sir William Mitchell Ramsay* (1923)35.

17. The speakcr quoted first in the text is Trajan, in Pliny, *Ep.* 10.34; cf. Trajan on the *eranoi* of Amisus: they are permissible if "not for the purpose of *turbae et illiciti coetus*" (*ibid.* 10.93); note in Dio Chrysos., *Or.* 45.8 and 50.3, passages describing ἑταιρεῖαι splitting a city into sections and supplying backing against the town council. In Rome, the Dionysiac artists of the second century are referred to as "a very arrogant class of men, and hard to keep in order" (Philostr., *Vit. soph.* 596.) This is the kind of evidence that explains the view of Tertullian quoted from *Apol.* 38.1f. The connection between the existence of societies, and riots in public places (above, n. 11), was seen also by Caracalla who, in Alexandria, "abolished the spectacles and συσσίτια," that is, *collegia*, sometimes also called *symposia* (see Waltzing 1.323 and n. 2, and *Dig.* 54.2.3, where Augustus dissolves συσσίτια in Rome; the word "must mean the *collegia*," according to M. Hammond, *The Augustan Principate* . . . [1933] 258n68). Compare the συμπόσιον of leatherworkers and makers of pontoons (for use to build barges) who supported Odenathus in 257–258 (H. Seyrig, *Annales archéologiques de Syrie* 13 [1963] 161f). On Tarsus' linenworkers, see Dio Chrysos., *Or.* 34.21f, quoted in the text; cf. *Griechische Papyri im Museum des Oberhessischen Geschichtsvereins zu Giessen*, ed. E. Kornemann, O. Eger, and P. M. Meyer (1910–1912) 40 II 21f, saying that fellahin, drifting into Alexandria, "disturb the city." They are to be found among the linenworkers, whose "appearance and dress" they have assumed. The mintworkers' revolt is known from SHA *Aurel.* 38.2, though no one takes the casualty figure at face value. In Cyzicus (Soz., *Hist. eccl.* 5.15, quoted in the text) troubles were anticipated among the workers organized in two τάγματα πολυάνθρωπα, permitted to live in the city under contract to deliver a yearly quota of uniforms and coins for the troops. Armsworkers in Caesarea also rioted (Greg. Naz., *Or* 43.57 = *PG* 36.569, quoted in the text) and were prominent in revolts at Hadrianople. Prominent—else why execute ten of them as punishment of the whole town? (Athanas., *Hist. Arianorum* 18). Ammianus says that the *fabricenses* were a *multitudo* there (31.6.2). The same reasoning applies to the fines and prison sentences levied against "the whole society of merchants" and "the traders" who supported Ambrose in Milan, in the anti-Arian riots of 385 (Ambrose, *Ep.* 20.6f). They were punished because, no doubt, they were the chief weapon of his authority. Further evidence of working-class unrest, between A.D. 362 and 392, comes from Liban., *Or.* 1.206f; 22.7; 29.3 and 6; 34.4; 56.4; cf. Philostr., *Vit. soph.* 526, in second century Athens "an uproar arose among the bakers' stores" in time of famine. Finally, sailors caused seditions. See Athanas., *Hist. Arian.* 81 (356?), "We adjure also the masters of vessels to publish these things everywhere, and to carry them to the ears of the most

pious Augustus." Compare Greg. Naz., *De vita sua* 1.840f and 887f, the sailors bribed to play partisan, in A.D. 380, and Soz., *Hist. eccl.* 8.17, and Soc., *Hist. eccl.* 6.15, an incident of A.D. 403.

18. On episcopal elections, see W. Smith and S. C. Cheetham, *A Dictionary of Christian Antiquities* (1875) 1.213–216. The violent battles involving Damasus in Rome and Athanasius in Alexandria, with hosts of other examples from the fourth and fifth centuries, come quickly to mind.

19. Mob weapons included house burning (Julian, *Misopogon* 370C; Amm. 14.7.6; Theodoret, *Hist. eccl.* 5.22; Ambrose, *Ep.* 40.13; Dio Chrysos., *Or.* 46.11f; Browning 15 and 19); massacres (as in Herodian 7.7.3, officials and judges the victims); and insult to carved or painted portraits, of the emperor (as in Liban., *Or.* 19.27f), or of a minister like Sejanus (Juv. 10.58–87), or of other hated individuals, such as Agrippa's daughters (Jos., *Ant. Jud.* 19.9.357f). All forms of mob attack grow more common, until we come to the urban prefect "whose administration suffered from turbulent seditions, but had nothing remarkable about it worth describing" (Amm. 17.11.5). Collections of evidence for the early Empire do not exist, nor have I made one myself. For the later Empire, besides Kohns, Browning, and Whittaker (Whittaker to be used with caution), see J. R. Martindale, *Public Disorders in the Late Roman Empire* . . . , (1960), which contains much material. Rome supplies the most, but should be somewhat discounted as atypical, with note taken of the disbanding of police forces in the city (above, n. 1). In Antioch, taxation caused a riot, described by Theodoret, *Hist. eccl.* 5.19; Zos. 4.41; and Browning 14f. On reaction to taxes in rural areas, see Chapter VI. Religious disputes are rare. In one mentioned in the text, the Cynopolites had the best of it: they ate a kind of fish, a pike, their enemies had to eat a dog (Plut., *Mor.* 380B-C, an event "in my own day"); for the second incident, see SHA *Had.* 12.1, also quoted in the text. The Greeks and Romans, as everyone knows, showed great religious tolerance, always provided it was reciprocated, and these two examples, adding a final case from southern Egypt (Juv. 15.33–83), are the only ones I can find of pagans fighting pagans. Christianity introduced a hotter standard of zeal, shown in pagans' defense of their own shrines by physical force, as, for example, in Julian, *Ep.* 115 (Bidez), in Edessa; in Rufinus, *Hist. eccl.* 2.22, Soz., *Hist. eccl.* 7.15, and Soc., *Hist. eccl.* 5.16, describing battles over the Sarapis temple in Alexandria in 391, followed by waves of armed resistance spreading into Syria, Galilee, and Lebanon (Martindale 59). More battles broke out in Sufes in Africa in 399 and 408 (*ibid.*). For the other side of the story, the destructive violence of Christians, see R. Van Loy, *Byzantion* 8 (1933) 395–397, on Liban., *Or.* 30, A.D. 390, and the incident connected with Ophitism, above, Chap. III n. 22. Of all heresies, Arianism gave birth to the most violence. See, for example, Bell, *Jews and*

Christians in Egypt 56–67; Martindale 3, 5, and 21f (episcopal election riots in Constantinople in 336, 337 or 338, 342, ca. 344, 345, 359, and ca. 370).

20. Kohns 89–92 (and, p. 79, specifically on the passages from Ammianus and Symmachus which show their train of thought, *copia = concordia*) notes the connection between scarcities and tumults or seditions. For food riots against those thought to be responsible, see Dio Chrysos., *Or.* 46.6f; Tac., *Ann.* 12.43; Suet., *Claud.* 18.2f; Philostr., *Vit. Apoll.* 1.15; Liban., *Or.* 29.4; and Amm. 14.7.5f. Great pressure was needed to make the rich unlock their stores (Philostr., *Vit. Apoll.* 1.15; Liban., *Or.* 18.195; Petit, *Libanius* 115; Downey, *History of Antioch* 388 and 421). For suspected complicity of bakers with rich hoarders, see Petron., *Cena Trimalch.* 44; Liban., *Or.* 1.207f; and Petit 115. On the cruelty of the rich growing yet richer from others' plight, see Ambrose, *De Nabuthe* 7.35; Greg. Naz., *Or.* 48.34; Basil, *Homil. in illud dictum evang.* 3 (*PG* 31.268); and other passages quoted by M. M. Fox, *The Life and Times of St. Basil . . .* (1939) 9f. But sometimes, as pointed out by Kohns 89 and 91f, and by Magie, *Roman Rule* 600, attacks were made on a man not because he was to blame for anything, but simply because he was rich.

21. Libanius (*Or.* 18.195; 27 *passim;* 36.4f; and 50 passim) and Julian (*Misopogon* 368C-D and 369C-D) show some sympathy for the poor, but a wider sense of social justice must be sought in Christian writers such as John Chrysos., *In ps. XLVIII* 4 (*PG* 55.228); Ambrose, *De Nabuthe* 1.2 and 12.53; S. Giet, *Les Idées et l'action sociales de saint Basile* (1941) 97f, 100, 106f, and 110f. They point to the dependence of the rich on the poor, in views to be studied in Giet 97 and John Chrysos., *In ep. I ad Cor. Homil.* 34.4 (*PG* 61.292f). They blame the rich for poor people's sins of desperation. See John Chrysos., *In ps. XLVIII* 2 (*PG* 57–58.591), supplying the quotation used in the text, and Asterius, *Homil. II adv. avarit.* (*PG* 40.209), "You [Avarice] fill the land with brigands and murderers, the sea with pirates, the cities with riots, the courts with perjurers, calumniators, betrayers, lawyers, and judges drawn whithersoever you attract them." That circumstances, not God's will, account for poverty, is emphasized by Greg. Naz., *Or.* 14.29 (*PG* 35.897), and condemnation of usury follows, in Greg. Nyssa, *Contra usurarios;* Clem. Alex., *Homil. in ps.* XIV 1f; John Chrysos., *Homil. in Matt. LXI–LXII* (*PG* 58.591f); Basil, *Homil. in ps. XIV* 1f (*PG* 29.250f). The rich are taught by sermons on charity. See John Chrysos., *Homil. in Matt. LXI–LXII* (*PG* 58.591); John Chrysos., *In ps. XLVIII* 3f (*PG* 55.516f); Ambrose, *De Nabuthe* 1.8 (*PL* 14.768); Clem. Alex., *Quis dives salvetur* 1f (*PG* 9.603f); Greg. Naz., *Or.* 14.36 (*PG* 35.906f); Greg. Nyssa, *De pauper. amandis* (*PG* 46.454–469, esp. 457); and in Giet 108. Church leaders set the example in succor of the helpless, for instance, Ephraim in Edessa (details and references in Appendix A, 4). For other

pauper hospitals established by Christian charity in Rome and Caesarea and its neighborhood, see Jerome, *Ep.* 77; Basil, *Ep.* 142; 143; and 150.3. On Christian aid to the distressed in Egypt, see Bell 44 and 72–78. Most of the monks described in these incidents were Copts. Their charity excluded not even criminals. Examples are not infrequent of ex-robbers and murderers turned monk; see R. MacMullen, *Aegyptus* 44 (1964) 197. Add E. A. T. W. Budge, *The Paradise of the Holy Fathers . . .* (1907) 1.339, 346, and 352.

22. For the view that class tensions were sharper in the late Empire, see Browning 13 and 19. A dozen references (p. 13) are all irrelevant—Thessalonican riots over theater matters, other tumults or loud speeches in religious matters, but nothing to show a class war. Whittaker's references and conclusions (*Historia* 13 [1964] 361f) are almost equally valueless. Other scholars quoted in Chapter VI, though they speak of class war, really mean only rural tensions. There is actually more evidence—but still not much—from the earlier Empire, for example, the quotation in the text from Plut., *Mor.* 822A, and Tac., *Hist.* 1.4.3—though, for remarks on the "low plebs," "brainless mob," and "plebeian vileness," see also late sources: Ausonius, *Ordo urb. nobil.* 4–5.4f, and *Cod. Theod.* 9.42.5. As early as Caligula's reign, a writer quoted in the text could regret the passage of good feeling between rich and poor (Philo, *Legat. ad Gaium* 11f, where it is clear in sections 8 and 14 that the interlude was contrasted with conditions before and after these seven blissful months).

23. In Philostr., *Vit. soph.* 531, early second century factions in the city are reconciled by the rhetor Polemo; *ibid.* 603, Naucratis is "divided into factions" in the second half of the same century; Philostr., *Vit. Apoll.* 4.2 and 8 describes stasis in Ephesus and Smyrna. In *IGRR* 4.914, dated under Claudius or Nero, Cibyra is threatened by a "major conspiracy, offering the greatest hurt to the city"; and Philostratus, in *Vit. Apoll.* 6.38, reports that the governor of Syria "had started an internal quarrel in Antioch, making the people suspicious of each other, and as they met together divided in their assembly," only an earthquake was adequate to remind them of the community of their interests; cf. Philostr., *Epp. Apoll.* 75f, referring to extreme stasis in Sardis. There were class disturbances at Rhodes under Antoninus Pius (Aelius Aristides, *Or.* 44, ed. Dindorf, vol. 1, p. 824 and *passim*). Dio Chrysos., *Or.* 39, adds examples from Nicaea, and stasis is implied at Nicomedia by its coin legends, ὁμόνοια, βουλή, and δῆμος (ca. A.D. 166, C. Bosch, *Die kleinasiatischen Münzen der römischen Kaiserzeit* vol. 2 pt. 1 [1935] 219). Plut., *Mor.* 824, says that faction in a city is terrible, and people with authority should do everything they can to restore peace. Some of these references, and an excellent short survey of the evidence, can be found in T. R. S. Broughton, in *An Economic Survey of Ancient Rome*, ed. T. Frank, 4 (1938) 810–812. For the distinction between urban and rural elements, see, for example, *IGRR* 3.69, of Prusias; Popescu, *Dacia*[2] 7 (1960)

285–287; Magie 857, 859, and 640. For contempt of οἱ ἀγροῖκοι and *agrestes*, see above, Chap. III n. 28; F. Halkin, *Analecta Bollandiana* 81 (1963) 11; Pliny, *Ep.* 7.25. The advice on concord given by Dio Chrysostom (*Or.* 34) to the Tarsians is discussed by Broughton 811 and Magie 640 and 1503n26. Tensions were sometimes exacerbated by rhetors. See Dio Chrysos., *Or.* 43.6, where I take δασμολογεῖν to mean "lay the country under taxation," evidently a measure directed against big landowners. On talk of redivision of land and abolition of debts, see above, Chap. IV n. 30; on the frequent interference of rhetors in local affairs, above, n. 12 and earlier in this same note; and on the inflammatory views of Cynics, see Chap. II at n. 16. A final example in Prusa is drawn from Magie 600, on Dio Chrysos., *Or.* 48.1 and 2f.

24. On town magistrates doubling as guild magistrates, see Waltzing 3.58 and 60; for Augustal high priests as benefactors to fullers of Acmonia and dyers of Sagalassus, see Waltzing 3.30; he gives similar instances at 3.51f. Much larger numbers are known in western cities, as in Waltzing 1.438, 444, 445 (*fabri* of a little town with 15 patrons, an Ostian society with ten Roman senators as patrons, and so on). For the high respect shown by the patron to the society that chose him, see Waltzing 1.435f.

25. Various forms of competition in Greek provinces—trumpet contests and the like—are reported by Magie 1525; A. M. Woodward, *BSA* 26 (1923–1925) 214–218; M. N. Tod, *BSA* 10 (1903–1904) 63–77; and L. Robert, *Revue de Philologie* 56 (1930) 49f. The law quoted in the text, against competitive building, is in *Dig.* 50.10.3 (Macer), where other reasons for restricting building are added. The claim of a city on a citizen's loyalty, even on his life, is a commonplace in, for example, Dio Chrysos., *Or.* 44.1; John Chrysos., *On the Statues, Homil.* 2.4; and Diog. Laert. 7.130. He was expected to advance its repute by ostentatious spending (Philostr., *Vit. soph.* 532, using just the arguments advanced by Alcibiades, Thuc. 6.16.3f) or by extravagant gifts to the city, which are praised by Dio Chrysos., *Or.* 40.2–9; 45.3, 5f, and 12 (on Prusa, which Dio intended to make "head of a federation of cities, and to bring together in it as great a multitude of inhabitants as I can"); 47.13, 16, and *passim* (praising fine buildings in other cities, to stir up local ambitions). Speeches in praise of cities, emphasizing among other points their visible grandeur, were an ancient genre. For those of the Roman period, besides the famous *To Rome* of Aelius Aristides, see, for example, Carthage praised by Apul., *Flor.* 18f, or the pages devoted to the *topos* in the third century handbook of Menander, *Rhetores graeci*, ed. L. Spengel, 3.358f; and in the fourth century, Liban., *Or.* 11.42f; John Chrysos., *On the Statues, Homil.* 17.14; 19.15; and Himer., *Or.* (7) 41 passim. On "buildings and games," a typical passage quoted in the text is Dio Chrysos., *Or.* 40.10. But competition could be carried too far. Quarrels περὶ τοῦ πρωτείου were deprecated by Ael. Arist., *Or.* 42 (ed. Dindorf vol. 1 p. 771 and *passim*) and by Dio Chrysos., *Or.* 38.24. Nicaea and Nico-

media, like Anazarbus and Tarsus, were *both* first (Bosch 225); B. V. Head, *Historia numorum* [1911] 717 and 733). For a definite ranking in the provinces, see Magie 636 and n. 17, and 1497. Ranking gave rise to ill-feeling, and so to rebuke (Dio 52.37.10; 54.23.8; Ael. Arist., *Or.* 42, ed. Dindorf vol. 1 p. 791; and Dio Chrysos., *Or.* 38.33). Note the adjudication of a dispute by Antoninus Pius, renewed in the next reign (Magie 636 and n. 17 and Broughton 742f, for much material on title rivalries). A ridiculous ambition was shown by Anazarbus. On its boastful coinage, see Bosch 221n60 (coins of 219–220) and Head 716–717. The abbreviations were first decoded by Waddington (P. LeBas and W. H. Waddington, *Inscriptions grecques et latines* . . . [1870] 3.349f). For the opposed tendency, to end rivalry and reconcile cities, see R. Mouterde, *Syria* 2 (1921) 280, on the Concord between two *poleis.* A relevant inscription is quoted in the text. The subject is further discussed *ibid.* 281f; and speeches on ὁμόνοια have survived by Aelius Aristides (*Or.* 42 and 44) and by Dio Chrysostom (*Or.* 39f). The same word is often invoked on coins (Bosch 118, 184, 219, and 237; *RE* s.v. Homonoia [Zwicker, 1913] col. 2268; and Magie 1499f).

26. Border disputes between cities are noted in Jos., *Ant. Jud.* 18.6.153; 20.1.2; Dio Chrysos., *Or.* 34.11 and 43–45; *IGRR* 4.571; *CIL* 3.586; *Inscriptiones graecae* 7.2870; F. F. Abbot and A. C. Johnson, *Municipal Administration in the Roman Empire* (1926) 344f; in Sardinia, *CIL* 10.7852; in Spain, *AE* 1952 no. 122; in Italy, *CIL* 9.2827 and 5420; cf. P. Veyne, *Latomus* 18 (1959) 578f. Egyptian villagers in the 380's battled each other over the water supply and "certain fields" (Budge 1.152 and 346), and in Africa, Oea and Lepcis in Vespasian's reign fought a war "begun among the peasants for mutual thefts of goods and herds, at the first trifling," Oea drawing in the Garamantes to her side, and the legions needed to enforce peace (Tac., *Hist.* 4.50). Sen., *De brev. vit.* 3.1, refers to boundary disputes breaking out at the slightest provocation. Western cities were thus as contentious as eastern ones, though perhaps for slightly different reasons. See above, n. 8, on Capua and Puteoli, and Philostr., *Vit. Apoll.* 5.13, on Sardinia in 68. Feuds interrupted commerce, whereas concord improved trade (Magie 638 and 1500f; Dio Chrysos., *Or.* 40.30f) and led to the exchange of gifts (Fronto, *Ep.* 1 p. 270, Loeb ed.) and of citizenship (Magie 538). Feuds, moreover, might result in the destruction of cities, as in Tac., *Hist.* 1.65, quoted in the text, where Vienne, though not razed, had to plead for peace. Byzantium actually did suffer, being "treated like a village" (Dio 75.14.3) and being stripped of its "theaters, baths, and every adornment, just as Antioch was given to Laodicea" (Herodian 3.6.9). For the effect of the wars of Septimius Severus, to exacerbate "mutual jealousy, envy, and hatred" in eastern cities generally, see Herodian 3.2.7f and 3.3.3, where Tyre and Beirut entered the war out of mutual hatred. Tyre had earlier been at war with Sidon, until both were disciplined by Rome (Dio

54.7.6, A.D. 20). In Phrygia, the emperor had to intervene to save Orcistus. It was given its independence from the *depraedatio potentiorum* of Nacolia (*CIL* 3.7000). How it came to be attributed to Nacolia in the first place is not known. A reverse instance is the deliberate handing over of one city to another for depredation (Soz., *Hist. eccl.* 5.3; Theodoret, *Hist. eccl.* 5.19f).

27. Robert, *Etudes anatoliennes* 203f.

28. Plut., *Mor.* 815D, instances troubles otherwise unexplained which "overtook the Pergamenes under Nero and the Rhodians under Domitian and the Thessalians earlier under Augustus, when they burned Petreius alive." Elsewhere, he urges concord (*Mor.* 824, quoted in the text). For Greek praise of the *pax Romana*, see Plut., *Mor.* 408B-C; Epict., *Diss.* 3.13.9; Ael. Arist., *To Rome* 70; and Euseb., *Laus Const.* 16.2-4, cited by J. Palm, *Rom, Römertum und Imperium* . . . (1959) 117. The Roman peace may actually have quieted rivalries and differences. The cities of Lycia illustrate a tendency (how widespread in the eastern provinces I cannot judge) toward a quiescent uniformity: quarreling with each other in the early Empire and roughly chastened by Claudius (Suet., *Claud.* 25.3; Dio 60.17.3), later showing an increasingly fraternal spirit (Magie 538). On the other hand, some revival of interest in the writing of local history, still later (end of third century), may indicate a loosening of ties to the empire. So W. von Christ, *Geschichte der griechischen Litteratur*[6] 2 (1924) 763. Rome's role as unifier is explicitly recognized in the passage quoted in the text, from Ael. Arist., *To Rome* 97, trans. J. H. Oliver, *Transactions of the American Philosophical Society* 43 (1953) 906. Compare Menander, *Rhetores graeci*, ed. Spengel, 3.360, "All the Roman cities [M. means, in the Greek provinces] are now administered by one" system of law; and Liban., *Or.* 30.5, the Romans "communicate to all cities their own form of government."

29. Ael. Arist., *To Rome* 65, trans. Oliver, who rightly interprets οἱ δυνατοί as municipal magnates. The passage, however, goes on to add, "But there is the indignation and punishment from you [Romans] which will come upon them immediately, if they themselves dare to make any unlawful change." For an exceptional mention of popular anti-Romanism, see Lucian, *De morte Peregrini* 19, "At one moment he counseled the Greeks to take up arms against the Romans," where D. Magie in the Loeb edition refers to SHA *Ant. Pius* 5.5, mentioning the suppression of some obscure rebellion in Achaea. Oliver 953–958 gathers most interesting material on Roman intervention in first century Greek cities, but the picture that emerges is of help given generally to the upper classes against an individual or a few men aspiring to virtual tyranny.

30. Disgust at gladiation is expressed by such men as Marcus Aurelius, in Dio 72.29.3; Quint., *Decl.* 9.6f; Sen., *Ep.* 7.3f; Sen., *De tranq.* 2.13; Dio Chrysos., *Or.* 31.121f, describing how gladiation in Athens was rebuked by

a philosopher, but a Roman one, and the crowds booed him away; Philostr., *Vit. Apoll.* 4.22, in an incident perhaps not historical; Plut., *Mor.* 822C, quoted by G. Schnayder, *Eos* 30 (1927) 139n3, who refers also (p. 143) to the probably antigladiatorial *Treatise on Gladiation* of Favorinus; add, further, Lucian and Artemidorous, cited by Robert, *Les Gladiateurs* 249f. Robert (esp. 241–266) throws a great deal of light on the whole subject, emphasizing how untypical were the views of the Hellenic purists. Philhellenism extended not only to the rejection of Roman culture but of Latin, too. See Lucian, *Demonax* 40; H. Fuchs, *Der geistige Widerstand gegen Rom in der antiken Welt* (1938) 49n60, and 50n62; and often later, in Libanius, on "the Italic speech" (*Or.* 1.214; 2.44; *Ep.* 951) and in Gregory of Nyssa (*PG* 46.1053). The movement in the field of language is typified by figures of the Second Sophistic such as Arrian, Herodes Atticus, and Claudius Hadrianus, discussed in Palm 131f, and Christ 2.694–696 and 746f. Their enthusiasm was shared by Hadrian, the cuirass of whose statue, set up in Athens, shows Athena riding on the Capitoline wolf! Other gibes at Rome, as at her greed for conquest, were heard from Romans as well as Greeks. See Sallust and Tacitus, quoted in Fuchs 16. Or Rome's origins and avarice might be attacked, as in Dio Chrysos., *Or.* 13.31f; 31.43 and 114 (more anti-Rhodian than anti-Roman; and cf. 41.9); Philostr., *Epp. Apoll.* 30 (rather constructive criticism), and 54 (plea for more Roman charitable attention to women and children). On Rome's origins, see Schnayder 114, 122, and 135f; for the same use of foundation legends against Rome by Christians, see Min. Fel., *Oct.* 25.2f (but note in 25.1 the admiration for Rome); Tert., *Ad nat.* 2.9.19; Tert., *Apol.* 25.14; Oros., *Hist.* 2.4; Lact., *Div. Inst.* 5.6. For the ambiguity of Romulus' fame—after all, a fratricide—in Cicero and Sallust, as well as in later anti-Roman writers, see O. Seel, *Römertum und Latinität* (1964) 219–221. The vulgarity or extravagance of the Roman aristocracy is pilloried by Juvenal and Ammianus, but also by Lucian, *Nigrinus*, the passages commented on by A. Peretti, *Luciano* (1946) 41–49 and 83. Peretti's arguments for Greek anti-Romanism are based on loose interpretations of the texts—of Dio Chrysostom, Plutarch, Philostratus, and especially Lucian—which I need not examine in detail, since they are answered by Palm's thorough good sense (pp. 45–51) and by V. Fumarola, *Parola del passato* 6 (1951) 196f and 204f, who emphasizes how commonplace are Lucian's themes and comments.

Chapter VI. The Outsiders

1. Bandits were common in ancient literature, as P. A. Mackay, *Greece and Rome*[2] 10 (1963) 152, points out, and they were even venerated in Christian times. See H. Hubert, *Les Celtes depuis l'époque de la Tène*

(1932) 185. For the stories of brigands cited in the text, see Appendix B.

2. The perfection of the *pax Romana* is acknowledged in Vell. Pat., *Hist. Rom.* 2.126, and Epict., *Diss.* 3.13.9, both quoted in the text.

3. Laws define the accomplices of brigands: Paul, *Sent.* 5.3.4 (cf. P. Ant. 87); *Cod. Theod.* 9.29.1 (374) and 2 (383–391); 7.18.7 (383); 1.29.8 (392). Rural inns were often bandits' headquarters, as we can see from Cyprian, *Ep.* 68.3.3; Liban., *Or.* 33.40; cf. the man murdered in 342 in a Syrian inn, *SEG* 20 (1964) 372.

4. For the atrocious conduct of military police, see R. MacMullen, *Soldier and Civilian in the Later Roman Empire* (1963) 86–89. On the connection between wars and the spread of brigandage, see Appendix B, 4; Tac., *Hist.* 1.46; *Cod. Theod.* 7.20.7; Symm., *Ep.* 7.38, A.D. 398; and Liban., *Or.* 18.104. On the *bellum desertorum,* see Appendix B, 11; on raids into Gaul in the 170's, some references are given in R. MacMullen, *Historia* 14 (1965) 102n33, including destruction attributed to *latrones.* A characteristic law, quoted in the text, licensed pursuit of criminous soldiers: *Cod. Theod.* 9.14.2 (391); cf. Basil, *Ep.* 268, writing of soldiers in Thrace in 377; Zos. 5.22, writing of Thrace in 401; and *Cod. Theod.* 7.1.12 (384) and 16 (398), on soldiers "wandering at large throughout the provinces" and in Italy, too (*Cod. Theod.* 7.18.1, A.D. 365, and 7.18.2–6, A.D. 379–382), as well as Pontus (*ibid.* 7.18.7, A.D. 383) and Gaul (*ibid.* 7.18.8–10, A.D. 383 or 391 to 400, and *Cod. Just.* 3.27.2, A.D. 403).

5. On stipulations that prisoners be returned, in treaties of A.D. 173 and 180 with the Iazyges and Buri, see Dio 72.13.4 and 73.3.2. Evagrius, *Hist. eccl.* 1.7.258, tells of Nestorius' capture by Blemmyes. Christian charity ransomed Numidian victims in 253 (Cyprian, *Ep.* 62), and inscriptions of the third century such as *CIL* 3.12455 (A.D. 239) offer thanks for return of captives. In *Inscriptiones graecae in Bulgaria* 1, a priest appears as captured by *barbari* and rescued; in *AE* 1949, 255, from Lydia in 263, a captive appears as restored from the Goths. A. Mocsy, *Archaeologiai ertesitö* 1963, p. 20, describes those inscriptions from Savaria of 167–177 where the subject's age is unknown, and the refuge caves are discussed by S. Gagnière and J. Granier, *Provence historique* 13 (1963) 234. For the details on the consequences of invasion mentioned in the text, see Greg. Thaumat., *Ep. canon.*, *PG* 10.1021, 1025, 1037, 1041, 1044f, dealing with problems in Pontus in the wake of raids of about 260, and compare *Cod. Just.* 8.51.4 (290) telling of litigation over property of a captive, and 8.51.18 (294) over a captive returned to his property. Amm. 31.6.5 offers the story of prisoners and captives of the Goths, especially gold miners "who could no longer endure the heavy burden of taxes," in 376–377 in Thrace, serving as scouts and traitors. Compare similar betrayals in Paulinus of Pella, *Eucharist.* 328–336 (A.D. 415, Bordeaux); Greg. Thaumat., *Ep. canon.*, *PG* 10.1040f; *Cod. Theod.* 9.14.3 (397), a law against persons "in criminal conspiracy with soldiers,

civilians, or even with barbarians," to kill any imperial agent (see below, on flight to join barbarians).

6. The quotation on the poor is from the anonymous *De rebus bellicis* 2.3, trans. E. A. Thompson, *A Roman Reformer and Inventor . . .* (1952), with his comments, pp. 33f. For similar statements by John Chrysostom and Asterius, see above, Chap. V n. 21. On the clustering of evidence for brigandage around Septimius Severus' reign, see Appendix B. Nothing, I think, is proved by the fact that reference to *latrones* in the *Digest* is most frequent in the earlier third century. That happened to be the era in which the jurists, later most cited, gave their opinions. Some of the *latrones* texts are *Dig.* 13.6.5.4; 17.2.52.3; 19.2.9.4; 23.3.5.4; 24.3.21; and 48.9.7, all Ulpian; of Paul, 41.2.3.8; 49.15.19.2; 49.16.14; of Marcian, 48.13.4; 48.19.11.2; of Callistratus, 48.19.28.15. A contributor to brigandage was third century *anachoresis,* often noted in Egypt, though it was endemic to the province. A. Calderini, *JEA* 40 (1954) 19f, stresses an interesting aspect, the people who have "fled into wandering." On social mobility in the late Empire, more generally, see R. MacMullen, *JRS* 54 (1964) 49–53, and the groups of visionaries mentioned above in Chapter IV.

7. On slave unrest, see above, Chap. V n. 6. Note SHA *Firmus, Saturninus, and Proculus* 12.2, where Proculus launches his revolt by arming 2,000 of his slaves; and note also the young men, evidently of the better classes, who are leaders of the slaves plundering around Bordeaux, about 415 (Paulinus of Pella, *Eucharist.* 328–336). Severan laws pertaining to fugitives, for the same reason of citation in the *Codes* as was offered in the preceding note, do not prove an increased incidence of flights of slaves in the period of Ulpian and later.

8. Herodian 7.4.3f is quoted on the arming of African peasants. At the orders of "their masters," they came "in great multitudes." Compare SHA *Gordiani* 7.2f, noting the involvement of *rustici* and *plebs urbana vel rusticana.* Popular support for the Palmyrene princes appears in the two phrases quoted in the text, from Oros., *Hist.* 7.22, and Jordanes, *Romana* 290; add Ruf. Festus, *Brev.* 23, *conlecta Syrorum agrestium manu.* Rural clientage is known from L. Harmand, *Un Aspect social et politique du monde romain: Le Patronat . . .* (1957) 231, 237, 272, 277, 279, 283. These third century examples of rural *patrocinium* outnumber the few of an earlier date (Harmand 211, 215, 239). In at least one case (*CIL* 10.521; Harmand 427) one of these later patrons apparently held no office, only lands. In another inscription (*IGRR* 3.1317, A.D. 294–295, Arabia) the patron helps the village to build a storage tank. Links between rural rich and poor appear also in later centuries (Harmand 422–466, esp. 424 and 454). On the subject of late Roman rural class relations, I suspect that much could be added—such as Jerome, *Vita Malchi* 2—if the writings of the Church Fathers were carefully searched. Much may be guessed from a score of laws threatening

landowners whose patronage conceals brigands and deserters. See *Cod. Theod.* 7.18 *passim* (364–412), with mention of estates requiring bailiffs and slaves, and therefore of a large size, whose owners are sometimes described as being of high rank.

9. Several studies of unrest among the elements excluded from society have appeared recently (those in Russian having been translated for me). To explore disagreement with them point by point would take too long. Some of my arguments are implied in notes 6 and 7 above or are made for me by Marxist writers themselves. See P. Oliva, *Pannonia . . .* (1962) 124n175, and 308n149; S. I. Kovalev, *Vestnik drevnei istorii* 1954, no. 3, p. 34. For the views contested in the text, besides the position of these last two writers, see A. D. Dmitriev, *Vestnik drevnei istorii* 1951, no. 4, pp. 62f *passim,* esp. p. 69 (on Africa); A. P. Kazhdan, *Vestnik drevnei istorii* 1953, no. 3, pp. 105f; J. Burian, *Studii clasice* 3 (1961) 173; H. J. Diesner, *Forschungen und Fortschritte* 36 (1962) 214; and H. J. Diesner, *Kirche und Staat im spätrömischen Reich* (1964). Oliva 114 rather emphatically leans on a Leipzig dissertation (1953) of D. Günther on brigandage. The director of the university library at Leipzig courteously informs me that the work is not to be found in the city, and my efforts to get in touch with Professor Oliva directly have not been rewarded.

10. The view that the *circumcelliones* were social revolutionaries appears in W. H. C. Frend, *The Donatist Church* (1952) 172 and 210; Diesner, *Forschungen und Fortschritte* 36 (1962) 214; cf. E. Tengström, *Donatisten und Katholiken* (1964) 69f and 74. They are called, if half ironically, *sancti,* or *agonistici* (Optatus Milevitanus 3.4; Aug., *Ep.* 108.6.18); and they were dressed *habitu monachorum* (Isidore, *PL* 83.796, quoted in Frend 174). Compare other texts cited by Frend 174f and by Tengström 58–60. Tengström insists they are not monks. The dispute degenerates into terminology. On their staffs, replaced by spears and swords, see Tengström 51, and Aug., *Contra litt. Petil.* 2.97.222. On their character as *latrones,* see the quotation in the text from Aug., *Ep.* 88.8; Aug., *Ep. ad Cath.* 20.54; and Aug., *Ep.* 43.8.24, mentioning the *publica latrocinia* of the Donatists. The words, however, are standard terms of abuse. Chief victims of *circumcelliones* were the rich, as is seen in Aug., *Ep.* 108.6.18, and *Cod. Theod.* 16.6.2, and in the example of the landowner whose house they would have burned had not his *coloni* defended him (Diesner, *Kirche und Staat* 70; cf. Frend, *Donatist Church* 210). They "reversed the position of master and slave" (Optatus Milevitanus 3.4, quoted in the text), and debtors joined them (Aug., *Sermo de Rusticano* 4; Aug., *Ep.* 108.19; 185.4.15, perhaps referring to circumcellions as well as to Donatists); but that the circumcellions did not generally consist of, but only sheltered, fugitives, is the view of Diesner, *Kirche und Staat* 75, and Tengström 54. Augustine tells us of *quotidianas violentias circumcellionum sub episcopis et presbyteris ducibus* (quoted in Teng-

ström 62; cf. p. 40). See also, on subordination to *possessores*, *PL* 11.1420A, quoted in Diesner, *Kirche und Staat* 55; further, *ibid.* 74 and Tengström 163; but the supposed masters of the circumcellions, the Donatists, were sometimes out of sympathy with, or frightened by, their violence. See Diesner, *Forschungen und Fortschritte* 36 (1962) 214; Frend 172, 176, 197; Tengström 68; and J.-P. Brisson, *Autonomisme et christianisme dans l'Afrique romaine* . . . (1958) 346f. And masters, even if Catholic, permitted or winked at circumcellion activity on their estates (Tengström 135–141 and 163). Possidius, *Vit. Aug.* 10, goes so far as to say that the circumcellions "spare neither their own kind nor others."

11. Cases of upper-class Donatists are discussed by Tengström 175 and Frend, *Donatist Church* 171. Compare above, n. 10, on breaks in sympathy between Donatist conservatives and radical circumcellions. Nearer the coast, Donatism may have appealed to rejected and tumultuous elements of the population (cf. Augustine's tendency to be suspicious of the poor, emphasized by Diesner, *Forschungen und Fortschritte* 36 [1962] 215), but in southern Numidia, Donatism blanketed the countryside and reflected the full social spectrum. Augustine gives his opinion of Optatus in *Contra litt. Petil.* 2.23.53, quoted in the text and discussed by Tengström 75–78, who connects the charges with Optatus' position, and with his abuse of the powers of guardian to heiresses and minors. The passage has, to my mind, been distorted by Frend and other writers (quoted *ibid.* 78). The quotation on the building of the great cathedral (200 × 50 feet) and its attribution to Optatus is by Frend 209.

12. Aug., *Contra litt. Petil.* 2.23.54, among many texts.

13. In the aspects of the dispute relevant to this chapter, concerning the nature and intent of Donatism, I depend mostly on the cool and careful scholarship of Tengström. See his full bibliography, pp. 195–200.

14. For the Moorish attacks, see R. Cagnat, *L'Armée romaine d'Afrique* . . . (1912) 47f; for interpretation, Dmitriev 69; Burian 171f, with much loose speculation on detail; and Oliva 119f, citing a text certainly worthless, SHA *Pertinax* 4.2, . . . *dicitur* (thus even the SHA doubts the fact). The inferences of class unrest drawn by all three writers are rightly dismissed by G. Charles Picard, *La Civilisation de l'Afrique romaine* (1959) 385. The cult of their kings among the African tribes is referred to by T. Kotula, *Travaux de la Société des sciences et des lettres de Wroclaw*, ser. A, no. 174 (1961) 107; for their rulers' titles, see J. Carcopino, *Le Maroc antique*[10] (1943) 303f, and P. Romanelli, *Hommages à Albert Grenier* (1962) 1360f.

15. T. Kotula, *Eos* 50 (1959–60) 198 and n. 5, argues for a sense at least of prideful separateness in the province, but his evidence is inadequate. Worship of the *dea patria* seems to prove nothing and, as he points out, one casualty in the rising felt that he died *pro amore Romano*, in opposition to the barbarian Maximinus. Worship of the goddess Africa, popular for sev-

eral centuries, received emphatic official approval. See M. Leglay, *Hommages à Jean Bayet* (1964) 374f and 380f. R. M. Haywood, *Transactions of the American Philological Association* 71 (1940) 175, concludes, "After a diligent search through all the evidence, I have been unable to find evidence of any feeling of common nationality or common patriotism among the Africans." Cf. also Brisson 27n4. I have made my own search, through studies on African pottery, lamps, and relief sculpture, for signs of the survival or revival of preclassical styles (I need not list a purely negative bibliography) without finding very much. I return to the subject below, in n. 40. On tribal incursions, see Kotula, *Travaux* 109, and Cagnat 60f—described as mere rapine by Amm. 28.6.2 and 29.5.27.

16. On support for Firmus, see Aug., *Ep.* 87.10; on Firmus' persecution of Rogatus and his fellow schismatics, Aug., *Contra Ep. Parm.* 1.10.16, and Aug., *Contra litt. Petil.* 2.83.184. Frend, *Donatist Church* 73 takes these passages to prove Donatist support of Firmus, but cf. Tengström 78–83. For shelter with villages, see Amm. 29.5.25 and 39. The opinion on Gildo's aims is quoted from Frend 221. He is called a mere "plunderer" in Claud., *De bello Gild.* 1.162, and Claud., *De cons. Stilich.* 1.358. Augustine's charges against Donatists, that their leader Optatus was Gildo's friend, is noted by Tengström 85, who cites also Aug., *Ep.* 43.8.24.

17. For these parallels, suggested by a number of writers, see, for example, W. H. C. Frend, *Cambridge Journal* 2 (1949) 491; Frend, *Donatist Church* 59; E. L. Woodward, *Christianity and Nationalism in the Later Roman Empire* (1916) 44f; E. R. Hardy, *Christian Egypt* (1952) 53. On Pelagianism, the views of J. N. L. Myres, *JRS* 50 (1960) 21–33, are sufficiently refuted by W. Liebeschuetz, *Historia* 12 (1963) 233f; on Egyptian heresies, arguing against the joint operation of religious and cultural motives, see R. MacMullen, *Aegyptus* 44 (1964) 193f.

18. For Donatist brigands, see Frend, *Donatist Church* 12; for a Montanist brigand, W. Schepelern, *Der Montanismus . . .* (1929) 35; for ritual drunkenness, *ibid.* 37 and Frend 174. On Egyptian pagan relics in Coptism, see B. R. Rees, *JEA* 36 (1950) 86–100, and other references in MacMullen, *Aegyptus* 44 (1964) 194f; on traces of Saturn worship among circumcellions, see Frend 103f; on orgiastic mysticism in Montanism, see W. M. Calder, in *Anatolian Studies Presented to Sir William Mitchell Ramsay* (1923) 64; W. M. Calder, *Bulletin of the John Rylands Library* 7 (1922–23) 329, on a pre-Montanist prophetess of Philadelphia honored by Montanists later. Schepelern 105f, 112, 123f, 128, and 159f, and K. Holl, *Hermes* 43 (1908) 253, deal with other pagan aspects of Montanism. The evidence of inscriptions is studied by A. M. Ramsay, in *Anatolian Studies* 336f; A. M. Ramsay in *Studies in the History and Art of the Eastern Provinces . . .*, ed. W. M. Ramsay (1906) 9 and 91; and *Monumenta Asiae minoris antiqua* 5 (1937) xxxiii. Contemporaneous revivals of older worships can be seen *ibid.*, *passim*,

on Zeus Bronton, his cult centered in Phrygia, and very ancient, but inscriptions mostly of A.D. 125–225. On the Tekmoreian Guest Friends, an obscure cult of a conservative cast whose records begin only in the second quarter of the third century, see W. M. Ramsay, in *Studies . . . of the Eastern Provinces* 346, 356 (dates which I would prefer to push back from ca. 250 to ca. 225), and 357–358 (arguing unconvincingly for a movement of population from cities to villages in this period); W. M. Ramsay, *Journal of Hellenic Studies* 32 (1912) 155, supposing that the cult existed throughout the Roman period; and E. N. Lane, *Berytus* 15 (1964) 56–58, and Magie 1326n44, 1548n35, and 1573n40, correcting some of Ramsay's speculations. Lane 5–58 and M. H. Hardie, *Journal of Hellenic Studies* 32 (1912) 115 and 120f, deal with the very ancient worship of Men, the records of which, however, at Pisidian Antioch, likewise become numerous only in the Roman era. A similar "taste for erudition and religious conservatism . . . a real regression," can be seen in the cult of Zeus at Mylasa (A. Laumonier, *Les Cultes indigènes en Carie* [1958] 65). For the vitality shown by the Phrygian language, see *Monumenta Asiae minoris antiqua* 7. xxviii and the map, p. xliv, showing its distribution in ca. 250; R. MacMullen, *AJP* 87 (1966) 13n29. Evidence of language and religion is sometimes used to argue for a Phrygian nationalism, by J. G. C. Anderson, for example, in *Studies . . . of the Eastern Provinces* 202. Tertullian, quoted in the text, sees in heretical deviations rather the work of magicians and charlatans (*De praescr.* 43, forgetful of I Corinthians 1.27). A like list of suspects occurs in *Cod. Theod.* 16.5.62 (425): "heretics, schismatics, astrologers (*mathematici*), and every sect inimical to the Catholics." Heresies especially flourished in this whole area. On those at Laodicea, see W. M. Calder, *Bulletin of the John Rylands Library* 13 (1929) 256; for laws against these sects, *Cod. Theod.* 16.5.2 and 7.

19. Various kinds of wandering ascetics and heretics are reported by Theodoret, *Hist. eccl.* 4.11 (A.D. 367–371); Calder, in *Anatolian Studies* 64; Synes., *Ep.* 67, the *vacantivi;* Jerome, *Ep.* 22.28; Liban., *Or.* 30.8f; and Praedestinatus 1.17 (*PL* 53.592). On the agitation of the circumcellions in *nundinae*, see Frend, *Donatist Church* 176. The lower-class nature of religious rioters, in such phrases as are quoted in the text, is emphasized by Athanasius, *Hist. Arian.* 55, speaking of Alexandria in 339, and by Frend 11, on a disputed church election in Cirta in 305, the richer townsfolk being locked up in a cemetery; cf. references to "tumultuous conventicles" of slaves (*Cod. Theod.* 16.4.5), Manichaeans proselytizing among "persons of the lowest classes" (*ibid.* 16.5.9), and the Arians' sending of four companies of soldiers into Paphlagonia against Novatianist peasants, who beat off the attack with reaping hooks and hatchets (Soc., *Hist. eccl.* 2.38, *PG.* 67.329).

20. Bans on various groups or sources of unrest include those against movements of tribes. See Frend, *Donatist Church* 40, on Berbers in the second century. Concerning tribes in northern provinces, see R. MacMullen,

AC 32 (1963) 552 and 554. For laws to control deserters, see above, n. 4; to tie down beggars, *Cod. Theod.* 14.18.1 (382); against heretics, *ibid.* Bk. 16 *passim.* The legislation quoted is found *ibid.* 16.4.1f, trans. Pharr.

21. On criminals and bankrupts turned monk, see above, n. 18, and Chap. V n. 21. Monks become agitators drew forth *Cod. Theod.* 9.40.15 (392), 16 (398), and 16.3.1 (390—repealed in 392, by 16.3.2). The role of monks in Antioch's troubles in 387 is touched on above, in Chapter V, and more fully by Theodoret, *Hist. relig.* 13 (PG 82.1404), and by John Chrysos., *On the Statues, Homil.* 17.2f; 18.4. For Shenute as a defender of the poor against officialdom and the rich, see MacMullen, *Aegyptus* 44 (1964) 197.

22. Sources for the Bagaudae are gathered in V. A. Sirago, *Gallia Placidia . . .* (1961) 377n1; W. Seston, *Dioclétien et la Tétrarchie* (1946) 68; and E. A. Thompson, *Past and Present* 2 (1952) 11n1, who (against Sirago 382) seems to be right in taking *omne paene Galliarum servitia in Bacaudam conspiravere* to refer to serfs, not slaves. On the activity of the Bagaudae in the Alps and Spain, see Sirago 377 and 382f and Thompson 16f; on their history in Gaul, see L. Hermann, *Querolus* (*Grognon*) (1937) 58, supplying the quotation in the text. The comedy is generally dated to the early fifth century. As to their leaders, Aelianus' coinage is in dispute. See Seston 69n1, who accepts its authenticity, though P. H. Webb, in H. Mattingly and E. A. Sydenham, *Roman Imperial Coinage* vol. 5 pt. 2 (1933) p. 595, hesitates. For Amandus' coins, see ibid. For the history of the movement in Armorica, see Zos. 6.5, quoted in the text, and Thompson 18.

23. Bagaudae are called nationalistic by Sirago 378, among many other scholars; but on Gallic nationalism generally, see MacMullen, *Historia* 14 (1965) 103, and Gallic orators protest their loyalty to Rome: *Paneg. vet.*, ed. Galletier 5.3.4; 8.5.2; 11.2.3; 8.2.4, the Heduans *consanguinitatis nomine* (that is, with Rome) *gloriati sunt*, and 8.3.1f, *simplex caritas* toward Rome in the second century B.C. They boast of their opposition to Gallic pretenders, *ibid.* 8.4.2; cf. 5.4.1, on the *latrocinio Batavicae rebellionis* against a *civitatem . . . fraternam populi Romani nomine gloriatam.* And there is evidence that the pretenders did not stand for separation from Rome, but for its salvation, as in SHA *Trig. tyr.* 5.5, calling Postumus, Lollianus, Victorinus, and Tetricus *adsertores Romani nominis; ibid.* 3.6, "a great love felt by all the Gallic peoples toward Postumus because, clearing away all the German tribes, he had recalled Roman rule to its former security." A good test of the advertised intentions of both Carausius and Postumus is to be made on their coinage; but their iconography, to say nothing of the legends, is classical, conservative, and imitative of that of legitimate rulers. See E. Fantecchi, *Rivista italiana di numismatica* 61 (1959) 134–137. Postumus so far accepted the traditional criteria of imperial success, in his competition with Gallienus, as to cheat in his enumeration in order to arrive at TRIB. POT. X, IMP. X, in only eight years of rule (L. Laffranchi, *ibid.*

43 [1941] 132f). For such reasons J. J. Hatt, *Histoire de la Gaule romaine* . . . (1959) 227, rightly says, "It would be a serious misunderstanding to consider [the Gallic empire] as an attempt at national liberation. In fact it was a desperate effort to defend at all costs, even at the edge of the Roman empire, a political and social State, a civilization that Rome had made but which Rome herself . . . could not preserve." L. Homo, *Essai sur le règne de l'empereur Aurélien* . . . (1904) 45, speaks in the same terms of the situation in 270.

24. For the interpretation of early events in Gaul as proofs of nationalism, see, for example, Sirago 378 and Hatt, *Histoire* 227. Yet the motives seem to have been simpler. See Tac., *Ann.* 3.40, and above, Chap. V n. 26. On the northern population under Vindex, see Tac., *Hist.* 1.51, quoted in the text; on the Treviri and Lingones, *ibid.* 1.53; for *libertas* as freedom from taxes, *ibid.* 4.17. The recruits to the revolt fought under their own leaders (*ibid.* 4.16 and 4.23—quoted in the text), and apparently only against conscription and the payment of tribute (*ibid.* 4.26 and 32).

25. One symptom of the weakness of the Gallic revolutionary movement is the desertions from it (*ibid.* 4.56, 66, 70, 79), and disunity is acknowledged among the tribes (4.69 and 74, key passages). On these and many other aspects—coinage, Roman ways among the rebels, motives—see G. E. F. Chilver, *JRS* 47 (1957) 29f, and especially P. A. Brunt, *Latomus* 18 (1959) 534 and 544–553, emphatic, trenchant, and thorough against any talk of nationalism. There are passages suggesting a contrary view, such as the mention of ancestral gods and the like, in Tac., *Hist.* 4.64 and 67; 5.17; cf., on the British rebellion, Tac., *Agr.* 21 and 30; but on the cliché nature of these speeches, note the points made by Walser and quoted in R. Chevallier, *Latomus* 20 (1961) 50. The same split treatment can be seen in Dio 62.3.1f, on Boadicea: δεσποτεία contrasted with τῆς πατρίου διαίτης; but the speech moves directly to the depredations and heavy taxes that come with Roman rule. Compare Dio 67.4.6, for A.D. 85 and 86, "Many of Rome's subjects revolted when money was raised from them by force. Among these were the Nasamones, who had killed the tax collectors and defeated the governor of Numidia." See also the outbreak of the Bucoli in the third century, outraged by the conduct of the army levy (MacMullen, *Aegyptus* 44 [1964] 185), and the revolt supporting Jotapianus against Philip, produced by weight of taxes (Zos. 1.20.2).

26. See the passages on the *pax Romana* cited in Chap. V n. 28, and Tac., *Hist.* 4.69 and 74.

27. On the use of the term "nation," see H. Dessau, ed., *Inscriptiones latinae selectae* 2316, 2893, and 2896. Though *natio* and *gens* are sometimes used interchangeably (Lewis and Short, *Dictionary* s.v. *natio*), only the former applies to really big units of people. Note the distinction in Tac., *Germ.* 2. *Nationes* were regularly, and crudely, characterized by contemporaries, as if all Syrians were luxury-loving, or the like (Herodian

2.10.7; 3.11.8; 4.8.7; Zos. 3.11.8; Aurel. Vict., *De Caes.* 42.17; Dio 78.6.1a, Loeb ed.; Julian, *Against the Galileans* 116A; on Egyptians, the references collected by MacMullen, *Aegyptus* 44 [1964] 190). Of 76 occurrences of *natio* that I find in *Inscriptiones latinae selectae,* 21 are easily datable: five references to a German origin, *natione,* one to an African, in the first century; in the second and third centuries, 15 references (Thracian, African, Gallic, Syrian, and so on). On the increasing use of ἔθνη, Kornemann is cited by A. N. Sherwin-White, *The Roman Citizenship* (1939) 270, who, p. 271, discusses recognition of the composition of the empire (*cunctae gentes*). Stoics tried to rise above smaller political loyalties to a patriotism higher than nationalism, as can be seen in the quotation in the text from Marcus Aurel., *Medit.* 4.23 (the same metaphor in Epict., *Diss.* 1.9.1). Obedience to a supranational law is urged in Origen, *Contra Cels.* 5.25f and 27; cf. Tert., *Ad nat.* 2.1, *nobis negotium est, adversus institutiones maiorum, auctoritates receptorum, leges dominantium . . . adversus vetustatem, consuetudinem, necessitatem;* whereas these same older national virtues were praised in Eunap., *Vit. soph.* 503, quoted in the text, as also Julian, *Or. to Sallust* 246B. Note further how Julian, in *Ep.* 111 (Bidez), defended πατρῴων δογμάτων, παλαιῶν θεσμῶν, versus Christianity, τὸ καινὸν κήρυγμα, and went on expressly to advocate national differences (*Against the Galileans* 116A, 131C, 134D–E, 138A, and the passage on "the presiding national god," 143B).

28. Though attribution of the *Book of the Laws of Countries* to Bardesanes is not certain, no one doubts that it represents fundamentally his views. See MacMullen, *AJP* 87 (1966) 4n8, for bibliography. The comments of S. Mazzarino, *Rapports du XIe Congrès international des sciences historiques* (1960) 2.37f, at points unclear or inconclusive, emphasize interestingly the sharper spiritual response to Rome to be found on the periphery of the empire, in Bardesanes and Hippolytus. I discuss Hippolytus in Chapter IV, above. For his meaning when he uses the word δημοκρατίαι, not "democracies" but "constituted states," see J. H. Oliver, *Transactions of the American Philosophical Society* 43 (1953) 92.

29. Tatian mentions the Roman haughtiness in *Or. ad Graecos* 35. Bardesanes' similar views appear in Euseb., *Praep. ev.* 6.10.35 and 41, or ed. Cureton (Syriac) pp. 27 and 30, and the views of Lucian emerge especially in *Nigrinus* 15–17. Cf. above, Chapter V n. 30. Jewish anti-Romanism, quoted in the text, can be seen in M. Hadas, *Philological Quarterly* 8 (1929) 373, though the Jews also show their anti-Hellenism, in E. M. Smallwood, *Historia* 11 (1962) 502, in a Mishnah quotation referring to the early second century.

30. For arguments against nationalist interpretations of third century Egyptian risings, see MacMullen, *Aegyptus* 44 (1964) 186f. For the measures taken against "nationalist" pretenders, see the quotation in the text from Dio 71.31.1. The only comment I have found on this interesting law is M. Hammond, *The Antonine Monarchy* (1959) 277n55, who says, "Dio's

'then,' τότε, perhaps indicates that the rule was no longer in force when he wrote." On Gordian's eastern origins, see A. R. Birley, *Britain and Rome*, ed. M. A. Jarrett and B. Dobson (1966) 000; on Celsus, and on Saturninus, Aemilianus, Bonosus, Firmus, Proculus, L. Domitius Alexander, and Magnus Maximus (the last seven being aliens to the province of their revolt) see Zon. 12.21; Victor, *Epit. de Caes.* 31.2 and 40.17; Zos. 2.1.2f and 4.35.3; SHA *Firmus* 3.1; 7.1; 12.1; and 14.1; SHA *Trig. tyr.* 29.2. For pretenders styled *latrones*, as the quotation in the text shows, see SHA *Firmus* 2.2, confirmed by scores of references in inscriptions and legal and literary sources, such as *ibid.* 5.3f; MacMullen, *Revue internationale des droits de l'antiquité*[3] 10 (1963) 223f; and above, n. 16. The term of contempt, *latro*, was not far wrong, in some cases: Proculus was the descendant of brigands, Trebellianus an Isaurian brigand (SHA *Trig. tyr.* 26.2), whose historicity is doubted for no good reason.

31. Coins and texts of Uranius Antoninus present great difficulties. See Mattingly and Sydenham vol. 4, pt. 3 (1949) pp. 204 and 206; R. Delbrueck, *Numismatic Chronicle*[6] 8 (1948) 27f; A. Calderini, *I Severi* (1949) 153.

32. On Palmyrene costume, see H. Seyrig, *JRS* 40 (1950) 2f, and H. Seyrig, *Syria* 18 (1937) 4–27; on the Archers, P. V. C. Baur and M. I. Rostovtzeff, *Excavations at Dura-Europus . . . Preliminary Report . . . 1928* (1929) 53f, and the Comte du Mesnil du Buisson, *Les Tessères et les monnaies de Palmyre* (1962) 445; on Vorod, H. Seyrig, *Annales archéologiques de Syrie* 13 (1963) 162f and 166f, and H. Ingholt, *Berytus* 3 (1936) 93f; and on Odenathus' expansion *Syrorum agrestium manu, collecta rusticorum manu*, see Ruf. Festus, *Brev.* 23, and Jordanes, *Romana* 290. On the popular opinion about that expansion, compare the two Palmyrene inscriptions in H. Seyrig, *Mélanges de l'Université St. Joseph* 37 (1961) 262f and 266f, seeming to reflect an Arab pride in Odenathus' achievements, and H. Seyrig, *Syria* 31 (1954) 217, mourning losses in Egypt. On the titles of Odenathus' heir, see Seyrig, *Syria* 18 (1937) 2, and A. Solari, *Philologus* 92 (1937–38) 241–243, where the Palmyrene relations with Persia and Rome are explored. Those with other provinces would have been injured by extreme anti-Romanism (Sherwin-White 281). On the lack of nationalism, I have M. Seyrig's authoritative opinion, from occasions when he permitted me to cross-question him on these matters. I here record my special thanks to him.

33. Victor, *De Caes.* 39.26, supplies the quotation on the Pannonians. See, further, A. Alföldi, *A Conflict of Ideas in the Late Roman Empire* (1952) 14–17. Distributions of command, office, and patronage similar to those of A.D. 365 and later may be presumed also in the third century, though there is little evidence, and what there is has not been discussed, to my knowledge. The hostility of the sources to the uncultivated emperors is analyzed by Alföldi 100–123.

34. For the market offered by military concentrations, see R. von Uslar, *Saalburg Jahrbuch* 8 (1934) 63, 83–88, and 96; R. von Uslar, *Klio* 28 (1935) 295f; F. Kiechle, *Historia* 11 (1962) 175; and MacMullen, *Soldier and Civilian* 96n70. The influence of soldiers in their role as patrons, customers, and recipients of imperial largesses, is discussed *ibid.*, chap. V; R. MacMullen, *Latomus* 21 (1962) 160–164. On the increasing number of barbarians in the highest ranks as in the lowest and on the consequent barbarization of the army, see R. Grosse, *Römische Militärgeschichte* . . . (1920) 41; E. Sander, *Hist. Zeitschrift* 160 (1939) 17f; and W. Grünhagen, *Der Schatzfund von Gross-Bodungen* (1954) 72. Soldiers had an influence also on other aspects of culture. See, for example, exhibitions of open rage by troops, Amm. 15.8.15; 21.13.16; 27.10.7; Zos. 4.51.4; 4.56.8f; on the freer expression of anger in the late Empire, see R. MacMullen, *Art Bulletin* 46 (1964) 452f.

35. On survival of preconquest culture in Illyricum, see T. Nagy, in *Huitième Congrès international d'archéologie classique (Paris 1963)* . . . (1965) 378f, showing native Pannonian gods still flourishing in the third century; E. Swoboda, *Carnuntum*[3] (1958) 101f; J. Klemenc, *Omagiu liu Constantin Daicoviciu* (1960) 303–310, discussing Celtic patterns in relief sculpture and costume; and for their survival and a mature stage in Antonine times, see E. Beninger, *Wiener Beiträge zur Kunst- und Kulturgeschichte Asiens* 9 (1935) 40. M. Grbic, *Carnuntina* (1956) 78–84, shows how resistance to full Romanization produced a truly independent native expressionism in early fourth century Moesia; I. Cremosnik, *Glasnik*[2] 15–16 (1960–61) 200–202, studies Bosnian pottery of the third and fourth centuries recalling late Latène styles, part of "a renaissance of autochthonous elements" carried over into costume and symbolism under the patronage of "a rich stratum of the local population, who raised funeral monuments to themselves bearing the traces of elements of Celtic culture." Compare Swoboda 102 and 185 on the strong dominance of Celtic elements in pottery after the Marcomannic wars, and the contemporary resurgence of native cults and burial customs.

36. For the "Celtic renaissance" in western provinces, see MacMullen, *Historia* 14 (1965) 95f, adding A. Frazer, *Essays in Memory of Karl Lehmann* (1964) 108, who discusses Celtic handling of decoration of a fourth century bowl from Cologne; also *RE* s.v. Grannus (Ihm, 1912) col. 1824–1826, mentioning a later second and third century revival of the cult of a Celtic oracular god, and R. Pettazzoni, *Journal of Celtic Studies* 1 (1949) 39 and 42f, detecting a revival of the Celtic three-faced god from 200 on in northern France. R. Laur-Belart, in *Huitième Congrès international d'archéologie classique (Paris 1963)* . . . 165, and especially 174, finds Celtic influence even on a gold cult statue of Marcus Aurelius; and S. J. De Laet, *Diogène* 47 (1964) 99, 103f, and 107, notes the passage of powers of patronage to the culturally conservative middle classes; cf. J. J. Hatt, *La Tombe gallo-romaine* (1951) 183 and 209. Similar phenomena can be detected in

Spain. See MacMullen, *Historia* 14 (1965) 96n11; H. Comfort, *Archivo español di arqueologia* 34 (1961) 11; and P. Palol de Salellas, *Settimane di Studio* . . . 3 (1955 [1956]) 114. But the whole subject remains relatively unexplored. Turning back to Gaul, to consider the question of language: the revived use of the Gallic *leuga* might mean no more than the extension of roads into less Romanized areas, and evidence for Gallic often has to do with magic and religion, as we might expect. As for the Druids of later times, they were openly permitted because so greatly fallen from their former importance. See MacMullen, *AJP* 87 (1966) 15f; G. Must, *Language* 36 (1960) 193 and 197; MacMullen, *Historia* 14 (1965) 99–103; and above, Chap. IV n. 28.

37. Cremosnik 200 shows the penetration of Belgic imports to Illyricum. On religious revivals, see MacMullen, *Historia* 14 (1965) 98f; above, n. 36, on Grannus; on Britain, Frend, *Cambridge Journal* 2 (1949) 494n1.

38. Cologne offers evidence of reviving commerce with barbarians. See M. Amand, *Latomus* 11 (1952) 482f, and the authorities cited by MacMullen, *Historia* 14 (1965) 101n31. The influence of barbarian tastes on Roman manufactures for export is clear from A. Alföldi, *Jahresbericht der Gesellschaft Pro Vindonissa* 1948–49, p. 20; S. J. De Laet, J. Dhondt, and J. Nenquin, *Etudes d'histoire et d'archéologie dédiées à Ferdinand Courtoy* (1952) 1.155f; Grünhagen 73n4; B. Stjernqvist, *Saalburg Jahrbuch* 13 (1954) 59f; and J. Werner, *Bonner Jahrbücher* 158 (1958) 398. Similar influences touched manufactures for internal markets: see MacMullen, *AC* 32 (1963) 553f and esp. 558–559; F. Behn, *Mainzer Zeitschrift* 30 (1935) 56–65; J. Pilloy, *Etudes sur d'anciens sépultures dans l'Aisne* (1895) 2.82f, 89, 305, 311, and 316f; Kiechle 190; A. France-Lanord, *Revue archéologique* 1963, p. 34; T. Pekary, *Archeologiai ertesitö* 82 (1955) 29; K. Sági, *Acta archaeologica academiae scientiarum Hungaricae* 12 (1960) 187f, 220–244, and 252; and L. Barkoczi, *ibid.* 16 (1964) 298. S. J. De Laet and A. Van Doorselaer, *Saalburg Jahrbuch* 20 (1962) 54–61, give an interesting catalogue of sites with the conclusion that the internal barbarians of the fourth and fifth centuries strengthened vestigial customs in the provinces going back to Latène times.

39. Mentions of desertions to the enemy that I find, in no very thorough search, are Petrus Patricius (ed. Müller) frg. 5, deserters to Decebalus under Trajan; Dio 71.11.2 and 72.2.2, to the Quadi and Marcomanni in the 160's and 170's; SHA *Proculus* 13.4; *Cod. Theod.* 7.1.1 (323); 5.7.1 (366); *Cod. Just.* 6.1.3; Amm. 28.3.8; 30.5.3 (368 and 370's); Jerome, *Ep.* 123.16 (406), Pannonii joining barbarian raiders; and several more fourth and fifth century mentions in n. 5 above.

40. I have in mind the relief sculpture of Tripolitania, in the semimilitary zone (access to the scattered sources through my *Soldier and Civilian* 19n43, and 20). W. H. C. Frend, *Antiquity* 16 (1942), 343f, argues for a revival of Berber art in the fourth and fifth centuries, but the material is scanty and his interpretations questionable. Low relief and chevron and rosette designs

do not, as he claims, identify Berber art alone, but are found also in Punic art, and what he calls Berber is perhaps better termed Neo-Punic. See (for Punic parallels) pp. 85f of the article by Guey cited by Frend himself (p. 352n); the opinions of Gsell and others also in Frend (p. 343); and P. Gauckler, *Nécropoles puniques de Carthage* (1915) 2. ccxliv and 5. G. Charles Picard, *Antike Kunst* 5 (1962) 30–37, detects native (principally Punic?) elements in local African art of Severan times and later but the arguments seem fragile, and are attacked by M. Floriani-Squarciapino, in *Huitième Congrès international d'archéologie classique (Paris 1963)* . . . (1965) 230f. The latter (pp. 231f) and Charles Picard (p. 33), however, agree in finding such characteristics as frontality, abstraction, and linear treatment, typical of late antique art in general, in African works of this period. Revivals of suppressed cultures are somewhat clearer in Asia Minor, as in cults, discussed by C. Bosch, *Die kleinasiatischen Münzen der römischen Kaiserzeit* vol. 2 pt. 1 (1935) 161f (quoted in the text); further, Bosch 170 on the reappearance of Asclepius from "the substratum." On Caria, above, n. 18; on Phrygia, see the same note, and G. Rodenwaldt, *Jahrbuch des deutschen archäologischen Instituts* 34 (1919) 84f, describing the cult of Zeus Bronton reviving in the later Empire, depicted in monuments of linear, flat, frontal treatment that recede from realism into ornament.

41. The quotation on Dacian culture comes from C. Daicoviciu and I. Nestor, *Rapports du Congrès international des sciences historiques* (1960) 2.128. D. Protase, *Dacia*[2] 7 (1964) 190f, though generally stressing the continuity of a mixed but mainly Romanized culture in Dacia after 270, nevertheless mentions (p. 181) the revival of indigenous pottery styles. On previous survival of Dacian culture, see M. Macrea, *Dacia*[2] 1 (1957) 205–220, emphasizing the importance of the unurbanized eastern parts of the province. For similar historical patterns, see Sherwin-White 287, on Zos, 3.33f: Nisibis is abandoned to Persia, and the city inhabitants, "after being educated for so many centuries in Roman civilization," emigrated to Amida, while "the folk of the tribes and strongholds remained to endure Persian rule." Compare also Petrus Patricius in C. Müller, ed., *Fragmenta historicorum graecorum* 4.192, "The nobility fled the city [of Antioch at the approach of the Persians], the great mass of the people remained, some well-disposed to Mariades [the traitor], some pleased by the thought of change." This took place about 253.

42. On the Jubaleni under Firmus, see above, at n. 16; on Ptolemais supported by the Blemmyes against Coptos, and on the Bucoli in like movements, see MacMullen, *Aegyptus* 44 (1964) 185n3, and Evagrius, *Hist. eccl.* 1.7.258.

43. See MacMullen, *AJP* 87 (1966) 7–11, on the language, and MacMullen *Aegyptus* 44 (1964) 194–198, on other aspects of early Coptism. For quite un-Romanized and un-Hellenized figures prominent in the Coptic

church, see S. Pachomius, S. Anthony, and Kalosirius, *ibid.* 198n6, and *ibid.* 197, on Shenute.

44. On the Church's social views, see above, Chap. V at n. 21; F. Schulz, *History of Roman Legal Science* (1946) 298, with ample bibliography on the Christian influence on secular law, 297n4; and E. Albertario, in *Scritti di diritto romano in onore di Contardo Ferrini*, ed. G. G. Archi (1946) 127f, whose views on *pretium iustum* are quoted in the text. On the democratic tone of much Church literature, see MacMullen, *Journal of Theological Studies* 17 (1966) 109–111, and above, Chap. V n. 17. On the use of interpreters in the Church, see *S. Silviae peregrinatio* 47; Euseb., *Mart. Pal.* 1.1 (long recension); Aug., *Sermo* 288.3; Aug., *Civ. dei* 19.7; Aug., *De haeres.* 87; Aug., *Ep.* 209.2f; cf. Irenaeus' earlier need of Celtic and Tatian's of Syriac. Yet in general it must be granted that the Church made no strong, systematic effort to overcome language barriers. See K. Holl, *Hermes* 43 (1908) 252f.

45. F. Wieacker discusses the popularizing aspects of law, drawing extremely suggestive parallels with the wider social and cultural developments of the late third and fourth centuries. See his article in *Sitzungsbericht der Heidelberger Akademie der Wissenschaft* 1955, no. 3, pp. 10–18, 22, and 47. A simultaneous toleration of minority languages in the courts is traced by MacMullen, *AJP* 87 (1966) 2f.

46. On imagery in Ammianus, see MacMullen, *Art Bulletin* 46 (1964) 435, 443f, 453, and 455.

47. The principal argument on the origins of late antique art favored the east. Among a score of discussions and (lately) refutations, see E. Will, *Etudes d'archéologie classique* 2 (1959) 134f, and M. Morehart, *Berytus* 12 (1956–57) 80f; H. P. L'Orange and A. von Gerkan, *Der spätantike Bildschmuck des Konstantinsbogen* (1939) 201–203; G. Rodenwaldt, *Jahrbuch des deutschen archäologischen Instituts* 51 (1936) 107f; and E. H. Swift, *Roman Sources of Christian Art* (1951) 158. For a few examples of this style (with local variations) to be seen in provincial art, see above, n. 40; also E. Diez, in *Huitième Congrès international d'archéologie classique (Paris 1963)* . . . (1965) 210 (Noricum); A. Schober, *JOAI* 26 (1930) 24, 46–51, emphasizing the Celtic contribution; and MacMullen, *Aegyptus* 44 (1964) 195f (Coptic). The contribution of Roman traditions carried on from the later Republic has been stressed by G. Rodenwaldt in a number of his writings, by Swift (140–163), and L'Orange and Gerkan (206f); by R. Bianchi Bandinelli, *Archeologia e cultura* (1961) 228 and 410f; R. Bianchi Bandinelli, *Hellenistic-Byzantine Miniatures of the Iliad . . .* (1955) 20; B. Schweitzer, *Die spätantiken Grundlagen der mittelalterlichen Kunst* (1949) 12; and G. Zinserling, *Klio* 41 (1963) 200f; but, in sum, it is a universal tendency, as is widely acknowledged, by L'Orange and Gerkan 198, for instance, and by G. C. Picard, *L'Information d'histoire de l'art* 7 (1962)

142. In Roman official art, its signs are first seen in Trajan's column, better in the Antonine column, and decisively under Septimius Severus; but its dominance comes only in the late third century (Bianchi Bandinelli, *Miniatures* 19; L. Franchi, *Ricerche sull'arte di età severiana in Roma* [1964] 37; Schweitzer 13; and Zinserling 201).

48. For the Church as a "vulgarizing" force in art, see Bianchi Bandinelli, *Archeologia* 416f, and *Miniatures* 22 and 24; T. Klauser, *Jahrbuch für Antike und Christentum* 1 (1958) 20; and H. Sedlmayr, in *Perennitas . . .* (1963) 107–115; cf. the entrance of biblical imagery into pagan literature of the fourth century, in MacMullen, *Art Bulletin* 46 (1964) 444 and 455.

49. Much of this reasoning, and the importance of social history for art history, is elaborated by Bianchi Bandinelli, *Archeologia* 197f and 412, and *Miniatures* 20–23; Franchi 43; and M. Bonicatti, *Scritti di storia dell'arte in onore di M. Salmi* (1961) 1.61. On the specific contribution of the army, see the references above, n. 34, and H. Schoppa, *Die Kunst der Römerzeit . . .* (1957) 43.

50. H. Bloch, in *The Conflict between Paganism and Christianity in the Fourth Century*, ed. A. Momigliano (1963) 202. For the best synthesis of the senatorial struggle against Christianity, see the whole of Bloch's essay. Though the heroes of this resistance could not be called "outsiders," they did support a pretender, Eugenius, a man of their own culture. It is noteworthy that he was the puppet of a Frankish general, Arbogast. For some of the propaganda that came out of the struggle, see the works of Alföldi cited by Bloch 194n4 and 202n1, and above, Chap. IV n. 31.

Chapter VII. Conclusion

1. St. Basil (*PG* 29.417) is quoted in the text; cf. Alexander of Tralles (sixth century) in Puschmann's edition 1.561 and 567; 2.377f and 583f; G. Schlumberger, *REG* 5 (1892) 85f; and the further quotation in the text from G. Must, *Language* 36 (1960) 193 and 197.

2. T. Nagy, *Huitième Congrès international d'archéologie classique (Paris 1963)* . . . (1965) 378, on Eraviscan culture; but the same point could be easily demonstrated from the history of Celtic culture under the Romans.

3. On acclamations, with a long history but greater prominence in the later Empire, see SHA *Claudius* 4.3f, quoted in the text; R. MacMullen, *Art Bulletin* 46 (1964) 437f; on partisan songs, R. MacMullen, *Journal of Theological Studies* 17 (1966) 111; SHA Aurelian 6.5; 7.2; on cities buying apotropaic magic, above, Chap. V at nn. 25–31. Conscription of *collegia* into an official role is too well known to require documentation.

Index

(Note: minor place names may be sought under major areas, Antioch under Syria, Carthage under Africa.)

Acts of the Pagan Martyrs, 84–90, 223, 314f
Africa, 4, 14, 89, 121, 123, 165, 194, 198, 200–207, 214, 222, 232, 250, 252, 255f, 262, 264, 266, 323, 335f, 344, 347f, 351–356, 358f, 362f
Agricola, Cn. Iulius, 47, 80, 312f
Alexander of Abonoteichus, 115–119, 322f
Ammianus Marcellinus, 135, 137, 238, 251, 364
Annaeus Cornutus, L., 23, 39, 41, 54, 68, 76
Annaeus Mela, L., 23, 29, 54, 68, 311
Annius Pollio, 54, 137, 312
Antoninus Pius, 60, 129, 194, 203, 257, 325, 332f, 346, 348
Apocolocyntosis, 38, 46, 69, 304
Apollonius of Tyana, 48, 73f, 88f, 92, 97, 112–115, 124, 126, 129, 253, 301, 310, 312, 316, 321f
Apuleius, 121–124, 126, 139, 165, 222, 324
Arianism, 104, 177, 180, 207, 319, 344, 356
Army, *see* Soldiers
Arria, 38f, 304
Artemidorus, 48, 65, 310
Arulenus Rusticus, Q. (?) Junius, 22, 41, 55, 62, 79, 307f
Asia Minor, 65f, 114–118, 134, 143f, 149, 154f, 174–177, 183–188, 194f, 198, 200, 207–209, 215, 225, 232f, 250–253, 257f, 260–264, 309, 319, 322f, 332, 336f, 339f, 342f, 346–349, 351, 355f, 360, 363
Asinius Pollio, 18, 20
Athanasius, 111f, 184, 236, 344
Athenodorus of Tarsus, 48, 305
Augustus, 5, 18f, 29, 33, 35, 37f, 48, 63, 129, 131f, 134, 158, 161, 170, 176, 263, 295, 299, 303f, 325f, 330
Aurelian, 129, 177, 225f, 260, 326
Avidius Cassius, 130, 223, 244

Bagaudae, 192f, 198, 211–213, 216, 232, 266, 357
Balbillus, Tiberius Claudius, 140, 142, 328
Barea Soranus, 54f, 76, 137, 141f
Bardesanes, 221f, 359
Brahmans, 97–99, 114, 316f
Britain, 140, 214, 227f, 256, 358, 362
Brutus, M. Junius, 1f, 5f, 8–20, 25, 27, 30f, 33f, 41, 47, 56, 71, 76, 78, 82, 94, 295–300, 305
Bulla Felix, 192f, 196, 216, 267

Caesar, 2–6, 8f, 13–19, 25, 30, 35, 242, 296–300
Caligula, 2, 19f, 30, 34f, 38, 61, 64, 75, 78, 96, 140, 170, 183, 302, 308, 313, 346
Canus, 75, 96, 316
Caracalla, 120, 126, 165, 170, 265, 311, 321, 329
Carausius, 212f, 225, 357
Cassius (C. Cassius Longinus, tyrannicide), 1, 13, 16, 18–22, 27f, 30f, 33, 47, 56, 78
Cassius Longinus, C. (consul A.D. 30), 21, 299
Cato, 2–6, 8, 14, 18–21, 25, 27–29, 33, 40, 52f, 67f, 77f, 80–82, 94, 295f, 299f, 313
Cato's and *Anti-Cato*'s, 5, 27, 75, 79, 295, 299
Censorship, 20, 35, 38f, 44, 130, 136, 148, 155, 304, 326f
Chaereas, Cassius, 30f, 54, 301
Chaldean Oracles, 106f, 323
Chaldeans, 97f, 106, 110, 128, 132–134, 139, 325, 327
Chion of Heraclea, 11f, 31, 52, 62, 72, 298, 307

Index

Christians and Christianity, 84, 89, 91–93, 99, 104f, 110, 130, 142, 145f, 152–154, 156, 158–161, 165, 176–179, 181f, 195, 208, 217, 219, 222, 235–237, 239, 246, 313, 315, 318f, 321, 324, 330, 332f, 335, 337, 342. 344f, 364f

Cicero, 3, 5f, 8–10, 12, 14, 17f, 23, 46f, 62, 80, 96, 110, 295–298, 350

Circumcellions, 198, 200–203, 206, 209, 216, 266, 353f, 356

Claudius, 2, 29, 32, 35f, 38, 40, 106, 140, 165, 250, 252, 263, 323, 327, 338, 346, 349

Coins, 1, 6, 9, 33, 101, 117f, 131, 157, 186f, 211, 216, 224, 239, 241, 296f, 302, 313, 317, 333, 343, 346, 348, 357, 360

Collegia, see Societies

Commodus, 2, 71, 85, 170f, 255, 260, 266f, 314, 340

Conspiracies, 2, 6f, 9, 16, 24, 27, 30, 54, 63, 67, 69, 72f, 137

Constantine, 73, 125, 129, 150, 155, 187, 197, 226, 231, 236, 251, 261, 319, 326, 330, 340

Constantius, 125f, 129, 317, 326

Coptism, 207, 210, 235f, 259, 346, 355, 363

Cornutus Tertullus, C. Julius, 41, 302

Cremutius Cordus, A., 19f, 28, 32, 39, 41, 82, 299, 310

Curiatius Maternus, 27, 39, 41, 63, 301, 303

Cynics and Cynicism, 49, 59–62, 65, 90, 92f, 99, 109, 184, 305f, 308f, 311, 314f, 320f

Decline of Rome, views of, 34f, 161, 303, 334f

Demetrius the Cynic, 22, 54, 61, 65, 74, 76, 82, 308, 310f

Dio Cassius, 66, 120, 127, 134, 137, 156, 323, 327

Dio Chrysostom, 48, 52, 61, 65f, 109, 113, 180, 183, 188, 306, 309f, 322

Diocletian, 129f, 202, 204, 226, 239, 241, 253, 326

Domitian, 35–40, 45, 48, 55, 61–68, 70f, 73f, 78–80, 88, 93, 113, 133f, 151, 170f, 301, 304f, 309, 312, 321, 325, 337, 339, 349

Donatism, 201–207, 253, 353–355

Druids and Druidism, 142, 155, 228, 332, 335, 362

Egypt, 60, 84–87, 91, 98, 101–103, 106, 112, 140f, 147, 149f, 159, 165f, 176f, 179, 182, 194, 207, 219, 223, 225, 235–237, 250–252, 256, 258, 263, 265, 314f, 317f, 330, 336, 339–346, 348, 351f, 355f, 358f, 363

Ephraim, 236, 254, 345

Epictetus, 48, 53, 55–57, 60, 64f, 75, 79, 82, 90, 310

Euphrates of Tyre, 48, 52, 306, 310

Fannia, 77, 312

Favorinus of Arles, 48, 66f, 310, 328

Firmus, 204f, 214, 355, 360, 363

Galba, 33, 187, 213, 302

Gallienus, 89, 159, 204, 333f

Gaul, 142, 174, 187, 195f, 211–216, 220, 222, 228, 230, 233, 244, 252, 256, 258, 260, 266f, 336, 342, 348, 351f, 357–359, 361f

Germany, 14, 142, 213, 227, 230, 258, 260, 266, 328, 359, 361f

Gildo, 202, 205f, 214, 220, 355

Gladiators, 16, 167, 169f, 189, 244, 267f, 299, 337–339, 349f

Greece, 10f, 37, 60, 65, 97, 99, 101, 104f, 112, 114–116, 143f, 167, 174, 185, 194, 200, 236, 252, 255, 257, 262, 264, 297, 337–339, 343, 349–351

Hadrian, 2, 65f, 101, 139, 141, 256, 313, 318, 326, 328, 333, 342, 350

Helvidius Priscus the elder, 41, 55–57, 63, 65, 77, 79, 301, 309, 312f

Helvidius Priscus the younger, 41, 53, 55, 68, 79, 305, 307, 310, 313

Herennius Senecio, 41, 51, 55, 77, 79, 301, 307, 312

Heresies, *see individual entries*

Hermetic Corpus, 107, 109, 150, 320

Index

Hippolytus, bishop of Rome, 151f, 331, 359
Hystaspes, 130, 148, 329f

Illyricum, 226–228, 240, 248, 361f
Italy (excluding Rome), 40, 56, 59, 65, 81, 104, 117, 120, 132, 137, 143, 158, 164, 167–171, 173–175, 185, 194f, 198, 200, 216, 230, 243, 249, 251, 256, 259, 261, 266–268, 304, 308, 319, 334, 337–339, 342f, 347f, 351

Jews and Judaism, 83–87, 93, 110, 121, 130, 145–149, 151, 153, 156, 159f, 222f, 264, 304, 314, 316, 323, 329–332, 338, 341f, 359
Josephus, 29f, 62, 301
Julian (emperor), 107, 111, 136f, 177, 181, 187, 217, 220–222, 251, 329, 335, 339
Julianus the elder (Chaldean), 106, 319
Julianus the younger (theurgist), 104, 107, 124, 126, 129, 319
Junius Mauricus, 29, 41, 55
Juvenal, 38, 139, 164

Laeti, 230–232, 234
Laws, 38, 79, 123–134, 155–157, 167, 171, 175, 178, 184, 186, 188, 194, 197, 223, 236–238, 241, 256f, 259, 324–327, 347, 351f, 357, 359, 364
Libanius, 136f, 177, 181, 183, 251, 258, 327, 341
Lucan, M. Annaeus, 23–26, 28, 31–34, 38, 40f, 44, 54, 63, 68, 76f, 105, 119, 121, 243, 300f, 303, 312, 323f
Lucian, 37, 99, 101, 111f, 115–117, 119, 222

Manichaeism, 130, 159, 326, 356
Marcus Aurelius, 85, 104, 107, 117, 130f, 133, 154, 219f, 223, 229, 251f, 255, 266, 319, 326, 349, 361
Martial, 40, 68, 77, 170, 304
Martyrologies, 39, 83f, 89–92, 314f
Maternus (sophist), 35, 301; *see also* Curiatius Maternus
Maximian, 211, 220, 226
Maximus (theurgist), 111, 126, 136, 320, 327
Meletianism, 182, 200
Monks and monasticism, 111f, 200, 209f, 217, 235, 266, 315, 318, 346, 352, 357
Montanism, 155, 200, 207–209, 326, 332, 335, 355
Musonius Rufus, 48, 53–55, 60f, 65f, 75f, 305–310, 312

Nationalism, 203–206, 212–215, 220f, 225, 356–360
Neoplatonism, *see* Platonism
Neopythagoreanism, *see* Pythagoreanism
Nero, 2, 19f, 22–27, 36, 38–40, 54, 59f, 63f, 69–71, 78f, 121, 137, 139–147, 151, 167, 170–172, 185, 187, 241, 296, 300f, 304f, 308f, 311–313, 319, 323, 327–329, 340, 346, 349
Nero, 37, 61, 301, 305
Nerva, 73f, 115, 171

Octavia, 37, 69, 304
Odenathus, 224f, 343, 352, 360
Ophitism, 118, 209, 322, 344
Optatus of Timgad, 202, 205f, 354f
Oracle of the Potter, 150f, 330

Pachrates, 101f, 126, 128, 318
Parthia (and Persia), 98f, 119, 130, 144–146, 153, 181, 329, 360, 363
Pelagianism, 207, 355
Peregrinus Proteus, 99f, 102, 136, 310, 317
Persius, A., Flaccus, 22f, 38f, 41, 44, 54, 304
Petronius, 76, 251, 303, 312
Phaedrus, 38, 44, 304
Platonism, 10, 12, 21, 47, 95, 105–108, 111, 120, 124, 136, 140, 150, 298, 305, 320, 323, 330, 334f
Pliny the younger, 29, 31f, 40f, 48, 65, 68, 79, 82, 120, 125, 156, 185, 302, 305, 307, 310, 313
Plotinus, 99–102, 105, 108, 120, 316–319, 323, 334

Police, 156, 163–167, 171, 194f, 257–260, 265, 336–340, 351; *see also* Laws
Pompey, 3f, 16, 18, 25
Pretenders and impostors, 17, 130, 143f, 223–225, 244, 250, 255, 263, 266, 299, 328f, 357f, 360
Pythagoreanism, 49, 95–98, 100–102, 104, 107f, 112–114, 118, 124, 140, 316f, 320f, 323

Quintilian, 47, 50, 71, 109, 303

Republicanism, 13f, 19, 27, 31f, 41, 46, 55, 63, 80, 299, 302, 307, 309
Rubellius Plautus, 37, 48, 54, 65, 308, 310

Second Sophistic, 190, 244, 350
Sejanus, 20, 38, 140, 344
Seneca the elder, L. Annaeus, 23, 33, 300, 303
Seneca (the younger, L. Annaeus), 19f, 22f, 27–29, 31–33, 36–40, 44, 46–48, 51, 53f, 58, 61, 63, 66, 68f, 75f, 82, 92, 96, 109, 139, 141f, 165, 243f, 295, 300f, 304–307, 309, 312f, 316
Sentius Saturninus, Cn., 30–33, 54, 64, 81, 309
Septimius Severus, 87, 132, 134, 156, 260, 264, 267, 326f, 333, 340, 348, 352, 365
Servilia, 2, 296
Shenute, 210, 236, 357, 364
Sibylline Oracles, 130, 145f, 149f, 154f, 159, 223, 326, 329f
Slaves, 154, 167, 180f, 183, 196, 198f, 201, 242, 260, 264, 267, 305, 321, 332, 337, 352f, 357
Societies (*collegia*), 165, 167f, 170, 173–178, 224, 247, 250, 336, 338f, 341–343, 347, 360, 365
Socrates, 4f, 10f, 46, 52, 59, 67, 75, 82, 84, 88, 90, 99, 300, 307, 312–315
Soldiers (including deserters), 164–166, 171, 194f, 199, 209, 214, 227, 230f, 233, 240, 253, 259–261, 263–265, 267, 326, 336f, 340, 351, 361f, 365
Spain, 23, 194, 211, 222, 228, 244, 258, 266f, 348, 357, 362
Stoics and Stoicism, 3f, 12, 14, 22f, 25f, 39, 45, 47, 49–53, 57–60, 62–64, 67, 76, 79, 84, 96, 110, 137, 141, 219, 295f, 298, 300, 305–309, 314, 316, 330, 359
Suicide, 4f, 18f, 22, 24, 40, 45, 67, 72, 75f, 96, 295, 310–312
Symmachus, 172, 180, 251, 268, 340
Syria, 83, 112, 151, 153f, 170, 177–179, 187, 194, 209, 216, 220, 223, 244, 251–253, 258, 261, 264, 318, 321, 332, 336, 339–342, 344, 346, 348, 351f, 357–360, 363

Tacitus, 31–33, 39, 45, 53, 63, 72, 80, 126, 134, 139, 214f, 238, 244, 246, 302–304, 311, 313
Theaters, 16, 30, 69–71, 168–176, 186, 304, 338–342, 348
Thessalus, 126, 319f
Thrasea Paetus, 21–23, 28, 31, 39, 41, 48, 51, 53f, 56, 61f, 65, 72, 75, 81, 299–301, 307f, 310, 312f
Thrasyllus, 140f, 328
Tiberius, 2, 19f, 22f, 29, 36–38, 45, 96, 129f, 139f, 156, 170, 193, 256, 259, 302–304, 310, 325, 327, 332, 337
Titinius Capito, 27, 80, 312f
Titus, 36, 40, 115, 144, 251
Trajan, 33, 48, 65, 86f, 106, 141, 153, 156, 165, 171, 175, 177f, 193, 256, 260, 314, 335, 343, 365
Tribes, 104f, 142, 192, 203f, 209, 212–215, 230f, 234, 255, 261f, 264, 266, 335, 348, 351, 354, 356–358, 362
Tyrants and tyrannicides, 4, 8–13, 20f, 24f, 27, 30, 32, 36, 56, 64, 66, 68, 72f, 82–85, 88, 91, 98, 297, 300, 303, 309, 313, 315

Valens, 135f, 177, 327
Vespasian, 2, 33, 35, 39, 55–57, 61, 63, 67, 133, 167, 252, 303, 307, 309, 348
Vettius Valens, 138f, 328
Vitellius, 133, 170, 213